South Wales S[port]

A rock climbing guideb[ook to] sport climbing in South Wales

Text and route information by Mark Glaister,
 Goi Ashmore, Roy Thomas, Gary Gibson
Crag photography by Mark Glaister
 and Adrian Berry
Action photography as credited
Edited by Alan James
Technical Editor Stephen Horne
Printed in Europe on behalf of Latitude Press
Limited (ISO 14001 and EMAS certified printers)
Distributed by Cordee (cordee.co.uk)

All maps by ROCKFAX
Some maps based on original
source data from openstreetmap.org

Published by ROCKFAX in November 2016
© ROCKFAX 2016

rockfax.com

All rights reserved. No part of this publication may be reproduced, stored in a retrieval system, or transmitted in any form or by any means, electronic, mechanical, photocopying or otherwise without prior written permission of the copyright owner. A CIP catalogue record is available from the British Library.

This book is printed on FSC certified paper made from 100% virgin fibre sourced from sustainable forestry

ISBN 978 1 873341 36 0

Cover: Rhoslyn Frugtniet on *Retrobution* (7b) - *page 107* - Trial Wall, Gower. Photo: Simon Rawlinson
This page: Naomi Buys breaking out of the final corner of the classic Dinas Rock testpiece *Berlin* (7a+) - *page 189*. Photo: Mike Hutton

Mark Glaister
Goi Ashmore
Roy Thomas
Gary Gibson

AWESOME WALLS
CLIMBING CENTRES

AWESOMEWALLS.CO.UK

AWESOME WALLS LIVERPOOL
ATHOL ST, LIVERPOOL, L5 9TN

AWESOME WALLS STOCKPORT
PEAR MILL, STOCKPORT, SK6 2BP

AWESOME WALLS STOKE
SEFTON RD, LONGTON, ST3 5LW

AWESOME WALLS SHEFFIELD
GARTER ST, SHEFFIELD, S4 7QX

WE CLIMB, WE CARE, WE'RE AWESOME!

In a back street in Liverpool a small wall was created in 1998 by a passion to prove to the world that climbing walls can be fun and inspiring places to climb and train. Awesome Walls Climbing Centres aim to provide frequent well set routes and boulder problems in a clean and friendly atmosphere.

DID YOU KNOW WE HAVE AN APP? DOWNLOAD IT HERE

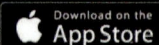 

Contents — South Wales Sport Climbs

Jen Stephens midway up the sustained off-vertical wall climbing on the excellent *Black Magic* (6b) - page 331 - at Navigation Quarry. Photo: Mark Glaister

- Introduction................4
  - The Rockfax App...........8
  - Symbol, Map and Topo Key....9
  - Previous Guidebooks........10
  - Acknowledgements..........12
- **South Wales Sport Logistics** 14
  - Getting Around and Map......18
  - Accommodation............20
  - Pubs...................22
  - Cafes, Gear Shops and Walls .24
- **South Wales Sport Climbing**...26
  - Access.................28
  - Gear and Bolting..........30
  - Grades.................32
  - Trad Climbing............34
  - Bouldering and DWS.......35
  - Limestone Graded List......36
  - Sandstone Graded List......40
  - Destination Planner........42
- **Carmarthenshire**............46
  - Telpyn Point.............48
  - Morfa Bychan............58
  - Pendine................70
  - Cwm Capel.............78
- **Gower**...................80
  - Rhossili Beach...........82
  - Trial Wall Area..........104
  - Third Sister to Zulu Zawn....112
  - Oxwich...............126
  - Watch House...........134
  - Foxhole..............140
  - Minchin Hole...........148
  - Bowen's Parlour Area......152
  - Bosco's Gulch Area.......158
  - Pwlldu Bay............166
  - Rams Tor.............168
  - Barland Quarry.........172
- **Inland and Coastal Limestone** 174
  - Dinas Rock............176
  - Taff's Well............194
  - Taff's Well West.........206
  - Gilwern..............214
  - Witches Point..........226
  - Temple Bay...........236
  - Castle Upon Alun.......248
- **The Valleys Sandstone**.......252
  - Dyffryn..............256
  - Abbey Buttress.........262
  - Treherbert Quarry.......266
  - Ton Pentre............274
  - Gelli................278
  - Ferndale.............284
  - Blaenllechau...........286
  - Dan Dicks............288
  - Trebanog............290
  - Coed Ely............292
  - Glynfach............296
  - Trehafod............298
  - The Darren..........302
  - Cwmaman..........306
  - Mountain Ash........312
  - The Gap............320
  - Navigation Quarry......328
  - Deri...............334
  - Bargoed............336
  - Llanbradach.........340
  - Crymlyn Quarry......352
  - Tyle y Coch.........354
  - Sirhowy............358
  - Tirpentwys..........368
- **Route Index**................368
- **Crag and General Index**......376

South Wales Sport Climbs — Introduction

South of the Brecon Beacons lies a wealth of sport climbing that spans from the River Wye on the Welsh Border to Pembrokeshire. Until now, it has been somewhat unknown, overshadowed by better known areas.

The Valleys Sandstone quarries and the spectacular sea cliffs of Gower have been climbed on for decades, resulting in many steel-fingered locals and numerous stunning trad sea cliffs respectively. However, since the late 1980s it has been the development of sport climbing that has been the major source of action in the area, firstly on the sandstone quarries and now across the inland limestone and coastal limestone cliffs.

The area offers a multitude of venues located in environments that vary from sea cliff to mountainside, and post-industrial landscapes to world heritage settings. This book covers the sport climbing that has been developed on this varied collection of natural and quarried crags of both limestone and sandstone.

The routes on offer cover the full grade span - ranging from easy-going 3s and 4s through to some state-of-the-art upper end grade 8s. There is plenty to keep both local and visitor busy for a long time, with 1750 fully bolted routes documented in this guide and potential for many more to come.

The area is conveniently situated - whether you are based in Cardiff or Swansea, travelling to or from Pembroke, or on a quick trip from London down the M4 corridor. There is plenty to appeal for quick evenings, full weekend trips or as an escape from bad weather elsewhere. Staying in the area is easily arranged, with the popular options of camping or modern hostel accommodation being widely available.

The climbing is easily split into four main areas - Carmarthenshire sea cliffs, Gower, Inland and Coastal Limestone and The Valleys Sandstone.

Gower's stunning beaches and cliffs will be a main draw for holidaying visitors and locals alike, whilst nearby Camarthenshire's remote sea cliffs will reward those prepared to try somewhere off of the beaten track.

The inland limestone and coastal cliffs are situated in a wide circle around the Valleys Sandstone. Some of them are long established and well used by locals, but have not been recognised by climbers coming from further afield and deserve much more attention.

Finally the sandstone quarries that line the sides of the valleys stretching up towards the Brecon Beacons bring a fascinating dimension to the area. The ambience is not always what many go climbing for, but lurking in the confines of these little known venues are some truly memorable pitches that will test technique and finger strength to the maximum.

So if you have enjoyed the sport climbing at Portland, North Wales, The Peaks or Yorkshire give South Wales a punt - rock up at Foxhole, Rhossili, Dinas Rock, Witches Point, Sirhowy, Tirpentwys, Navigation Quarry or Gilwern and you might well be in for a pleasant surprise.

Mark Glaister, October 2016

Introduction **South Wales Sport Climbs** 5

Cai Bishop-Guest hanging out on the lip of Foxhole's Top50 classic *Pioneers of the Hypnotic Groove* (7b) - *page 143*. Foxhole is one of a number of fine sport climbing venues on Gower and offers opportunities for cragging throughout the year. It also has the benefit of being non-tidal and sheltered from the rain. Photo: Simon Rawlinson

South Wales Sport Climbs — Introduction

Coverage

This book covers virtually all the worthwhile sport climbing to be found on the limestone and sandstone crags and quarries of South Wales. It isn't a definitive coverage in the traditional style of guidebook, and the area is constantly developing hence there are always likely to be new routes being added. However, it is the most comprehensive documentation of sport climbing in this area yet published and will be added to and improved in both print and digital formats over the coming years.

The trad climbing in the area has not been covered. In some places we have listed a few trad routes, and you would be well advised to pack a trad rack if visiting the crags since there are a number of semi-sport routes and fully trad challenges amongst the sport routes. In most cases these are in the harder grades.

The coverage is in the now familiar format designed so that you should never have to turn more than a few pages to first get to the crag, then get to the buttress and finally locate the start of your chosen route. All route descriptions are on the same page as their topo and listed from left to right. There are many other features to help choose suitable routes and crags depending on specific weather conditions or your ability level. You can select a crag from the crag tables on page 42. Each topo also has crag symbols for a quick glance check - see key on page 9.

This book is also available in digital form on the Rockfax App - see page 8 for more information.

Sundown at Three Cliffs Bay, Gower. Photo: Simon Rawlinson

Introduction **South Wales Sport Climbs** 7

Guidebook Footnote

The inclusion of a climbing area in this guidebook does not mean that you have a right of access or the right to climb upon it. The descriptions of routes within this guide are recorded for historical reasons only and no reliance should be placed on the accuracy of the description. The grades set in this guide are a fair assessment of the difficulty of the climbs. Climbers who attempt a route of a particular standard should use their own judgment as to whether they are proficient enough to tackle that route. This book is not a substitute for experience and proper judgment. The authors, publisher and distributors of this book do not recognise any liability for injury or damage caused to, or by, climbers, third parties, or property arising from such persons seeking reliance on this guidebook as an assurance for their own safety.

South Wales Sport Climbs — The Rockfax App

This South Wales Sport Climbs guidebook is also available on the Rockfax App which brings together all the Rockfax climbing information with UKC Logbooks and presents it in a user-friendly package for use on Apple iOS devices (Android version available from early 2017).

The heart of the app is the Rockfax crag and route information which is downloaded by way of paid in-app purchases for individual crags, or bundles of crags, in 'Areas' which correspond roughly to printed guidebooks. You can purchase each crag or area individually, or the whole book. The main data on the app is downloaded and stored on your device so you don't need any signal to be able to read the descriptions and see the topos and maps. There is a free sample crag for each area and some of these are quite extensive, enabling you to get a really good impression of what the app is like without shelling out any money.

The Rockfax App itself is a free download and incredibly useful in its own right. It contains a detailed crag map linked to the UKClimbing crags database (currently with basic information and routes lists for around 20,000 crags worldwide). The map also displays all the 4,000+ listings from the UKClimbing Directory of climbing walls, outdoor shops, climbing clubs, outdoor-specific accommodation and instructors and guides amongst others.

To find the app, search for 'Rockfax app' in Google or in the appropriate app store.

UKC Logbooks

An incredibly popular method of logging your climbing is to use the **UKClimbing.com** logbooks system. This database lists more than 383,000 routes, over 20,500 crags worldwide and, so far, more than 31,000 users have recorded over 4.9 million ascents! To set up your own logbook all you need to do is register at **UKClimbing.com** and click on the logbook tab. Once set up you will be able to record every ascent you make, when you did it, what style you climbed it in and who you did it with. Each entry has a place for your own notes. You can also add your vote to the grade/star system linked to a database on the Rockfax site used by the guidebook writers. The logbook can be private, public or restricted to your own climbing partners only.

The Rockfax App can be linked to your **UKClimbing.com** user account and logbook so that you can record your activity while at the crag and look at photos, comments and votes on the routes. To do this you will need a 3G/4G data connection. You can also look at the UKC logbooks to see if anyone has climbed your chosen route recently to check on conditions.

Symbol, Map and Topo Key — South Wales Sport Climbs

Route Symbols

 A good route which is well worth the effort.

 A very good route, one of the best on the crag.

 A brilliant route, one of the best in the area.

 A significant route which is one of the best of its type and grade in the book.

 Technical climbing requiring good balance and technique, or complex and tricky moves.

 Powerful climbing; roofs, steep rock, low lock-offs or long moves off small holds.

 Sustained climbing; either lots of hard moves or steep rock giving pumpy climbing.

 Fingery climbing with significant small holds on the hard sections.

 Fluttery climbing with big fall potential and scary run-outs.

 A long reach is helpful, or even essential, for one or more of the moves.

 Some loose rock may be encountered.

Crag Symbols

 Angle of the approach walk to the crag with approximate time.

 Approximate time that the crag is in the direct sun (when it is shining).

 The crag is exposed to bad weather and will catch the wind if it is blowing.

 Some or all of the routes can only be reached at certain states of the tide.

 The crag can offer shelter from cold winds and it may be a good suntrap in colder weather.

 The crag suffers from seepage. It may well be wet and unclimbable in winter and early spring.

 The crag is steep and may well offer some dry rock to climb when it is raining.

 Some or all of the routes have a restriction due to nesting birds. Details in the crag information.

 Some or all of the routes are affected by an access problem. Details in the crag information.

 Deserted - Currently under-used and usually quiet. Fewer good routes or remote and smaller areas.

 Quiet - Less popular sections on major crags, or good buttresses with awkward approaches.

 Busy - Places you will seldom be alone, especially at weekends. Good routes and easy access.

Crowded - The most popular sections of the most popular crags which are always busy.

Topo Key

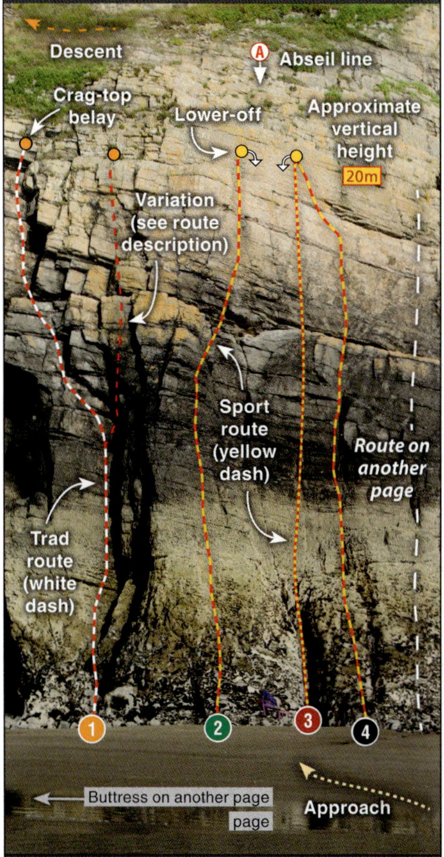

Map Key

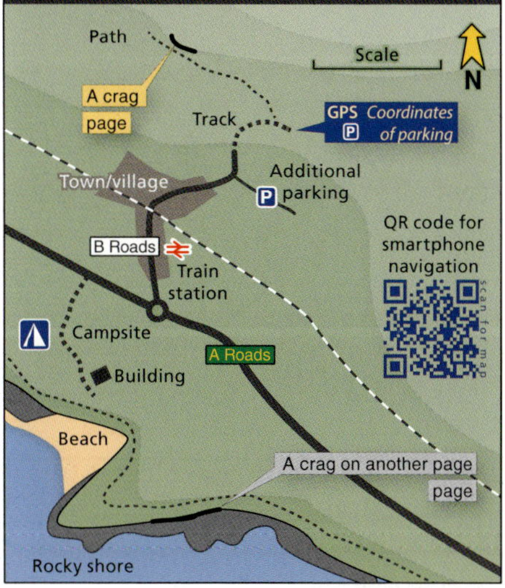

South Wales Sport Climbs — Previous Guidebooks

Key Previous Guidebooks and Route Information Sources

Trad and sport climbing on the sandstone and limestone crags of South Wales has been documented since the 1970s. We are very grateful to all those who have worked on previous guidebooks and those who have taken the trouble to record their endeavours. The key books and web-based information sites are listed below.

Guidebooks

Gower
J.O.Talbot (West Col 1970)

Southeast Wales
J.C.Horsfield (SWMC 1973)

Southeast Wales
John Harwood (SWMC 1978)

Gower and Southeast Wales
M.Danford, Tony Penning (SWMC 1983)

Gower & S.E.Wales
A.E.Richardson (SWMC 1991)

Southeast Wales Sandstone
Goi Ashmore, A.Senior (JDMEL 1991)

Southeast Wales Sandstone
Goi Ashmore (JDMEL 1995)

Gower Sport Climbs
Adrian Berry (1997)

Southeast Wales Sandstone, Limestone & Gower Sport Topos
Gary Gibson (Climb High 1997)

Gower & S.E.Wales
Goi Ashmore, Roy Thomas (SWMC 2003)

Gower Sport Climbing MiniGuide and Rockfax App
Adrian Berry (Rockfax 2010, 2013 and 2016)

Gower Rock
Stuart Llewellyn, Matt Woodfield (Pesda Press 2012)

Websites

UKClimbing.com - The UKC Logbook route database for all areas (including trad) covered in this guidebook.

southwalesmountaineering.org.uk - A wiki covering the trad and sport climbing in the area. A good spot to look for new developments.

swbg.co.uk - A guide to bouldering in the area.

Acknowledgements **South Wales Sport Climbs** 13

Dave Pickford moving up the steep *Staple Diet* (7b) - *page 229* - at the beachside Witches Point. Witches Point, along with its close neighbour Temple Bay, offers some great climbing straight off the beach. Photo: Mark Glaister

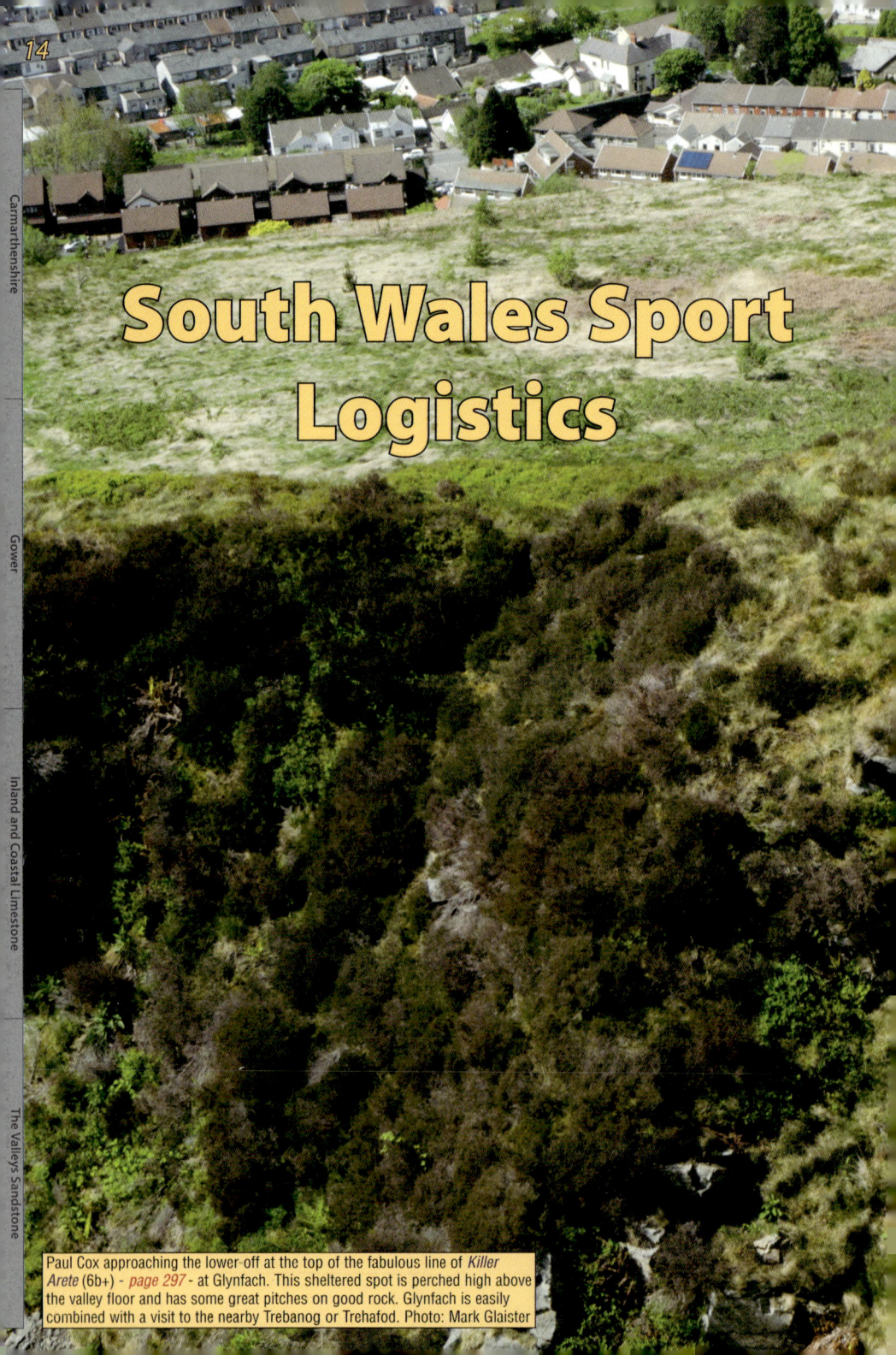

South Wales Sport Logistics

Paul Cox approaching the lower-off at the top of the fabulous line of *Killer Arete* (6b+) - *page 297* - at Glynfach. This sheltered spot is perched high above the valley floor and has some great pitches on good rock. Glynfach is easily combined with a visit to the nearby Trebanog or Trehafod. Photo: Mark Glaister

South Wales Sport Logistics

Mountain Rescue and Coastguard
In the event of an accident requiring the assistance of Mountain Rescue:

Dial 112 and ask for 'MOUNTAIN RESCUE'
or
Dial 112 and ask for 'COASTGUARD RESCUE' for sea cliffs

This is very important since just asking for 'Police' will redirect you to a switchboard which could be a long way from your current location. This can cause delays in the rescue procedure as the authorities try and track down where the injured party is. Asking for 'Mountain Rescue' or 'Coastguard' will redirect you to people who know the area well.

Mobile Phones
Mobile phone coverage is good at the majority of the crags featured in this book. Remember that even if you cannot get a signal from your provider, emergency calls will still get through in many instances where there is some coverage from any provider.

Tourist Information Centres and National Park Centres
If you are short of ideas about what to do on a wet day or need some accommodation, take a look at the Tourist Information Centres. They contain a lot more useful information than it is possible to include in these pages.

Abergavenny - The Tithe Barn, Monk Street, NP7 5ND. Tel: 01873 853254
Blaenavon - Blaenavon World Heritage Centre, Church Road, NP4 9AS. Tel: 01495 742333
Cardiff - Unit 1, Wales Millennium Centre, CF10 5AL. Tel: 02920 877927
Crickhowell - Crickhowell Information Centre, Beaufort Street, NP8 1BN. Tel: 01873 812105
Swansea - Plymouth Street, SA1 3QG. Tel: 01792 468321
Caerphilly - The Twyn, CF83 1JL. Tel: 02920 880011
Carmarthen - Castle House, Carmarthen Castle, SA31 1AD. Tel: 01267 231557

More information and other travel tips are at **information-britain.co.uk** and **visitwales.com**

Temperature °C	Jan	Feb	Mar	Apr	May	Jun	Jul	Aug	Sep	Oct	Nov	Dec
Average Max Temp (°C)	8	8	9	12	15	18	20	20	18	14	11	9
Average Min Temp (°C)	4	4	5	6	9	12	14	14	12	10	7	5
Average Rain Days/Month	15	11	14	11	10	10	10	11	10	15	15	14

When to Go
The climbing sites covered in this guide are geographically diverse, ranging from exposed mountain tops to sheltered seaside suntraps. As a result there is scope for climbing in good conditions throughout the year. The climate data given above is for Gower and it is here that the most reliable conditions are to be found during the cooler months. The other areas are best climbed on from Spring until Autumn, heading to the higher crags such as Treherbert and Gilwern for fresher conditions when things become very hot lower down.

18 South Wales Sport Logistics   Getting Around and Map

Getting Around
The main artery roads of the M4 leading on to the A48, A465 and A40 bisect the area and provide quick and easy access to most of the crags if travelling from afar. The starting points for approaches to the crags are all easily reached by car and the approach descriptions are written assuming you have access to a car.

Satellite Navigation
All the parking spots are indicated with a precise GPS location. This is in the form of two decimal numbers as in the sample blue box. Different GPS devices accept these numbers in alternative formats, although this is the standard format and it can be cut and pasted directly into Google Maps.

QR codes have been included with the approach maps. You can scan the QR code using an app such as **Scan** (for iOS) or **Google Goggles** (for Android) and choose to open the result direct into the **Google Maps** navigation app on your phone.

GETTING AROUND AND MAP — South Wales Sport Logistics

Public Transport

The area has some of the easiest crags to get to by public transport in the UK. The cliffs of Gower, The Valleys Sandstone, Witches Point and Dinas Rock are all simple to reach from either Cardiff, Bridgend or Swansea by rail and bus. Nearly all The Valleys Sandstone crags are within striking distance of railway stations. Gower is very well serviced by bus from Swansea. Cardiff and Swansea are on the mainline from London and Bristol.

Buses - the website traveline.info is an excellent place to get a quick idea of links and times of bus services. The tourist information centres are also useful for travel information.

Trains - The cities of Cardiff, Swansea and many of the towns in The Valleys can all be easily reached by train. For timetable information go to **thetrainline.com**

South Wales Sport Logistics — Accommodation

Carmarthenshire

The Valley Campsite - *See map on page 47*
The Valley, Amroth Road, Llanteg. SA67 8QJ
Tel: 01834 831720   thevalleycampsite.co.uk
Basic site close to the climbing at Pendine, Morfa Bychan and Telpyn.

Gower

Pitton Cross Camping - *See map on page 80*
Rhossili, Gower. SA3 1PT
Tel: 01792 390593   pittoncross.co.uk
Nice site that is well positioned for all the areas on Gower. Best to book ahead at busy times.

Eastern Slade Barn - *See map on page 80*
Oxwich, Gower. SA3 1NA. Tel: 01792 391374
easternsladebarngower.co.uk
Superb accommodation plus a basic camping field. Book ahead for the bunkhouse.

Limestone and Valleys

Lone Wolf Campsite - *See map on page 175*
Glyn Y Mul Farm, Aberdulais. SA10 8HF
Tel: 01639 638551   glynymulfarm.co.uk
Out of the way site. No groups. Well placed for Dinas Rock and Dyffryn. No pubs nearby.

Park Farm - *See map on page 175*
Llangattock, Crickhowell. NP8 1HT.
Tel: 01873 770589   parkfarm-campsite.co.uk
Excellent site good for Gilwern and dropping over into the sandstone crags of the Valleys. Easy walk into Crickhowell for good pubs, restaurants, cafes and takeaways. No need to book ahead.

Wern Watkin Bunkhouse - *Map on page 175*
Llangattock, Crickhowell NP8 1LG
wernwatkin.co.uk
High quality accommodation in a stunning setting. Need to book in advance. Good for Gilwern and dropping over into the sandstone crags of the Valleys. Remote and no facilities nearby.

Pwll Du Adventure Centre - *Map on page 214*
Blaenavon, NP4 9SS Tel: 01495 791577
pwllduadventurecentre.co.uk
Bunkhouse within walking distance of Gilwern.

Acorn Camping - *See map on page 175*
Ham Lane South, Llantwit Major. CF61 1RP
Tel: 01446 794024   acorncamping.co.uk
Well positioned for Witches Point and crags just off of the M4. Quiet site close to beaches. No groups allowed. Book ahead at busy times.

Southerndown - *See map on page 227*
Three Golden Cups, Southerndown, CF32 0RW.
Tel: 01656 880432   thethreegoldencups.co.uk
Seasonal site, close to Witches Point.

Heritage Coast Campsite - *Map on page 175*
Monknash, Vale of Glamorgan. CF71 7QQ
Tel: 01656 890399   heritagecoastcampsite.com
Good site near to Witches Point. No Groups.

Cwmcarn Forest Camping - *Map on page 255*
Cwmcarn, Crosskeys. NP11 7FA
Tel: 01495 272001   your.caerphilly.gov.uk/cwmcarnforest/
Nice camp site with 10 'glamping' pods available. Good mountain bike opportunities and only a 20 minute walk to the local pub - the Philanthropic Inn. Book in advance.

The Lone Wolf campsite.
Photo: Mark Glaister

Accommodation **South Wales Sport Logistics** 21

Marti Hallett on *Debbie Reynolds* (7a) - *page 116* - at Deborah's Zawn, Gower. Deborah's Zawn is one of Gower's tougher venues that, along with Shipwreck Cove, Foxhole and neighbouring Zulu Zawn, contain the pick of its harder climbs. Photo: Mark Glaister

Carmarthenshire

Springwell Inn - *See map on page 70*
Pendine, Carmarthen. SA33 4PA
Tel: 01994 453274. Nice friendly spot close to the beach.

Gower

The Joiners Arms - *See map on page 172*
50 Bishopston Road, Bishopston. SA3 3EJ
Tel: 01792 232658 - Handy spot for crags at the eastern end of Gower.

King Arthur Hotel
Reynoldston, Gower. SA3 1AD
Tel: 01792 390775. Excellent venue. Good food and beer garden. Not particularly close to the coast but worth the effort to get to.

Worm's Head Hotel - *See map on page 82*
Rhossili, Gower, West Glamorgan. SA3 1PP
Tel: 01792 390512. Fine location overlooking the beach and Worm's Head. Decent food and great outside terrace.

Limestone and Valleys

Gwaelod Y Garth Inn - *See map on page 206*
Taffs Well, Gwaelod-y-Garth. CF15 9HH
Tel: 02920 810408 - Close to Taffs Well crags. Nice, rustic and homely.

The Bear Hotel
Crickhowell. NP8 1BW. Tel: 01873 810408
Good hotel bar with decent food. Close to Gilwern crags and Park Farm camping.

The Three Golden Cups - *Map on page 227*
Southerndown, Bridgend. CF32 0RW
Tel: 01656 880432. Small pub close to Witches Point and the beach.

Plough and Harrow
Monknash, Cowbridge. CF71 7QQ
Tel: 01656 890209. Ancient country pub with good food. Close to Witches Point.

The Pelican - *See map on page 227*
Ogmore-by-Sea, Bridgend. CF32 0QP
Tel: 01656 880049. Upmarket venue with food and a lively atmosphere. Close to Witches Point and Castle Upon Alun crags.

Prince of Wales
Ton Kenfig, Bridgend. CF33 4PR
Tel: 01656 740356. Good pub with food midway between Witches Point and Abbey Buttress.

Greenhouse Inn
Newport Road, Llantarnam. NP44 3BP
Tel: 01633 866911. On the western side of the Valleys and a good spot for Tirpentwys.

Glantaff Inn - *See map on page 320*
Quakers Yard, Treharris. CF46 5AH
Tel:01443 410822. Good friendly spot central to many of the Valleys crags especially The Gap. Good food and beer.

The King Arthur Hotel in Reynoldston. Photo: Mark Glaister

BUIS-LES-BARONNIES

Accommodation in the heart of Haute Provence

- Open all year
- 2/4 person studio apartment
- 13 person bunkhouse
- 7/9 person gite
- 12m Heated pool
- WIFI throughout
- Children's playground
- World-class, year-round climbing within 20 mins
- New via-ferrata just 20 mins away
- Great cycling - on and off-road
- Mountain bike hire on site
- Large groups and clubs welcome

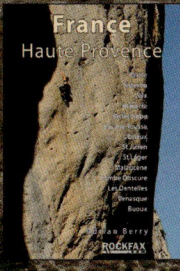

Owner Audrey Seguy hanging out at the local crag Baume Rousse, with a snow-capped Mt. Ventoux in the distance.

Our pool is open May through Sept.

La Bergerie - a 7/9 person gite

The dining room

www.alauzon.com | +33 9 87 88 65 77

Cafes

Plenty of options on the Pendine seafront in Carmarthenshire and in The Valleys. Four cafes in other areas worth a mention are:

The Bay Bistro and Coffee House - In Rhossili with great views over the beach and close to the parking. Good coffee.

Three Cliffs Coffee Shop - In Southgate next to the parking. Has a shop with post office and cash machine.

Number 18 - On the High Street in Crickhowell. Good coffee and atmosphere.

Dunraven Beach Cafe - A seasonal cafe in Southerndown (Witches Point car park).

Gear Shops

Up and Under
490 Cowbridge Road East, Cardiff.
CF5 1BL   Tel: 02920 578579
upandunder.co.uk
See advert opposite

Crickhowell Adventure - Crickhowell.
crickhowelladventure.co.uk
There are also **Blacks**, **GoOutdoors** and **Cotswold Outdoor** shops in Cardiff, Swansea and/or Carmarthen.

Climbing Walls

Boulders
Pengam Road,
Cardiff CF24 2RZ.
Tel: 02920 484880
Large centre with leading and bouldering.
bouldersuk.com
See advert on front cover flap

The Hangout
Haverfordwest
Leisure Centre,
Haverfordwest SA61 1QX.
Tel: 01437 776676
pembrokeshire.gov.uk/leisure
See advert inside back cover

Other walls include **Dynamic Roc**k in Swansea, **Rock UK** in Trelewis near Merthyr Tydfil, **Cragfit** in Abergavenny, **Spot** in Treforest south of Pontypridd, **The Cube** in Port Talbot YMCA and **Llangorse Activity Centre**.

The Bay Bistro and Coffee House in Rhossili. Photo: Mark Glaister

South Wales Sport Climbing

Dave Henderson making quick work of the steep and fingery orange-stained wall on *Cointreau* (7a+) - *page 314* - at Mountain Ash. Photo: Mark Glaister

28 South Wales Sport Climbing — Access

In common with most climbing areas in the UK, there have always been access issues on the limestone and sandstone cliffs of South Wales. Clashes over nesting birds, flora, historical sites, land ownership, gardening and dogs have all been causes for disagreement in the past. Other issues such as drilling, path erosion and parking have also caused conflict. Despite this, and thanks to the great work of the BMC and its volunteers, the majority of the crags covered in this book currently have good access arrangements.

🚫 There are some restrictions and warnings so please keep a look out for the red 'Restrictions' symbol (left). These are usually attributed because of nesting birds and the dates generally range from the beginning of February to the end of July. Other crags have very precise parking and approach requirements, whilst others have strict rules on what can and cannot be done due to the presence of historic artefacts. At some sandstone quarries access is less well defined (often due to liability concerns) and has led to signs being erected that state that climbing is not allowed. In these cases climbing has often gone on unhindered for many years, but, should you be asked to leave, please do so politely and send details of the owner and circumstances to the BMC access officer.

Individual crag access is covered in the respective chapters. Please read this information carefully and take great care to follow the described approaches so as not to infringe any restrictions. If in any doubt contact the BMC (Tel: 0161 445 6111), or check the access section of the BMC website - **thebmc.co.uk/modules/RAD/**.

John Warner and Jen Stephens on *Bowen to the Inevitable* (6a) - *page 157* - at Bowen's Parlour, Gower. Photo: Warner Collection

South Wales Sport Climbing — Gear and Bolting

Prolific new router and bolter Gary Gibson on the fine wall climbing of *Asset Manager* (6c) - *page 61* - at Morfa Bychan. Maintaining the bolts in South Wales has been a massive undertaking and is ongoing. Please consider donating to the South Wales Bolt Fund (SWBF) through **UKBoltFund.org**. Photo: Mark Glaister

Gear

The vast majority of the sport routes featured in this book have good solid bolts and lower-offs in place. For most of the routes a 60m rope and 14 quickdraws is sufficient. However, there are a small number of lines that will require a longer rope to get down (and more quickdraws). **To avoid any doubt, always tie a stopper knot in the dead end of the rope to ensure that it will not pass through the belay device.**

If you intend to climb any of the trad routes described then you will need a full rack of wires and cams.

Bolting

The work of maintaining the bolts has been carried out by a few individuals and has been a huge task.

A plea from the bolt equippers

Please do not top-rope or repeatedly lower from the lower-off bolts/ring/maillon/krab as this increases the wear on these fixed items which may then need premature replacement. If you are going to top-rope, or make multiple ascents, please do so using your own quickdraws in the lower-off with only the last person threading the rope through the fixed lower-off point.

South Wales Bolt Fund

The South Wales Bolt Fund (SWBF) was formed to help with the replacement of protection bolts and lower-offs throughout South Wales - **southwalesboltfund.co.uk**

If you have enjoyed the sport routes in this book then consider donating an evening's beer money to the SWBF. You can find the link to the PayPal page via **UKBoltFund.org**. Proceeds from a proportion of the sales of this guidebook will go towards the SWBF.

UKBoltFund.org
Support local bolting volunteers

South Wales Sport Climbing — Grades

Most of the routes in this book are sport routes which are given a **Sport Grade**. A sport route is defined as one where all the major protection comes from gear fixed in the rock (bolts).

There are a few trad routes covered where the majority of the gear is carried by the lead climber and is hand-placed. These are given a **British Trad Grade** and a red and white dotted line on the topo (instead of the normal red and yellow dotted line).

Sport Grade
The sport grade is a measure of how hard it is going to be to get up a certain section of rock. It makes no attempt to tell you how hard the hardest move is, nor how scary a route is.

British Trad Grade
1) Adjectival grade (Diff, VDiff, Severe, Hard Severe (HS), Very Severe (VS), Hard Very Severe (HVS), E1... to E10). An overall picture of the route including how well protected it is, how sustained and a general indication of the level of difficulty of the whole route.

2) Technical grade (4a, 4b, 4c... to 7b). The difficulty of the hardest single move, or short section.

Colour Coding
The routes are given a colour-coded dot corresponding to a grade band. The colour represents a level that a climber should be happy at, hence sport routes tend to be technically harder than the equivalent coloured trad routes because the climber doesn't need to worry about the protection.

❶ Up to 4c (Up to Severe)
Mostly these should be good for beginners and those wanting an easy life.

❷ 5a to 6a+ (HS to HVS)
General ticking routes for those with more experience.

❸ 6b to 7a (E1 to E3)
Routes for the experienced and keen climber. A grade band which includes many of the area's great classics.

❹ 7a+ and above (E4 and above)
The really hard stuff including some top sport routes.

Sport Grade	British Trad Grade	UIAA	USA
1	Mod (Moderate)	I	5.1
2	Diff (Difficult)	II	5.2
2+	VDiff (Very Difficult)	III	5.3
3	HVD (Hard Very Difficult)	III+ / IV-	5.4
3+	Sev (Severe) 3c	IV	5.5
4a	HS (Hard Severe) 4b BOLD	IV+	5.6
4b	VS (Very Severe) 4b/5a	V-	5.7
4c	HVS (Hard Very Severe) 5a/5b	V	5.8
5a		V+	5.8
5b	E1 5c BOLD/SAFE	VI-	5.9
5c	E2 6a/5b	VI	5.10a
6a	E3 6a/5c	VI+	5.10b
6a+		VII-	5.10c
6b	E4 6b/6a	VII	5.10d
6b+		VII+	5.11a
6c	E5 6b/6c	VIII-	5.11b
6c+		VIII	5.11c
7a	E6 6c	VIII+	5.11d
7a+	E7 6c/7a	IX-	5.12a
7b		IX-	5.12b
7b+	E8 7a	IX	5.12c
7c		IX+	5.12d
7c+		IX+	5.13a
8a	E9 7a	X-	5.13b
8a+		X	5.13c
8b	E10 7b	X	5.13d
8b+		X+	5.14a
8c		XI-	5.14b
8c+		XI	5.14c
9a		XI	5.14d
9a+		XI+	5.15a

Grades **South Wales Sport Climbing** 33

Jordan Buys enjoying the 'black spot' route *Palace of Swords Reversed* (8a) - *page 143* - at Foxhole on Gower. Photo: Mike Hutton

South Wales Sport Climbing — Trad Climbing

There are many well established trad venues in South Wales that are not covered in this book. The variety of styles and grades is vast, ranging from easy-going multi-pitch expeditions, to extremely serious lines in the upper E grades. Below is a list of the best venues and some brief information that will give an idea of what to expect. All the cliffs and routes can be found on the SWMC and UKClimbing databases and in the guidebooks **Gower Rock** and **Gower & S.E. Wales**.

Lewes Castle (Gower) - *On map on page 104*
Mid-grade limestone coastal cliff set above a fine beach. **Best routes** - *Isis* HVS 5a, *Osiris* VS 4c, *Southwest Diedre* HVS 5a.

Yellow Wall (Gower) - *On map on page 104*
A big steep limestone sea-cliff with strenuous multi-pitch routes in the E grades. Tidal with an abseil approach. **Best routes** - *Yellow Wall* E3 5c, *Transformer* E3 5c.

Great Tor and Three Cliffs Bay (Gower)
Beautiful seaside limestone cliffs with many lower and mid-grade lines both single and multi-pitch. Tidal. **Best routes** - *Great Tor East Ridge* HS 4a, *Scavenger* VS 4c, *Arch Slab* VS 4c.

Ogmore (near Witches Point)
Adventurous single-pitch sea cliff trad climbing. Pumpy banded limestone, and not well travelled but memorable. Abseil approach and tidal. **Best routes** - *Flash Harry* HS 4a, *Pluto* VS 4c, *Pinnochio* HVS 4c, *Glycogen* E1 5a, *Spellbinder* E5 6a.

Dinas Rock - *See page 176*
Home to a small number of difficult limestone trad lines. **Best routes** - *Groovy Tube Day* E1 5b, *Spain* E4 6a, *Dina Crac* E9 7a.

The Sandstone
Spread about all over the multitude of sandstone quarries are some worthwhile trad lines - although they see little traffic and may need a brush-off before an attempt. All of the routes listed below are covered in the Valleys Sandstone section of this guidebook.
Best routes - *Lamb Leer Diease* E2 5c, *Thumbsucker* E5 6a, *Just Hanging Around* E1 5b, *The Owl and the Antelope* E2 5c, *The Expansionist* E3 5b, *Crack Basher* E3 5c.

Bridget Collier finishing the brilliant corner of the classic Ogmore trad route *Pluto* (VS 4c). Photo: Mark Glaister

Bouldering and DWS — South Wales Sport Climbing

There is plenty of bouldering on offer all over the area covered in this guidebook, but the main developed venues are listed below. The venues listed are covered on the UKClimbing and SWMC databases and topos and information on these and many other bouldering spots in the area is available at **swbg.co.uk**

Oxwich (Gower) - *On map on page 127*
Seashore limestone boulders of all shapes and sizes that are the remnants of a huge rock slide. Now developed to give many problems that range from f4 to f7c+. Tidal approach and bring a mat as the boulders sit on a rocky platform.

Pwlldu East, Caswell Bay (Gower)
Two good limestone areas south of Bishopston. Lots to do in the f5s and f6s plus some harder stuff.

Limeslade Bay (Gower) - *Map on page 169*
An area near Rams Tor with a good range of problems.

Dinas Rock - *See page 176*
The epicentre of limestone bouldering in the area with many problems throughout the grades up to f8a+. Most popular spot is the Kennelgarth Wall - an undercut smooth wall cut by a few cracks.

Ogmore-by-Sea (near Witches Point)
Lots of very good seashore problems on wave sculpted limestone. Grades from f5 to f7b+. Slightly tidal and bring a mat as there are rocky landings.

Neath Abbey Quarry - *See map on page 257*
A good sandstone boulderfield, but with some access issues.

Sully Island - *See map on page 255*
A tidal limestone bouldering area close to Cardiff. Lots to do across the grades.

The scope for Deep Water Soloing is wide given a good high tide on many of the sea cliffs, but the most popular spots are Sheepbone Wall at Rhossili Bay (good for easier lines), Giants Cave on Gower (Steep stuff over good water), Ogmore (wild, high and serious top-end venue).

Alex Mannion on *Coup De Tat* (f6c+) at the seashore boulders of Oxwich, on Gower. Photo: Simon Rawlinson

Graded Lists
These graded lists cover many of the popular routes in the guidebook. They have been put together by the four main authors paying close attention to the UKC Logbook votes. Eagle-eyed readers will spot that routes on the sandstone crag Telpyn appear in the limestone list. This is deliberate due to the crag's location and the climbing style being similar to the other nearby Carmarthenshire crags.

Limestone Graded List — South Wales Sport Climbing

8 b+
- [ ] Helvetia 89
- ** [ ] Surplomb de Ray 142

8 b
- [ ] Mortal Kombat 186
- *** [ ] Achilles' Wrath 89

8 a+
- *** [ ] Dog Days are Over 116
- ** [ ] Mr.T. 229
- *** [ ] Air Show. 86
- * [ ] Cannonade 89
- *** [ ] Masada 229
- ** [ ] Black Wall Direct. 106

8 a
- *** [ ] The Black Pearl 188
- ** [ ] Palace of Swords
  Reversed. . . . . *25, 33* . 142
- ** [ ] Captain Barbarossa. 188
- [ ] Zulu Wall. . . . . *225* . 124
- ** [ ] Vennerne. . . . . *85* . . 86
- ** [ ] Delta Dagger 89

7 c+
- *** [ ] Bellerophon. . . . . *166* . 167
- ** [ ] Under Arrest 116
- ** [ ] Super Size Me. 229
- *** [ ] Kestrel. 150
- ** [ ] Hydraulic Lunch 118

7 c
- * [ ] The Milkier Way 130
- [ ] Grow-Up! 230
- [ ] Ultimatum 124
- ** [ ] Chives of Freedom . . . *opposite* . 190
- *** [ ] Smashed Rat 184
- * [ ] Turkey Lurking 144
- [ ] Bitchin' 130

7 b+
- ** [ ] Basilica 184
- ** [ ] Department of Correction 116
- [ ] Resisting Arrest 116
- *** [ ] Wide Eyed and Legless. . . . *113* . 116
- ** [ ] Still Life. 188
- [ ] One Ton Depot 86
- ** [ ] Rotbeest 173
- [ ] This God is Mine. . . . . *226* . 229
- *** [ ] Harlem 191

7 b
- [ ] Wrecking Ball 86
- [ ] The Sharp Cereal Professor. *177* . 191
- ** [ ] Popped In, Souled Out 115
- [ ] Trailblazer 211
- *** [ ] Retrobution. . . . . *cover* . 106
- ** [ ] Red River Rock. 130
- *** [ ] Rat on a Hot Tin Roof. 184
- [ ] Parlour Games 154
- [ ] Red with Rage . . . . *126* . 130
- [ ] Pioneers of the
  Hypnotic Groove. . . . . . . *5, 140* . 142
- [ ] Staple Diet . . . . *13* . 229
- *** [ ] Berlin Extension 188

7 a+
- * [ ] Munsterosity. 182
- ** [ ] Scream for Cream. . . . . . *206* . 211
- [ ] Berlin . . . . *1, 174* . 188
- * [ ] Fuelled by Pies 225
- *** [ ] Jump the Sun 149
- * [ ] It's a Black World 209
- ** [ ] Sink or Swim . . . . *213* . 211
- * [ ] Jezebel 167
- ** [ ] When I'm 64 154
- * [ ] Pump Action 138
- * [ ] The Inflated Roundhead 180
- * [ ] Ducky Lucky 144
- * [ ] The De-Regulators 182
- *** [ ] Marine Layer. 86
- ** [ ] King George verses
  the Suffragettes. . . . . *39* . . 89
- * [ ] Touch and Go 138
- ** [ ] The Conneticut Connection. 198
- [ ] The Raven. . . . . *151* . 150

7 a
- ** [ ] The World-v-Gibson 230
- ** [ ] Tufa at the Top 230
- [ ] Joy de Viva . . . . *139* . 144
- ** [ ] The Hant . . . . *105* . 106
- ** [ ] Foxy Lady 144
- ** [ ] The Hooker . . . . *146* . 144
- *** [ ] Jacky Fisher's Phobia 72
- * [ ] Pugsley 182
- ** [ ] She's Slipping Away . . . . . *46* . . 60
- *** [ ] Melting Man 198
- * [ ] Tribulations 106
- * [ ] Jump to Conclusions . . . . *135* . 138
- ** [ ] French Undressing 115
- ** [ ] Normal Norman 211
- * [ ] Stray Cats 186
- ** [ ] Debbie Reynolds. . . . . *21* . 116
- ** [ ] The Cool Crux Clan 170
- * [ ] Inspector Gluescau 130
- * [ ] Bristol Beat 209
- ** [ ] Rob Roy 178
- * [ ] The Drilling Fields 136
- ** [ ] LA Confidential 198
- * [ ] Tragic Moustache 229
- * [ ] Gorilliant 186
- * [ ] Marmalade Skies . . . . *11* . 142
- ** [ ] Ashes to Ashes 167
- * [ ] Liassic Lark. 229

6 c+
- * [ ] St. Vitus's Dance 136
- ** [ ] There's Life in the Old Dog Yet. . 230
- ** [ ] Fats Waller 84
- * [ ] Five O'Clock Shadow 229
- *** [ ] Blockiness. 90
- * [ ] Diagnosis Made Easy 222
- ** [ ] El Camino Del Roy 192
- * [ ] Chinese Whispers 208
- * [ ] Beware of Poachers 182
- [ ] Genghis Khan . . . . *194* . 198
- * [ ] Thousand Yard Stare 182
- ** [ ] Look Over Yonder 200
- ** [ ] Thin Lizzy 234
- [ ] Goose in Lucy. . . . . *80* . 142
- * [ ] Gentlemen Prefer Bolts. 156

6 c
- * [ ] Totally Radish . . . . *193* . 186
- ** [ ] Sophie's Wit Tank 74
- ** [ ] Decades Apart. 167
- * [ ] Clip Joint. 138
- ** [ ] Battle of the Bulge 222
- * [ ] Call a Spade a Spade 186
- ** [ ] Organised Chaos. 198
- ** [ ] Par 3. 90
- ** [ ] Black Adder. 84
- ** [ ] Glucosamine and Chondroitin. . 225
- * [ ] Charlie's Rusks. 180
- * [ ] Any Old Iron 212
- *** [ ] Half Pipe Dream 218
- [ ] Hanging by a Thread. 230
- [ ] Asset Manager . . . . . . *30, 62* . . 60
- * [ ] Kissin' the Pink. . . . . *132* . 130
- ** [ ] Dream Academy 192
- *** [ ] Twilight World. . . . . *119* . 115
- * [ ] Deadly Nightshade 180
- * [ ] Spider 154
- [ ] Vladimir and the Pearl . . . *49* . . 52
- * [ ] Miss You. 173
- * [ ] Crock Block. 167
- ** [ ] Daggers 200

Jordan Buys on the super technical Chives of Freedom *(7c) - page 190 - at Dinas Rock. Photo: Mike Hutton*

Carmarthenshire | Gower | Inland and Coastal Limestone | The Valleys Sandstone

37

South Wales Sport Climbing — Limestone Graded List

6 b+

	Credit Squeeze . . . . *59* . .	60
*	The Day the Sky Fell In	144
***	Off the Peg	120
**	Croeso I Gymru	230
*	Rum Thieves	84
*	Gwest y Gymru 7 Inch Mix	200
*	Taurus Bulbous	198
***	Selling Short . . . . *62* . .	60
*	Breccial Motion . . . . *153* . .	154
**	Tread Gently	136
*	Open Roads	182
*	Rock Bottom	120
**	Reaction Series	156
*	Jaded Locals . . . . *137* .	136
*	Squash the Squaddie	182
*	Sideburn	229
*	Triple Sigh	149
	Sidewinder	220
*	Wij Zitten…Een Sneeuwstorm . .	173
**	Cheesy Rider	178
**	Red Square	198
*	Creme de Roquefort	178
**	Rag And Bone	212

6 b

*	Beyond the Fringe	149
**	Fergie's Folly	216
**	Soapy Dahl . . . . *77* . .	74
*	Miss Alto	182
*	All's Well	211
**	A Freem of White Horses . . *248* .	251
**	John's Route	90
*	The Deflated Dickhead	180
**	Unleashed	74
*	Good Gear, Good Cheer	200
**	Magic Carpet . . . . *219* .	218
*	Cod Liver Oil	225
**	Threadbare	120
**	Bolus Feed	64
**	Fiesta	115
*	Straining Pitch	138
*	Flow Job	222
**	Feud For Thought	156
**	Hot Flush	120
*	Great Expectorations	234
*	Left Wing Rebolt	138
*	Anonymous Bosch	136
**	Smoke and Mirrors	234
*	Bottom Drawers	92
*	Fly	154
**	Tea Leaves	222
**	Magic Touch . . . . *232* .	229
**	A Starke Reminder	160
*	Straight as a Dai	72
*	Scarface	120
*	Sand Man	90
*	Steel Yourself	130

6 a+

**	No Beer, No Fear	4
	Southeast Wall	115
*	Reverted Revisionist . . . *237* .	243
*	Mr Potato Head	
**	3D Dog	74
**	Christian Broke My Flake	222
*	Sorcerer's Assistant	234
**	Rudaceous Ramble	154
**	Parlour Vous le Sport	156
*	First Handout	90
**	Hanger Then High	163
*	Knackers Yard	212
	Hung Over . . . . *122* .	120
**	Y'all Come Back Now . . . . *164* .	163
*	Stinking of Fish	173
*	Pelagic Mush	229
*	You Sane Bolter . . . . *66* .	64
**	Aur of Glory	160
***	Don't Jis on My Sofa	173
*	Unholy Alliance	142
*	Pillars of the Earth	106

6 a

*	Gentleman's Relish	156
*	Johnny Takes a Tumble	225
**	Bowen to the Inevitable . . . *28* .	156
*	Clair de Lune	209
*	Wreckers ball	212
*	Bowen Arrow	156
*	Landfill Tax	212
*	Once Upon a Time	208
*	Go With The Flow	222
*	Spit it Out	111
**	Under the Mattress	98
*	Black Night's Rein	216
*	Sport Wars (Watch House)	136
*	All of a Quiver	156
*	Snap Crackle 'n' Pop	225
**	Sister Mary's Blessed Finger *114* .	115
*	Cinders Catch	92
	Lemon Soul . . . . *82* .	98
*	Megalodon	196
*	Gentleman's Retreat	156

5 c

*	There's No Business Like… . . .	222
*	Under a Blood red Sky	225
*	Blow Me, Another One . . *239* .	238
*	Fromage Frais	178
*	Salty Dog	74
*	Pwll Du Crack . . . . *215* .	222
*	Sallies of Youth	156
*	Mega Mix	200
*	Angry Pirate	196
*	Nietzche's Niche	243
*	Stalag Luft	204
*	No Fathers Day	98
**	Monica's Dress	111
*	Heading South	60
*	Take me up the Hindu Kush . . .	225
*	The Enema Affair	115
*	Descarte's Dithers . . . . . *244* .	243
*	Abra-Ker-Fucking-Dabra	234
*	Kiss the Gunner's Daughter . . .	196
*	Tickety-Boo	136
*	Poppin' in the Poop Deck	196

5 b

*	Buckets of Bubbly	106
**	A Mermaids Tale	98
**	The Plumb . . . . *217* .	220
**	Holds May Spin . . . . *101* .	98
*	Wedgling	106
*	Cash in the Attic	98
*	Wedge Dew Bin . . . . *108* .	106
*	Blockbuster	111
**	Telefunken U47 . . . . *172* .	173
**	Dawson's Creek	98
*	Atomic Wedgie	106

5 a

*	Back, Crack and Sack	225
*	The Road to Eldorado	186
***	Dawson's Corner	98
*	Wisdom of Age	156
*	White Noise	225
*	Excavation	136

4 c

*	Wittle Thieving Lankers	84
*	Sharktopus vs Megapotamus . . .	196
	Fistful of Tenners . . . . . *102* .	98
*	Basil Brush	142
*	Brittle Biscuit	225

4 b

*	Jug Fest	222
*	Schengen	94
*	Border Control	94
*	Bulbus Tara	198
*	The Trevena Fish Hotel	98

3 a

*	The Power of the Leopard Skin Leg Warmers	142

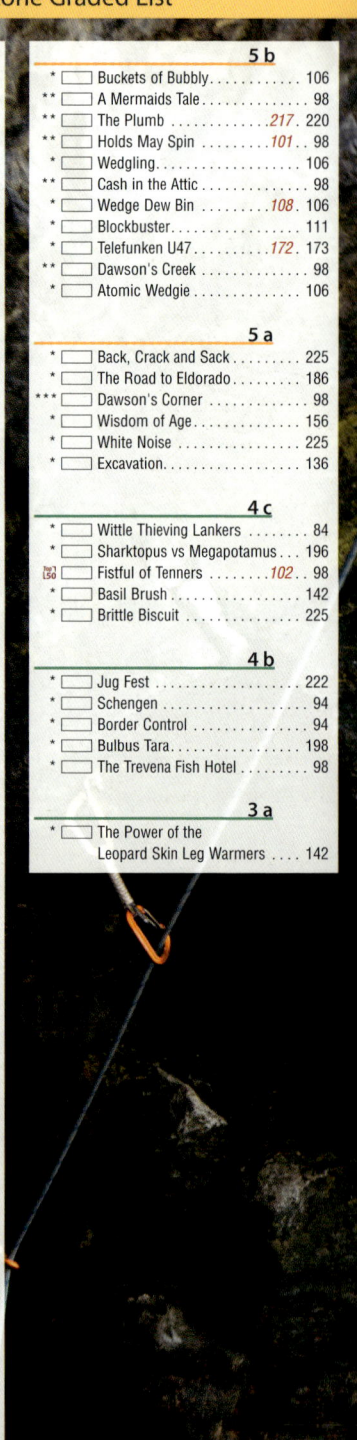

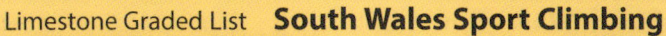

Limestone Graded List **South Wales Sport Climbing** 39

Anya Forino enjoying the steep and juggy ground on the popular *King George verses the Suffragettes* (7a+) - *page 88* - at Shipwreck Cove, Gower. Photo: Simon Rawlinson.

40 **South Wales Sport Climbing** Sandstone Graded List

The compact wall of excellent sandstone at Coed Ely has some worthwhile lines that pack in the moves, despite their relatively modest height. The quarry is sheltered and a suntrap. In this picture Paul Cox is tackling the surprisingly steep finishing crack of *Campaign For See-through Bikinis* (6a+) - *page 295* . Photo: Mark Glaister

Sandstone Graded List — South Wales Sport Climbing

7c
- *** Contraband 342
- ** Mad at the Sun 324

7b+
- ** The Basildon Snapper 304
- ** Sharpy Unplugged 304
- ** Encore Magnifique 324
- *** Face 360

7b
- ** Rise 304
- ** Dai Hard 297
- ** Skanderbeg 360
- * 'King Ada 360
- ** Butcher Heinrich 360
- ** Salmon Running, Bear Cunning .. 324

7a+
- *** King Zog 360
- *** Mother of Pearl 308
- ** Pleasant Valley Sunday ...321. 324
- * Cointreau 26. 314
- ** Get Flossed 324
- ** Lyddite 338
- ** Pastis on Ice 314
- ** Outspan 314
- ** Round Are Way 304
- ** Scared Seal Banter 327
- *** Slip into Something Sexy ..341. 351
- ** Propaganda 308
- ** Eastern Block Rock 332
- ** Blowing For Tugs 338
- ** Sheer Heart Attack 364
- ** Food for Parasites 348

7a
- ** Western Front Direct 252. 332
- ** Misadventure 318
- * Gott in Himmel 360
- ** Mawr, Mawr, Mawr 361. 360
- ** The Uninvited 294
- * Rhubarb Lets Fly 300
- ** Leave it to Me (Dyffryn) 258
- ** One Track Mind 326
- ** Demi Moore 300
- ** Turn Off the Sun 297
- ** Young Free and Single 294
- ** Banog's Barmy Army 291
- ** Killer Queen 364
- * Hail Mary 369. 372
- ** Nosepicker 267. 269
- ** Supertramp 371

6c+
- * Shaken but not Stirred 304
- ** Fairies Wear Boots 357. 355
- ** Enema of the Affair 356
- ** Hair of the Dog 291
- ** Great Expectations 331
- ** Our Man In Bargoed 338
- ** Gorki's Zygotic Mynci 300

6c
- ** Deus Ex Machina 328. 331
- ** The Relaxed Ladybird 331
- * Behind the Lines 293. 294
- * Scrotum Oil 326
- ** Hostility Suite 362
- ** Molybdenum Man 314
- ** Moses Supposes His Toeses Were Roses 297
- * So Uncool 322
- ** Leave it to Me (The Gap) 324
- ** The Mastic Mick 327
- ** Strange Little Girl 359. 360
- * Elf and Safety 300
- ** The Grout Of San Romano 327
- ** Controlled Emission 326

6b+
- ** Peachy 355
- ** Killer Arete 14. 297
- ** Queens of the Stone Age 365. 364
- ** Beware the Burly Butcher of Bargoed 338
- * Yikes 322
- ** Raving Queen 364
- * Piano Dentist 353
- ** Gaz 316. 264
- ** Slip into the Queen 364
- ** The Bolt Fund Blues 331
- * Flakes and Chips 373
- ** Twisted Logic 372
- * Crock Licker 272

6b
- * Enigma 258
- ** Black Magic 3. 331
- ** Rattle Those Tusks 324
- ** Nappy Rush 343
- ** High Moon 356
- ** Half Man, Half Machine 331
- ** Bad Bad Boy 258
- * The Tactless Teacher 372
- * Pepperatzi 338
- ** Lundy Boy 374. 371
- ** Firewater 291
- ** Land of the Dinosaurs 324
- ** Blood Sweat and Beers 331
- * A Poxy Queen 364
- * Post Expressionist 346
- * Don't Blame Me 322
- ** Terry Forkwit 270. 272
- * Balthazaar's Ball Sac Bulges .. 338
- * Ring of Confidence 324
- ** The Cragmeister 371
- ** Greased Balls 326
- ** Catch The Pigeon 289
- ** A Certain Peace 317. 318
- * Brittania 338
- * Diamond Dog 372
- * Bluster 322
- * Sorry Lorry Morry 304
- * Dirtbag Arete 287
- * Dirty as a Dog 343

6a+
- ** Rising Sap 316
- * Galvanised 280
- * The Godfather 327
- * I Came 314
- * Beavers at Bargoed 338
- * Campaign For See Through Bikinis ....opposite. 294
- * Earl of Porth 300
- ** Marlin on the Wall 322
- * Kabuto Mushi 322
- * Fluster 323. 322
- * The Chimney Finish 373
- ** Poker in the Eye 324
- * Baldy Walks to Ponty 300
- * Hawk's Cheep 338
- ** Discount Included in the Price 299. 300
- * Shackles of Love 324
- * Drag Queen 364

6a
- * Leading Edge 372
- * Grout Expectations 324
- * Yank the Plank 310
- ** Up Yours 327
- * Hey Mister 310
- * Crash Landing 332
- * Groping For Jugs 337. 338
- * Rocky 371
- * Mister Faraday 324
- * Twice Shy 343

5c
- * Rockover Beethoven 331
- ** Little Queen 367. 364
- ** Pocket Battleship 258
- ** The Forgotten Route 310
- * Dicky Dyson 287
- * Newton's Apple 327
- * Mental Mantles 372
- * Generation Gap 324

5b
- * Weeping Stump 313. 316
- * Looking for Leather 310
- * Per Rectum 326

5a
- * He Sawed 314
- * Leaky Ball Cock 287

4c
- * Down Under 280
- * Fairy Godmother 287
- * Raspberry Ripple 287

3a
- * Ripple Slab 287

Destination Planner

Region	Location	Routes	up to 4+	5 to 6a+	6b to 7a	7a+ and up
Carmarthenshire	Telpyn Point	41	–	20	17	4
Carmarthenshire	Morfa Bychan	55	2	24	22	7
Carmarthenshire	Pendine	54	–	18	23	13
Carmarthenshire	Cwm Capel	11	1	6	4	–
Gower	Rhossili Beach	124	23	53	31	17
Gower	Trial Wall Area	36	–	18	12	6
Gower	Third Sister to Zulu Zawn	46	–	8	22	16
Gower	Oxwich	47	–	7	22	18
Gower	Watch House	20	–	5	13	2
Gower	Foxhole	26	3	3	10	10
Gower	Minchin Hole	12	–	1	6	5
Gower	Bowen's Parlour Area	32	1	11	12	8
Gower	Bosco's Gulch Area	28	–	7	16	5
Gower	Pwlldu Bay	10	–	–	3	7
Gower	Rams Tor	14	–	–	5	9
Inland and Coastal Limestone	Barland Quarry	14	–	5	7	2
Inland and Coastal Limestone	Dinas Rock	108	1	11	43	53
Inland and Coastal Limestone	Taff's Well	71	9	13	40	9
Inland and Coastal Limestone	Taff's Well West	49	1	15	18	15
Inland and Coastal Limestone	Gilwern	77	5	29	40	3
Inland and Coastal Limestone	Witches Point	64	3	10	29	22
Inland and Coastal Limestone	Temple Bay	62	3	40	19	–
Inland and Coastal Limestone	Castle Upon Alun	37	7	15	15	–

Approach	Sun	Sheltered	Dry in Rain	Restrictions	Seepage	Tides	Summary	Page
10 min	Sun and shade				Seepage	Tidal	A remote but friendly sea cliff, composed of hard vertical sandstone, and within easy reach of the Pembroke trad crags.	48
2-10 min	Sun and shade	Sheltered			Seepage	Tidal	A good discovery that, although slightly tidal, should become popular. Easy access and with many fine routes in the mid-grades.	58
10 min	Lots of sun					Tidal	Restricted access due to a tight tide window, but well worth the effort needed in planning a visit. Substantial climbs that take strong lines on good quality limestone.	70
1 min	Early morning	Sheltered					A small sandstone quarry with some easier routes that are useful if you are passing, or looking for a local evening venue.	78
12-14 min	Early morning		Dry in the rain		Seepage	Tidal	Lots of routes across the grade spectrum, straight off of one of Wales's finest beaches. The crags are tidal and conditions are not always ideal.	82
8-10 min	Afternoon						A collection of walls set high above the beach, with wide ranging appeal from grade 5s to grade 8s. Reliable conditions, little in the way of seepage and only a short distance from the car or beach.	104
25-40 min	Sun and shade	Sheltered	Dry in the rain		Seepage	Tidal	A stunning section of coast dotted with some fine sport crags that offer plenty of routes in the mid and higher grades. Excellent rock and the cliffs have the ambience of sea cliff climbing.	112
10-15 min	Sun and shade	Sheltered	Dry in the rain	Restrictions	Seepage	Tidal	An impressive venue with easy access and a good set of (mainly) hard routes. There are two areas - one is an impressive leaning wall and the other a smaller hidden wall in the woods - an SSSI.	126
10 min	Afternoon					Tidal	Two contrasting crags near Southgate. Watch House Slab has some fierce slabby pitches. The overhanging Watch House East has more conventional fare.	134
10 min	Afternoon	Sheltered	Dry in the rain		Seepage		Superb sport crag that offers some of the best steep climbing in the area, on excellent rock. Climbing is possible in the rain and on sunny days in winter if seepage is not present. Short approach.	140
10 min	Sun and shade			Restrictions			An unusual setting in a large sea-level cave/zawn with a number of atmospheric lines. Cliff is of historic importance so some restrictions on what can and cannot be done.	148
10-12 min	Sun and shade	Sheltered	Dry in the rain		Seepage	Tidal	A collection of walls, overhangs and small zawns with a good spread of grades. Some sections are tidal but there is always something to climb in calm seas. Awkward to find your way around on first acquaintance.	152
15 min	Sun and shade	Sheltered		Bird		Tidal	An interesting set of tidal sea cliffs with a range of routes across the grades. A little awkward to navigate around the various cliffs on a first visit. A bird restriction on one wall.	158
20 min	Morning	Sheltered					One good hard section of quarried cliff with a number of tough grade 7s. There are other easier lines on the same wall, but these are covered in mud that has washed down over the face.	166
10 min	Sun and shade						A wide crag that has bands of fierce overhangs running across it. Tricky to reach since the descent path is overgrown - the best access is now via abseil.	168
5 min	Early morning	Sheltered		Restrictions			A gloomy inland old quarry working that has some intense slab climbs. Access problems.	172
2-12 min	Morning	Sheltered	Dry in the rain	Restrictions	Seepage		One of South Wales's premier crags that has lots of hard climbs on excellent limestone, and is set in a lovely quiet valley. Also home to some accessible easier climbing.	176
1-5 min	Afternoon	Sheltered			Seepage		Impressive walls and close to Cardiff. A good number of long face routes that are generally on good rock. The drawback is the road noise from the A470. Some easier routes.	194
10-13 min	Not much sun	Sheltered	Dry in the rain		Seepage		Two main sections of contrasting cliff, one steep and the other slabby. The setting is off putting but the climbing is good. In summer the dense tree canopy shelters some of the cliff from rainfall.	206
5-12 min	Morning	Windy			Seepage		A series of quarried bays located high above the Usk Valley and with stunning views. Plenty here for those climbing in the lower and mid-grades. Very good rock.	214
5-6 min	Evening				Seepage	Tidal	A steep, high standard cliff set next to a fine surf beach. Many excellent routes that need crisp conditions to be enjoyed to the full. Only marginally tidal at its landward end.	226
15 min	To mid afternoon					Tidal	A long line of low walls just around the headland from Witches Point. Many steep and sharp lines on solid rock. Tidal and next to a quiet beach.	236
15 min	Sun and shade	Sheltered					A hidden quarried wall of good, steep slabs. It is prone to getting dirty and the approach path is overgrown.	248

Faded symbol means that only some of the routes are sheltered / dry in the rain / restricted / suffer from seepage / tidal

Carmarthenshire

Gower

Inland and Coastal Limestone

The Valleys Sandstone

Destination Planner

	Routes	up to 4+	5 to 6a+	6b to 7a	7a+ and up
Dyffryn	45	1	27	17	-
Abbey Buttress	25	-	6	16	3
Treherbert Quarry	39	2	21	13	3
Ton Pentre	14	-	6	8	-
Gelli	50	9	27	14	-
Ferndale	9	-	1	6	2
Blaenllechau	17	7	4	6	-
Dan Dicks	14	-	2	8	4
Trebanog	8	-	-	7	1
Coed Ely	9	1	2	6	-
Glynfach	11	-	5	5	1
Trehafod	19	-	8	11	-
The Darren	21	-	2	10	9
Cwmaman	29	-	14	9	6
Mountain Ash	56	-	19	24	13
The Gap	55	-	21	24	10
Navigation Quarry	34	-	8	22	4
Deri	15	-	1	9	5
Bargoed	27	-	7	18	2
Llanbradach	87	3	7	62	15
Crymlyn Quarry	18	-	6	10	2
Tyle y Coch	22	8	2	9	3
Sirhowy	56	-	23	26	7
Tirpentwys	30	2	16	11	1

Approach	Sun	Sheltered	Dry in Rain	Restrictions	Seepage	Summary	Page	
13 min	Morning	Sheltered				A good local spot with lots of short but interesting lines in a quiet location.	256	
10 min	Afternoon	Windy				An old quarry with plenty of climbs close to the M4 and overlooking the steelworks at Port Talbot.	262	Carmarthenshire
20 min	Afternoon	Windy				A quiet venue with some good climbs. It is perched high above the valley and has stunning views. Has the feeling of a mountain cliff and therefore is a warm weather venue.	266	
10 min	From mid morning	Sheltered				A compact and steep quarry that is easily combined with a visit to nearby Gelli. A local venue.	274	
10 min	Sun and shade					Lots of lower-grade routes good for locals on a summer evening. The approach is a bit grotty initially, but the crag itself is quiet and pleasant.	278	
10 min	Sun and shade	Sheltered				A series of vertical walls in a quarry high above the valley.	284	
10 min	Afternoon	Sheltered				A good little quarry for some easier lines. Quiet spot.	286	
10 min	Morning	Sheltered		Bird		An easily accessed crag with some impressive lines, but prone to becoming vegetated. Restriction due to nesting birds early in the year.	288	
1 min	From mid morning	Windy				A small local spot good for a workout. Plenty of sun in winter and dries quickly.	290	Gower
4 min	Afternoon	Sheltered		Restrictions		A nice little quarry with a handful of tough lines on good rock. Sunny and sheltered but with some access issues.	292	
13 min	Afternoon					A small quarry high on the hillside with a limited number of routes. Worth a look for the climbs on the Killer Arete buttress.	296	
Roadside	From mid morning	Sheltered	Dry in the rain			A small cliff with some stiff problems that is only a minute from the railway station platform. Good for grabbing some quick routes when passing.	298	
5 min	Sun and shade	Sheltered	Dry in the rain			Local training crag that has a wall of super-steep climbs in the 7th grade.	302	
10 min	Afternoon	Sheltered			Seepage	A vertical blank wall at the far end of the quarry that is home to some finger searing testpieces. Some of the easier lines are also worthwhile.	306	Inland and Coastal Limestone
3-4 min	From mid morning	Sheltered			Seepage	A collection of quarried walls shrouded by trees and quick to get to. Many decent routes across the grades.	312	
2-4 min	Not much sun					The old forcing ground of hard climbing in the Valleys. Still gets attention which keeps it in good condition. Some classic pitches on reliable well-equipped rock. Very fingery and technical climbing.	320	
13 min	Lots of sun	Sheltered		Bird		A lovely spot with good sport routes and also some trad. Sunny aspect and with excellent rock. Variable restriction due to nesting birds early in the year.	328	
7 min	Evening		Dry in the rain	Bird		A fine little crag located on the edge of a country park. It has a steep wall of grade 7s. Access has been a problem in the past but is now fine. Restriction due to nesting birds early in the year.	334	
1 min	Afternoon				Seepage	A small quarry, set in woods, with lots of routes. Something here for most climbers, but the grades are quite stiff.	336	
10-20 min	Morning	Sheltered			Seepage	A massive quarry with impressive walls. Good routes, but much of the quarry is now reverting back to nature although some of the walls have stayed relatively clean.	340	
4-12 min	Sun and shade	Sheltered				A local crag that has been extensively cleaned but needs traffic to stay in condition.	352	The Valleys Sandstone
4 min	Morning	Sheltered	Dry in the rain	Restrictions	Seepage	A small fierce little crag with good routes. Seepage can be a problem. No official access but climbing is usually tolerated.	354	
2-5 min	Afternoon	Sheltered		Restrictions		One of the Valleys's best. A lovely spot with brilliant climbs on its two best walls - The Rust Curtain and Western Walls. Sensitive access - keep the noise down and pay attention to parking information.	358	
12 min	Lots of sun	Sheltered		Restrictions		An excellent little quarry that has lots of good lines on clean and well-bolted rock. A very pleasant spot to hang out and climb. No official access but climbing is usually tolerated.	368	

Faded symbol means that only some of the routes are sheltered / dry in the rain / restricted / suffer from seepage

Tom Skelhon enjoying a fine evening on the sustained *She's Slipping Away* (7a) at the remote sea cliff of Morfa Bychan - *page 61*. Photo: Mark Glaister

Carmarthenshire

Telpyn Point, Morfa Bychan, Pendine, Cwm Capel

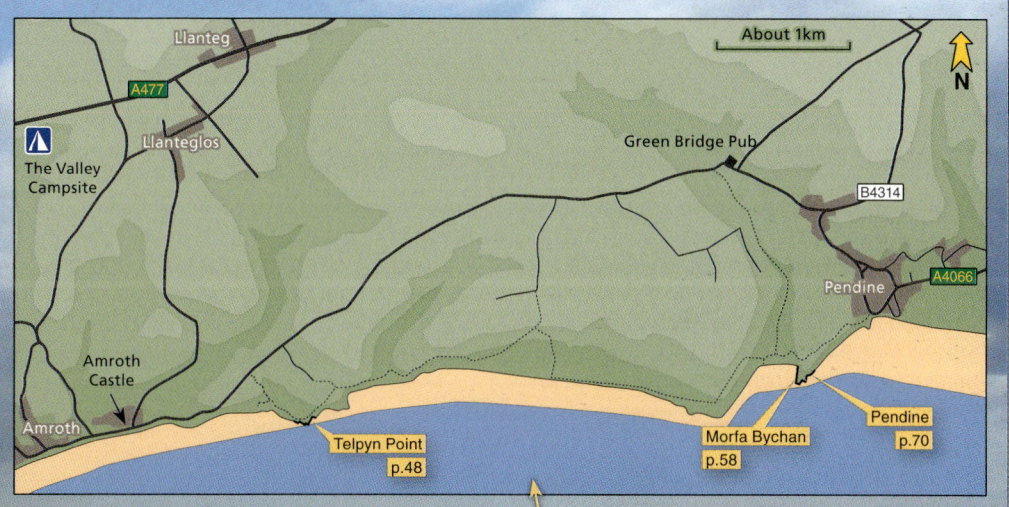

Telpyn Point

	No star	🟢	🟠	🔴
up to 4c	-	-	-	-
5a to 6a+	12	8	-	-
6b to 7a	2	10	4	1
7a+ and up	-	3	1	-

Set between Pembroke and Gower is this surprising sport climbing sea cliff venue. Telpyn, like its nearby neighbours Morfa Bychan and Pendine, offers plenty of sport climbs on well-equipped rock in a beautiful setting. The rock is a hard sandstone and provides both technical and strenuous lines. The routes close to the descent scramble are excellent and provide a good range of mid-to-hard grade routes that will appeal to many. Lurking around the corner is a wall with a totally different feel - radically steep, covered with stacked overhangs and only really appealing to those who like their sport climbing with a heavy dose of adventure.

Approach   Also see map on page 47

From the roundabout on the A40 at St Clears, take the A477 to Tenby. After 8 miles turn left signed to Amroth, a small seaside village. From the seafront at Amroth, follow the road east towards Pendine for around 1.5 miles to a parking layby (with a large coastguard warning sign) on the right, just before the Carmarthenshire border sign, and opposite two gates. Follow a footpath down towards the sea, and as the path veers right, go down steps on the left to a small footbridge and over a stile. Continue along the coast path for 200m until a two metre high vertical wooden fence post appears on the right (there are lots of smaller fence posts). The cliff lies below this post. Walk down right from the post to good rock ledges above the cliff and scramble down below these (easiest to the right, looking out) to ledges at sea level. The cliffs are to the left (looking out).

Tides

The base of the cliff is tidal and can only be accessed for 4 hours on either side of low water. The Mollusc Wall can be reached by abseil and its base is usually above high tide in calm sea conditions.

Conditions

The cliff gets plenty of sun from midday onwards and is clean, although seepage can be a problem after prolonged rainfall. The gently shelving rock platform at the base of the cliff is extremely slick when wet and walking over it requires great care.

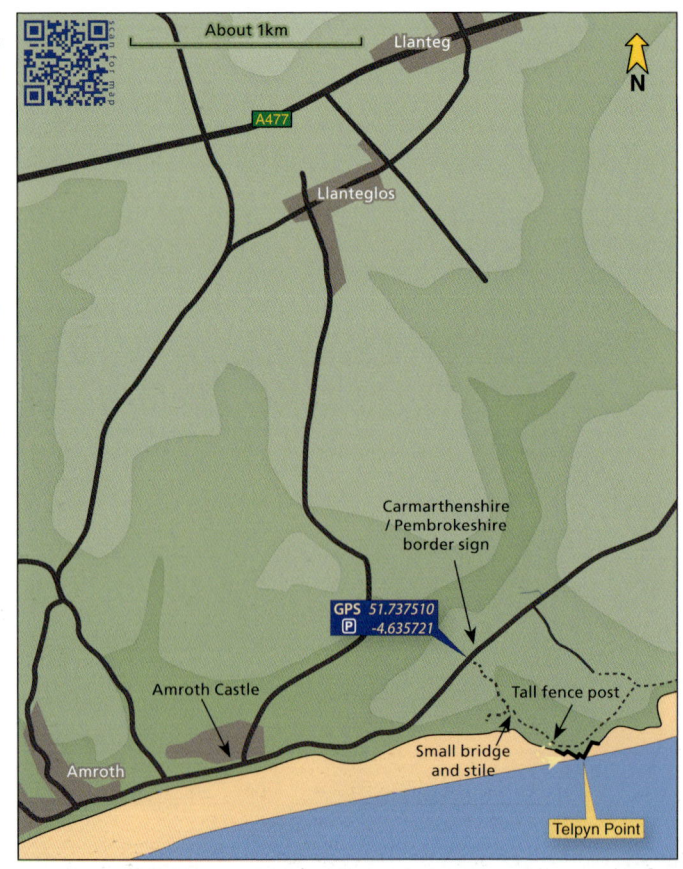

Telpyn Point 49

Tom Skelhon on the excellent thin crackline of *Vladimir and the Pearl* (6c) - *page 52* - on The Mollusc Wall at the sea cliff of Telpyn Point. Photo: Mark Glaister

50 | **Telpyn Point** Fisherman's Wall

Carmarthenshire | Gower | Inland and Coastal Limestone | The Valleys Sandstone

Liz Collyer pulling past the overhang on *Hook, Line and Stinker* (6a+) - *opposite* - on the Fisherman's Wall at Telpyn Point. Photo: Simon Rawlinson

Fisherman's Wall Telpyn Point 51

Fisherman's Wall
A fine section of perfect rock situated above a tidal platform - this can be treacherously greasy when wet.
Approach - Either abseil directly into the wall or (just as easily) scramble down ledges on the right (facing out).
Tides - The ledge under the wall is only accessible for 4 hours on either side of low water.
Conditions - The walls face southwest and dry very quickly after rain. They take little seepage.

1 Little Shrimp . . . . **6a+**
An isolated wall with two hard moves. Very short.
FA. Roy Thomas, Gary Gibson 27.8.2006

2 Small Fry **6a**
A tight line that takes a corner crack up a to a ledge on the left then finishes direct up the wall.
FA. Roy Thomas, Matt Hirst, Nick O'Neill 28.7.2008

3 Cure for Crabs **5c**
The vague crackline on the left-hand side of the wall passing an old peg. A stiff pull over the overhang above the ledge is needed.
FA. Roy Thomas, Gary Gibson 26.8.2006

4 Wrasse . . . . **6b+**
A short fingery wall which leads to a shallow juggy groove above. Much harder if you cannot span to the ledge (**6c+**).
FA. Gary Gibson, Roy Thomas 26.8.2006

5 Cast Adrift . . . . **6a+**
A stiff pull left of the cave gains the juggy upper wall.
FA. Gary Gibson, Roy Thomas 25.6.2006

6 Hook, Line and Stinker . . . . . **6a+**
Steep climbing but with superb hidden holds. *Photo opposite*.
FA. Gary Gibson, Roy Thomas 26.8.2006

7 A Fisherman's Tackle **6b**
A shallow groove line with a hard move to pass the overlap.
FA. Gary Gibson, Roy Thomas 26.8.2006

8 Sprats from the Captain's Table . **5c**
Two tricky moves below the ledge. Easier above.
FA. Roy Thomas, Gary Gibson 26.8.2006

9 Top Mouth Gudgeon **5c**
The left-hand thin crack in the side wall complete with overlap.
FA. Roy Thomas 2006

10 Leger System **5a**
The thin crack above the overhang.
FA. Roy Thomas 2006

11 Cunning Ling **5b**
The thin crack just left of the large corner.
FA. Roy Thomas 2006

12 Tough Carapace . . . . **VS 4c**
The corner. Use the bolt belay on the right or escape left to and top-out.
FA. Roy Thomas 2006

The Mollusc Wall

A good wall of sheer rock with routes that are sustained and fingery - the crux moves are nearly always in the final few metres.

Approach - Either abseil in or walk across the platform from below the Fisherman's Wall.

Tides - The approach to the wall is tidal and can only be accessed for around 4 hours on either side of low water. The base of the wall is not tidal, and in calm seas can easily be reached via abseil, even at high tide.

Conditions - The walls face southwest and dry relatively quickly. They do suffer from seepage, most surprisingly in humid weather when it really makes the routes significantly harder. When a westerly breeze blows it provides the ideal venue.

1 Barnacles at Dawn 6c
A technical, balancy start with better holds on the upper section. Suffers from seepage.
FA. Gary Gibson 27.8.2006

2 Pray for the Cray . . . . . . 7a+
The left-trending crackline has a final difficult pull.
FA. Gary Gibson 25.6.2006

3 Lobster Bisque 7b
Another vague crackline which is reasonable until the desperately fingery finale.
FA. Gary Gibson 25.6.2006

4 Oyster Party 7a
A super little wall climb with technical moves away from gear at the top.
FA. Gary Gibson, Roy Thomas 18.6.2005

5 Vladimir and the Pearl . . 6c
The central line of the wall leftwards via a prominent crackline.
Photo on page 49.
FA. Gary Gibson, Roy Thomas 18.6.2005

6 Shellin' Out. 7b
A sustained affair with, as usual, a sting in the tail.
FA. Gary Gibson 24.6.2006

The Mollusc Wall — Telpyn Point 53

7 King Prawn . . . . 🔩2 ▭ **7a**
A fine series of thin cracks with good holds until the last move.
FA. Gary Gibson, Roy Thomas 18.6.2005

8 Man or Mollusc . . . . 🔩 🧗 ▭ **7b**
The final route of the wall once again saves the hardest to last.
FA. Gary Gibson 24.6.2006

9 Telpyn Corner . . . . ▭ **HVS 5a**
The prominent corner proves a little unnerving.
FA. Nick O'Neill, Roy Thomas 2006

10 Mussel Man . . . . 🔩1 ▭ **5c**
The arete on the right-hand side of the wall.
FA. Roy Thomas, Gary Gibson 24.6.2006

11 Moule Mariniere . . . . 🔩1 ▭ **6a**
Start up a left-facing corner.
FA. Roy Thomas, Gary Gibson 24.6.2006

12 Ma Moule Don't Like U Laffin . . ▭ **5c**
The wall, moving left from the last bolt to the lower-off.
FA. Roy Thomas, Gary Gibson 24.6.2006

The Zawn
The next four routes are on a south-facing wall in a small zawn/cave 30m to the right.

13 Taxi to the Ocean . . . 🔩1 🧗 ▭ **7a**
Tackle the arete full on, finishing via some bizarre moves on its right-hand side.
FA. Gary Gibson 27.8.2006

14 Diving for Pearls . . . . 🔩1 ▭ **6b**
The fine overlapped wall. Short but excellent on lots of jugs.
FA. Gary Gibson, Roy Thomas 27.8.2006

15 Sea Fairer. . . . . 🔩1 ▭ **6a+**
Start up a groove and continue up the overlaps above it.
FA. Gary Gibson, Roy Thomas 27.8.2006

16 Glug, Glug, Glug . . . . ▭ **6a+**
The wall to the right to a shared lower-off with *Sea Fairer*.
FA. Gary Gibson, Roy Thomas 27.8.2006

Tom Skelhon on *Spectre of Love* (6c+) - *page 56* - on the Tremors Wall at Telpyn Point. Although spectacular, this wall should be approached with caution as the rock quality is questionable. Photo: Mark Glaister

Telpyn Point

55

Telpyn Point — Tremors Wall

Tremors Wall

A big imposing wall with an intimidating atmosphere. It is composed of a series of slim grooves split by some hostile-looking overhangs. The current routes tackle the weaknesses in the roofs at relatively amenable grades. Any future additions are likely to be much harder. This is sport climbing with a large dose of adventure thrown in and is not a playground for the weak of spirit or those not used to handling loose rock.

Approach - Continue round the corner from The Mollusc Wall and down some ledges to the base of the cliff.
Tides - The base of the wall is tidal and can only be accessed for around 3 hours on either side of low water.
Conditions - The wall takes a little seepage towards its right-hand side which takes a while to dry. The climbs here can be very greasy in humid weather. The wall faces southeast and receives the sun until about 2pm.

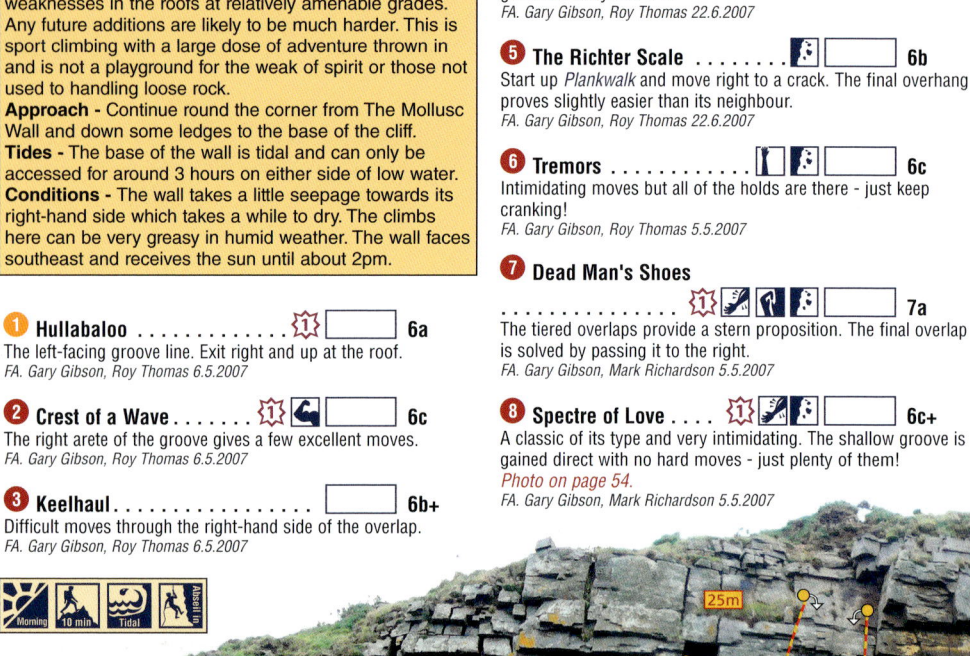

1 Hullabaloo 6a
The left-facing groove line. Exit right and up at the roof.
FA. Gary Gibson, Roy Thomas 6.5.2007

2 Crest of a Wave 6c
The right arete of the groove gives a few excellent moves.
FA. Gary Gibson, Roy Thomas 6.5.2007

3 Keelhaul .... 6b+
Difficult moves through the right-hand side of the overlap.
FA. Gary Gibson, Roy Thomas 6.5.2007

4 Plankwalk .... 6a+
The thin crackline springing from the right-hand side of the ledge is difficult to get established in. An airy pull and long reach gains the belay above it.
FA. Gary Gibson, Roy Thomas 22.6.2007

5 The Richter Scale 6b
Start up *Plankwalk* and move right to a crack. The final overhang proves slightly easier than its neighbour.
FA. Gary Gibson, Roy Thomas 22.6.2007

6 Tremors 6c
Intimidating moves but all of the holds are there - just keep cranking!
FA. Gary Gibson, Roy Thomas 5.5.2007

7 Dead Man's Shoes
.... 7a
The tiered overlaps provide a stern proposition. The final overlap is solved by passing it to the right.
FA. Gary Gibson, Mark Richardson 5.5.2007

8 Spectre of Love .... 6c+
A classic of its type and very intimidating. The shallow groove is gained direct with no hard moves - just plenty of them!
Photo on page 54.
FA. Gary Gibson, Mark Richardson 5.5.2007

Cave Wall **Telpyn Point** 57

Cave Wall

This wall surrounding the cave at the right-hand side of the Tremors Wall offers a handful of easier grade routes, together with one big pumpfest up the edge of the brooding cave. The rock quality here is better than on Tremors Wall.

Approach - Traverse the platform below Tremors Wall to the routes.

Tides - The base of the wall is tidal and can only be accessed for around 3 hours on either side of low water.

Conditions - The main cave takes seepage but the routes described are usually unaffected. The cliff faces west and gets afternoon sunshine, but the routes can be greasy in humid conditions.

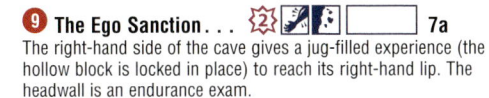

9 The Ego Sanction . . . 7a
The right-hand side of the cave gives a jug-filled experience (the hollow block is locked in place) to reach its right-hand lip. The headwall is an endurance exam.
FA. Gary Gibson 23.6.2007

10 Mental Message . . . 6b
The shallow groove line to a steep upper wall passing a mid-height lower-off.
FA. Roy Thomas, Gary Gibson 4.5.2007

11 Men From Boys E2 5b
A trad line up the lower groove system to a belay ledge on the right (5a). Then the fine hand-jamming crack to the top (5b).
FA. Roy Thomas, Stuart Llewellyn 6.2008

12 Safe Connection 5c
The centre of the wall via a thin crack system.
FA. Roy Thomas, Gary Gibson 23.6.2007

13 Innocents Abroad. 6a
Branch right from *Safe Connection* to climb the wall.
FA. Roy Thomas, Stuart Llewellyn 6.2008

Morfa Bychan

	No star	☆	☆☆	☆☆☆
up to 4c	2	-	-	-
5a to 6a+	15	8	1	-
6b to 7a	5	6	8	3
7a+ and up	-	7	-	-

Morfa Bychan is tucked away in a tranquil cove and adjacent to a nice beach. It has some superb rock and climbing and makes a worthwhile venue within easy reach of the Pembrokeshire crags, or when combined with a visit to the nearby Telpyn Point or Pendine. The cliff is limestone and very steep in its central section. This initially appears quite intimidating but on closer inspection it all feels quite friendly. Morfa Bychan has a good grade mix - in the centre are harder routes whilst on its right-hand side the cliff is less steep.

Approach   Also see map on page 47

From the roundabout on the A40 at St Clears, take the A477 to Tenby. After 8 miles turn left signed to Amroth. From the seafront at Amroth, follow the road east towards Pendine, for around 4 miles. Turn right opposite some standing stones (only a footpath sign). The turning is 100m before the Green Bridge pub. Go down a rough unmade road which leads past a caravan park on the left to a very tranquil cove in 1.5 miles. The crag is easily seen from here.

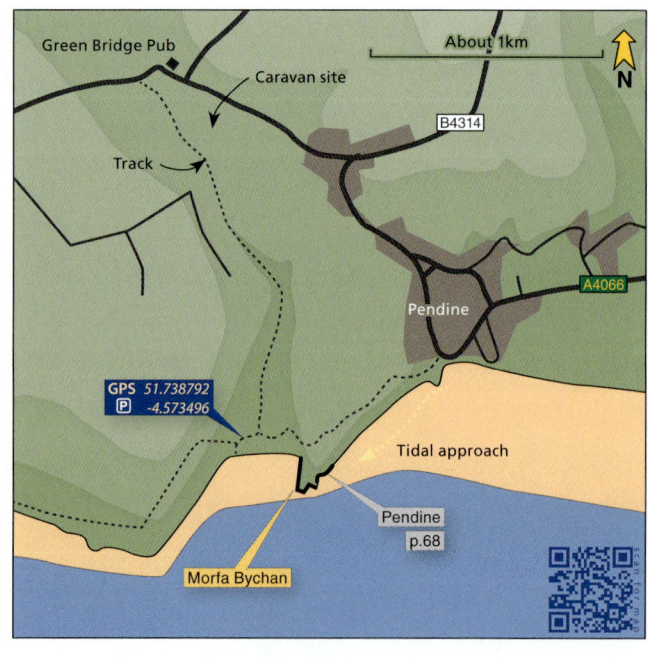

Tides

The crag is tidal. The right-hand side of the Main Cliff can only be accessed for 4 hours on either side of low tide. It is possible to climb on the left-hand side when the tide is in (although access and escape is cut-off). Due to the steep vegetated slopes above the cliff, an abseil approach is not recommended. Sunnyside is accessible for 2 to 3 hours on either side of low tide and Zero Zawn for 1.5 to 2 hours on either side of low tide.

Morfa Bychan 59

Conditions
The Main Cliff faces west and gets the sun from mid-afternoon onwards making it an ideal summer venue. Sunnyside and Zero Zawn have a southerly aspect. The Main Cliff takes relatively little seepage, except in winter, and can be climbed upon even after a light shower. The rock can feel soapy in humid weather before the sun has moved onto the face to dry it out.

John Warner on the fantastic rock and very sustained climbing of the pumpy *Credit Squeeze* (6b+) - *page 61* - at Morfa Bychan. Photo: Mark Glaister

Morfa Bychan — Main Cliff

Main Cliff
A good, well-equipped cliff in a lovely cove. It has a selection of steep and sustained routes in the 6th and 7th grades. The rock is good on the whole, although some sections on the steeper lines are a little fragile.

Approach - From the parking, walk along the pebble and sand beach to the rocky platform at the base of the cliff.
Tides - The base of the crag is tidal and can only be accessed for 4 hours on either side of low water.
Conditions - The rock can feel soapy in humid weather or before the sun has moved onto the face. The cliff does offer the possibility of climbing in showery weather, although it is exposed to westerly gales.

1 Dish the Dirt 6c
A fingery and powerful lower bulge is followed by much easier pleasant moves above.
FA. Gary Gibson, Roy Thomas 28.6.2008

2 Less is More ...... 7a+
A complicated sequence through the lower bulge precedes another tricky sequence via the short arete higher up.
FA. Gary Gibson 15.8.2008

3 More than Enough 7a
A very fine stamina exercise.
FA. Gary Gibson 29.6.2008

4 More More More 7a
Very overhanging with a tough central section.
FA. Gary Gibson, Roy Thomas 24.5.2009

5 Moreland .... 7a+
Brilliant stamina climbing via a mid-height hanging corner. Low in the grade.
FA. Gary Gibson 24.5.2009

6 Burn After Reading..... 6c+
Fine climbing from bottom to top with an amenable finale.
FA. Gary Gibson, Roy Thomas 7.6.2008

7 Morfa, Morfa, Morfa...... 7a
At present the pillar under the top roof is dangerously loose. A tough and draining sequence through the lower bulge. The upper overlap has a good rest just before it.
FA. Gary Gibson 8.6.2008

8 Listing Badly 7a
A demanding start leads to an easier middle section and difficult finale through the capping overlap.
FA. Gary Gibson 7.6.2008

Main Cliff **Morfa Bychan** 61

9 Wreckage .... 7a+
A very complex start, easier middle and then an even more difficult finish requiring a big wingspan.
FA. Gary Gibson 6.6.2008

10 She's Slipping Away 7a
A butch lower overhang complements a complex finale. A good taster for the harder routes. *Photo on page 46*.
FA. Gary Gibson, Roy Thomas 6.6.2008

11 Credit Squeeze .... 6b+
A gem of a route with excellent moves that are deceptively pumpy. The initial corner is sometimes damp. *Photo on page 59*.
FA. Roy Thomas, Gary Gibson 8.6.2008

12 The Pinch is On .... 7a+
Direct up the leaning headwall above the start of *Credit Squeeze* with a hard finale.
FA. Gary Gibson 24.5.2009

13 Selling Short .... 6b+
A fine sister route to *Credit Squeeze* that breaks right after its initial corner. *Photo on page 62*.
FA. Roy Thomas, Gary Gibson 7.6.2008

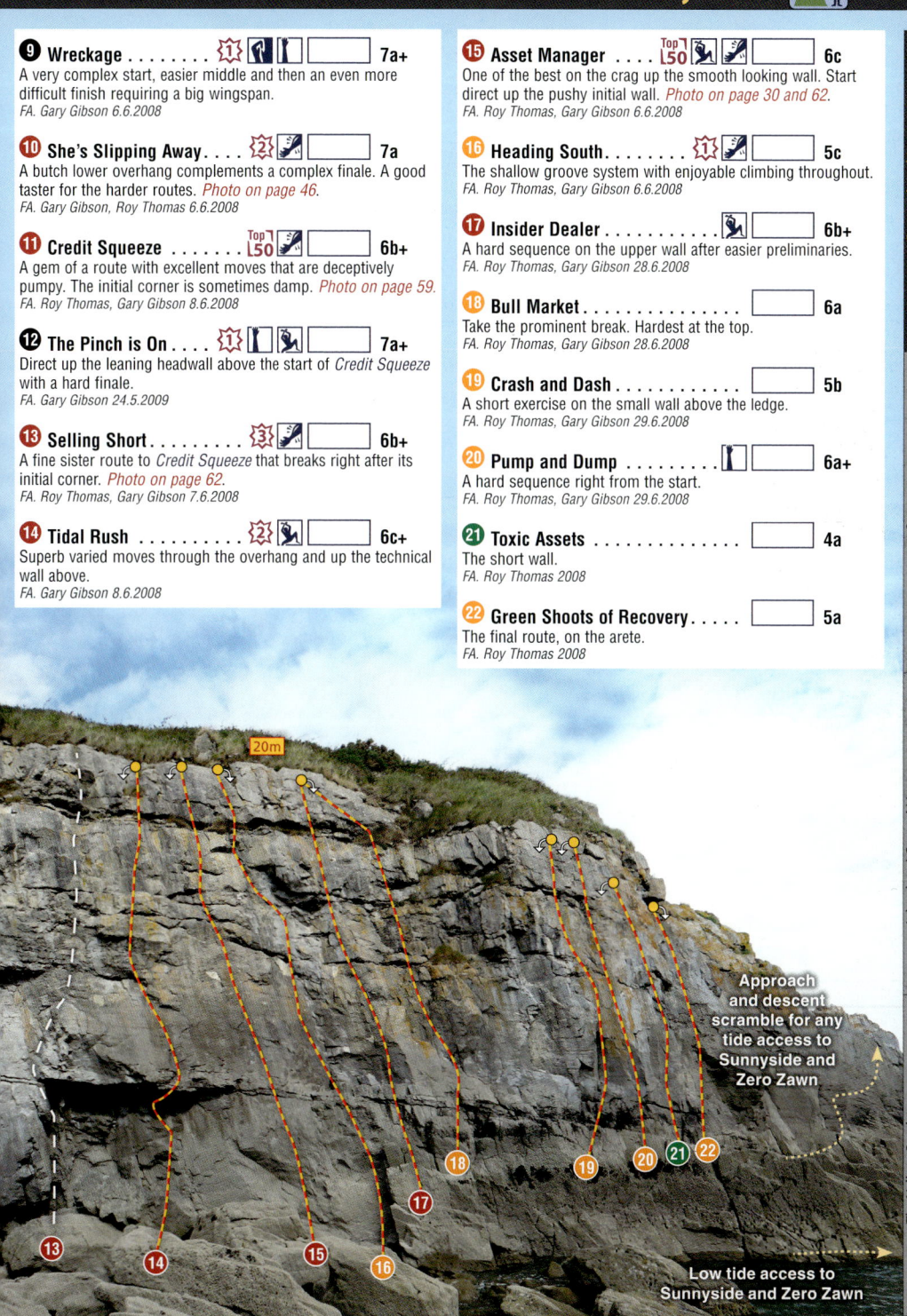

14 Tidal Rush .... 6c+
Superb varied moves through the overhang and up the technical wall above.
FA. Gary Gibson 8.6.2008

15 Asset Manager 6c
One of the best on the crag up the smooth looking wall. Start direct up the pushy initial wall. *Photo on page 30 and 62*.
FA. Roy Thomas, Gary Gibson 6.6.2008

16 Heading South 5c
The shallow groove system with enjoyable climbing throughout.
FA. Roy Thomas, Gary Gibson 6.6.2008

17 Insider Dealer .... 6b+
A hard sequence on the upper wall after easier preliminaries.
FA. Gary Gibson 28.6.2008

18 Bull Market 6a
Take the prominent break. Hardest at the top.
FA. Roy Thomas, Gary Gibson 28.6.2008

19 Crash and Dash 5b
A short exercise on the small wall above the ledge.
FA. Roy Thomas, Gary Gibson 29.6.2008

20 Pump and Dump .... 6a+
A hard sequence right from the start.
FA. Roy Thomas, Gary Gibson 29.6.2008

21 Toxic Assets 4a
The short wall.
FA. Roy Thomas 2008

22 Green Shoots of Recovery 5a
The final route, on the arete.
FA. Roy Thomas 2008

Approach and descent scramble for any tide access to Sunnyside and Zero Zawn

Low tide access to Sunnyside and Zero Zawn

Morfa Bychan

John Warner on the steep mid section of *Selling Short* (6b+) - *page 61* - and Jean Marc Agnonistidis on *Asset Manager* (6c) at Morfa Bychan. Photo: Mark Glaister

Morfa Bychan *63*

Morfa Bychan — Sunnyside

Sunnyside

An isolated bay with some smart little sport pitches on good rock. Careful timing of the approach and exit with regard to the tides is needed to get the best from a visit.

Approach and Tides - The cliff can be gained at very low tide along the beach from the base of the Main Cliff but, in order to get plenty of climbing time in, the best access is via the higher approach. From the seaward end of the Main Cliff, scramble up cracks, ledges and walls to the top of the cliff and walk around to abseil bolts above the cliff edge. To exit, climb up the easy *Get Out Claws* and reverse the scramble back to the Main Cliff.

Conditions - It faces roughly south and gets plenty of sun but can be greasy in humid weather.

1 Squeeze that Lemon 5c
Climb the pillar via the vague arete.
FA. Roy Thomas, Goi Ashmore 12.5.2016

2 The Golden String 5c
Start up the enclosed deep crack then head directly up the pillar.
FA. Roy Thomas, Goi Ashmore 26.7.2014

3 Noah's Arse 5b
Climb the wall to a steepening, then step right to a shared lower-off with *Knee Jerk*.
FA. Roy Thomas, Eugene Travers-Jones 24.8.2014

4 Knee Jerk 6a
Contains some amusing moves to pass the overlap
FA. Roy Thomas 27.7.2014

5 Lucas Numbers 6c
An awkward start gains a groove and roof. The line goes directly up to the first bolt, via a slot to a hand rail. Starting up the groove to the left is far easier and doesn't qualify for a tick.
FA. Goi Ashmore 31.5.2014

6 Bonacci's Sequence 7b
The overhanging right wall of the arete of *Lucas Numbers*. Technical with a huge lurch to finish.
FA. Goi Ashmore 27.7.2014

7 Mistaking Cassini's Identity .... 7a+
The groove between *Bonacci's Sequence* and *All For Nothing*. Oddball climbing that involves a powerful lock off on a sloper.
FA. Goi Ashmore 29.9.2014

Sunnyside **Morfa Bychan** 65

8 All For Nothing .... 6a+
Start at the base of the ramp and climb the red wall and overlap.
FA. Roy Thomas, Eugene Travers-Jones 5.7.2014

9 Get Out Claws 2c
The staircase right of *All For Nothing*.
FA. Roy Thomas 28.7.2014

10 Zero Inclination .... 6a+
The faint rib and groove is quite tricky.
FA. Roy Thomas, Goi Ashmore 6.7.2014

11 Recurring Nightmare 5a
Left of *A Question Of Rabbits* a short stapled wall leads to the ledge of the following routes and a shared ring lower-off.
FA. Roy Thomas, Goi Ashmore 6.2014

12 A Question of Rabbits ...... 6b+
The short wall. Start left of the arete and move into the centre of the face before heading upto the ledge.
FA. Roy Thomas 27.7.2014

13 My Slice of Pie 6a
The arete, big ledge and high groove.
FA. Roy Thomas, Goi Ashmore 6.2014

14 Sad Little Nutter .... HVS 5b
The thin crack in the left side of the pillar.
FA. Roy Thomas, Goi Ashmore 6.2014

15 Off at a Tangent .... 6a+
The wall to the right of the thin crack. Joins the other routes after the ledge.
FA. Roy Thomas 6.2014

16 Smart Keas 6a
Left of the crack of *Daft Nutter*, take the sidewall then stick to the arete until tricky moves gain the ledge.
FA. Roy Thomas, Nik Goile, Gareth James 9.2014

17 Daft Nutter .... HVS 5b
The thin crack up the wall left of *You Sane Bolter* has good rock and a couple of hard moves.
FA. Roy Thomas 5.2013

18 You Sane Bolter .... 6a+
The groove on the right-hand side of the central pillar leading to a pedestal and lower-off above the break. Interesting moves.
Photo on page 66.
FA. Roy Thomas, Goi Ashmore 6.2014

19 Bolus Feed 6b
The pillar on the left-hand side of the zawn.
FA. Roy Thomas, Goi Ashmore 6.2014

20 Nil By Mouth .... 6a+
A tricky start off of the ledge at the start of the zawn.
FA. Roy Thomas, Goi Ashmore 6.2014

Morfa Bychan

Mark Glaister enjoying perfect summer conditions at Morfa Bychan's Sunnyside area. The dark recess of Zero Zawn is to the right of the climber who is nearing the top of the entertaining *You Sane Bolter* (6a+) - *page 65*. Photo: Glaister Collection

Morfa Bychan

67

Morfa Bychan — Zero Zawn

Zero Zawn
An impressive gash in the cliff that abuts the right-hand end of the Sunnyside crag The routes take time to come into condition but once climbable are excellent.
Approach and Tides - As for the Sunnyside crag.
Conditions - Shady and needs a dry spell to come into condition. The bed of zawn has a pool in it.

1 Continued Nursing Care . . . . . . 6a+
A short hard section.
FA. Roy Thomas 31.5.2014

2 P.E.G Feed 5c
The groove has an awkward start.
FA. Roy Thomas, Goi Ashmore, Eugene Travers-Jones 6.7.2014

3 Labrynthitis . . . . 6a+
Deep inside the dark confines of the zawn. Usually wet.
FA. Roy Thomas, Goi Ashmore 8.2015

4 The Quest for the Origins of Place Holder Notation
. . . . 6b+
The left-hand line on the right wall of the Zawn. Start as for *Turing's Sum* and take a rising traverse in.
FA. Roy Thomas 27.7.2014

5 Disraeli's Curl 7a
The vague groove towards the left of the wall, reached via the rising traverse from *Turing's Sum*.
FA. Goi Ashmore 6.6.2014

6 Disraeli's Curl Direct 7a
The awkward left-hand groove leading up into *Disraeli's Curl* is much harder than first appearances suggest. Very rarely dry - only seen dry to date on midwinter spring tides when the angle of the sun is low enough to dry it out.
FA. Goi Ashmore 21.2.2015

7 Kitchener's Nabla . . . . 7a+
The start is usually wet so either use the first bolt as an aid point, or gain the upper section from *Turing's Sum*.
FA. Goi Ashmore 5.7.2014

8 Turing's Sum . . . . 6c+
The bomb bay chimney and harder-than-expected continuation groove. The start is feasible in wet conditions which is why it is used to reach the upper sections of the routes to the left.
FA. Goi Ashmore 6.7.2014

9 Blank Dark Thirty 6b
The hanging set of grooves split by sloping shelves.
FA. Roy Thomas, Goi Ashmore 22.4.2015

10 Joys of a Tethered Goat . 6b
Climb the pocketed rib left of the start of *Central Integrator*, and then head leftwards to gain and finish up *Blank Dark Thirty*.
FA. Roy Thomas, Goi Ashmore 22.5.2015

11 Central Integrator 6b
Start up a short corner to a ledge and then follow the groove.
FA. Roy Thomas, Rich Phillips 5.2014

Zero Zawn **Morfa Bychan** 69

12 Dismal Differentiator .... 6a+
The flake crack before heading left to a lower-off shared with *Central Integrator*.
FA. Roy Thomas Goi Ashmore 15.04.2014

13 Napier's Bones 6a
A short line up the pillar to the right of the zawn entrance.
FA. Roy Thomas, Eugene Travers-Jones 8.2.201

Pendine

	No star	★	★★	★★★
up to 4c	-	-	-	-
5a to 6a+	9	8	1	-
6b to 7a	-	12	8	2
7a+ and up	-	4	7	2

To the west of the tiny resort of Pendine, and its famous expanse of sand, is an excellent little sport cliff which has some of the area's best routes. The rock is excellent, the lines appealing and the location fabulous, however your approach needs careful planning to ensure that you squeeze the most out of a visit. The left-hand crag, known as Dark Side, is a long wall covered with narrow overhangs. It has plenty of quality climbing in the 7s. The right-hand Platform Cliff is taller but less steep and has numerous grade 6s that tackle some fine grooves, thin cracks, overlaps and steep slabs.

Approach   Also see map on page 47

From the roundabout on the A40 at St Clears, take the A477 towards Tenby. After 6 miles turn left onto the B4314 (signed Red Roses) and follow it to Pendine. Park in the centre of the seaside village (roadside parking or car parks). Walk down on to the beach and head west for 10 minutes until the cliff is reached just before the headland.

Tides

Careful planning is needed. The simplest approach is to walk in as soon as you can as the tide goes out, climb for four hours, then walk out. Another option is to walk in at low tide and climb on the Platform Area as the tide comes back in (the platform is above high water level in calm seas) and walk out during the following low tide, although this makes for quite a long day. Another option for those familiar with the area is to walk in on a falling tide, climb a route or two at Pendine and then nip around the headland at low water to gain Sunnyside/Zero Zawn at Morfa Bychan. You could then work your way along that cliff as the tide comes in, reversing the high approach from the Main Cliff, and complete the day here before the tide cuts off access to Morfa Bychan beach. Then simply walk back along the cliff top path to Pendine.

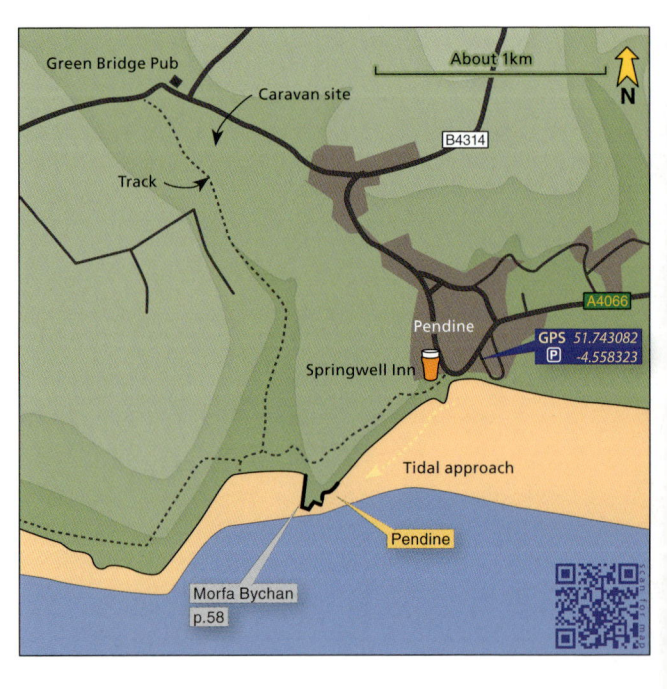

Conditions

The cliff gets plenty of sun until mid afternoon and dries quickly. Seepage can be a problem after rainfall.

Pendine 71

Goi Ashmore working on the first ascent of *Gladstone's Deficit* (7b) - *page 72* - one of many fine pitches established on The Dark Side section of Pendine. Photo: Mark Glaister

Pendine — The Dark Side

The Dark Side
The roof-dotted wall that dips towards the sea is a fine section of cliff with some excellent grade 7s. The routes give powerful, technical and sustained climbing on excellent rock.

Approach - Walk along the beach and then over boulders to below the cliff.
Tides - The base of the wall is uncovered for around 2 hours on either side of low tide.
Conditions - The cliff gets the sun until early afternoon.

1 Short Sharp Sock 6b
The short finger biting wall.
FA. Roy Thomas, Goi Ashmore 1.10.2015

2 Juice Runs Down My Leg 5c
Another short and fingery wall right of a crack.
FA. Roy Thomas, Goi Ashmore 25.3.2016

3 Straight as a Dai 6b
Make some difficult moves up the barnacle band before the good stuff arrives.
FA. Roy Thomas, Goi Ashmore 16.4.2014

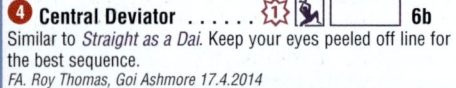

4 Central Deviator 6b
Similar to *Straight as a Dai*. Keep your eyes peeled off line for the best sequence.
FA. Roy Thomas, Goi Ashmore 17.4.2014

5 Silver Surfers Sermon ..... 6c+
A broken looking line that takes the pillar and crack.
FA. Eugene Travers-Jones 6.7.2015

6 Before Planck's Time ... 7a+
The seam and hanging groove has a distinct crux. The lower-off is well above the band of vegetation.
FA. Goi Ashmore, Eugene Travers-Jones 5.6.2015

7 Salisbury's Crowd ..... 7b+
Where the bolt lines split, keep up and left into the groove. Difficult to work out although reasonable to redpoint.
FA. Goi Ashmore 10.7.2015

8 Gladstone's Deficit 7b
Climb *Salisbury's Crowd* past its first overhang before stepping right to gain a break with difficulty. A further difficult couple of moves leads to good holds above the overlap and an easier finish up the flake. High in the grade. *Photo on page 71.*
FA. Goi Ashmore 14.6.2015

The Dark Side **Pendine**   73

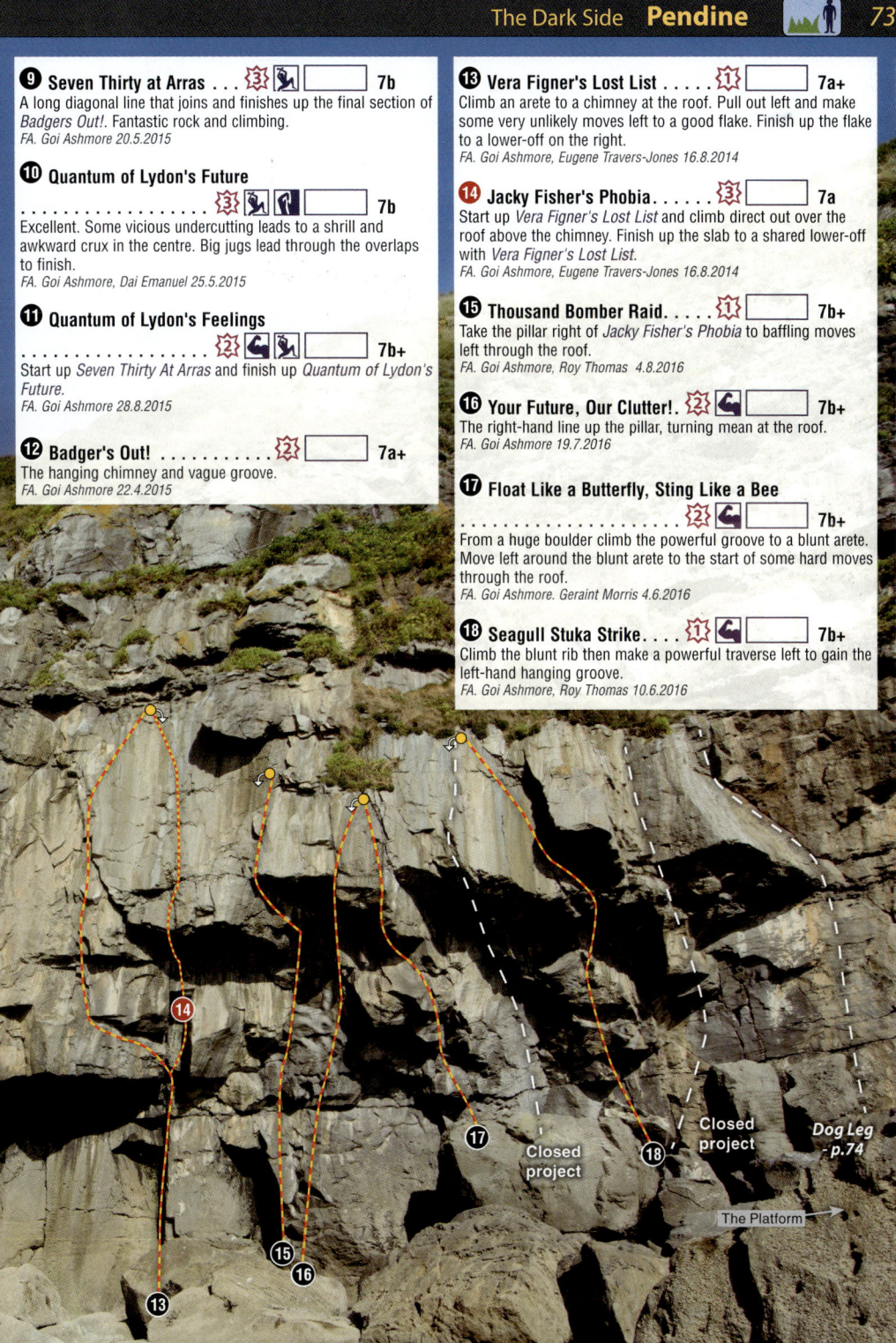

9 Seven Thirty at Arras 7b
A long diagonal line that joins and finishes up the final section of *Badgers Out!*. Fantastic rock and climbing.
FA. Goi Ashmore 20.5.2015

10 Quantum of Lydon's Future
. . . . 7b
Excellent. Some vicious undercutting leads to a shrill and awkward crux in the centre. Big jugs lead through the overlaps to finish.
FA. Goi Ashmore, Dai Emanuel 25.5.2015

11 Quantum of Lydon's Feelings
. . . . 7b+
Start up *Seven Thirty At Arras* and finish up *Quantum of Lydon's Future*.
FA. Goi Ashmore 28.8.2015

12 Badger's Out! . . . . 7a+
The hanging chimney and vague groove.
FA. Goi Ashmore 22.4.2015

13 Vera Figner's Lost List . . . . . 7a+
Climb an arete to a chimney at the roof. Pull out left and make some very unlikely moves left to a good flake. Finish up the flake to a lower-off on the right.
FA. Goi Ashmore, Eugene Travers-Jones 16.8.2014

14 Jacky Fisher's Phobia. 7a
Start up *Vera Figner's Lost List* and climb direct out over the roof above the chimney. Finish up the slab to a shared lower-off with *Vera Figner's Lost List*.
FA. Goi Ashmore, Eugene Travers-Jones 16.8.2014

15 Thousand Bomber Raid. . . . . 7b+
Take the pillar right of *Jacky Fisher's Phobia* to baffling moves left through the roof.
FA. Goi Ashmore, Roy Thomas 4.8.2016

16 Your Future, Our Clutter!. . . 7b+
The right-hand line up the pillar, turning mean at the roof.
FA. Goi Ashmore 19.7.2016

17 Float Like a Butterfly, Sting Like a Bee
. . . . 7b+
From a huge boulder climb the powerful groove to a blunt arete. Move left around the blunt arete to the start of some hard moves through the roof.
FA. Goi Ashmore. Geraint Morris 4.6.2016

18 Seagull Stuka Strike. . . . . 7b+
Climb the blunt rib then make a powerful traverse left to gain the left-hand hanging groove.
FA. Goi Ashmore, Roy Thomas 10.6.2016

Pendine — The Platform

The Platform

A very good wall that has a large choice of worthwhile grade 6s. The rock is generally excellent and the routes follow subtle lines of corners and grooves.
Approach - Walk along the beach and up over boulders.
Tides - The base of the wall is above high tide in calm seas, but the approach is cut off.
Conditions - The cliff gets sun until late afternoon.

① Dog Leg 6a
The left most bolt line moving leftwards up a narrow rampline.
FA. Roy Thomas, Goi Ashmore 9.7.2015

② Dog Wuff 6b
Climb a crack and finish direct.
FA. Roy Thomas, Goi Ashmore 9.7.2015

③ Doggy Style Deviant .... 6a+
Start up *Doggy Style* and finish up the ramp on left.
FA. Roy Thomas, Eugene Travers-Jones 21.7.2015

④ Doggy Style 6b
A fine bit of climbing starting up a crack
FA. Roy Thomas, Rich Phillips 18.7.2015

⑤ Doggy Bag 6a
Take the crack left of the large block that leans against the face - 'The Tombstone' - and continue up bubbly holds.
FA. Roy Thomas, Rich Phillips 18.7.2015

⑥ Little Runt 6a
From the top of the 'Tombstone', make difficult moves up wall.
FA. Roy Thomas, Nick O'Neill, Eugene Travers-Jones 2.8.2015

⑦ Table Scraps 6a
From the top of the 'Tombstone', climb wall left of crack - dirty.
FA. Roy Thomas, Gary Gibson 6.9.2015

⑧ Give the Dog a Bone 5b
Start just to the right of the 'Tombstone' and climb the arete and its left side to a lower-off.
FA. Roy Thomas, Gary Gibson, Hazel Gibson 6.9.2015

⑨ Salty Dog 5c
Move up the technical groove to steeper ground. Big holds lead up left to a shared lower-off.
FA. Hazel Gibson, Roy Thomas 8.6.2015

⑩ Bitch 6b
The smooth depression leads to steep pulling in upper section.
FA. Gary Gibson, Hazel Gibson 8.6.2015

⑪ Snuffle Hound .... 6b+
Technical climbing past the mid-height slab.
FA. Gary Gibson, Hazel Gibson 9.6.2015

⑫ Unleashed 6b
Excellent varied moves.
FA. Gary Gibson, Hazel Gibson 9.6.2015

The Platform **Pendine** 75

13 3D Dog . . . . 6a+
Make a difficult pull to enter the steep and technical groove.
FA. Gary Gibson, Hazel Gibson 9.6.2015

14 Soapy Dahl 6b
A striking line. The smooth groove with a diversion right.
Photo on page 77.
FA. Gary Gibson, Hazel Gibson 7.6.2015

15 Man Machine . . . . 6c+
The corner groove has some perplexing moves midway.
FA. Gary Gibson, Roy Thomas, Hazel Gibson 7.6.2015

16 Cross Country Booty Call. 7a+
The arete to a big round pocket and low lower-off.
FA. Alan Rosier, Rob McAllister 15.5.2016

17 Sophie's Wit Tank . . 6c
Brilliant climbing and line up thin crack on face of buttress.
FA. Roy Thomas, Gary Gibson, Hazel Gibson 8.6.2015

18 Perfect Prude . . . . 6b+
Bridge and layback up the corner right of *Sophie's Wit Tank*.
FA. Roy Thomas 6.2015

19 Stroking the Lizard . . . . 6a+
The pillar corners and exposed roof. A long pitch.
FA. Roy Thomas, Eugene Travers-Jones 6.7.2015

20 Milking the Snake 6a
Follow corners to a roof. Pull over and move left to join and finish as for *Stroking the Lizard*.
FA. Roy Thomas, Goi Ashmore 10.7.2015

21 Stroke of Good Luck. 6c
Climb the short arete and its left wall direct.
FA. Roy Thomas, Rich Phillips 24.6.2015

22 Rubble Escalator 5b
The chimney.
FA. Roy Thomas 18.6.201

23 Blood Spunker . . . . 6a+
The crack and wall to the right of *Rubble Escalator*. Finish via a hand traverse right to gain the lower-off.
FA. Dai Emanuel 2015

24 Dishonourable Discharge 5c
Layback up to join *Spunk Welder*.
FA. Roy Thomas, Rich Phillips 8.2015

25 Spunk Welded 6a
A steep crack and slab. Technical.
FA. Dai Emanuel 2015

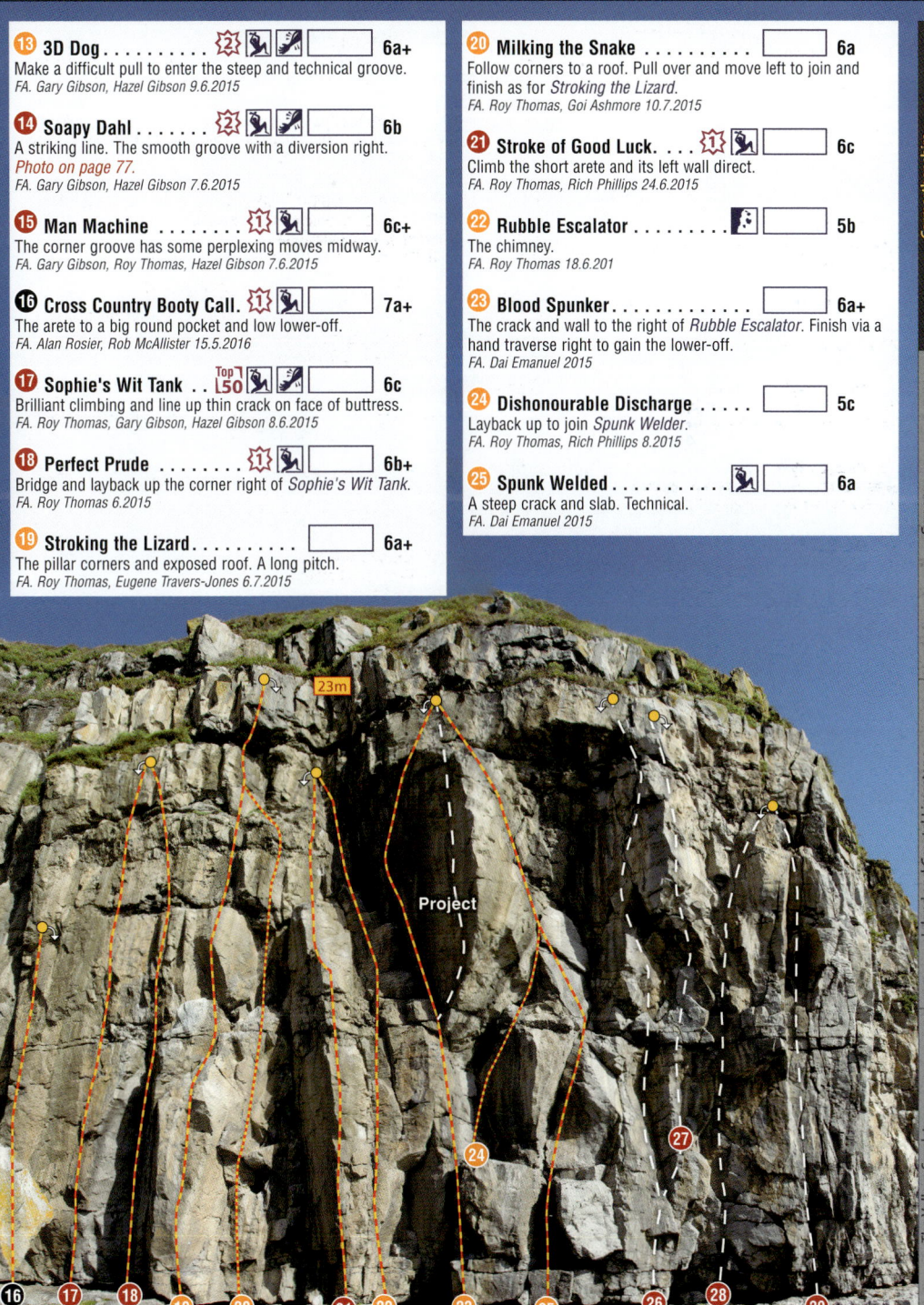

Pendine The Platform

26 Stuck Up Bitch 6c
Take the groove to a strenuous crack in the headwall.
FA. Roy Thomas 1.10.2015

27 Waxing Lyrical. .... 6b+
Start as for *Stuck Up Bitch* and move right to climb a rib then back left to gain a single bolt lower-off.
FA. Roy Thomas, Eugene Travers-Jones 1.11.2015

28 Mary Hinge's Close Shave ... 6b+
The corner/groove is very steep.
FA. Roy Thomas 20.5.2015

29 Nothing in it 6b
The groove/crack to the left of the arete.
FA. Roy Thomas 21.2.2015

30 McGoohan Loses Six ... 6c+
The arete is technical low down. A great line and position.
FA. Goi Ashmore 21.7.2014

31 The Amount of Fun to be had by a Bear with a Broken Baculum .. 6a
The slab right of an arete on pockets and reinforced flakes.
FA. Roy Thomas, Eugene Travers-Jones, Goi Ashmore 22.3.2015

Down and right of The Platform are some more routes.

32 Wristlock 6b
The wall and roof to a to a lower-off.
FA. Roy Thomas, Goi Ashmore 2.9.2016

33 Alpha Blocker .... 6a+
Climb the wall starting at a pointy handhold. Move directly over the small roof and head on up to join *Beat A Block, Ha!* at the top of its diagonal crack.
FA. Roy Thomas, Goi Ashmore 7.2016

34 Beat A Block, Ha!. 6b
Climb the short wall to a ledge, step up from the ledge to a steep crack. Move up to gain a stacked block pillar before launching up the final wall to a shared lower-off.
FA. Roy Thomas 7.2018

35 Hypertension. .... 6a+
Start up *Beat A Block, Ha!* and then take the hanging groove and diagonal crack to a shared lower-off.
FA. Roy Thomas, Eugene Travers-Jones 10.7.2016

36 ACE Inhibitors .... 6b+
Follow *Beat A Block, Ha!* to a ledge and then take the orange wall on the right.
FA. Roy Thomas, Goi Ashmore 23.7.2016

The Platform **Pendine** 77

Carmarthenshire

Gower

Inland and Coastal Limestone

The Valleys Sandstone

Bridget Collier checking out the clean-cut corner of the fine *Soapy Dahl* (6b) - *page 75* - at The Platform crag. Pendine Sands in the background is where many early land speed records were attempted. Photo: Mark Glaister

Cwm Capel

	No star	★	★★	★★★
up to 4c	1	-	-	-
5a to 6a+	6	-	-	-
6b to 7a	4	-	-	-
7a+ and up	-	-	-	-

A small sandstone quarry with some easier routes that are useful if you are passing or for a local evening venue.

Approach Also see map on page 18
The quarry is in the village of Craig, near Burry Port. From Llanelli, follow the A484 towards Pembrey. Just after passing the Pemberton Arms is a chapel. Turn right here to Craig and follow the road past the Farmers Arms, trending right, past some housing. Park adjacent to an old chimney (Cwm Capel Colliery). Do not obstruct access to the yard. The quarry is opposite the chimney. Go around the fence on the left not over it.

Conditions
The quarry is set amongst dense tree cover. This offers some shelter from light rain but also holds in any damp.

Access
Do not top out or make lots of noise as there are residential gardens close by.

① Mini Mission 5b
First short route on the far left of the wall.
FA. Roy Thomas 6.2016

② Nocturnal Emission .... 6b+
Star up a fingery wall to gain a shattered section and shared lower-off with *Seamanship Mission*.
FA. Roy Thomas, Dai Emanuel 6.2016

③ Seamanship Mission 6b
Follow the corner/groove.
FA. Roy Thomas 6.2016

④ Vile Proposition 4a
The stepped corner/groove to a chain lower-off.
FA. Dai Emanuel, Roy Thomas 6.2016

⑤ Premonition 5a
Climb to a lower-off below the oak tree. The shale band is very loose.
FA. FA. Dai Emanuel, Roy Thomas 6.2016

⑥ Requisition .... 6a+
Mantelshelf above the shale band to a lower-off below oak tree.
FA. FA. Dai Emanuel, Roy Thomas 6.2016

⑦ Superstition 6b
Haul over the small roof above the shale band on a sloping jug.
FA. FA. Dai Emanuel, Roy Thomas 6.2016

⑧ Man on a Mission 5a
The corner - a decent pitch.
FA. Roy Thomas, Dai Emanuel 6.2016

Cwm Capel

9 Crime of Omission 6a
The wall of small overlaps just to the right of the corner.
FA. Roy Thomas, Dai Emanuel 6.2016

10 Working on Commission 6b
The wall on a variety of holds to a shared lower-off with *Crime of Omission*.
FA. Roy Thomas, Dai Emanuel 6.2016

11 Attrition .... 6a+
Move into a corner then ramble up to a high lower-off.
FA. FA. Dai Emanuel, Roy Thomas 6.2016

Gower

Rhossili Beach, Trial Wall Area, Third Sister to Zulu Zawn, Oxwich, Watch House, Foxhole, Minchin Hole, Bowen's Parlour Area, Bosco's Gulch Area, Pwlldu Bay, Rams Tor, Barland Quarry

Rhossili Bay
Rhossili Beach p.82
Trial Wall Area p.104
Third Sister to Zulu Zawn p.112
Pitton Cross Camping
Rhossili
Reynoldston
Eastern Slade Barn
Port Eynon
Oxwich p.126
Watch House p.134
Foxhole p.140
Minchin Hole p.148
Southgate
Bowen's Parlour p.152
Bosco's Gulch Area p.158
Barland Quarry p.172
Bishopston
Pwlldu Bay p.166
Rams Tor p.168
West Cross
Swansea Bay
The Mumbles

About 4km

Carmarthenshire
Limestone
Valleys Sandstone

Naomi Buys on the powerful *Goose In Lucy* (6c+) - *page 143* - one of a host of superb sport climbs at Foxhole on Gower. Photo: Mike Hutton

Rhossili Beach

	No star	⭐	⭐⭐	⭐⭐⭐
up to 4c	14	8	-	1
5a to 6a+	22	22	7	2
6b to 7a	4	19	7	1
7a+ and up	4	3	4	6

The development of the sport climbing potential on the beachside sea cliffs at Rhossili has led to it becoming one of South Wales' most popular climbing destinations in recent years. The climbing is excellent, diverse and spans the grades from easy to desperate, but it is its situation next to one of Wales' finest beaches that really ramps up its appeal - get the tides right, some decent summer weather and a fantastic day of climbing, swimming and relaxation is guaranteed.

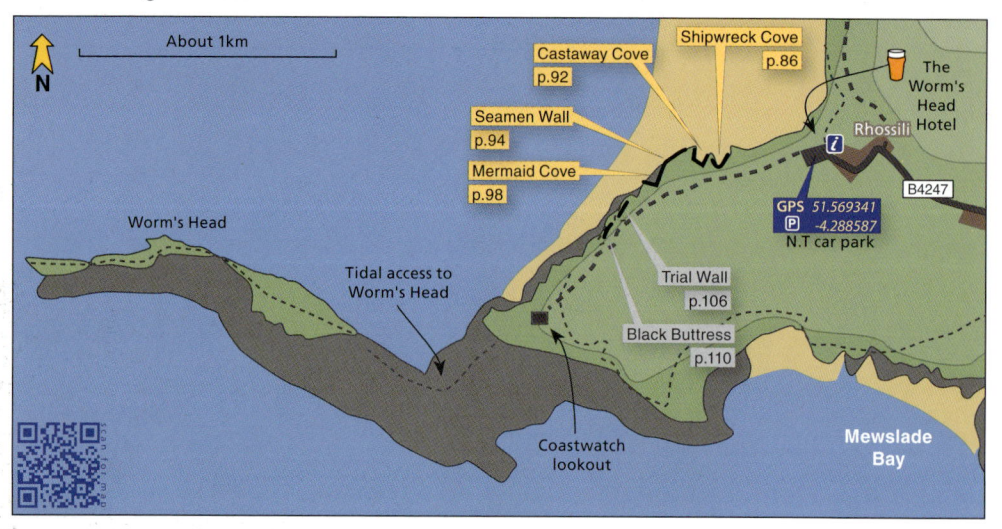

Approach and Tides   Also see map on page 80

From the National Trust car park entrance, take the signed footpath down to the beach. Once on the beach head left. This is a tidal venue and care needs to be taken to ensure that you don't get caught out. The high water level varies considerably during neaps and springs and can shorten the times for access. The state of the sea and air pressure can have an influence, and in rough seas access is sometimes impossible.

Black Wall and Shipwreck Cove - Accessible for around 6 hours at low water.
Castaway Cove and Seamen Wall - Accessible for around 4 to 5 hours at low water.
Mermaid Cove - Accessible for around 3 to 4 hours at low water.

Rhossili Beach 83

The headland at the southern end of Rhossili Beach is one of the major sport climbing destinations in South Wales, having a large number of superb and challenging lines across the grades. The location of the crags overlooking the beach is sublime and makes this a great spot for climbing and relaxing alike. Here Royston Thomas takes on one of Mermaid Cove's many enticing lines *Lemon Sole* (6a) - *page 99*. Photo: Mark Glaister

Conditions
Sandy bases at all the crags means that a rope bag and mat are very useful. First bolts are high and the sand level varies so a stick clip is very handy. At times it can be helpful to allow time for the sun to dry the rock and helps get rid of lingering moisture.

Access
Be aware that this is a busy beach - make sure other users are aware of the dangers of falling rock and please watch your language.

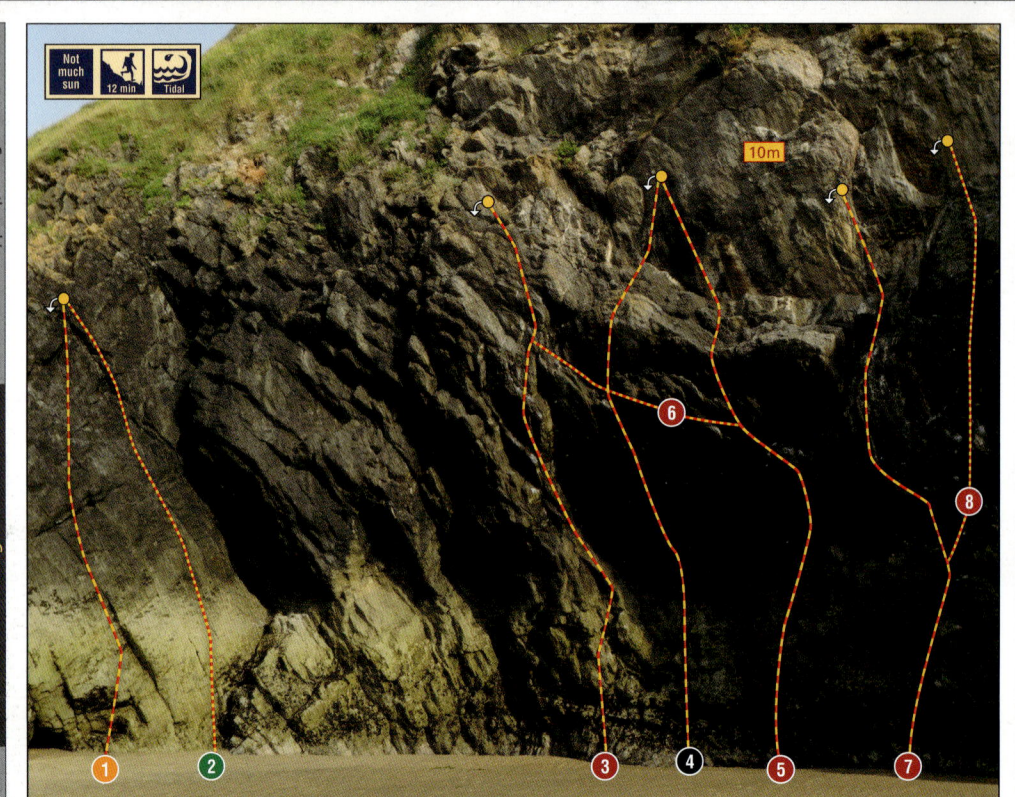

Rhossili Beach — Black Wall

Black Wall
A short overhanging wall with some tough lines. It is the first of the beach crags to be clear of water, so is useful if waiting for the tide to retreat.
Tides - Accessible for 6 hours at low water.
Conditions - The wall gets little sun except very early and late in the day during summer months. There is some possibility of climbing during rain, but the routes are harder in humid/greasy conditions.

1 Thieving Little Parasites. 6a
The left-hand line on the angled wall. Start steeply up diagonal breaks and then head more easily up right to a lower-off.
FA. Roy Thomas 5.2014

2 Wittle Thieving Lankers 4c
The right-hand line on the angled wall to the shared lower-off.
FA. Roy Thomas 5.2014

3 Fats Waller 6c+
The slim leaning corner is a fine but short-looking line. However, its bite is tougher than its bark!
FA. Rob Lamey 26.8.2012

4 The Route with Two Pockets 7b
Easy climbing leads to the steep wall that has only two pockets to cover a large distance.
FA. Simon Rawlinson 8.2012

5 Black Adder 6c
Small edges lead to a steep finale, which thankfully delivers large holds when they are needed. Easy once you know how, but harder for the short.
FA. Simon Rawlinson 8.2012

6 This ain't Pretty 6c+
A link-up. From near the end of *Black Adder* traverse left along the rail to finish up *Fats Waller*.
FA. Simon Rawlinson 10.3.2014

7 The Strongbow Flyer 6b
An awkward start leads to some less-than-brilliant climbing. Much harder if the sand level is low.
FA. Simon Rawlinson 8.2012

8 Rum Thieves 6b+
Much better than its neighbour. Move directly up the smooth shield on good edges and sidepulls. Much harder if the sand level is low.
FA. Simon Rawlinson 8.2012

Kel Vargas on one of Shipwreck Cove's classic lines *Vennerne* (8a) - *page 87* . Since the first lines at Shipwreck Cove were established in 2012 it has become one of the most popular sport crags in South Wales. Photo: Simon Rawlinson

86 Rhossili Beach Shipwreck Cove

Shipwreck Cove **Rhossili Beach** 87

Shipwreck Cove

Shipwreck Cove is a brilliant sport climbing destination with some excellent routes from the mid grade 7s to high 8s. Most of the rock is sound, clean and STEEP! The far side of the cove has some good routes in the 6s that are best attempted in non-humid conditions or in the early morning sun. Some of the lines can be a touch sandy. Although tidal, the amount of time that access is possible will normally be longer than your arms will last out!

Tides - Accessible for 5 to 6 hours at low water. Wading in gives a little more time at the crag as the sand level in the cove is slightly higher than that crossed on the approach.

Conditions - The cove sees sun in the morning and evening and is often in condition during the drier months. It does seep after prolonged rainfall. Climbing during rainfall is possible. It can retain greasiness in some damp weather and is best if there is a light breeze to dry it out.

❶ Stuart's Line Left Finish . 6c
The left-hand finish takes the final sting out of the mother line - not quite as good but more balanced.
FA. c.2014

❷ Where Has Stu Gone? 6c+
A good intro to the style of climbing on this wall, with a tough final few moves to reach the lower-off.
FA. c.2014

❸ Mutiny Crack E4 6a
The overhanging crack and niche is a tough mission.
FA. Simon Rawlinson 11.2012

❹ Wrecking Ball . . 7b
A pitch of three parts - a fingery thin crack followed by some steep pulls to a puzzling finish.
FA. Rob Lamey 1.9.2012

❺ Attrition E5 6a
The long right-to-left leaning crackline builds to a very steep ending and lower-off.
FA. Pat Littlejohn 1997

❻ Marine Layer. . . . . 7a+
An unusual pitch - strenuous and with some unusual sequences along the way.
FA. Rob Lamey 25.5.2013

❼ One Ton Depot. . . . . 7b+
The first of the big lines saves its crux for the very top, though there are some good rests on the way. Start up *Marine Layer*.
FA. Rob Lamey 9.8.2012

❽ Vennerne 8a
A superb pitch named after the wreck of the ship 'Vennerne', the remains of which are visible in Castaway Cove. *Photo on page 85*.
FA. Rob Lamey 11.8.2012

❾ Air Show. . . . . . 8a+
An incredibly sustained line with a few tricky moves thrown in. Start as for *Vennerne* and head right. Slightly easier for the tall.
FA. Adrian Berry 7.7.2013

Rhossili Beach — Shipwreck Cove

10 Helvetia .... Top 50 **8b+**
Not your typical British hard route, more European in style. A hard crux guards the upper wall which is unrelenting in difficulty. The route is named after the shipwreck on the main beach.
FA. Ben West 19.8.2014

11 Delta Dagger......... **8a**
Steep, but with good holds. Possibly **7c+**.
FA. Dave Pickford 15.8.2014

12 Cannonade .... **8a+**
Good use of the knees gets you through the lower crux. Easier climbing up the groove gains access to the upper crux and tricky moves turning the lip.
FA. Rob Lamey 9.6.2015

13 Achilles' Wrath **8b**
The central line through the super-steep wall is a wrestling match from start to finish! Knee bars and heel hooks are just some of the trickery required for success!.
FA. Simon Rawlinson 11.2012

14 King George verses the Suffragettes
.... **7a+**
A tricky start involving a wobbly jug leads through some impressive terrain. Move right to finish up the grey ramp.
Photo on page 39.
FA. Simon Rawlinson 2013

15 Cocky Black Chauffage **6c**
A long rising traverse following the lower of two breaks. Can only be stripped on a top-rope.
FA. Adrian Berry 2014

16 Cross Incontinents **6c**
Start up *Cocky Black Chauffage* and continue along the upper of the two breaks. Can only be stripped on a top-rope.
FA. Adrian Berry 2014

Above the start of Cocky Black Chauffage are three bolted lines. They are loose and have been omitted since any rock dislodged may hit people below.

Three link-ups have been recorded - these are not shown on the topo.

17 Gunshow................ **8a+**
Start up *Helvetia*, moving left to join *Air Show* at its fourth bolt. Now follow *Air Show* to below the final overlap before traversing out left to finish as for *Vennerne*.
FA. Dave Pickford 2014

18 Euro Fighter **8b**
Climb *Air Show* past its crux (at half height), then move right into the finish of *Helvetia*.
FA. Dave Pickford 2014

19 Fata Morgana **8b**
Climb *Delta Dagger* to its fifth bolt and then break left into *Helvetia*, which is climbed to the rest before its final crux on two undercuts. Now move left again to finish up *Air Show*.
Photo on page 91.
FA. Dave Pickford 5.2016

Shipwreck Cove **Rhossili Beach**

Three loose bolted lines here not described as any rock that is dislodged may end up hitting people standing on the beach.

Rhossili Beach — Shipwreck Cove

⑳ Blockiness — 6c+
Good and steep - especially at the start. Things become a little more technical higher up.
FA. Rob Lamey 1.6.2013

㉑ Sand Man — 6b
Climb up to the corners. It can be very sandy at times but, if clean, it is a good pitch.
FA. Simon Rawlinson 2013

㉒ Par 3 — 6c
Climb the lower wall to a steep mid-height section that leads to a final pull to the lower-off. A good route that stays free of sand.
FA. Simon Rawlinson 2013

㉓ John's Route — 6b
Start up a ramp before heading up the wall and past the left side of the small cave. Sustained climbing.
FA. John Bullock, Roy Thomas 10.2013

㉔ First Handout — 6a+
Pleasing climbing passing the ramp and niche to a lower-off out to the right and lower than that of *John's Route*.
FA. Roy Thomas, John Bullock 10.2013

㉕ Hand Shandy/Make a Splash — 6a+
The right-hand line moving leftwards to a shared lower-off with *First Handout*.
FA. Roy Thomas 2013

Shipwreck Cove **Rhossili Beach** 91

Dave Pickford making the first ascent of *Fata Morgana* (8b) - *page 88* - at Shipwreck Cove, Rhossili. Photo: Mark Glaister

Rhossili Beach — Castaway Cove

92

Shipwreck Cove

9m — ① ② ③
18m — ④ ⑤ ⑥

Castaway Cove
The cove is adjacent to Shipwreck Cove and has some easier lines on generally good rock.
Tides - Accessible for 4 hours at low water.
Conditions - The climbs get sun in the morning on the right-hand side, and on summer evenings on the left. There is no possibility of climbing in the rain.

① Top Drawer 5c
The left-hand side of the slab via a couple of small roofs.
FA. Dai Emanuel, Roy Thomas 10.2014

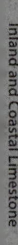

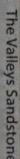

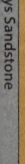

② Bottom Drawers 6b
Follow the easy slab, then make harder moves to pass the overhang and finish at the same lower-off as *Top Drawer*.
FA. Roy Thomas, Dai Emanuel 10.2014

③ Dirty Drawers .... 6b+
The right-hand side of the slab past two small roofs. A steep start.
FA. Roy Thomas, Ed Rees 5.7.2015

④ Sticky Tissue Issue .... 7a+
The left-hand side of the wall over the bulge to a shared lower-off.
FA. Rossili Bolt Project c.2014

⑤ La Doux Parfum de la Lingerie Utilisé 6c
Cross the bulge to the right of *Sticky Tissue Issue*.
FA. Dai Emanuel, Roy Thomas 10.2014

⑥ Secret Drawers 5b
The corner is not recommended.
FA. Dai Emanuel, Roy Thomas 6.2014

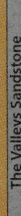

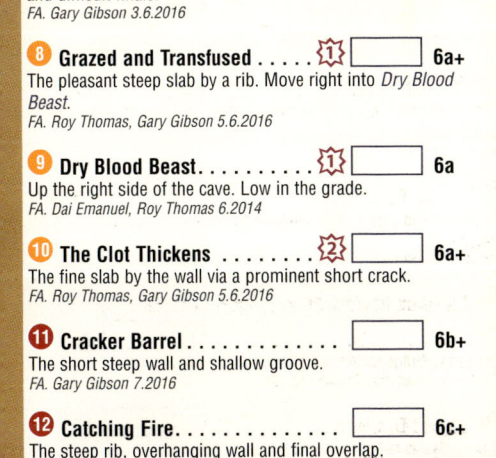

Castaway Cove — Rhossili Beach

7 Cast Me Away 6c
Climb the overhanging rib and shallow groove to an out-there and difficult finale.
FA. Gary Gibson 3.6.2016

8 Grazed and Transfused ..... 6a+
The pleasant steep slab by a rib. Move right into *Dry Blood Beast*.
FA. Roy Thomas, Gary Gibson 5.6.2016

9 Dry Blood Beast 6a
Up the right side of the cave. Low in the grade.
FA. Dai Emanuel, Roy Thomas 6.2014

10 The Clot Thickens .... 6a+
The fine slab by the wall via a prominent short crack.
FA. Roy Thomas, Gary Gibson 5.6.2016

11 Cracker Barrel .... 6b+
The short steep wall and shallow groove.
FA. Gary Gibson 7.2016

12 Catching Fire .... 6c+
The steep rib, overhanging wall and final overlap.
FA. Gary Gibson 7.2016

13 Cinders Catch 6a
A nice pitch up the black rock on good but fairly spaced finger edges at first. Finish left of a small shattered corner.
FA. Dai Emanuel, Roy Thomas 6.2014

14 Dirty Innuendo 5c
Climb the black wall and then move left to join *Cinders Catch* just below the shattered corner.
FA. Roy Thomas, Dai Emanuel 6.2014

15 Geez Louise 5c
A teasing little exercise. Climb easily to the final wall and move up it before stepping right to the lower-off avoiding the ledge on the right.
FA. Roy Thomas, Dai Emanuel 6.2014

16 Mini the Minx 5a
A short but pleasant wall.
FA. Roy Thomas, Gary Gibson 3.6.2016

Seamen Wall →

Rhossili Beach — Seamen Wall

Seamen Wall
A long, short wall with some steep sections which runs between Castaway Cove and Mermaid Cove.
Tides - Accessible for 4 hours at low water.
Conditions - The wall gets some early morning and late afternoon sun in the summer months. There is no possibility of climbing during rain.

1 Bored of Toad Hall 6a
An isolated line on the right-hand side of the first cave.
FA. Dai Emanuel, Roy Thomas 9.2014

2 The King's Shilling 6b
The overhanging crack in the bay.
FA. Dai Emanuel, Roy Thomas 10.2014

3 Captain Jacque Hoff . . . . 6b+
A direct assault on the overhang via its right-hand side, finishing at the same lower-off as *The King's Shilling*.
FA. Roy Thomas, Dai Emanuel 27.9.2014

4 Concrete Cows 6a
Start up the corner via a roof with a hard start.
FA. Roy Thomas, Dai Emanuel 9.2014

5 Smeaton's Stump 5c
Enter the corner from the right more easily.
FA. Roy Thomas, Dai Emanuel 10.2014

6 Good Ship Venus 5c
Climb right of the crack, stepping left to the lower-off.
FA. Dai Emanuel, Roy Thomas 10.2014

7 Lamisil 6a
The pleasant face and juggy overhang.
FA. Gary Gibson 7.2016

8 Zeuwit 6b
An easy start precedes a tricky black face.
FA. Gary Gibson 7.2016

9 Atraumen 5b
The shallow black groove.
FA. Gary Gibson 7.2016

Seamen Wall **Rhossili Beach** 95

10 El Cino .... ☐ 4b
The shallow groove.
FA. Gary Gibson 7.2016

11 Frappacino .... ☐ 4b
A shallow groove and slab.
FA. Gary Gibson 7.2016

12 Pure Cino .... ⚠ ☐ 4b
The blunt rib and face.
FA. Gary Gibson 7.2016

13 Giraffacino .... ☐ 5c
A steady black slab and final overlap.
FA. Gary Gibson 7.2016

14 Elephantacino .... ☐ 6a
The black slab and overlaps.
FA. Gary Gibson 7.2016

15 Catapult .... ⚠ ☐ 4b
The square-cut rib is very good.
FA. Gary Gibson, Roy Thomas 5.6.2016

16 Schengen .... ⚠ ☐ 4b
Climb direct via a shallow groove.
FA. Gary Gibson, Roy Thomas 5.6.2016

17 Border Control .... ⚠ ☐ 4b
The pleasant wall right of *Schengen*.
FA. Gary Gibson, Roy Thomas 5.6.2016

18 Checkpoint Checkout .... ⚠ ☐ 5b
The shallow black groove.
FA. Gary Gibson 5.6.2016

19 Ma Maid's Mermaid .... ⚠ ☐ 5b
A shallow groove and pleasant finishing slab.
FA. Gary Gibson 4.6.2016

20 Andre Marriner .... ☐ 5b
The black right-facing corner.
FA. Gary Gibson 4.6.2016

21 Marinieri .... ☐ 6a+
The smooth looking black face.
FA. Gary Gibson 4.6.2016

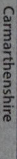

Rhossili Beach — Seamen Wall

22 Black Sea Shanty 5a
Take the easy wall to gain and finish up a pleasant shallow groove.
FA. Gary Gibson, Roy Thomas 7.8.2016

23 Sea Shanty Rib 4b
Climb up the blunt rib to a tricky clip at the lower-off.
FA. Gary Gibson, Roy Thomas 7.8.2016

24 Seaman's Sea Shanty 5a
The arete and shallow groove.
FA. Gary Gibson, Roy Thomas 7.8.2016

25 Seaman in the Groove 5b
The groove gives an excellent little line.
FA. Gary Gibson, Roy Thomas 7.8.2016

26 Them's Be Barnacles, Them's Be
.... 6a
The fine arete finishing at a lower-off on the right.
FA. Gary Gibson, Roy Thomas 7.8.2016

27 No Tar 5a
The right-hand finish to *Them's Be Barnacles, Them's Be*.
FA. Gary Gibson, Roy Thomas 7.8.2016

28 Operation Seaman 5a
Climb the arete right of the deep chimney.
FA. Gary Gibson, Roy Thomas 7.8.2016

29 Me Harty's 4b
Follow the pleasant rib and fine black wall.
FA. Gary Gibson, Roy Thomas 7.8.2016

30 Seaman Limbo 6a
The excellent right arete of the wall.
FA. Gary Gibson, Roy Thomas 7.8.2016

31 Kickback Tar 4b
The wall and shallow black groove.
FA. Gary Gibson, Roy Thomas 7.8.2016

Seamen Wall Rhossili Beach 97

32 Barnacle Bill 6a
Good climbing up the side-wall of the chimney.
FA. Roy Thomas, Gary Gibson 7.8.2016

33 Whispering Whelks 4a
The blunt rib is a nice outing.
FA. Roy Thomas, Gary Gibson 7.8.2016

34 Pump My Bilge 6a
The wall and overhang tucked into the back of the recess.
FA. Roy Thomas, Gary Gibson 7.8.2016

35 All Hands on the Sea Cocks.... 3a
Follows the easy wall and well-positioned rib above.
FA. Gary Gibson, Roy Thomas 7.8.2016

A climber enjoying some perfect late afternoon conditions on the hanging corner/groove of *Fought to the End* (5c) - *page 98* - at Mermaid Cove, Rhossili. Photo: Mark Glaister

Rhossili Beach — Mermaid Cove

Mermaid Cove

A lovely isolated cove with a fine line-up of lower-grade sport climbs on good rock.
Approach - Walk out across the beach and the cove is just beyond the Seamen Wall.
Tides - Accessible for 3 hours at low water. **Keep an eye on the water level as access for those hoping to stay dry is quickly cut off!**
Conditions - The wall gets the sun from mid-afternoon onwards.

1 Crass Word Pizzle 4a
A low-angled slab that is quite pleasant but has a run-out on easy ground to reach the lower-off out to the right.
FA. Roy Thomas, Nick O'Neill 4.2014

2 Landlubber 4a
Straightforward climbing direct to a shared lower-off.
FA. Rhossili bolt project 2014

3 The Naughty Corner 4a
The corner, moving right to the belay shared with *Ursula*.
FA. Rhossili bolt project 2014

4 Ursula 4a
Climb the wall right of *The Naughty Corner* to a shared lower-off.
FA. Rhossili bolt project 2014

5 Ceasg 4a
An independent line up the wall via large and thin cracks.
FA. Rhossili bolt project 2014

6 Turtle Apocalypse 4a
The wall right of the cracks of *Ceasg*.
FA. Rhossili bolt project 2014

7 No Father Day 5c
Follow the slab passing a hard move using a crystal pocket.
FA. Roy Thomas Rich Phillips 2014

8 Lara 5a
The edge right of the slender groove. A nice line.
FA. Joe Squire, Simon Rawlinson 2014

9 Scurvy Dog 5c
The centre of the pillar left of the first cut-out.
FA. Joe Squire, Simon Rawlinson 2014

10 Crimp Paddle .... 6b+
Start up *Paternal Love* and then pull out left onto the wall above.
FA. Simon Rawlinson, Joe Squire 2014

11 Paternal Love 6b
Follow the left edge of the pale pillar and wall above.
FA. Roy Thomas, Rich Phillips 2014

12 Bye Dad .... 6b+
An excellent series of moves up the centre of the pillar.
FA. Roy Thomas, Rich Phillips 7.2014

13 Filial Duty 5c
A tough number that takes the right-hand arete of the pillar.
FA. Roy Thomas, Rich Phillips 7.2014

14 Fought To The End 5c
The hanging groove right of the pillar. *Photo on page 97*.
FA. Roy Thomas, Rich Phillips 2014

15 This Vicar's Tea Party .... 6b+
Mount the ledge then climb the sidewall via some tricky moves to join *Stingray* above its crux.
FA. Roy Thomas 2014

16 Stingray 6c
Move up to and boulder through the block overhang.
FA. Rhossili bolt project 2014

Mermaid Cove **Rhossili Beach** 99

⑰ Lemon Soul............ Top 50 ☐ 6a
A lovely pitch. Climb the arete and continue up the face before moving left to finish up a short groove. *Photo on page 82*.
FA. Rhossili bolt project 2014

⑱ A Mermaid's Tale........ ☐ 5b
Climb left of the chimney, moving right to finish up a groove.
FA. Adrian Berry 2014

⑲ Dawson's Corner....... ☐ 5a
Start up left of a chimney crack and then follow the exposed corner on superb holds.
FA. Adrian Berry 2014

⑳ Dawsons Creek....... ☐ 5b
Start up *Dawson's Corner* and finish direct.
FA. Gordon Jenkin 2014

㉑ Fistful of Tenners...... Top 50 ☐ 4c
The line of the cove. Climb the front of the narrow pillar and finish up the short tricky wall above. *Photo on page 102.*
FA. Roy Thomas, Eugene Travers-Jones 2014

㉒ Under the Mattress..... ☐ 6a+
Climb to a high roof and pull onto the upper wall to finish at a lower-off on the right.
FA. Roy Thomas, Eugene Travers-Jones 2014

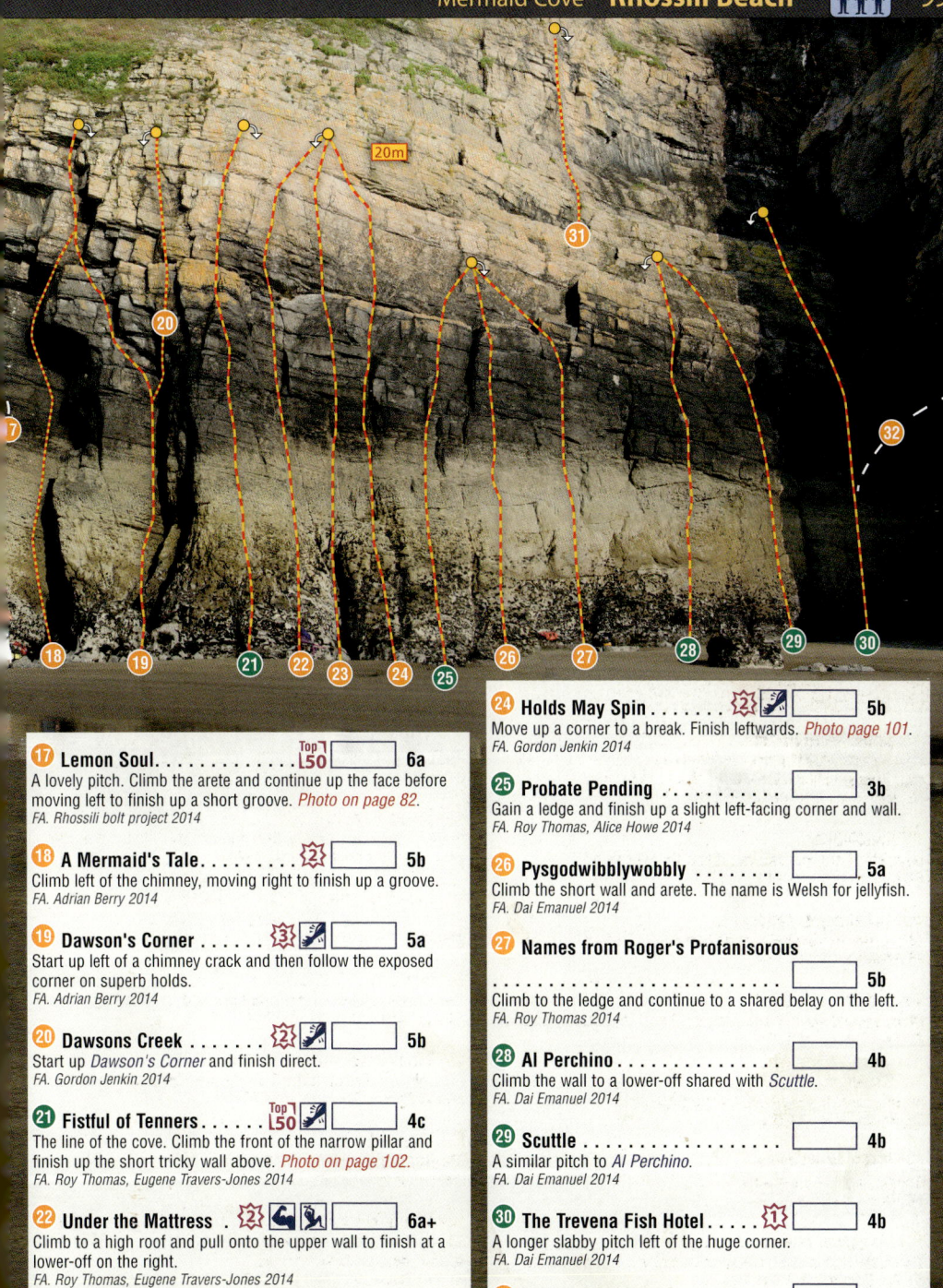

㉓ Cash in the Attic...... ☐ 5b
Climb up to, and surmount a bulge to reach the upper wall.
FA. Roy Thomas, Eugene Travers-Jones 2014

㉔ Holds May Spin....... ☐ 5b
Move up a corner to a break. Finish leftwards. *Photo page 101*.
FA. Gordon Jenkin 2014

㉕ Probate Pending........ ☐ 3b
Gain a ledge and finish up a slight left-facing corner and wall.
FA. Roy Thomas, Alice Howe 2014

㉖ Pysgodwibblywobbly........ ☐ 5a
Climb the short wall and arete. The name is Welsh for jellyfish.
FA. Dai Emanuel 2014

㉗ Names from Roger's Profanisorous
.... ☐ 5b
Climb to the ledge and continue to a shared belay on the left.
FA. Roy Thomas 2014

㉘ Al Perchino........... ☐ 4b
Climb the wall to a lower-off shared with *Scuttle*.
FA. Dai Emanuel 2014

㉙ Scuttle.............. ☐ 4b
A similar pitch to *Al Perchino*.
FA. Dai Emanuel 2014

㉚ The Trevena Fish Hotel..... ☐ 4b
A longer slabby pitch left of the huge corner.
FA. Dai Emanuel 2014

㉛ Scarfish............. ☐ 5c
A line on the upper wall, the belay of which is on a ledge best reached via *Al Perchino*.
FA. Dai Emanuel 2014

100 Rhossili Beach — Mermaid Cove

Early morning · 14 min · Tidal

Project

The right-hand wall of the cove is much steeper and the barnacles are more of a hindrance on the starts. It is probably best to climb here in the morning when the sun has been on the wall.
Tides - Accessible for 1.5 hours on either side of low water. Keep an eye on the water level as access for those hoping to stay dry is quickly cut off!

32 The Naughty Step . . . . . . 6a+
Start up *The Trevena Fish Hotel* and then move right and climb the sustained groove. Intimidating.
FA. Roy Thomas, Rich Phillips 16.8.2014

33 The Naughty Step Direct Start
. . . . 6b
The direct start is very bouldery.
FA. Roy Thomas, Rich Phillips 16.8.2014

34 A Mermaid's Footwork 6b
The left-hand line up the pillar to the left of the wide crack.
FA. Roy Thomas, Rich Phillips 16.8.2014

35 Flounder 6b
Climb just to the left of the wide crack to a shared lower-off.
FA. Roy Thomas 16.8.2014

36 Somewhere in her Smile She Knows
. . . . 6b+
The centre of the leaning pillar on pockets, then the face above.
FA. Roy Thomas 16.8.2014

37 Besetting Fears 6a
Follow the pocketed pillar to join *Somewhere in her Smile She Knows* close to the top.
FA. Dai Emanuel, Roy Thomas 6.2014

38 Horse Flavoured Shadows . . 5c
Climb to a large ledge and then take the arete.
FA. Dai Emanuel, Roy Thomas 6.2014

39 Triton Left 5b
The left-hand finish.
FA. Dai Emanuel, Roy Thomas 6.2014

40 Triton Right 5b
The right-hand finish.
FA. Dai Emanuel, Roy Thomas 6.2014

Rhossili Beach *101*

Royston Thomas on *Holds May Spin* (5b) - *page 99* - at Mermaid Cove, Rhossili. Photo: Mark Glaister

Rhossili Beach

Mermaid Cove lies at the end of Rhossili Beach - one of the UK's finest. The cove is tidal but is quickly accessed across the beach once the water has receded and contains many excellent lower grade sport climbs that are well equipped and on great rock. Here Bridget Collier heads up the initial pillar of the stunning Top50 *A Fistful of Tenners* (4c) - *page 99*. Photo: Mark Glaister

Rhossili Beach 103

104   Trial Wall Area

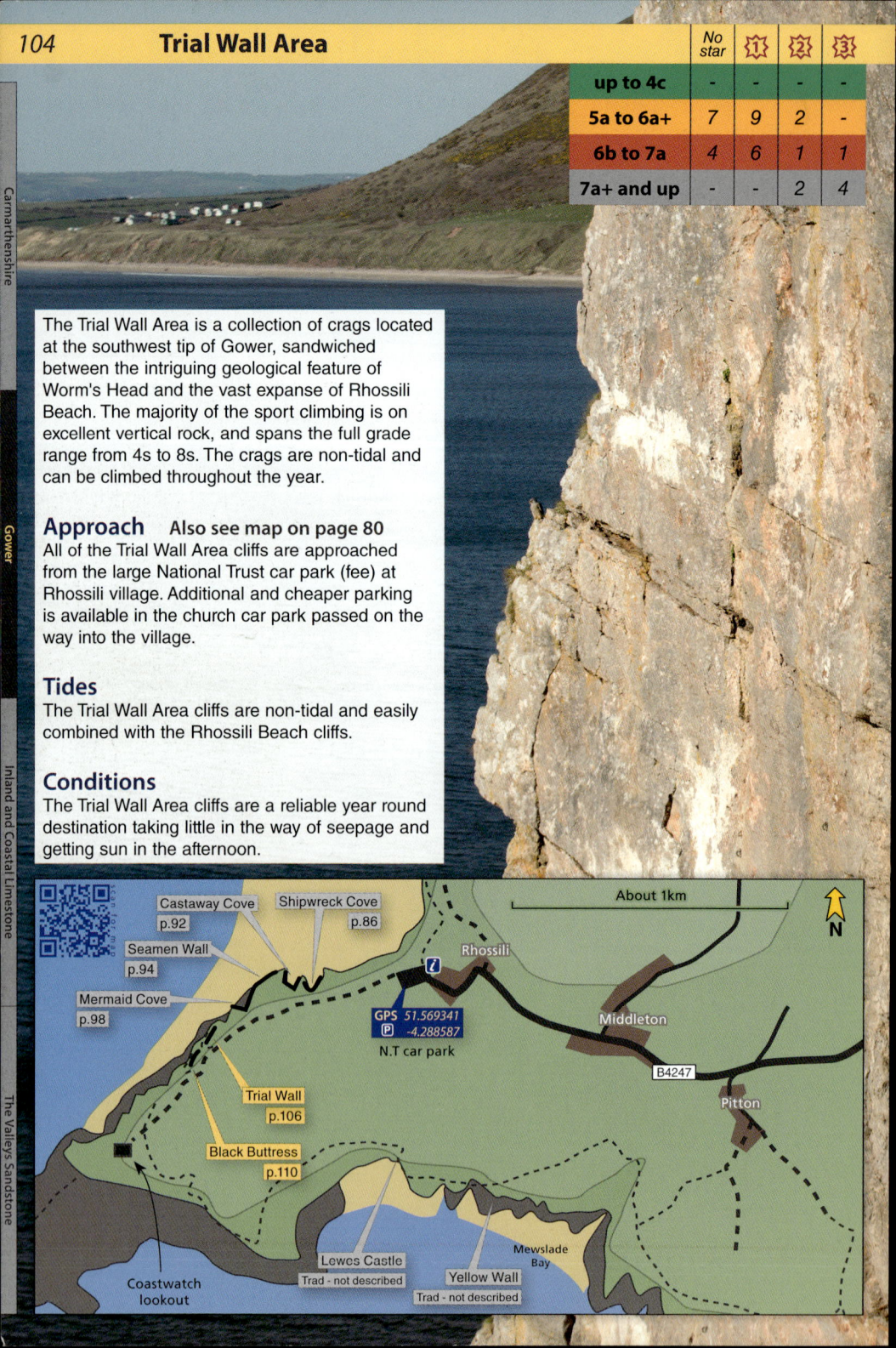

	No star	★	★★	★★★
up to 4c	-	-	-	-
5a to 6a+	7	9	2	-
6b to 7a	4	6	1	1
7a+ and up	-	-	2	4

The Trial Wall Area is a collection of crags located at the southwest tip of Gower, sandwiched between the intriguing geological feature of Worm's Head and the vast expanse of Rhossili Beach. The majority of the sport climbing is on excellent vertical rock, and spans the full grade range from 4s to 8s. The crags are non-tidal and can be climbed throughout the year.

Approach   Also see map on page 80
All of the Trial Wall Area cliffs are approached from the large National Trust car park (fee) at Rhossili village. Additional and cheaper parking is available in the church car park passed on the way into the village.

Tides
The Trial Wall Area cliffs are non-tidal and easily combined with the Rhossili Beach cliffs.

Conditions
The Trial Wall Area cliffs are a reliable year round destination taking little in the way of seepage and getting sun in the afternoon.

- Castaway Cove p.92
- Shipwreck Cove p.86
- Seamen Wall p.94
- Mermaid Cove p.98
- Rhossili
- GPS 51.569341 -4.288587
- N.T car park
- Middleton
- B4247
- Pitton
- Trial Wall p.106
- Black Buttress p.110
- Coastwatch lookout
- Lewes Castle — Trad - not described
- Mewslade Bay
- Yellow Wall — Trad - not described
- About 1km N

Trial Wall Area

A climber on the more positive holds of the top wall on *The Hant* (7a) - *page 107* - at the perfectly positioned Trial Wall, Rhossili, Gower. Trial Wall has a quality line-up of hard sport style lines a couple of which need some wires. Photo: Simon Rawlinson

Trial Wall Area — Trial Wall

Trial Wall

One of the older sport crags on Gower that has some tremendous pitches which require good technique and finger strength. The trad lines are also good and most require only a smallish rack. The wall is fairly sheltered as it lies on a northwest-facing slope. There is little chance of staying dry in the rain. Also covered are two smaller outlying walls with some reasonable low- and mid-grade sport routes. Both crags have good ledges at the bottom.

Approach - Head out of the National Trust car park on the road/track towards Worm's Head. After 5 minutes at a point where a distinct 'S' - bend in the track gets close to the cliff edge keep an eye out down on the right for the wall. The Retribution Wall is just around the corner from the Trial Wall. The Wedge Wall is 50m across the small scree slope in front of Trial Wall.

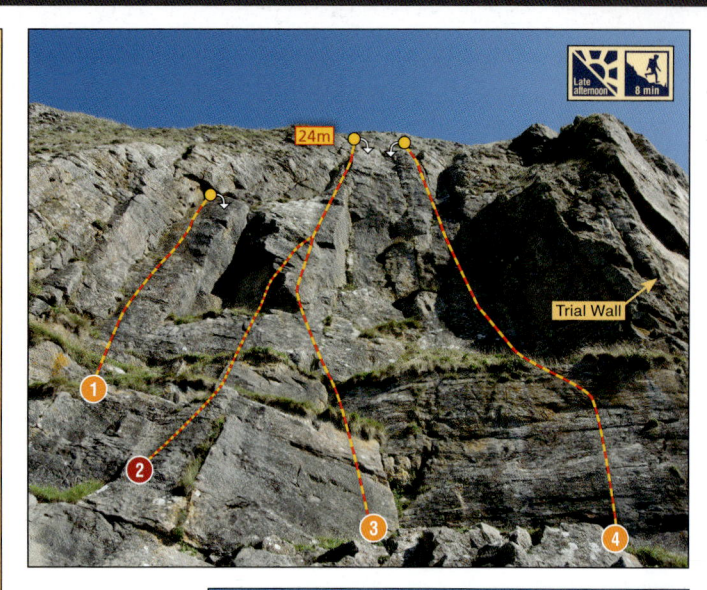

Retribution Wall

1 Spades of Glory 5c
The corner on the left-hand side of the wall. Some of the bolts are a bit of a stretch.
FA. Matt Woodfield 21.8.2011

2 World Without End 6b
A left-hand variation to *Pillars of the Earth*.
FA. Stuart Llewellyn 21.8.2011

3 Pillars of the Earth . . . . . 6a+
Good moves that are about right at the grade if the best line is followed. Direct is harder and weaving around may be slightly easier.
FA. Stuart Llewellyn 21.8.2011

4 Buckets of Bubbly 5b
Climb the short wall to the big grassy ledge, then follow the bolts leftwards to the belay.
FA. Steve Warrington 21.8.2011

Wedge Wall

5 The Fin End of the Wedge . . . 5c
Deceptive. Balance up and left onto the arete. Climb the arete, move right and then pull up to a ledge and lower-off.
FA. Stuart Llewellyn 9.9.2011

6 Wedgling 5b
Move up past a narrow ledge and either head up right to the lower-off (the tall persons way), or go up to the top of the wall and hand traverse right to the lower-off.
FA. Stuart Llewellyn 9.9.2011

7 Wedge-egade Master . . . 6a
Make a couple of insecure moves to gain and pass the second bolt, before better holds quickly lead to the lower-off.
FA. Stuart Llewellyn 9.9.2011

8 Wedge Dew Bin 5b
The thin seam/crack is a pleasant line climbed via a series of crimps and ledges. *Photo on page 108.*
FA. Matt Woodfield 9.9.2011

9 Atomic Wedgie 5b
The right-hand line of bolts is a good wall climb. No bridging out right at the start.
FA. Matt Woodfield 9.9.2011

Trial Wall — **Trial Wall Area** — 107

Trial Wall

10 The Adulteress — E2 5c
The series of thin cracks up the left-hand side of the wall with a difficult section to pass the overhang. Great position.
FFA. Andy Sharp, John Harwood 8.11.1981

11 Blackman's Pinch — E4 6a
The wall and overhang below the upper crack of *The Adulteress* has a couple of bolts in place.
FFA. Andy Sharp, John Harwood 5.12.1981

12 Skull Attack — Top 50 — 7c
The long thin wall and overlap is a stunning climb.
FA. Andy Sharp, Pete Lewis 15.4.1984

13 Retrobution — 7b
A superb pitch of escalating difficulty that is high in the grade. Some thin moves link the initial groove of *Crime and Punishment* to the upper section of *Skull Attack*.
Photo on cover.
FA. Martyn Richards, Andy Sharp 5.1.2013

14 Crime and Punishment — E5 6b
The natural line up the middle of the wall - classic. Almost a 7a+ sport route, but it requires a few of wires for the upper crack.
FA. Andy Sharp, John Harwood 18.10.1981

15 Black Wall Direct — 8a+
The blank wall and capping overhang is a fingery and powerful mission. The move to pass the overhang is the crux.
FA. A.Forster, Andy Sharp 1988

16 Black Wall — 7b+
The easier, right-hand finish to *Black Wall Direct*. Very good.
FA. Andy Sharp 2011. In newly cleaned and bolted state.

17 The Hant — 7a
A tough nut with good moves. This is a modern take on an older line that finished up easier ground after the difficult initial wall.
Photo on page 105.
FA. Andy Sharp, Pete Lewis 4.1987

18 Tribulations — 7a
Climb the right edge of the crag via some tricky moves. The line is pretty tight but the climbing is worthwhile.
FA. Roy Thomas 20.9.1998

108   Trial Wall Area

Carmarthenshire

Gower

Inland and Coastal Limestone

The Valleys Sandstone

Bridget Collier nipping up *Wedge Dew Bin* (5b) - *page 106* - on the Wedge Wall, a good little spot for soaking up some sun and warming up, or whilst waiting for the tide to go out before a visit to the beachside cliffs. Photo: Mark Glaister

Trial Wall Area 109

Trial Wall Area — Black Buttress

Black Buttress
A collection of good walls with a number of worthwhile grade 5s and 6s. The walls have good grassy bases and share the same awesome views of all the other Trial Wall Area cliffs.

Approach - Either take a contouring path from Wedge Wall along the base of the upper cliffs or walk along the cliff top until the Black Buttress comes into view and descend an easy path on its left (looking out).

Conditions - The cliffs are sheltered from southwesterly winds and get the sun from mid-afternoon onwards.

1 The Axe E1 5a
The spectacular arete has little in the way of gear.
FA. Tony Penning, Andy Sharp, John Harwood 26.5.1985

2 Blockbuster 5b
The bolt-line to the right of *The Axe* has some good moves in a fine situation. Single bolt lower-off.
FA. N.Williams, P.Williams 1978

3 Hatchet Man .... 6b+
The sustained wall to a shared lower-off with *Blockbuster*.
FA. Roy Thomas, Ed Rees 5.2011

The next two lines are on the taller wall on the left of the main buttress.

4 Left line .... 6b+
Start at a square-cut corner and follow the left-hand line of bolts passing some hollow rock.
FA. Stu Llewellyn 2011

5 Right 6b
The right-hand line of bolts from the square-cut corner, again with plates of hollow rock.
FA. Stu Llewellyn 2011

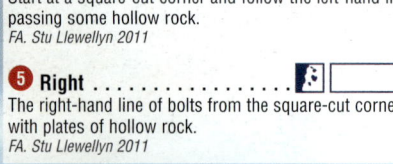

To the right is a more substantial buttress with a number of well-bolted lines up cracks, walls and aretes.

6 Spittle and Spume 6c
The blunt technical rib right of the slim corner is climbed direct.
FA. Gary Gibson, Roy Thomas 5.2016

7 Fiff and Faff .... VS 5a
The jamming crack.
FA. Gary Gibson, Roy Thomas 5.2016

8 Footsie 6a
Short but pleasant climbing starting from the right side of the raised platform.
FA. Gary Gibson, Roy Thomas 5.2016

9 Pied Noir .... 6c+
The short corner and tough technical slab above. Avoid straying onto larger holds at this grade.
FA. Gary Gibson, Roy Thomas 5.2016

Black Buttress — Trial Wall Area 111

10 Wonderful Land .... 1 ▢ 6c
A fine route direct up the slab with a tricky start. Easier if you wander off line.
FA. Gary Gibson, Roy Thomas 5.2016

11 Monica's Dress .... 2 ▢ 5c
The exciting overhang and crack above.
FA. Roy Thomas, Gary Gibson 5.2016

12 Spit it Out .... 2 ▢ 6a
The hanging corner complete with flake.
FA. Roy Thomas, Gary Gibson 5.2016

13 Black Friday .... 1 ▢ 7a
The desperate face to the right requires a humongous reach.
FA. Gary Gibson 5.2016

14 Can't Swallow That ...... 1 ▢ 5a
The crackline on the right trending left at the top to the lower-off.
FA. Roy Thomas, Gary Gibson 5.2016

15 Down in One .... ▢ 5a
The right-hand crack to a ledge. Finish up the arete.
FA. Joe Squire 2012

16 The Beautiful People ..... 1 ▢ 6a+
The left-hand side of the arete is a very good little exercise.
FA. Geraint Morris, Adrian Berry 2000s

17 Spit'n Polish .... 1 ▢ 6a
The right-hand side of the arete via a groove.
FA. Roy Thomas, Richie Phillips 2014

18 Spic'n Span .... ▢ 6a
The slabby face and arete on the far right.
FA. Roy Thomas, Gary Gibson 5.2016

Third Sister to Zulu Zawn

	No star	★	★★	★★★
up to 4c	-	-	-	-
5a to 6a+	3	2	1	2
6b to 7a	2	9	9	2
7a+ and up	-	1	9	6

A visually stunning section of coast dotted with some fine sport crags that offer plenty of routes in the higher grades as well as some lovely grade 6s. The rock is excellent and the cliffs have the ambience of sea cliff climbing.

Approach   Also see map on page 80

Please pay close attention to the approach descriptions as it is easy to misjudge the number of gates to be crossed and the distances between them. From Scurlage, drive 1.3 miles to parking on the right at Pilton Green (a National Trust sign) opposite a white house - the parking is on grass next to the track (can be boggy if wet). Cross the road and take a footpath on the left of a white house across fields towards the coast. As the path nears the coast it dips into a small valley and a green gate is encountered. From here each cliff's approach is described separately.

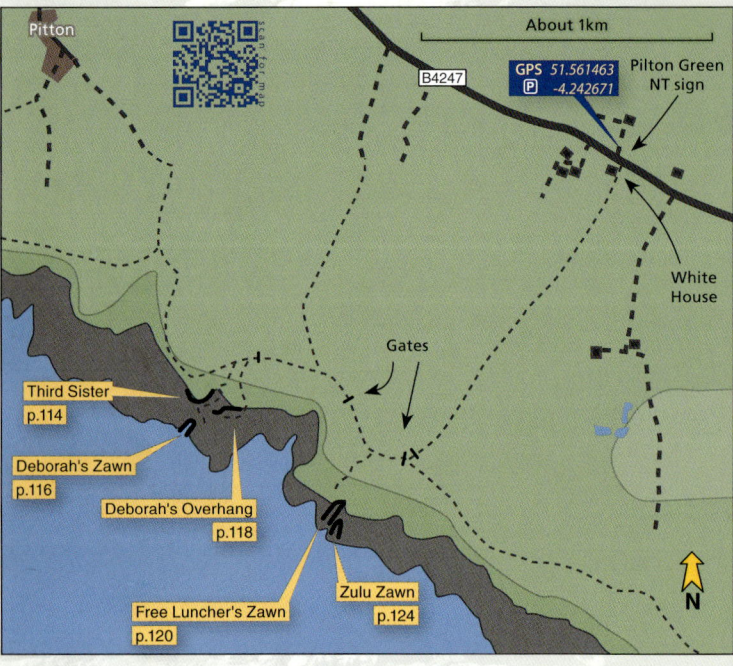

Third Sister and Deborah's Zawn - Go through the green gate and then right through another gate. Follow the coast path through a further two gates, and, 100m past the second gate, take the left fork out to the headland. A wide easy-angled grassy gully leads down to the sea. Descend the grassy gully and the Third Sister is on the right. For Deborah's Zawn keep descending leftwards until it is possible to break back right on rock to the bed of the Zawn.

Deborah's Overhang - From the final gate on the approach to Third Sister continue along the coast path for 20m and then head left down a valley (it has a small pinnacle on its right-hand side) to sea level. The crag is on the right (non-tidal, but the base can be wave washed).

Free Luncher's Zawn and Zulu Zawn - Go through the green gate and then right through another gate. Walk up a short slope and then head out towards the cliff top. Between two headlands descend a wide easy-angled grassy depression and the slit of Free Luncher's Zawn is at the bottom on the right. Scramble down the left side (looking out to sea) and then back right to the base of the climbs. For Zulu Zawn follow the approach to Free Luncher's Zawn and as the scramble steepens, Zulu Zawn lies down to the left. Either make an exposed scramble across the top of the zawn and down to the base of the wall or abseil in - gear needed to set up the abseil.

Conditions

Third Sister is high above the sea but the rest of the cliffs are at sea level and will not be accessible in high seas even at low tide. Both Zulu Zawn and Deborah's Zawn need time to dry out as well as crisp weather to be in the best condition.

Third Sister to Zulu Zawn

Andy Sharp on his own route, the fine *Wide Eyed and Legless* (7b+) - *page 116* - at Deborah's Zawn. Photo: Simon Rawlinson

Third Sister

A great little crag set in a commanding position that has some intense pitches on excellent rock. A good spot on a sunny winter's day. There are also some trad routes on this wall which have not been described.

Approach - This is the face on the right-hand side of the wide descent gully. The routes are on a narrow overhung ramp which becomes cramped and exposed to the left of *French Undressing*.

Conditions - The crag is very exposed to the sun and wind but it does not seep and dries rapidly.

❶ Chilean Flame Thrower . . 7b+
Start at the top of the ramp below a wedged boulder. Make bouldery moves up the severely overhung wall to easier ground.
FA. Goi Ashmore 23.4.2010

❷ World in Action . . . . 7b+
The line of bolts midway up the ramp. A sequence of hard moves gains a rest at the mid-height easing. Finish up the easier overhang and wall above.
FA. Andy Sharp 1989

Paul Cox high up on the steep headwall of *Sister Mary's Blessed Finger* (6a) - *opposite* - at Third Sister. Photo: Mark Glaister

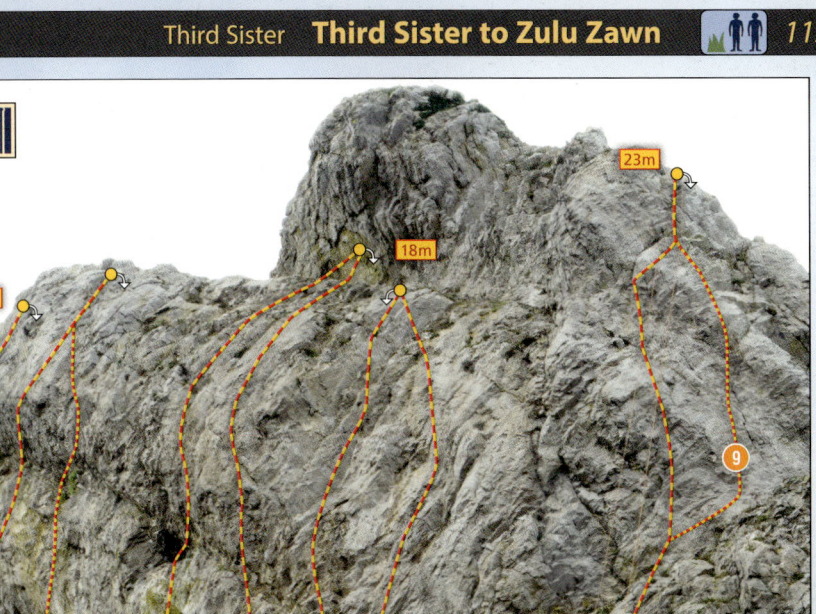

Third Sister to Zulu Zawn

Third Sister — 115

③ Popped In, Souled Out
.... 7b
The line of bolts left of the mid-height cave.
FA. Andy Sharp, Pete Lewis, John Harwood 6.2.1988

④ French Undressing .. 7a
Climb the wall to the small cave at mid-height. Pull out of the cave and move steeply up and right to finish easily. The lower-off is in the upper wall.
FA. Andy Sharp, Pete Lewis 10.10.1987

⑤ Twilight World 6c
An exciting pitch. Move up to where the rock starts to bulge. Climb up through the bulge past a jug and finish up the less steep wall above. *Photo on page 119.*
FA. Andy Sharp, Pete Lewis, John Harwood, A.Wilson, Bob Powles, A.Hughes 10.10.1987

⑥ Southeast Wall .... 6a+
A deceptively steep exercise on good but sharp holds. Climb the crisp lower wall to some unexpected jug hauling to finish.
FA. Jeremy Talbot, R.Corbett 1963. FFA Andy Sharp, Pete Lewis 1986

⑦ Fiesta 6b
Similar to *Southeast Wall* but more technical. The upper section can be climbed to the left or right of the bolts at the same grade.
FA. Andy Sharp, Pete Lewis, John Harwood 10.10.1987

*Just to the right is a thin steep crack (**Bob's Your Uncle**, E3 5c) - this may be bolted in the future.*

⑧ Sister Mary's Blessed Finger
.... 6a
A worthwhile pitch with a spectacular upper wall. Climb the lower buttress direct with a tough move past the overlap. Move up to the steep headwall and climb it on (mostly) good jugs, moving right near the top to a lower-off. *Photo opposite.*
FA. Roy Thomas 2009

⑨ The Enema Affair 5c
Follow *Sister Mary's Blessed Finger* to the headwall and then follow the right-hand line of bolts steeply to a lower-off.
FA. Roy Thomas 2009

Third Sister to Zulu Zawn — Deborah's Zawn

Deborah's Zawn
A very narrow zawn with some fine routes on excellent rock.

Approach - As for Third Sister but continue down the wide grassy gully leftwards to a point where it is possible to cut back right over rock to the zawn, which lies almost directly below Third Sister.

Tides - Climbing is possible for 6 to 7 hours at low water.

Conditions - Good conditions can be elusive since the enclosed zawn is both tidal and pretty shady. It takes time to dry once the tide has retreated and sees little sun but is often at its best when the sun is low in the sky from autumn to spring. Seepage is only a problem after prolonged rainfall.

① Debbie Likes It Wet .... 6a+
The line on the far left of the zawn has some butch moves on very steep ground. The first bolt is best stick-clipped.
FA. Roy Thomas, Rich Phillips 9.2015

② Silent Echo E1 5a
Climb the long left-to-right rampline starting on the left and finishing at a staple lower-off.
FA. Andy Sharp, Pete Lewis 1985

③ Charlie Barking 7a
The short slim groove that rises from the long left-to-right rampline.
FA. Martyn Richards, Andy Sharp. Mike Shewring, D.Morris. 5.2011

④ Prison Bitch 7b
The upper wall features some bouldery pocket pulling. Short-lived, but with some tough moves.
FA. Andy Sharp, Martyn Richards 6.6.2015

⑤ Debbie Reynolds 7a
The flake and wall. A good pitch with escalating difficulties. *Photo on page 21.*
FA. Martin Crocker 21.8.1988. Bolted later on.

⑥ Valley Uprising .... 6c+
An interesting line crossing the diagonal rampline of *Silent Echo*.
FA. Andy Sharp, Martyn Richards 6.6.2015

The next routes are in the enclosed landward end of the zawn.

⑦ Bolder Boulder 7a
Start at a low arch. From its right-hand side, make difficult moves up leftwards to better holds and continue to below the rampline of *Silent Echo*. Now head steeply rightwards, keeping below the rampline, to a lower-off.
FA. Andy Sharp, Pete Lewis, John Harwood 11.10.1987

⑧ Under Arrest .... 7c+
From just to the right of *Bolder Boulder*, climb up rightwards with difficulty to meet *Wide Eyed and Legless*. Cross it via a hard sequence on pockets and crimps to good holds at a junction with *Resisting Arrest*. Move out right and then up to a lower-off.
FA. Martyn Richards, Andy Sharp 25.9.2010

⑨ Wide Eyed and Legless .... 7b+
A classic. Follow the lower left-rising diagonal line joining *Bolder Boulder* to finish. *Photo on page 113.*
FA. Andy Sharp, Pete Lewis, John Harwood 1.10.1987

⑩ Resisting Arrest. Top 50 .... 7b+
A great line that is both powerful and technical. Climb the left-rising line to finish up *Bolder Boulder*.
FA. Andy Sharp, Pete Lewis 1985

⑪ Underdog 8a
From first bolt on *Resisting Arrest*, move up right into *Dog Days are Over* and finish up it.
FA. Martyn Richards, Andy Sharp 18.6.2016

⑫ Department of Correction
.... Top 50 .... 7b+
An awesome series of moves lead up the lower wall and into a prominent groove high up. Stick-clip the initial bolt.
FA. Martyn Richards, Andy Sharp 28.2.2010

⑬ Deputy Dawg... .... 7b+
Start up *Support Your Local Sheriff* below a break. Pull up to the break and clip the second bolt then move leftwards along a line of undercuts to meet up with *Department of Correction* at its fourth bolt. Finish up this.
FA. Martyn Richards, Andy Sharp 17.4.2010

Deborah's Zawn Third Sister to Zulu Zawn

14 Support Your Local Sheriff 7b+
The impressive line on the far right of the wall has a powerful start and finish.
FA. Andy Sharp, Martyn Richards 11.6.2010

15 Dog Days are Over 8a+
A stunning diagonal line across the inner zawn's steepest and blankest territory. Start up *Support Your Local Sheriff* and follow it to its junction with *Department of Correction*. Hard moves to gain and then leave a two-finger pocket are followed by a pumpy finish that joins *Under Arrest* near the top.
FA. Martyn Richards, Andy Sharp 5.6.2011

Not much sun | 40 min | Sheltered | Tidal

Carmarthenshire | Gower | Inland and Coastal Limestone | The Valleys Sandstone

Third Sister to Zulu Zawn — Deborah's Overhang and TV Zawn

Deborah's Overhang

Once the preserve of aid climbing, Deborah's Overhang is now the home of a few steep sport routes.

Approach - From the second gate mentioned in the approach to Third Sister, continue along the coast path for 20m and then head left down a valley (a small pinnacle on its right-hand side is a good landmark) to sea level. The crag is on the right.

Conditions - Prone to seepage after wet weather but it is relatively sheltered.

1 Going Down On Deborah.   **6c**
An unlikely start and a lurch gives access to the slim groove.
FA. Roy Thomas, Goi Ashmore 1997

2 Deborah . . . .   **6c+**
A powerful extended boulder problem.
FA. Andy Sharp 1985

3 Hydraulic Lunch. . . .   **7c+**
The original aid route from the 60s was hand-drilled with removable bolts. The modern result is a series of one finger lock offs, the top one requiring a little finger.
FA. Goi Ashmore 3.5.1996

4 Three Minute Hero . . . . .   **7a+**
A short technical problem to gain the groove.
FA. Andy Sharp 1985

TV Zawn

TV Zawn has a few lines and a couple of projects.

Approach - Drop down to sea level from below Deborah's Overhang.

Conditions - TV Zawn is very tidal and suffers from seepage, splash and condensation. It does come into condition in early autumn, when a visit might prove worthwhile.

5 Down Under Deborah **7a**
The far left line is a groove.
FA. Roy Thomas 17.7 1999

6 Debauching Deborah **6c**
FA. Roy Thomas 1997

7 New Zawn. . . . .   **6a+**
The roof and slab.
FA. Goi Ashmore 15.11.1996

8 Voyage of the Zawn Treader . . .   **5b**
Pull over the roof and then head left to a shared lower-off with *New Zawn*.
FA. Goi Ashmore 15.11.1996

The two lines on the left are closed projects.

Third Sister to Zulu Zawn

On the steep section of *Twilight World* (6c) - *page 115* - at Third Sister. Photo: Glaister Collection

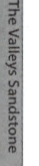

Third Sister to Zulu Zawn — Free Luncher's Zawn

Free Luncher's Zawn

A really good venue with a quality set of mid-grade 6s. The rock is excellent and the zawn a nice place to spend a day.

Approach - Scramble down the left side of the zawn (facing out) and work back down to the base of the zawn.

Conditions - Can be cold if the sun is not out and there is a wind blowing. Suffers seepage in winter after rain.

① Dai's Route 5c
Slightly tidal at the start. Pull up and left steeply and then continue up the pleasant black wall to a lower-off.
FA. Dai Emanuel 2011

② Cold Inconvenience . 6b
Lean in from the right to clip the first bolt and then make some stiff pulls to get established on the wall. Finish up the leaning wall on surprisingly good holds.
FA. Roy Thomas, Goi Ashmore 2.2012

③ Hung Over .... 6a+
A lovely steep pitch that gives a good introduction to the flavour of the routes on the cliff. From the top left of the pinnacle, pull across onto the wall on jugs and then move up to and past a small overhang (with difficulty) to a smooth hole. Finish steeply on good holds. *Photo on page 122.*
FA. Roy Thomas, John Bullock 4.1988

④ Threadbare 6b
Pull onto the steep wall and climb it past pockets to a fingery right-hand move to finish.
FA. John Bullock. Gwyn Evans 15.2.1987

⑤ Nematode .... 6b+
Pull onto the wall and make a sharp sequence over the square-cut overhang. Take the steep wall above on finger pockets and a good finger-flake.
FA. Roy Thomas, John Bullock, L.Moran 2.5.1988

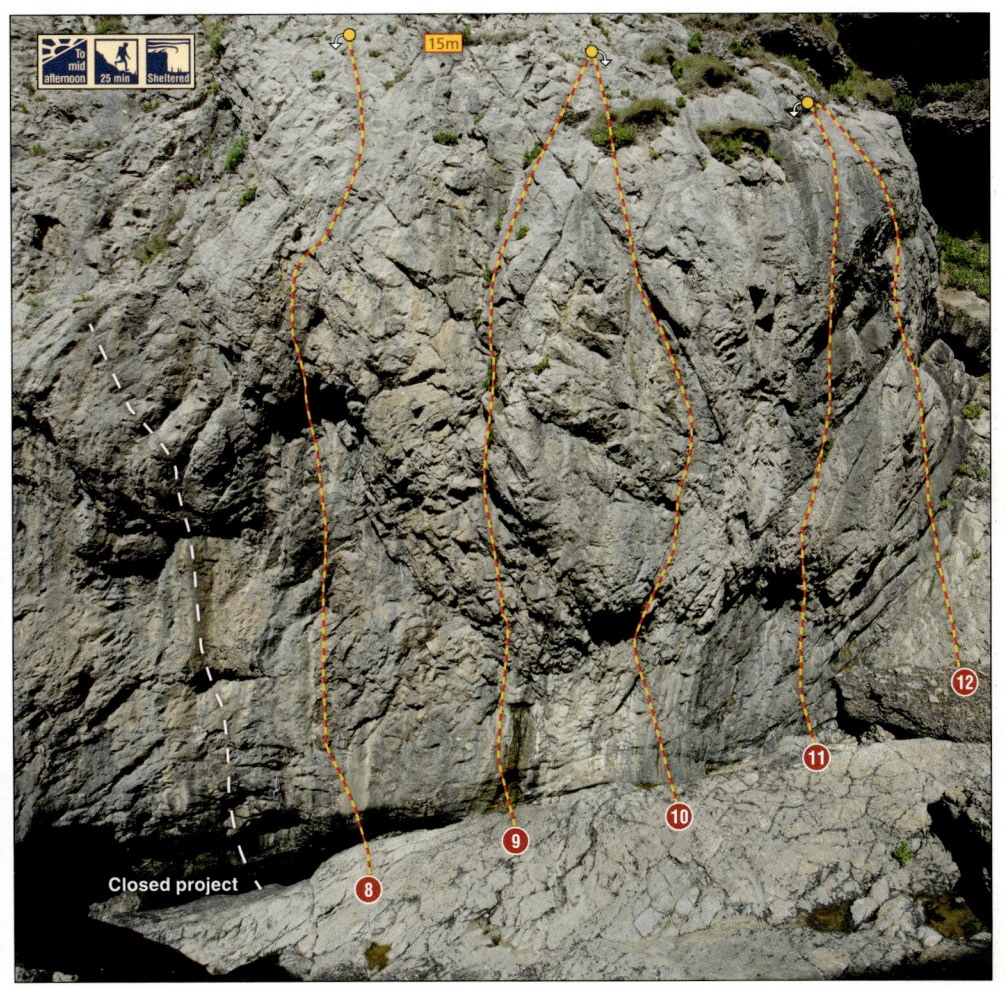

Free Luncher's Zawn — Third Sister to Zulu Zawn — 121

6 Rock Bottom .... 6b+
Start above a wedged chockstone. Step onto the apron of slabby rock and move up to a shallow depression. Exit via fingery moves to better holds.
FA. John Bullock, Gwyn Evans 24.4.1988

7 Chock a Block 6b
Follow the wall right of the slabby apron to steeper ground that is overcome on good holds.
FA. John Bullock, L.Moran, Roy Thomas 5.1988

8 Off the Peg .... 6b+
An excellent sustained pitch. Climb the leaning lower wall to an overhung hole. Pull out and then left with difficulty to easier ground leading to a lower-off.
FA. John Bullock, L.Moran, Roy Thomas 5.1988

9 Scarface 6b
Climb the difficult initial wall to gain an easier corner/groove that holds some vegetation.
FA. John Bullock, L.Moran, Roy Thomas 5.1988

10 Hot Flush 6b
Make a hard sequence of moves up the steep lower wall to gain the base of a slim corner. Finish more easily up it.
FA. Roy Thomas, Goi Ashmore 12.4.2012

11 Stonewall .... 6b+
Move up steeply to reach the diagonal break and then continue up the fingery wall above it.
FA. John Bullock, L.Moran, Roy Thomas 5.1988

12 Ledger 6b
The last line of bolts on the wall is not easy to spot. Climb up to and past the diagonal break to finish at the lower-off shared with *Stonewall*.
FA. Roy Thomas, John Bullock, L.Moran 2.5.1988

Third Sister to Zulu Zawn

Mark Glaister on the final steep section of the Top50 pitch *Hung Over* (6a+) - *page 120* - at the secluded Free Luncher's Zawn. The zawn has some great little routes on superb rock - a lovely spot to spend a day or two, or for a quick warm-up before embarking on the harder lines in the adjacent Zulu Zawn. Photo: Bridget Collier

Third Sister to Zulu Zawn *123*

Third Sister to Zulu Zawn — Zulu Zawn

Zulu Zawn

An extremely impressive and intimidating venue. The routes follow lines of weakness up the severely overhanging back wall of the zawn.

Approach - Follow the approach to Free Luncher's Zawn, and, as the scramble steepens, Zulu Zawn lies down to the left. Either make an exposed scramble across the top of the zawn, and down to the base of the wall, or abseil in - gear needed to set up the abseil.

Tides - Non-tidal in calm conditions.

Conditions - The zawn is not a good place to be in heavy seas even at low tide. Seepage can be a problem.

❶ Zulu Wall 8a
An impressive natural line that tackles the central section of the severely overhanging back wall of the zawn. Follow a line of good holds to a high crux section. *Photo opposite*.
FA. Adrian Berry 2010

❷ Ultimatum 7c
A tricky sequence leads up the wall until a big flake is reached. From here launch rightwards with a beautiful drop knee (or a wild slap), to a rampline that leads to the lower-off.
FA. Simon Rawlinson 3.6.2010

Zulu Zawn **Third Sister to Zulu Zawn** *125*

Rob Lamey on the super-steep line of *Zulu Wall* (8a) - *opposite* - at Zulu Zawn. Photo: Simon Rawlinson.

Oxwich 126

	No star	⚙1	⚙2	⚙3
up to 4c	-	-	-	-
5a to 6a+	2	5	-	-
6b to 7a	3	18	1	1
7a+ and up	2	6	7	2

Mid crux on the super sustained *Red with Rage* (7b) - page 130 - on the Sea Wall at Oxwich. Photo: Mark Glaister

Oxwich

Oxwich's Sea Wall is an impressive venue with easy access and a surprising sense of isolation despite the proximity of one the area's most popular beaches. The Sea Wall presents an impressive leaning wall of high quality limestone running above a sloping platform. The routes are all in the higher grades, from the upper 6s to some stunning routes in the 7s. The excellent sandy beach is a nearby distraction and the sea good for swimming. A little further along the beach is the shy Oxwich in the Woods cliff which has a good supply of grade 6s, though good conditions are not easy to find. There is plenty of bouldering on the huge boulders below the cliff.

Approach   Also see map on page 80

From the A4118, turn left just after the village of Nicholston and follow the road across the marsh to Oxwich. On the left-hand side of the road is a parking area (fee). From the beach, contour the right edge for 500m until the crag is visible on the right after a short spur of rock. For Oxwich in the Woods, continue along the shore from the Sea Wall for another 300m and, at a low overhang, head up into the woods on a hidden path. The crag is 100m from the shore.

Tides

Both crags are accessible for at least 6 hours at low water. Neither crag is actually under water at high tide so it is possible to walk in at low water, climb when the tide is in and then walk out again as the tide falls.

Conditions

The Sea Wall faces northeast and only receives sun until about 11am. It suffers from seepage after heavy rain but is an ideal summer venue when dry. Oxwich in the Woods is shaded by a dense tree canopy and is very greasy and unclimbable in humid conditions. It is also prone to getting dusty if traffic has been thin so may need to be cleaned.

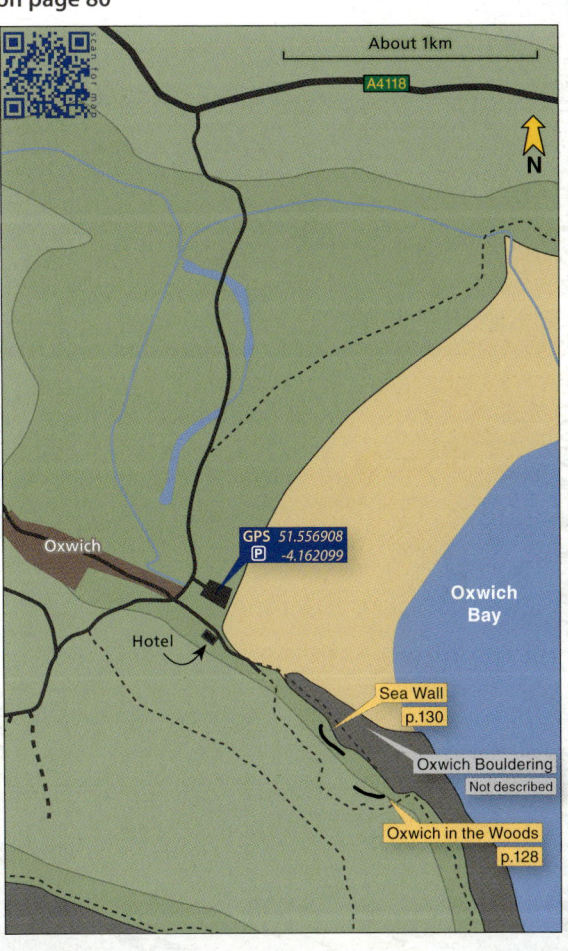

Oxwich — In the Woods

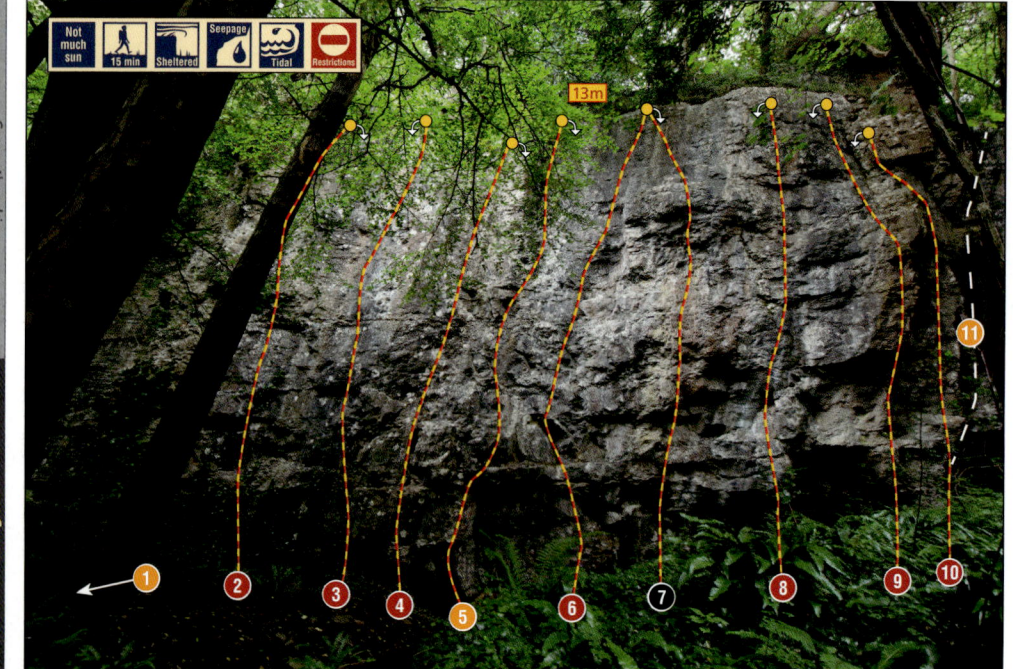

In the Woods

A compact wall of vertical and slightly leaning rock that gives some decent climbing when clean and dry.

Approach - Walk a further 300m along the shoreline from the Sea Wall and, at a low slit overhang in a section of cliff that juts out from the hillside, head up 100m into the woods.

Tides - The approach to the cliff is accessible for around 6 hours at low water, though the base of the cliff is non-tidal.

Conditions - Only head to this crag in dry weather and bring a brush. The rock is prone to gathering dust and becomes very greasy and unclimbable when it is humid. The crag lies below a dense tree canopy which holds the moisture in.

Access - The cliff is in a SSSI and should not be approached from above.

1 Load of Bullocks .... 6a+
20m to the left of the main crag is a route up a barrel-shaped buttress. Overgrown at the start.
FA. Roy Thomas 2005

2 Underneath the Larches .... 6b+
Nice climbing with a tough initial sequence passing a thin crackline. Can get overgrown.
FA. Gary Gibson 2005

3 Life's Too Short 6c
Super fingery climbing up the right-hand side of the wall.
FA. Gary Gibson 2005

4 Snatched from the Cradle
.... 6b
Very worthwhile fingery wall climbing. Keep out of the groove of *Cradle Snatcher* to the right.
FA. Gary Gibson 2005

5 Cradle Snatcher 6a
Make hard pulls to gain the good-looking groove above.
FA. Gary Gibson 2005

6 Baby Going Boing Boing
.... 6b+
Hard moves are needed to pass the low overhang which then accesses a smooth groove and awkward finish.
FA. Gary Gibson 2005

7 Laughing Boy .... 7b+
Powerful fingery pulls lead to a desperate twisting finale.
FA. Gary Gibson 16.7.2005

8 Baby Bouncer .... 6c+
A powerful undercut start gains good sustained climbing above.
FA. Gary Gibson 17.7.2005

9 Teenage Kicks .... 6c+
An impressive line. Start up the low hanging arete and then continue up the bulging rib above.
FA. Gary Gibson 17.7.2005

10 My Inheritance 6b
A tight line that is squeezed into the wall to the right, gained from the start of the groove of *Ox-Over Moon*.
FA. Gary Gibson 17.7.2005

In the Woods **Oxwich**

11 Ox-Over Moon . . . . 6a+
The open groove has a steep and tricky start
FA. Gary Gibson 17.7.2005

12 Dynamo Kiev . . . . . . 7b+
A powerful bouldery start that features a flying leap, is followed by fingery moves above.
FA. Gary Gibson 17.7.2005

13 Grated Expectations
. . . . 7a
Excellent thin moves following on from a fierce start.
FA. Gary Gibson 17.7.2005

14 Anonymous Flare . . . 6c
The left-leaning groove system.
FA. T.Dhallu 2004

15 Suppose I Try 6a
The shallow groove and thin crackline.
FA. Roy Thomas 2004

16 Anal Gesia 6b
Sustained and technical face climbing
FA. Roy Thomas 2004

17 Nice Groove . . . . 6a+
The groove is very nice when clean and dry.
FA. Nick O'Neill 2004

18 Toxicology . . . . 6c+
The short steep wall is very thin in places.
FA. Gary Gibson 16.7.2005

19 Hubble, Rubble 6b
Take the wall leading to the bottomless groove
FA. Roy Thomas, Gary Gibson 16.7.2005

20 Soil and Shuvel . . . . . . 6a+
The shallow groove-line behind a fallen large tree.
FA. Roy Thomas 2004

21 Anoek Clear Missile . 6b
The narrow pillar via some thin face moves.
FA. Goi Ashmore, Roy Thomas 10.11.2004

22 Dirt Box . . . . 6b+
The hard wall to an easier crack above.
FA. Roy Thomas, Gary Gibson 17.7.2005

23 Filthy Snatch 6b
The wall passing the bolts just to their left.
FA. Roy Thomas 12.7.2005

24 Cauldron of Satyr 6b
The crackline and slight groove finishing up the steeper wall via a break.
FA. Gary Gibson 16.7.2005

25 Devil's Brew . . . . 6a+
The low bulge and thin crackline to easier ground.
FA. Roy Thomas 16.7.2005

Oxwich Sea Walls

Sea Walls
A wide sheet of leaning red and grey streaked limestone composed of unusual bubbly rock, with plenty of routes in the higher grades.
Approach - Walk along the right edge of Oxwich beach, past the church, to the cliff.
Tides - Access via the beach is at low to mid tide only.
Conditions - The crag faces northeast and only receives sunshine until about 11am. The face also suffers from seepage after heavy rain but is an ideal summer venue when dry. It is possible to climb during light rainfall.

1 Beyond All Resin . . . 6c
The crack in the arete has a problematic entry when taken direct. The ivy occasionally needs to be cleaned from the start.
FA. Roy Thomas, Gary Gibson 28.5.1995

2 Resin d'être . . . . 7a+
The clean-cut line above a hole. Keep some strength for the finale up the blind open groove. A good pitch which packs a punch.
FA. Roy Thomas 1995

3 Two of a Perfect Pair . . . . . . 7b+
A shallow groove and wall just right of the arete with an unusual bolted-on flake.
FA. Eugene Travers-Jones 29.7.1996

4 Red River Rock 7b
A worthwhile pitch that follows small edges and crimps up a bubbly wall. The name is appropriate if you know the crag it refers to.
FA. Gary Gibson 16.8.1997

5 The Milkier Way . . . 7c
A mean pitch up the blank-looking face above the end of the ledge with a tough crux sequence.
FA. Gary Gibson 28.8.1997

6 Mars Attacks . . . . . . 7a+
An interesting creation. The grey and red-flecked wall finishing via a slight arete on the left. Absorbing and steeper than it appears.
FA. Gary Gibson 19.7.1997

7 Red with Rage . . . . . Top 50 7b
Classic stuff that is jam-packed with good climbing. The steep wall, ramp and final groove require a variety of techniques and subtleties for success. *Photo on page 126.*
FA. Gary Gibson, Roy Thomas 1.7.1995

8 Red Letter Day . . . . 7b+
A direct line finishing via a blunt arete. Steep stuff.
FA. Gary Gibson 19.7.1999

9 Written in Red 7b
The original right-hand finish to *Red Letter Day* via a big rock-over move.
FA. Gary Gibson 6.7.1997

The main wall presents a bald leaning face with few features and holds, which only a handful of routes connect.

10 Red Snapper . . . . 7b+
The left-hand line of the main wall with one desperate and fingery move.
FA. Gary Gibson 19.7.1999

11 Starkly Nameless . . . 7c+
A very impressive pitch arcing rightwards across the face.
FA. Tom Stark 2004

Sea Walls **Oxwich** 131

12 Bitchin' .... Top 50 — 7c
The superb central line of the wall builds to a committing but safe finale.
FA. Gary Gibson 26.8.1997

13 The Morgue the Merrier . — 7b+
A direct line via a shallow and very problematic depression.
FA. Gary Gibson 2.7.1997

14 Missin' the Drink ...... — 7b
The groove is one of the very few features of the wall. Gaining it proves quite tough.
FA. Gary Gibson 2.8.1997

15 Kissin' the Pink .... Top 50 — 6c
Classic features. The right arete of the groove has tufas, pockets and wrinkles. All very French. *Photo on page 132.*
FA. Eugene Travers-Jones, Roy Thomas, Gary Gibson 9.10.1994

16 Milkin' the Link .... — 6b
A useful starter. Head out right after starting up the initial wall of *Kissin' the Pink*.
FA. Stuart Llewellyn, Steve Warrington 25.3.2012

17 Pissin' the Sink ...... — 7b
A fine steep wall with a desperate finale to clip the belay. Great if you like slopers.
FA. Gary Gibson 20.7.1997

18 Foamin' at the Gusset . . . . . — 7a+
A short leaning wall and a tiny problematic groove above.
FA. Roy Thomas 1997

19 Inspector Glueseau .... — 7a
A technical little groove/ramp above the ledge.
FA. Roy Thomas, Gary Gibson 1.7.1995

20 Glue Year .... — 7a
A gem of a route with a straightforward entry which escalates to a fine intricate finale.
FA. Roy Thomas, Gary Gibson 1.7.1995

21 Settin' Stone .... — 7b
The wall below the prominent capping roof proves technical. Overcoming it requires a little ingenuity.
FA. Gary Gibson 25.8.1997

22 Steel Yourself .... — 6b
The right arete above the cave, accessed from the ledge above the cave. A direct start is **6c+**.
FA. Roy Thomas, Gary Gibson 1.7.1995

Oxwich

John Warner on Oxwich's most popular pitch *Kissin' the Pink* (6c) - *page 131* - Oxwich Sea Walls have a large number of difficult face climbs that are often in condition and provide some shelter from rain. Photo: Mark Glaister

Oxwich *133*

Watch House

	No star	★	★★	★★★
up to 4c	-	-	-	-
5a to 6a+	2	3	-	-
6b to 7a	3	8	2	-
7a+ and up	-	1	1	-

The Watch House crags are just two of the set of bolted sea cliffs that are clustered around the village of Southgate, to the east of Three Cliffs Bay. The two neighbours offer differing climbing styles. Watch House Slab has some fierce pitches that should not be approached too casually, especially if out of practice on slabby territory! The overhanging Watch House East has more conventional fare, mostly with steep starts leading to more vertical walls.

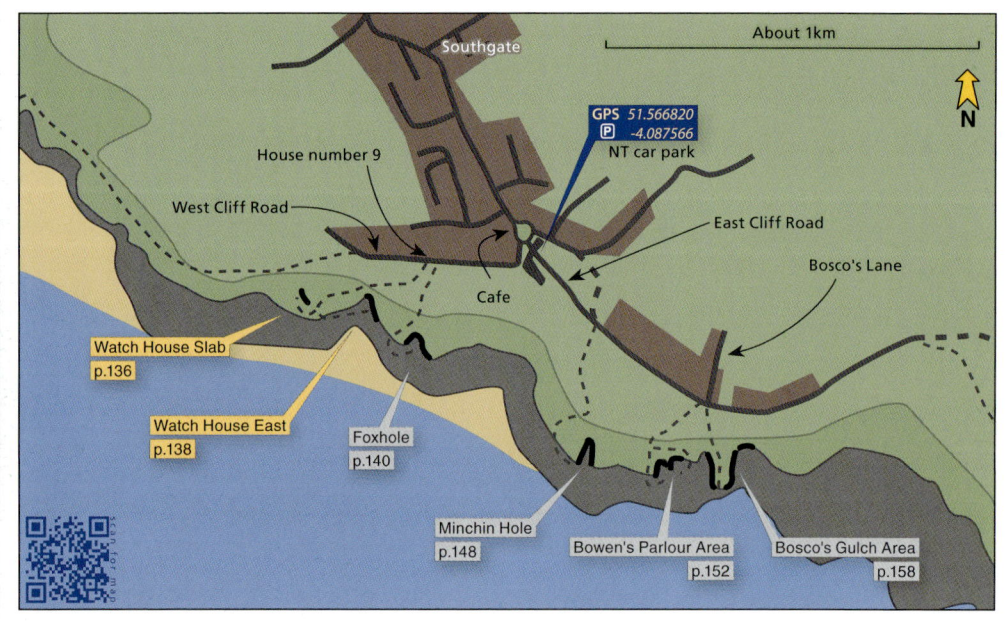

Approach   Also see map on page 80
From the National Trust car park (fee) at Southgate village (handy cafe and shop), walk west along the small road on the edge of the houses for 250m, and at house number 9, break left across the field to the edge of the plateau. Descend to the right of two grassy knolls to above a gully. Go down its east side (left looking out to sea) and then cut back right into the grassy gully and cliff. Take care on first acquaintance with the approach as the crags are not easily seen from above and the approach slopes are composed of steep grass, scree and rock. At lowish tide it is easy to walk between Foxhole and Watch House East - useful for taking a look at what is available or a quick change of venue.

Tides
Watch House Slab is non-tidal. During calm seas, climbing on Watch House East is possible on the landward lines at all times. The lines on the right are accessible for around 6 to 7 hours at low-water.

Conditions
Watch House Slab is well above the sea. Watch House East is best avoided in rough weather. Neither crag offers the possibility of climbing whilst it is raining and both suffer seepage after prolonged rainfall.

Watch House 135

Paul Walters on the lower moves of *Jump to Conclusions* (7a) - *page 138* - at Watch House East. Photo: Adrian Berry

Watch House — Watch House Slab

Watch House Slab
A compact slab located in a steep grassy gully. The rock is reasonable and the bolting is good. The climbing tends to be fairly fierce and those not good at slabs should think about heading elsewhere.

Approach - From Southgate car park walk west along the small road on the edge of the houses for 250m. At house number 9 break left across the field to the edge of the plateau. Descend to the right of two grassy knolls to above a gully. Go down its east side (left looking out to sea) and then cut back right into the grassy gully and cliff.

Conditions - There is some seepage after rain.

1 Excavation — 5a
The blunt rib with pleasant moves. Climb right of the bolts at this grade - a more direct line is **6a**.
FA. John Bullock, Danny McCarroll 2008

2 Tickety-Boo — 5c
A good little slab. Follow the slabby wall just to the right of the right-facing shallow groove.
FA. John Bullock, Danny McCarroll 2008

3 Sport Wars — 6a
Start just left of the bolt-line. A nice pitch.
FA. Dan Cook, Danny McCarroll 2008

4 Tread Gently — 6b+
An intense and insecure start gains another tricky sequence that eventually relents to steadier climbing up the final wall.
FA. John Bullock, Danny McCarroll 2008

Watch House Slab **Watch House** *137*

5 St. Vitus's Dance... 6c+
An extremely thin and technical lower wall eases above the white streaks.
FA. Danny McCarroll, Dan Cook 2008

6 The Drilling Fields..... 7a
A tough slabby start gains much easier ground above.
FA. John Bullock, Danny McCarroll 2008

7 Anonymous Bosch.. 6b
A good route up the overlapping walls.
FA. John Bullock, Danny McCarroll 2008

8 Jaded Locals...... 6b+
The best pitch at the crag. Follow *Anonymous Bosch* to its second bolt and then head right and up through the bulges.
Photo on this page.
FA. John Bullock, Danny McCarroll 2008

9 I Bolt, Therefore I Am... 6c+
Climb the technical lower face to the bulge. Make some fingery pulls through the bulge to finish.
FA. John Bullock, Danny McCarroll 2008

10 Trad Man............... 6a+
Cross the white streak from left to right via some technical climbing and then continue up less good rock.
FA. John Bullock, Danny McCarroll 2008

Liz Collyer pulling over the final bulge of *Jaded Locals* (6b+) - *this page* - at the Watch House Slab. Photo: Adrian Berry

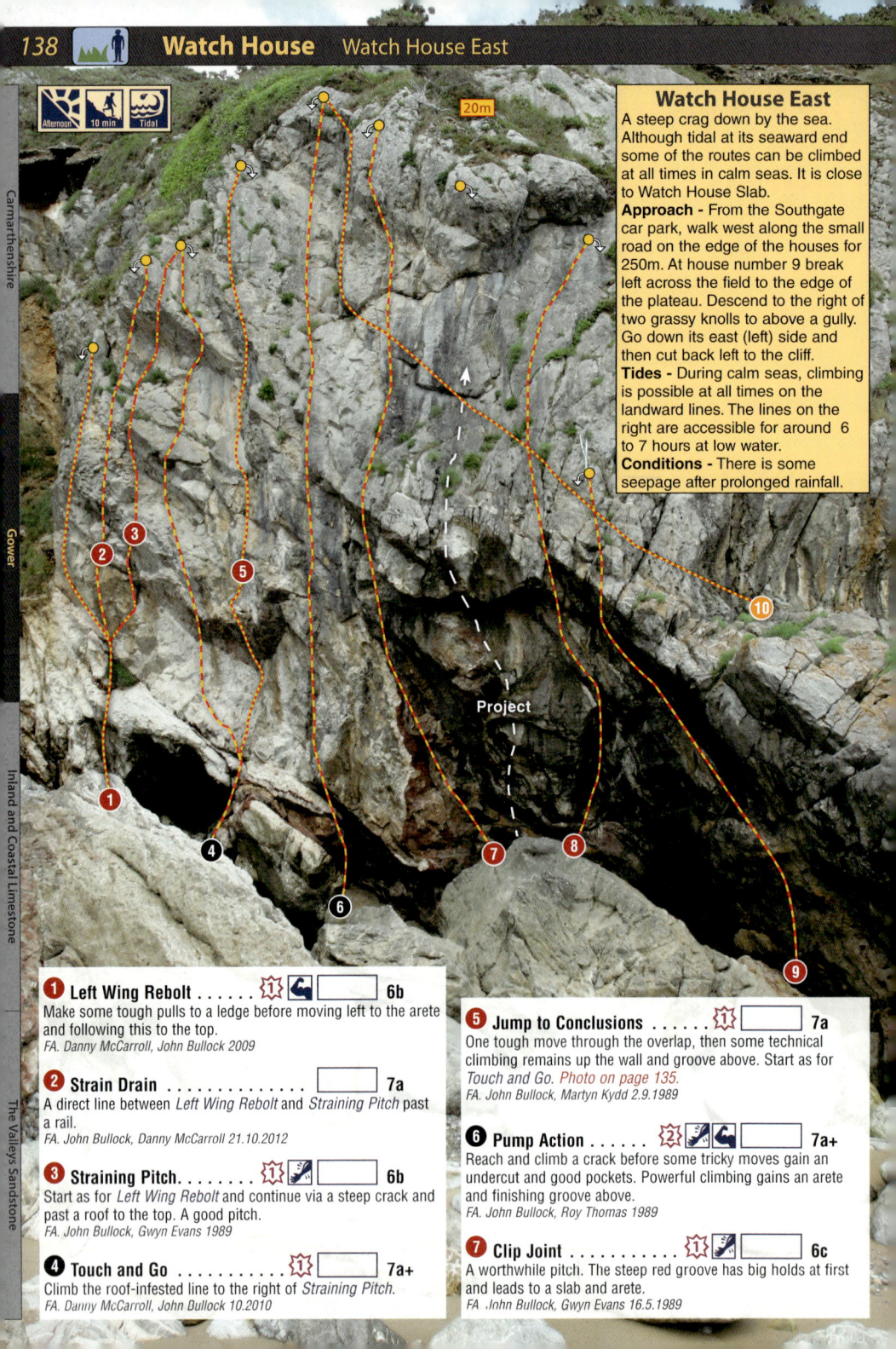

138 Watch House — Watch House East

Watch House East

A steep crag down by the sea. Although tidal at its seaward end some of the routes can be climbed at all times in calm seas. It is close to Watch House Slab.

Approach - From the Southgate car park, walk west along the small road on the edge of the houses for 250m. At house number 9 break left across the field to the edge of the plateau. Descend to the right of two grassy knolls to above a gully. Go down its east (left) side and then cut back left to the cliff.

Tides - During calm seas, climbing is possible at all times on the landward lines. The lines on the right are accessible for around 6 to 7 hours at low water.

Conditions - There is some seepage after prolonged rainfall.

❶ Left Wing Rebolt 6b
Make some tough pulls to a ledge before moving left to the arete and following this to the top.
FA. Danny McCarroll, John Bullock 2009

❷ Strain Drain 7a
A direct line between *Left Wing Rebolt* and *Straining Pitch* past a rail.
FA. John Bullock, Danny McCarroll 21.10.2012

❸ Straining Pitch 6b
Start as for *Left Wing Rebolt* and continue via a steep crack and past a roof to the top. A good pitch.
FA. John Bullock, Gwyn Evans 1989

❹ Touch and Go . . . . 7a+
Climb the roof-infested line to the right of *Straining Pitch*.
FA. Danny McCarroll, John Bullock 10.2010

❺ Jump to Conclusions 7a
One tough move through the overlap, then some technical climbing remains up the wall and groove above. Start as for *Touch and Go*. *Photo on page 135.*
FA. John Bullock, Martyn Kydd 2.9.1989

❻ Pump Action . . . . . . 7a+
Reach and climb a crack before some tricky moves gain an undercut and good pockets. Powerful climbing gains an arete and finishing groove above.
FA. John Bullock, Roy Thomas 1989

❼ Clip Joint 6c
A worthwhile pitch. The steep red groove has big holds at first and leads to a slab and arete.
FA. John Bullock, Gwyn Evans 16.5.1989

Watch House East **Watch House** 139

8 No Rest for the Wicked 7a
Start down behind the boulder - which is avoided at this grade.
FA. Adrian Berry 1995

9 Too Many Fingers 7a
A pumpy line avoiding the arete. From the belay it is possible to continue along *Nia Miss*.
FA. Danny McCarroll, John Bullock 2008

10 Nia Miss 5c
An adventurous outing that requires careful route finding and some long slings. Start on the ledge at the right-hand side of the crag at a bolt belay. Step around the corner, and creep leftwards across the slab, then continue round to bridge up the corner.
FA. John Bullock, Danny McCarroll 2008

Jen Stephens on one of Foxhole's finest lines *Joy de Viva* (7a) - *page 144* - Foxhole along with all the other crags close to the coastal village of Southgate provide the highest concentration of lines on Gower. As an added benefit the cafe next to the car park is very pleasant and a must for a pre- or post-climb snack. Photo: John Warner

140 Foxhole

	No star	★	★★	★★★
up to 4c	1	2	-	-
5a to 6a+	2	1	-	-
6b to 7a	1	5	2	2
7a+ and up	-	3	6	1

Chris Savage dispatching the classic Gower sport climb *Pioneers of the Hypnotic Groove* (7b) - *page 143* - at Foxhole. Photo: Mark Glaister

Foxhole 141

Gower's coastline is peppered with well-hidden bays. Foxhole is one of these with a back wall that lends itself both to climbing and isolation - a real gem. The left-hand side of the recess is formed by the roof of an old cave, whilst the right-hand side provides a fine wall of excellent fused limestone. There is a variety of climbing styles on offer here that ranges from some easy-angled slabs to super steep cave lines. All the routes are worthwhile but the best climbing is in the mid-to-higher grades. The crag is rainproof, very close to the parking and cafe and can be climbed on all year round as long as it is not seeping.

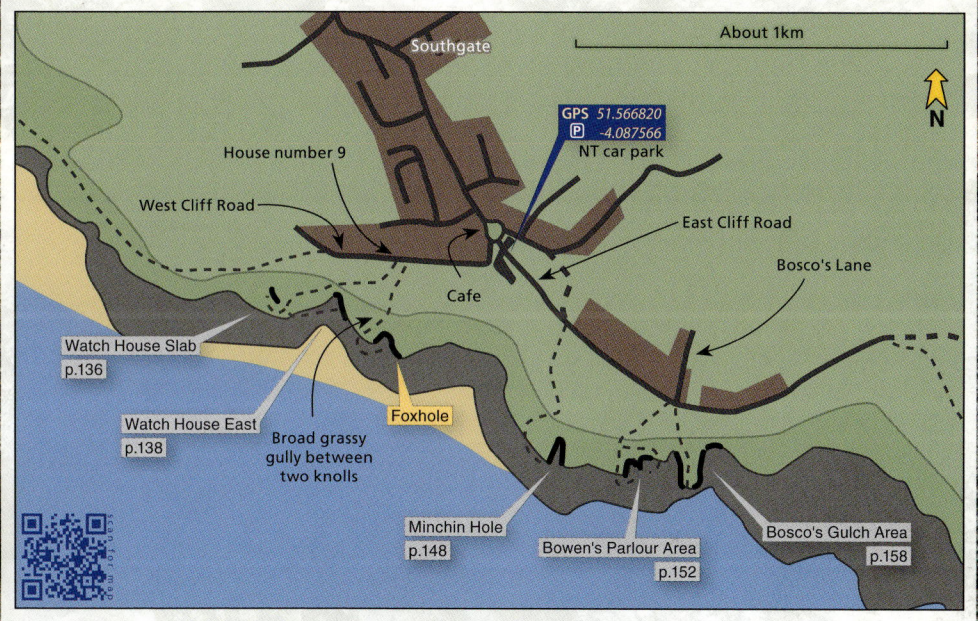

Approach Also see map on page 80

Follow the road through Southgate to the National Trust car park (Fee). From here, walk west along the small road on the edge of the houses for 250m and at house number 9 break left across the field to the edge of the plateau. Descend between two grassy knolls via a broad grassy gully until the cliff edge is gained. From here there are two options: either traverse left (looking out) above the cliff and then descend a vague track, taking care not to dislodge rocks and stones or, better, continue slightly rightwards down a fisherman's track and contour back left to the cliff.

Conditions

The cliff faces southwest and gets sunshine from mid-morning onwards. The overhanging nature means the crag can give shade, but it is not an ideal venue when the weather is hot and sunny. It does, however, make it an ideal spring and autumn venue. The crag suffers from seepage after long spells of rain during the winter months, but when dry, it stays so for long periods and can even be climbed on in rain. The cliff is completely non-tidal.

142 Foxhole

Foxhole 143

The first two routes are outliers located 50m down and left of the crag above a zawn.

1 The Power of the Leopard Skin Leg Warmers
.... 3+
The left-hand side of the gentle slab.
FA. Rhoslyn Frugtniet 3.2010

2 A Leopard Cannot Change His Spots
.... 2
The right-hand side of the gentle slab.
FA. Rhoslyn Frugtniet 3.2010

Just to the left of the main crag is a broken area of overlapping rock that has a few easier bolted lines on it.

3 Cunning Little Fox 5a
The left of two lines up the broken rock.
FA. Stuart Llewellyn 25.5.2010

4 Never Out Fox the Fox 5a
The right-hand line up the broken rock.
FA. Stuart Llewellyn 10.6.2010

5 Basil Brush 4c
The first climb on the main section of crag.
FA. Danny McCarroll, John Bullock 5.3.2013

6 Unholy Alliance .... 6a+
Steep climbing up the white pillar on the fringe of the main crag. Hardest towards the top.
FA. Martin Crocker, John Harwood 1.5.1994. Bolted at a later date.

7 Marmalade Skies. 7a
A tight line that follows the deceptively steep orange streak with a tough pull just above mid-height. *Photo on page 11.*
FA. Danny McCarroll, John Bullock 2.3.2013

8 Connard Canard. ... 7b
A very steep route up a grey streak with two bouldery sections.
FA. Gary Gibson, Michelle Gouze 1.9.1998

9 Goose in Lucy .... Top 50 6c+
Popular and very good when dry. A bouldery start past some finger pockets leads onto a rail and jug-riddled wall.
Photo on page 80.
Lucky Lizzy, 6c+ - It can be extended to the top of the crag by moving right and climbing the upper section of *Surplomb de Ray / Pioneers of the Hypnotic Groove*.
FA. Roy Thomas, S Coles 11.5.1996
FA. (Lucky Lizzy) Simon Rawlinson 23.4.2010

10 Surplomb de Ray ... 8b+
The toughest at the crag. Make desperate bouldery moves to a good tufa jug and continue to finish up *Pioneers of the Hypnotic Groove*.
FA. Simon Rawlinson 20.6.2010

11 Pioneers of the Hypnotic Groove
.... Top 50 7b
A brilliant sustained exercise tackling the leaning groove in the back of the cave. Summon your energy levels and keep some for the final moves before the steadier headwall above the first lower-off. *Photo on page 5 and 140.*
FA. Goi Ashmore, Simon Coles, James Tracey 19.4.1996

The next two lines are a project and an old line that lost a hold and hasn't been reclimbed.

12 Palace of Swords Reversed
.... 8a
The impressive bulging wall provides one of the testpieces of the area and requires an almighty effort. *Photo on page 25 and 33.*
FA. Goi Ashmore 8.9.1996

Foxhole

⓭ Chicken Licken .... 6c+
A short, sharp shock to the system via the overhanging arete. Climb just left of the arete to the mid-height easing and a lower-off.
FA. Roy Thomas 19.7.1996

⓮ Fowl Play 7a
A left-to-right diagonal taking in some steep terrain. Climb *Chicken Licken* to its fourth bolt, moving right to the concreted jug on *Joy de Viva*. Do the crux of this, and then move right again to some flat holds. Climb directly to gain jugs and a lower-off. Some long quickdraws are needed.
FA. Martyn Richards, Andy Sharp 15.4.2010

⓯ No Epoxy Au Oxley .... 6b+
Climb the steep cracks just right of the arete to the mid-height easing. Traverse leftwards and finish up the headwall as for *Pioneers of the Hypnotic Groove*. Take some long slings to reduce rope drag.
FA. Roy Thomas 1994

The next routes start up No Epoxy Au Oxley to gain the mid-height easing.

⓰ Gypsy Eyes .... 6b+
The headwall to the right of *No Epoxy Au Oxley*. Take some long slings to reduce rope drag
FA. Stuart Llewellyn 30.3.2013

⓱ Little Miss Lover 7a
The headwall 2m left of some conglomerate.
FA. Martin Crocker 1.5.1994. Bolted at a later date.

⓲ Foxy Lady 7a
A superb route with plenty of good moves and climbing. Climb the leaning wall to a tough finishing sequence. A logical link-up of *Chicken Licken* into the upper section of *Foxy Lady* gives **Foxy Chicken, 7a+**.
FA. John Bullock, Roy Thomas 5.1990

⓳ The Hooker 7a
Similar to its neighbour with great climbing. Start as for *Foxy Lady* and continue to some pushy moves up and left to finish.
Photo on page 146.
FA. John Bullock, Roy Thomas 6.1990

⓴ Joy de Viva 7a
The best of the trio of 7as requiring stamina and ingenuity. Climb to the hole before pulling out right and up to some conglomerate. A further hard move gains better holds and a race for the lower-off. *Photo on page 139.*
FA. Gary Gibson, Roy Thomas 5.7.1997

There are two projects here, the left one has just one bolt.

㉑ Power Struggle ..... 7b+
A tough and innocuous pitch on crisp little edges and side-pulls.
FA. Martin Crocker, John Harwood 1.5.1994

㉒ Ducky Lucky ... 7a+
Superb climbing with a long reach or technical move.
FA. Roy Thomas 10.8.1996

㉓ The Day the Sky Fell In .. 6b+
The steady looking groove on the right-hand side of the crag is much more involved and strenuous that first impressions suggest.
FA. Roy Thomas 18.5.1996

Foxhole

145

Many variations have been climbed, the following three are the most popular.

㉔ Turkey Lurking....... 7c
As for *Power Struggle* to the good holds after its crux (4th bolt), then make a hard move leftwards to a series of stiff pulls on good holds Make a final cruxy rockover to gain the lower-off of *Foxy Lady*.
FA. Eugene Travers-Jones 10.8.1996

㉕ Poultry in Motion...... 7b+
A rising traverse of the crag from bottom right to top left. Follow *The Day The Sky Fell In* to its 3rd bolt. Move left past *Ducky Lucky* and *Power Struggle*, continuing along *Turkey Lurking* to finish.
FA. Martiyn Richards, Andy Sharp 6.2000

㉖ Where the Fox That?... 7b+
Another right to left diagonal! Climb *The Day The Sky Fell In* to its 4th bolt, then follow the upper break approximately 1m below the top with hard moves between *Power Struggle* and *Fowl Play*. From the jug in the bulge of *Fowl Play*, move leftwards past the final bolt of *Joy De Viva*, making tricky moves to the belay of *The Hooker*.
FA. Martyn Richards, Andy Sharp 15.4.2010

146 **Foxhole**

Carmarthenshire

Gower

Inland and Coastal Limestone

The Valleys Sandstone

Ali Martindale finishing off the powerful upper section of *The Hooker* (7a) - *page 144* - at Foxhole. Foxhole is only a short step from the village of Southgate where many excellent cliffs are approached from and home to a good cafe. Foxhole has an exquisite set of routes that get plenty of sun and can be climbed on for much of the year. Although the crag does seep after prolonged rainfall it provides plenty of shelter from the rain. Photo: Glaister collection

Foxhole 147

Minchin Hole

	No star	☼	☼☼	☼☼☼
up to 4c	-	-	-	-
5a to 6a+	-	1	-	-
6b to 7a	2	3	1	-
7a+ and up	1	1	-	3

An intriguing crag with some fine pitches in an unusual and atmospheric setting. Please pay close attention to the access notes.

Approach See map on page 152

From the car park at Southgate, walk east along East Cliff Road for 300m road to where a track comes in from the left. Head out towards the highest point of the cliff top (a rocky knoll) and then descend a steep path just to its right. Where the grass and scree turn to rock, a faint path leads left to the entrance of Minchin Hole.

Conditions

Minchin Hole does see sun on both walls and is often dry, but it is not a place to head for in cold weather or high seas.

Access

Remains of lions, spotted hyena and wild boar have been excavated here and it contains the remains of a richly fossiliferous sequence. It is a 'Site of Special Scientific Interest' and as such has some specific areas of concern.
> The 'stuck-on' conglomerate features are important from a conservation perspective and should be avoided.
> No loose rock is to be removed, the cave deposits go right up to the roof clinging to the sides outside as well as inside the cave.
> Gardening is not permitted and the cliff face must be left undisturbed.
> Bolt replacement on existing routes should be on a like-for-like basis only and no new routes should be added.
> Avoid the flying buttress of debris left of the start of *The Raven*. It is part of the bone-bearing 'cave earth' and has been left there to show how the sediments inside the cave link with those in the entrance.
> Should you see any fossils or bones (do not dislodge if partially buried) please notify the National Trust.
> Only the routes presented here should be climbed.

A view out from the back of Minchin Hole, once the lair of lions and hyena but now just an intriguing sport climbing venue.

Minchin Hole 149

Fringe Benefits

23m

Bolt belay

There is an old line on the left **Fringe Benefits, 6a+** that is not bolted at present but may be restored in the future.

❶ Beyond the Fringe 6b
From a bolt belay, climb up the wall past a small tufa boss, to steeper climbing up the headwall to finish. A pleasant pitch.
FA. Roy Thomas, Gary Gibson 4.5.1998

❷ Triple Sigh . . . . 6b+
Climb up right past the large conglomerate lump to gain the steep rib above.
FA. Roy Thomas, Gary Gibson 14.5.1998

❸ Swim With The Sharks 6c
An excellent pitch via a small overhang and leaning wall.
FA. Roy Thomas 10.5.1998

❹ Jump the Sun . . . . . 7a+
A good climb up the wall and upper overhang to a some tough finishing moves. The lower staples are hard to spot.
FA. Roy Thomas, Gary Gibson 1.9.1998

Minchin Hole

150

26m

15m

Routes 1 to 4

Flying buttress of debris - DO NOT TOUCH

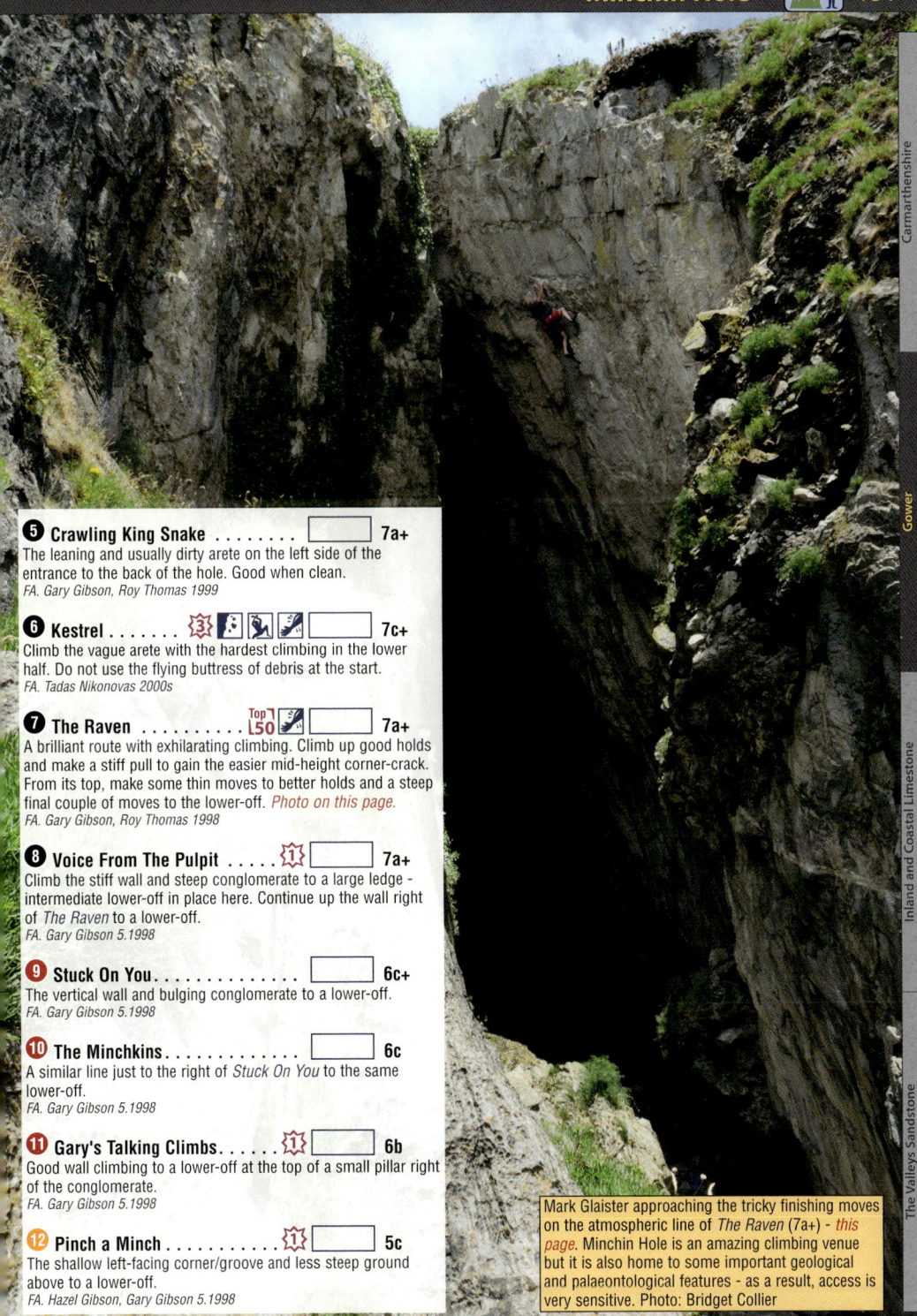

Minchin Hole 151

❺ Crawling King Snake . . . . ▢ **7a+**
The leaning and usually dirty arete on the left side of the entrance to the back of the hole. Good when clean.
FA. Gary Gibson, Roy Thomas 1999

❻ Kestrel . . . . 3️⃣ 🔒🔨 ▢ **7c+**
Climb the vague arete with the hardest climbing in the lower half. Do not use the flying buttress of debris at the start.
FA. Tadas Nikonovas 2000s

❼ The Raven . . . . Top 50 🔨 ▢ **7a+**
A brilliant route with exhilarating climbing. Climb up good holds and make a stiff pull to gain the easier mid-height corner-crack. From its top, make some thin moves to better holds and a steep final couple of moves to the lower-off. *Photo on this page.*
FA. Gary Gibson, Roy Thomas 1998

❽ Voice From The Pulpit . . . . . 🔒 ▢ **7a+**
Climb the stiff wall and steep conglomerate to a large ledge - intermediate lower-off in place here. Continue up the wall right of *The Raven* to a lower-off.
FA. Gary Gibson 5.1998

❾ Stuck On You . . . . ▢ **6c+**
The vertical wall and bulging conglomerate to a lower-off.
FA. Gary Gibson 5.1998

❿ The Minchkins . . . . ▢ **6c**
A similar line just to the right of *Stuck On You* to the same lower-off.
FA. Gary Gibson 5.1998

⓫ Gary's Talking Climbs . . . . . 🔒 ▢ **6b**
Good wall climbing to a lower-off at the top of a small pillar right of the conglomerate.
FA. Gary Gibson 5.1998

⓬ Pinch a Minch . . . . 🔒 ▢ **5c**
The shallow left-facing corner/groove and less steep ground above to a lower-off.
FA. Hazel Gibson, Gary Gibson 5.1998

Mark Glaister approaching the tricky finishing moves on the atmospheric line of *The Raven* (7a+) - *this page*. Minchin Hole is an amazing climbing venue but it is also home to some important geological and palaeontological features - as a result, access is very sensitive. Photo: Bridget Collier

Bowen's Parlour Area

152

	No star	✱	✱✱	✱✱✱
up to 4c	1	-	-	-
5a to 6a+	-	9	2	-
6b to 7a	2	7	3	-
7a+ and up	-	2	5	1

A further three sport crags lurk below the grass and scree slopes to the east of Minchen Hole. They all offer worthwhile climbing from lower end 6s to some very steep 7s. There is a mix of both tidal and non-tidal sectors and sun and shade can be found throughout the day. A bit of forward planning will pay dividends here in order to squeeze the most out of a visit. It is worth noting that Minchen Hole cannot be reached safely without returning to the top of the approach slope.

Approach   Also see map on page 80

Prawn Zawn and Bowen's Parlour - From the Southgate car park head east along East Cliff Road road for 700m until Bosco's Lane is reached. Face out to sea and head rightwards to a bench on the edge of the cliffs. Descend to above some inlets and scramble down, then right for Prawn Zawn or left for Bowen's Parlour (see photo below).

The Pantheon - Traverse left above the inlets, past a massive hole in the ground. Then head down and back right to below the routes.

Conditions

The lower sector of Bowen's Parlour and Prawn Zawn are tidal, meaning that they are not accessible during high seas at any tide state. The Pantheon is set well back from the sea. Seepage does occur mainly during the winter months. In rain there is the possibility of dry climbing at The Pantheon and on the steep routes at Bowen's Parlour.

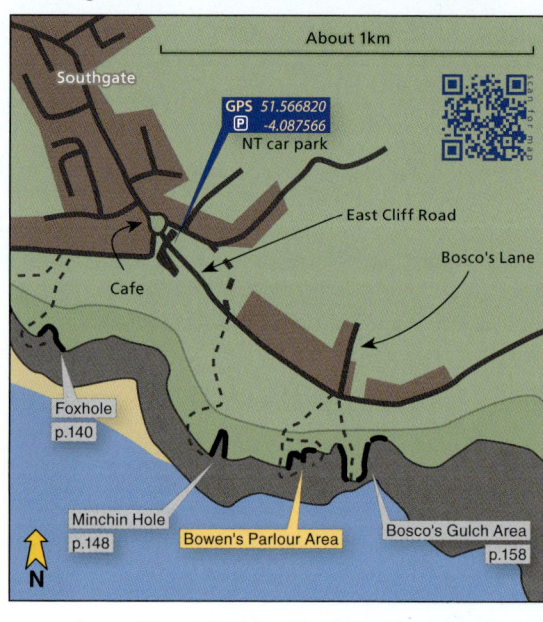

Bowen's Parlour Area 153

Paul Walters topping out on the steep finish of *Breccial Motion* (6c+) - *page 154* - at Bowen's Parlour. Photo: Adrian Berry.

Bowen's Parlour Area — Prawn Zawn

Prawn Zawn

A small inlet with some reasonable lines which are useful if it is busy at Bowen's Parlour.

Approach - The zawn is about 100m west of Bowen's Parlour, reached by a scramble at the base of the main approach.

Tides - The zawn is tidal (4 hours at low water). Aim to arrive at around low tide as the base takes time to dry.

Conditions - The routes are west facing and get afternoon sun.

❶ Bull Fighter .... 7b+
A wild test of roof and mantel skills. You may need a spotter for the move around the lip!
FA. Simon Rawlinon 12.5.2012

❷ Rush Hour .... 7b+
From the second bolt of *Bull Fighter*, move right and follow a parallel line.
FA. Ashleigh Wolsey-Heard 12.5.2012

❸ Prawn Star .... 6b+
A good pitch that takes the wall to the right of the overhang, moving right to the lower-off.
FA. Roy Thomas, Paul Hadley 1999

❹ Prawnsite 6b
The crack and groove.
FA. Roy Thomas, Paul Hadley 1999

❺ Hard Prawn .... 6c+
The harder direct version of *Prawnsite*.
FA. Roy Thomas, Paul Hadley 1999

❻ Soft Prawn .... 6a+
The flake and thin sharp wall above it. High in the grade.
FA. Roy Thomas, Paul Hadley 1999

❼ For King Trad Prawn E1 5a
Follow the crack up and right.
FA. Paul Hadley 1999

❽ Prawn Cock Tale 6a
The wall with a barnacled start.
FA. Roy Thomas, Paul Hadley 1999

❾ Teen Prawn .... S 4a
Easy climbing leads left to the belay.
FA. Roy Thomas, Paul Hadley 1999

Bowen's Parlour

❿ Rudaceous Ramble .... 6a+
The rubble is more solid than it looks, and the corner much steeper than expected.
FA. John Bullock, Danny McCarroll 2009

⓫ Breccial Motion .... 6b+
Swing right to borrow the delightful last few moves of *Parlour Games*. *Photo on page 153.*
FA. John Bullock, Danny McCarroll 2009

⓬ Parlour Games 7b
A direct line with a powerful crux.
FA. Danny McCarroll, John Bullock 2010

⓭ Parlour Français 7c
Start up the previous route and break through the overhang.
FA. Martyn Richards, Andy Sharp 2010

⓮ Spider 6c
The arete gives a fine, but short climb.
FA. John Bullock, Danny McCarroll 2009

Bowen's Parlour Area

Bowen's Parlour

An impressive bowl of steep limestone and conglomerate provides the harder lines; whilst below is a tidal zawn with two walls of easier lines. Moving around on the ledge below the upper walls is a little tricky.

Approach - at sea level head right (looking inland) to ledges below the upper walls and above the zawn. The zawn is accessible for around 2 hours on either side of low water. Enter the zawn either by a scramble down or abseil. Keep an eye on the water level as it quickly floods the base of the zawn.

Conditions - Sun and shade can be found throughout the day and during light rain climbing is possible on the steeper lines above the ledge.

15 Fly 6b
Unusual climbing using flowstone features. Beware - if you step on the 'roof' it is very awkward to get back on the route!
FA. Danny McCarroll, John Bullock 2009

16 Still Nifty at Fifty ... 7a+
Move up the faint rib to the left of *When I'm 64* to where the good holds end, then break horizontally left with a tough move to the lower-off.
FA. Danny McCarroll 2010

17 When I'm 64 ...... 7a+
The steepening diagonal is climbed on very positive holds to a wild finale off the 'house brick' hold.
FA. John Bullock, Danny McCarroll 2010

18 Aspidistra .... 6b+
Pull over the small roof using a high undercut. Some dodgy rock. Harder for the short.
FA. John Bullock, Danny McCarroll 2009

19 Maud 6b
Very steep climbing, but the holds are good. Some dodgy rock.
FA. Danny McCarroll, John Bullock 2010

Bowen's Parlour Area — The Zawn

The Zawn

The Zawn is below the approach ledge to the upper climbs. The first two routes are on the east wall of the zawn.

Approach - The zawn is accessible for around 2 hours on either side of low water. Enter the zawn either by a scramble down or abseil. Keep an eye on the water level as it quickly floods the base of the zawn.

Conditions - Sun and shade can be found throughout the day although the majority of the lines get the sun in the afternoon.

❶ Wisdom of Age 5a
The left line on the east-facing wall. Nice moves.
FA. Danny McCarroll, John Bullock 2010

❷ Sallies of Youth 5c
The right line on the east-facing wall. Best in the sun otherwise it can be a bit greasy.
FA. Danny McCarroll, John Bullock 2010

The rest of the routes in the zawn are all on its west wall.

❸ All of a Quiver 6a
The steep cracks from the sloping platform left of *Bowen Arrow*.
FA. Roy Thomas 7.2010

❹ Bowen Arrow 6a
The corner and flake starting from the slippery slope.
FA. Danny McCarroll, John Bullock 2010

❺ Reaction Series .... 6b+
Layback up the big corner and attack the overlaps.
FA. Danny McCarroll, John Bullock 2010

The Pantheon   **Bowen's Parlour Area**   157

6 **Bowen to the Inevitable** .... 🛡 ▢ **6a**
Great climbing up to and over the apex of the arch. Steeper than it looks. *Photo on page 28.*
FA. John Bullock, Danny McCarroll 2010

7 **Parlour Vous le Sport** ... 🛡 ▢ **6a+**
Straight up the steep ground right of the arch. It now has a hard start where there used to be a boulder - either clipstick past this or come in from the left. There are also some perplexing moves before the final overlap.
FA. Danny McCarroll, John Bullock 2010

8 **Feud For Thought**...... 🛡 ▢ **6b**
Sustained climbing through the overlaps.
FA. John Bullock, Danny McCarroll 2010

9 **Gentlemen Prefer Bolts.** . 🛡 ▢ **6c+**
The steep wall via the 'boss'. The start is reachy and the difficulties continue above.
FA. John Bullock, Danny McCarroll 2010

10 **Gentleman's Relish** .... 🛡 ▢ **6a**
Follow the groove to a hard finish.
FA. Roy Thomas, Goi Ashmore 2010

11 **Gentleman's Retreat** ...... 🛡 ▢ **6a**
Start just right of *Gentleman's Relish* and climb the wall to a belay on the upper ledge.
FA. Roy Thomas, Dai Emanuel 10.10.2010

The Pantheon
A compact section of very steep rock tucked away at the back of a boulder-filled cove.
Approach - Traverse left above Bowen's Parlour, past a massive hole in the ground, and head down and back right to below the routes.
Conditions - It is shady in the afternoon, non-tidal and also stays dry in rain. Seepage does occur but only after prolonged rainfall.

12 **Pegasus** .... 🛡 ▢ **7c**
Technical wall climbing on conglomerate holds leads to the first of three stepped roofs. Burly undercutting over these leads to the lower-off below the conglomerate cornice.
FA. Simon Rawlinson 9.2.2009

13 **Orion** .... 🛡 ▢ **7b**
Start up *Pegasus* and move right to below a roof. Cross the roof using undercuts and a sharp two-finger pocket to gain good jugs under the second roof. Finish on more conglomerate holds to a gripping finale.
FA. Simon Rawlinson 10.1.2009

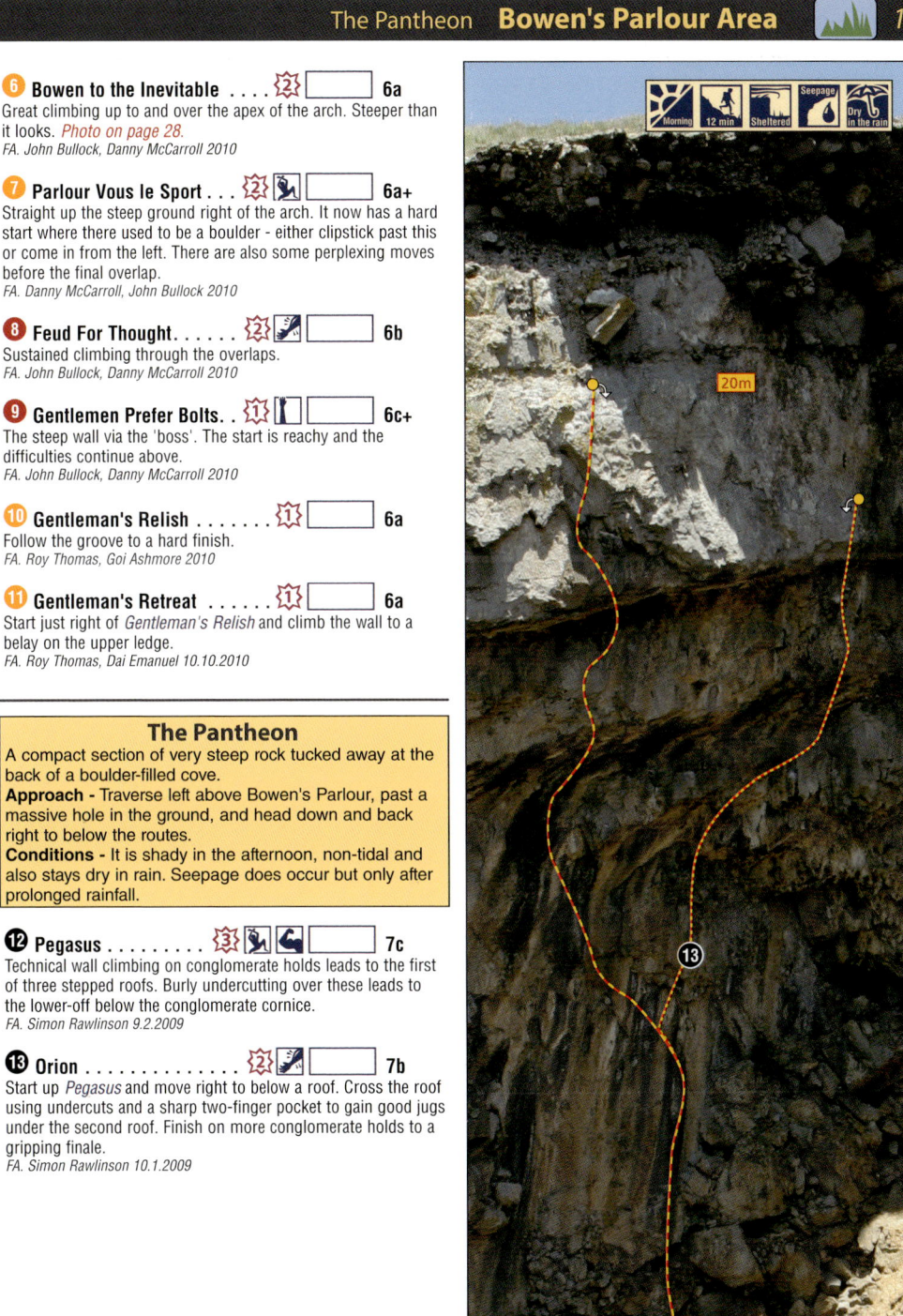

Bosco's Gulch Area

	No star	★	★★	★★★
up to 4c	-	-	-	-
5a to 6a+	1	3	4	-
6b to 7a	3	9	4	-
7a+ and up	1	2	2	-

A collection of small zawns and walls with some good routes. It has a slightly more awkward approach to other crags hereabouts. Golden Wall and Golden Gulch offer routes at either end of the grade spectrum, whilst Bosco's Gulch has plenty of good lines that see little attention and might need a brush before an ascent.

Approach and Tides   Also see map on page 80

From the Southgate car park, head east along East Cliff Road road for 700m to Bosco's Lane. Face out to sea and head slightly left to the edge of the cliffs. Descend the slope to a small square-cut quarry. Bosco's Gulch is to the left and can be reached by a scramble down to sea level (3 to 4 hours at low water) or by abseiling from a prominent spike/bolts on the left rim of the quarry. If abseiling, leave a rope in place to allow an escape when the tide comes in. It is also worth checking that the base is clear of water when abseiling in as the abseil is free-hanging.

Golden Wall and Golden Gulch are on the right side of the quarry and accessed by a scramble down (3 to 4 hours at low water). Alternatively an easy scramble down from the base of the approach to The Pantheon is possible and useful if approaching from Bowen's Parlour - also 3 to 4 hours at low water.

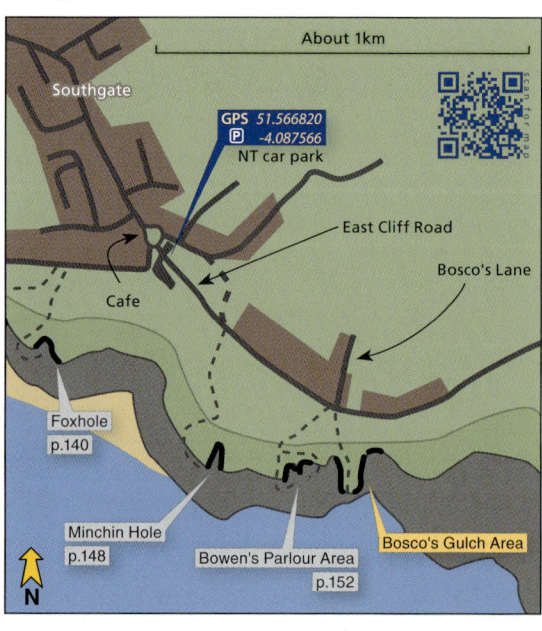

Bosco's Gulch Area 159

Simon Rawlinson picking his way up the unusual ground found on *Conglomeration* (7a) - *page 162* - at Bosco's Gulch. Photo: Adrian Berry

Conditions
Bosco's Gulch is fairly sheltered but it takes time for seepage to dry out. Golden Wall and Golden Gulch are more exposed to the elements but dry quickly.

Access
No climbing in the upper cave at the back of the zawn ('The Den') due to rare geology/artefacts. There is a bird restriction on the routes in The Cave from 1st March to 1st August.

Bosco's Gulch Area — Golden Gulch

Golden Gulch

An interesting compact cliff that has some good short climbs on fine rock. Easily combined with Bosco's Gulch.

Approach - Scramble down from the quarry to the boulder beach, or via the Pantheon crag approach (see page 157 for this approach).

Tides - Accessible for 3 to 4 hours at low water.

Conditions - The routes are west-facing so get afternoon sun. The base takes time to dry out once the tide has gone out.

① The Gold Rush .. 7a
A rising traverse finishing on the far left of the crag. There is a project that crosses the big overhangs.
FA. John Bullock, Danny McCarroll 1.9.2012

② The Midas Touch ... 6c+
The wall and overlaps. Very good
FA. Danny McCarroll, John Bullock 10.2010

③ A Starke Reminder 6b
Named after Tom Starke - an erstwhile local German/Austrian climber. Continue up the upper wall to the belay. Nice climbing.
FA. Danny McCarroll, John Bullock 10.2010

④ Aur of Glory .... 6a+
Enjoyable climbing on good holds.
FA. Danny McCarroll, John Bullock 10.2010

⑤ Aur of Need 6a
A similar route to *Aur of Glory* but a touch easier.
FA. Danny McCarroll, John Bullock 10.2010

⑥ Golden Boy 5c
The unusual runnel feature and upper wall.
FA. Roy Thomas 2.2016

⑦ Golden Hour 5c
Make steep moves to easier and less steep ground.
FA. Roy Thomas 2.2016

Golden Wall **Bosco's Gulch Area** *161*

Golden Wall
The Golden Wall is a severely leaning and compact sheet of stone that has a collection of quite short (but very hard) routes strung across it.
Approach - The wall is accessible for 3 to 4 hours at low water. Scramble down to the boulder beach via the Pantheon crag approach (see page 157 for this approach), or down from the quarry. Do not try and abseil in since the ground above the crag is loose.
Tides - The routes are mostly non-tidal.
Conditions - The wall faces west and gets the afternoon and evening sun.

8 Bye Bye Eddy . . . . 6b+
Super short, but good and powerful.
FA. Simon Rawlinson 14.6.2010

9 All that Glitters is not Gold
. . . . 7b+
Short and cruxy along the vague right-leading groove.
FA. Simon Rawlinson 21.6.2010

10 Au . . . . 7c+
The left-hand line out of *Shining Dawn* is not bolted. This line was done on pre-placed wires to a lower-off.
FA. Tom Starke 2000s

11 Shining Dawn 7c
Start up the diagonal flake and finish via a hard boulder problem.
FA. Tom Starke 2000s

12 Golden Wonder 7b
Climb *Shining Dawn* to its second bolt, then move right and up. The best route on the wall.
FA. Andy Sharp 2009

To the right are three bolted projects, the first is a direct start to *Golden Wonder*.

13 Gold Digger. 6c
Great climbing starting up the steep line of weakness at the seaward end of the ledge. A tough start leads to some good holds and a balancy finish.
FA. Roy Thomas 2011

14 Gilded Cage 5b
Steep groove at the seaward end of the wall.
FA. Roy Thomas 1.2016

Bosco's Gulch Area — Bosco's Gulch

162

A 25m — Abseil spike and bolts on rim of quarry

Leave rope in place to enable escape up final slope if you are planning on climbing once the tide has cut off access

'The Den' Climbing banned

Low tide approach from quarry

Easy scramble up to cave

Bosco's Gulch Area

Bosco's Gulch

A long wall of interesting rock and some harder pitches up in a shallow cave to the right. A good spot on a sunny morning that is easily combined with Golden Gulch.

Approach and Tides - The crag is accessed by an easy scramble for around 3 to 4 hours at low water. It is also possible to approach and retreat by abseil and leave a rope in place to allow escape up the final wall back to the abseil point. The Cave is reached via an easy short scramble.

Conditions - Fairly sheltered but takes time for seepage to dry out, especially in the back of the gulch.

⛔ **Access** - No climbing or access to the 'The Den' due to rare geology/artefacts. There is a bird restriction in the The Cave from 1 March to 1 August.

❶ Simple Simon E2 5c
Climb straight up (2 bolts), move left and then climb rightwards following an unstable overlap to a lower-off.
FA. Roy Thomas 29.5.1999

❷ Clapham Injunction . 6b
Start as for *Simple Simon*, and at the second bolt, move right and climb the wall. The direct start up a thin flake is **6c+** (one through-bolt at the start).
FA. Roy Thomas 29.5.1999

❸ Philandering Fillipino ... 6c
The flake and wall to the right have a powerful sequence to gain the overlap. Above the overlap, trend left to the lower-off.
FA. Gary Gibson 2004

❹ Gold Teeth In Them Thar Hills 6a+
Climb juggy flakes and then make steep moves to gain the easier-angled (but still interesting) upper wall and lower-off.
FA. Roy Thomas 29.5.1999

❺ Hanger Them High .... 6a+
Start left of the prominent boulder. Move up and make some harder moves out right onto the grey upper wall. Finish up this more easily on excellent rock to a lower-off. *Photo on page 164.*
FA. Roy Thomas 6.6.1999

❻ Y'All Come Back Now ... 6a+
From the boulder climb up to and over the small overhang and then take the wall above slightly leftwards to the lower-off.
FA. Roy Thomas 6.6.1999

❼ The Clampetts 6c
Start right of the boulder and climb the wall trending leftwards to the lower-off.
FA. Gary Gibson, Roy Thomas 6.1999

❽ Jump Over My Shadow
.... 7a
Layback up to join the slab. Continue past the overlap and up the headwall to finish.
FA. Gary Gibson 6.1999

❾ Conglomeration 7a
The wall via a worrying-looking but sound block of conglomerate. *Photo on page 159.*
FA. Gary Gibson 6.1999

❿ Standing on a Beach 6c
An easy corner gains a ledge. From the ledge, move left onto the wall and follow the left-hand line of bolts to a lower-off.
FA. Gary Gibson 6.1999

⓫ Reign of the Deer... 7a
The right-hand finish on the upper wall to *Standing on a Beach*.
FA. Gary Gibson 3.2000

The Cave

The Cave can be reached by an easy scramble.

⓬ Snatch .... 6c+
The left-hand route in the upper cave is equipped with staples.
FA. Gary Gibson , Roy Thomas 2000

⓭ Starter for Ten 7c
The central crack/groove. Sustained climbing to the roof precedes a powerful crux and an easier finish.
FA. Martyn Richards, Andy Sharp 6.2.2010

⓮ Squeal Like a Hog 6c
The impressive diagonal line is awkward, with spaced bolts.
FA. John Bullock, G.Morris 2000

⓯ The Millennium Thug ... 7a
Crosses the previous route with some powerful moves.
FA. Gary Gibson, Roy Thomas 3.3.2000

Bosco's Gulch Area

Paul Cox on the excellent upper wall of *Hanger Them High* (6a+) - *page 163* - at Bosco's Gulch. Along with the neighbouring Golden Gulch and Golden Wall, Bosco's Gulch offers an atmospheric venue with some great climbing. Careful planning with regard to tide times allows plenty to be done without abseil approaches. Photo: Mark Glaister

Bosco's Gulch Area

Pwlldu Bay

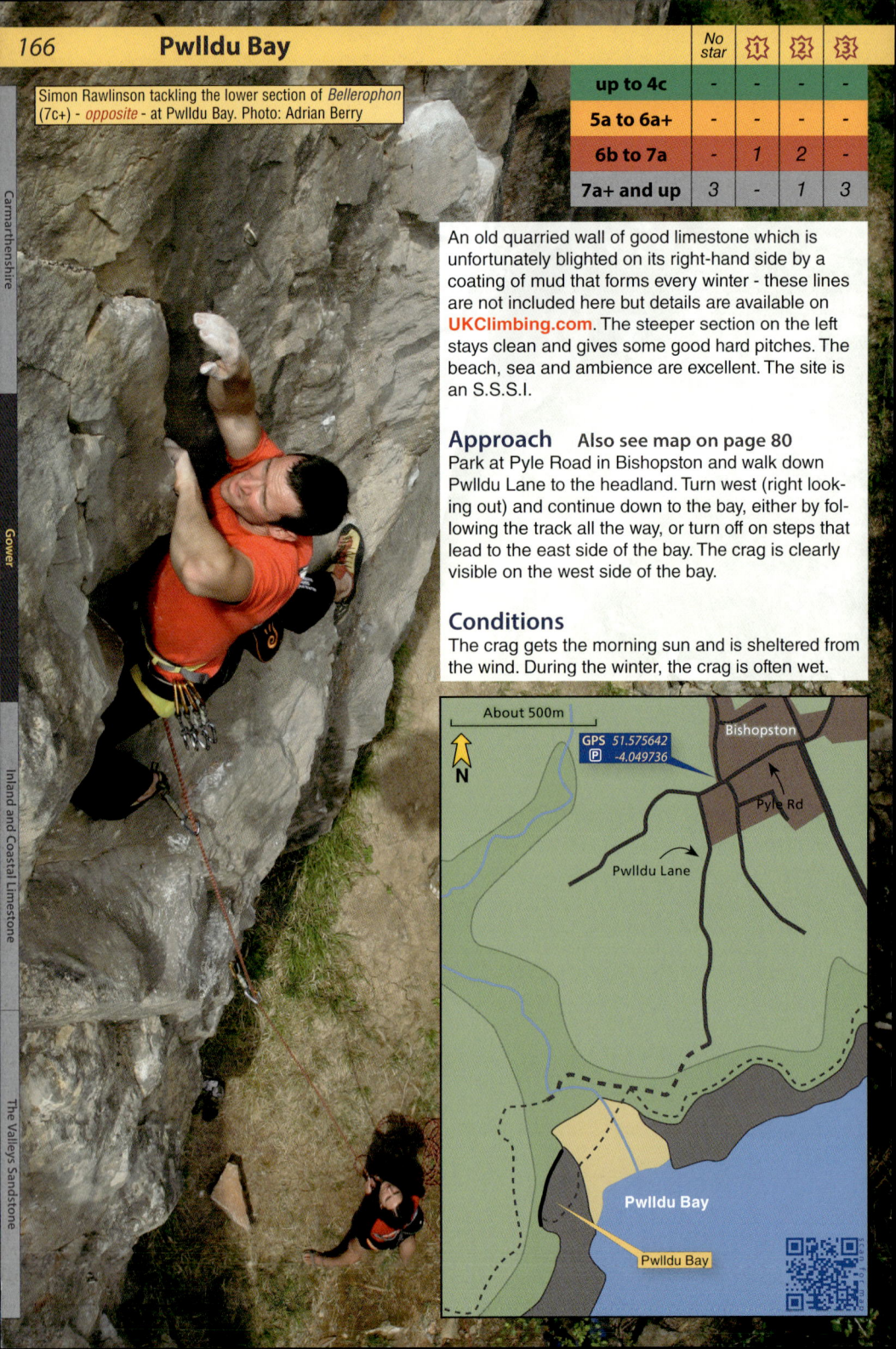

Simon Rawlinson tackling the lower section of *Bellerophon* (7c+) - *opposite* - at Pwlldu Bay. Photo: Adrian Berry

	No star	★	★★	★★★
up to 4c	-	-	-	-
5a to 6a+	-	-	-	-
6b to 7a	-	1	2	-
7a+ and up	3	-	1	3

An old quarried wall of good limestone which is unfortunately blighted on its right-hand side by a coating of mud that forms every winter - these lines are not included here but details are available on **UKClimbing.com**. The steeper section on the left stays clean and gives some good hard pitches. The beach, sea and ambience are excellent. The site is an S.S.S.I.

Approach   Also see map on page 80
Park at Pyle Road in Bishopston and walk down Pwlldu Lane to the headland. Turn west (right looking out) and continue down to the bay, either by following the track all the way, or turn off on steps that lead to the east side of the bay. The crag is clearly visible on the west side of the bay.

Conditions
The crag gets the morning sun and is sheltered from the wind. During the winter, the crag is often wet.

Pwlldu Bay 167

1 Ashes to Ashes 7a
A good little route. Reaching the belay can be a bit hard/mucky at times - better to finish at the last bolt in these conditions **6c**.
FA. Roy Thomas, John Bullock, Len Moran 20.10.1986

2 Decades Apart 6c
Sustained, with long reaches between mostly good holds.
FA. Gary Gibson, Roy Thomas 2011

3 Bellerophon ...... 7c+
An excellent line with a desperate finishing sequence. Up to the first lower-off is **Forty for Three, 7b+**. *Photo opposite.*
FA. Martyn Richards, Andy Sharp 7.8.2010
FA. (Forty for Three) Martin Crocker, Roy Thomas 1994

4 Senser .... 7c+
Great climbing up the centre of the buttress. To the first lower-off (widely-spaced staples) weighs in at **7b+**.
FA. Martin Crocker 24.7.1994

5 Jezebel .... 7a+
Never desperate, but has some big moves. Superb climbing.
FA. Martin Crocker 9.7.1994

6 Crock Block 6c
The block has to be more secure than it looks.
FA. Roy Thomas 7.1994

7 Old Slapper .... 7a+
Very bouldery.
FA. Roy Thomas 1994

8 Skedaddle .... 7a+
Another bouldery little number.
FA. Martin Crocker 24.7.1994

The next routes are on walls to the right of the main quarry.

9 Cross the Rubicon .... 7b+
The left-hand line has no lower-off in place.
FA. Martyn Crocker 1990s

10 Fin 8a
The bouldery arete is worth tracking down.
FA. Adrian Berry 1994

168   Rams Tor

	No star	★	★★	★★★
up to 4c	-	-	-	-
5a to 6a+	-	-	-	-
6b to 7a	-	4	1	-
7a+ and up	1	4	2	2

Simon Rawlinson on the final moves of *Renaissance* (6c+) - *page 171* - at Rams Tor. Photo: Alan Rosier

Rams Tor   169

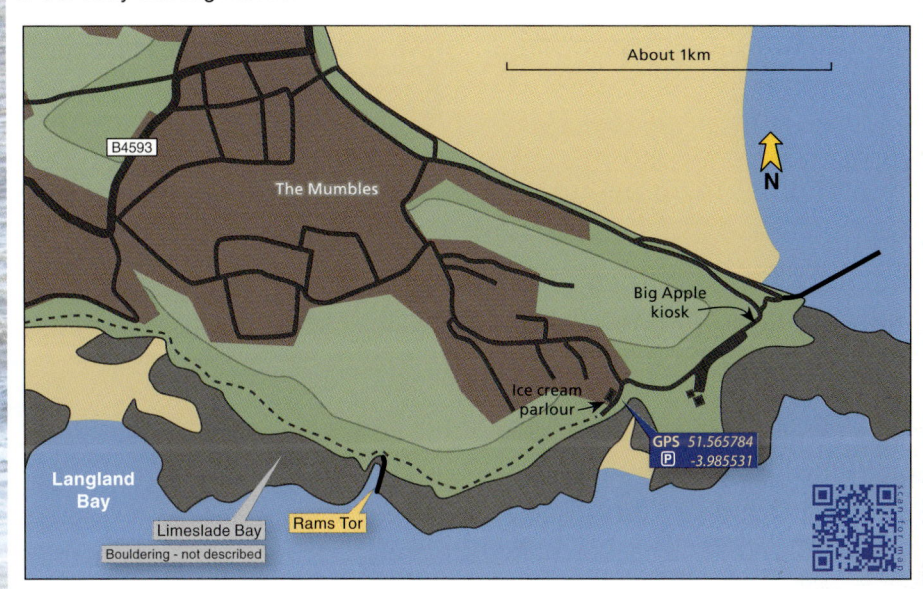

Rams Tor is a wide sea cliff that has some ferocious square-cut overhangs guarding its base. Above the overhangs are thin walls which offer technical finishes in contrast to the burly starting moves.

Approach   Also see map on page 80
Drive through Mumbles, past the 'Big Apple' (a kiosk) and the coastguard lookout, until the road ends at Bracelet Bay (ice cream parlour). Park here and follow the coast path west for 500m to some steps. Continue up the steps and, from the top, the crag is visible down on the left. Either scramble down opposite (steep and often overgrown), or abseil from the belay of *Nostradamus* (there are also belay stakes).

Conditions
The crag faces west and gets afternoon and evening sun. It dries quickly and is usually sheltered from the wind. Although non-tidal, heavy seas will encroach up the ramp below some of the lines.

170 Rams Tor

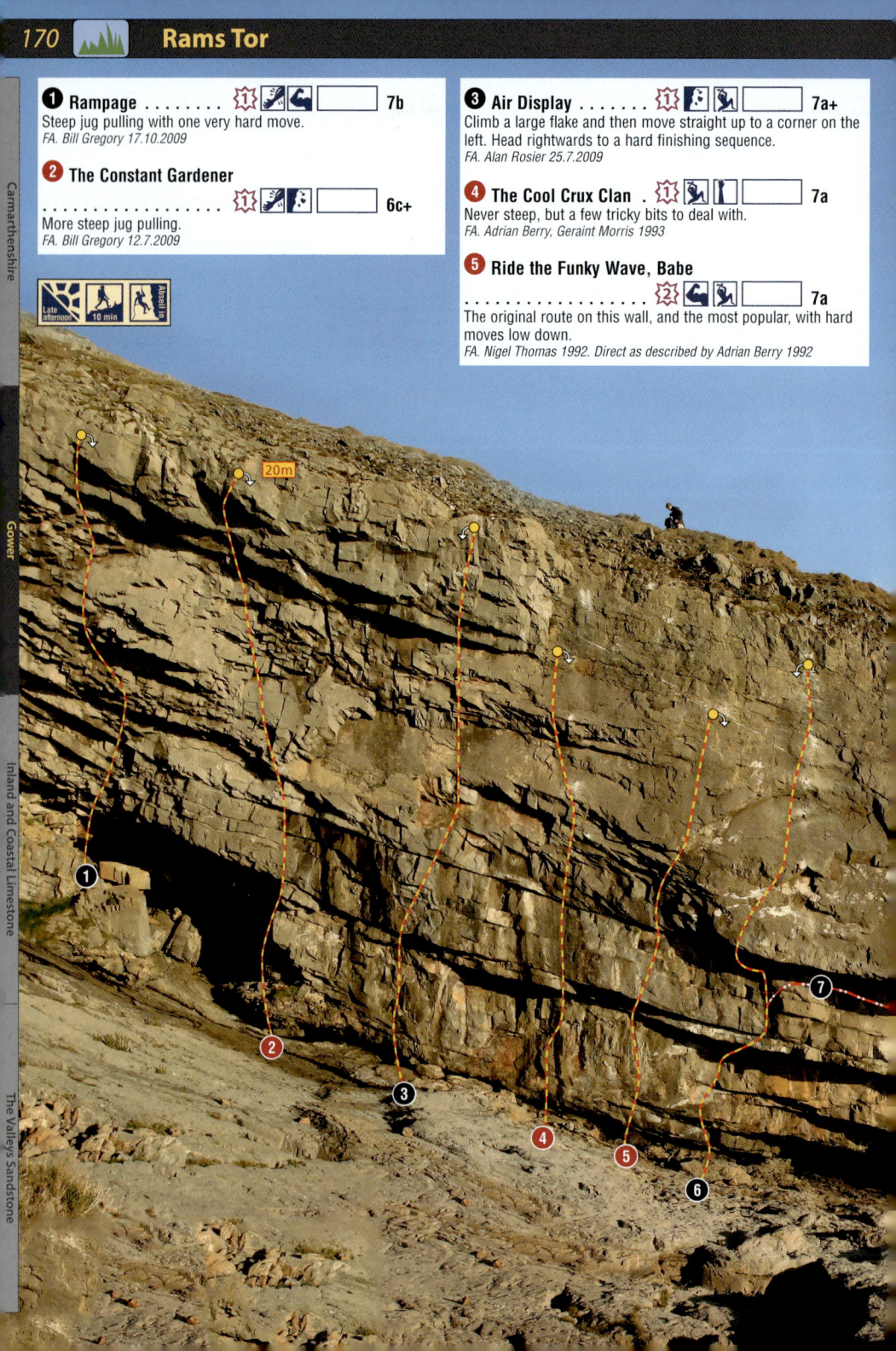

❶ Rampage 7b
Steep jug pulling with one very hard move.
FA. Bill Gregory 17.10.2009

❷ The Constant Gardener
.... 6c+
More steep jug pulling.
FA. Bill Gregory 12.7.2009

❸ Air Display .... 7a+
Climb a large flake and then move straight up to a corner on the left. Head rightwards to a hard finishing sequence.
FA. Alan Rosier 25.7.2009

❹ The Cool Crux Clan . 7a
Never steep, but a few tricky bits to deal with.
FA. Adrian Berry, Geraint Morris 1993

❺ Ride the Funky Wave, Babe
.... 7a
The original route on this wall, and the most popular, with hard moves low down.
FA. Nigel Thomas 1992. Direct as described by Adrian Berry 1992

Rams Tor 171

6 Rain Dance 7b
A good juggy start leads to a fingery pull onto the slab.
FA. Adrian Berry 1993

7 Girdle Traverse E4 6b
Start up *Ride the Funky Wave, Babe* and then follow the break below the roof all the way past the sport routes until easy ground leads to the top.
FA. Adrian Berry 1996

8 Hypocritical Mass ..... 7b+
A fingery boulder problem gains the break and is followed by another tough pull to turn the lip of the overhang.
FA. Adrian Berry 21.12.2008

9 Renaissance .... 6c+
Clip-stick the first bolt and use the rope to pull up to the jug. From here, follow good holds. The jug on the lip of the overhang is huge, but leaving it is not easy. *Photo on page168.*
FA. Adrian Berry 1993

10 Captain Hook 7b
Start up *Nostradamus* and finish as for *Renaissance*.
FA. Adrian Berry 1993

11 Nostradamus 7b
One of the best routes at the crag. Turning the lip is hard to read on the onsight.
FA. Adrian Berry, N.Thomas 1993

12 The Loneliness of the Long Distance Runner
.... 7b+
A seriously long reach around the roof at the start may prove insurmountable for some.
FA. Adrian Berry, Jason Brown 1993

13 Totally Clips ... 7c
The first of the pure sport routes here, before the crag was re-bolted.
FA. Adrian Berry 1993

14 One Small Step E3 6a
The start is either a jump to the jug, or a fingery pull. Could possibly be a deep water solo on a high tide.
FA. Adrian Berry, Jason Brown 1993

Barland Quarry

172

	No star	☆	☆☆	☆☆☆
up to 4c	-	-	-	-
5a to 6a+	2	2	-	1
6b to 7a	1	3	3	-
7a+ and up	1	-	1	-

An old disused quarry that is not very picturesque, but does have some quality hard slab routes. The rock and style of climbing is more akin to slate than limestone.

Approach
Also see map on page 80
Barland Quarry is passed just before you reach the village of Kittle. Park in Kittle and walk back down the hill to find the quarry entrance on your left. Walk around the quarry along the wide track until you reach the base of the slabs. Do not park in the quarry entrance or in the large lay-by just up the hill.

Conditions
The slabs face northeast so do not get much sun, but this is an advantage in hot weather. It is worth noting that gear goes missing here from time to time and some of it is now very old.

Access
The quarry is privately owned and climbing is not allowed by the owners. The information and descriptions presented here are only included for reasons of completeness. If asked to leave please do so immediately without fuss.

Liz Collyer taking on the delicate climbing to be found on *Telefunken U47* (5b) - *opposite* - at Barland Quarry. Photo: Adrian Berry

Barland Quarry 173

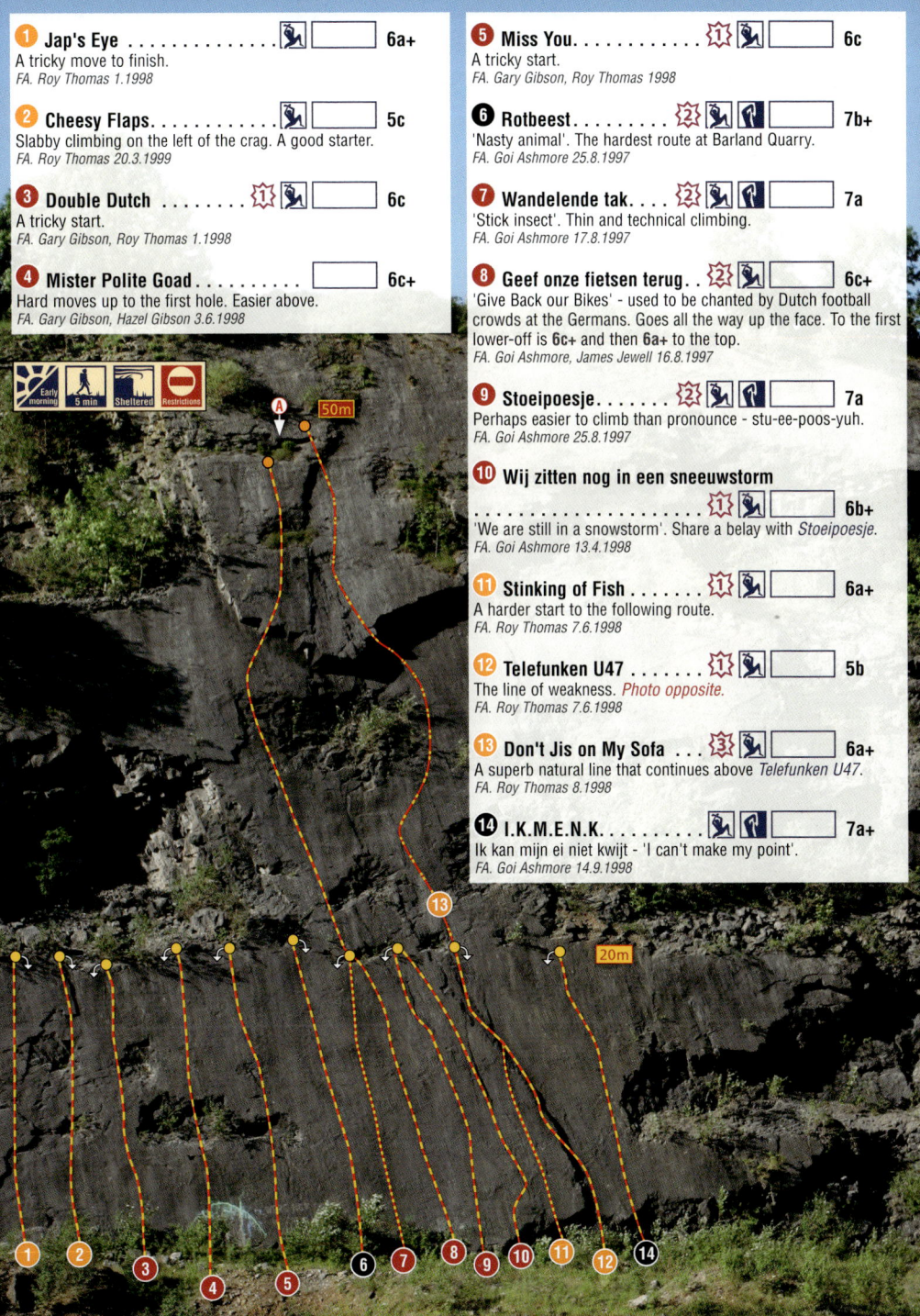

1 Jap's Eye .... 6a+
A tricky move to finish.
FA. Roy Thomas 1.1998

2 Cheesy Flaps 5c
Slabby climbing on the left of the crag. A good starter.
FA. Roy Thomas 20.3.1999

3 Double Dutch 6c
A tricky start.
FA. Gary Gibson, Roy Thomas 1.1998

4 Mister Polite Goad .... 6c+
Hard moves up to the first hole. Easier above.
FA. Gary Gibson, Hazel Gibson 3.6.1998

5 Miss You 6c
A tricky start.
FA. Gary Gibson, Roy Thomas 1998

6 Rotbeest .... 7b+
'Nasty animal'. The hardest route at Barland Quarry.
FA. Goi Ashmore 25.8.1997

7 Wandelende tak 7a
'Stick insect'. Thin and technical climbing.
FA. Goi Ashmore 17.8.1997

8 Geef onze fietsen terug .. 6c+
'Give Back our Bikes' - used to be chanted by Dutch football crowds at the Germans. Goes all the way up the face. To the first lower-off is 6c+ and then 6a+ to the top.
FA. Goi Ashmore, James Jewell 16.8.1997

9 Stoeipoesje 7a
Perhaps easier to climb than pronounce - stu-ee-poos-yuh.
FA. Goi Ashmore 25.8.1997

10 Wij zitten nog in een sneeuwstorm
.... 6b+
'We are still in a snowstorm'. Share a belay with *Stoeipoesje*.
FA. Goi Ashmore 13.4.1998

11 Stinking of Fish .... 6a+
A harder start to the following route.
FA. Roy Thomas 7.6.1998

12 Telefunken U47 .... 5b
The line of weakness. *Photo opposite.*
FA. Roy Thomas 7.6.1998

13 Don't Jis on My Sofa ... 6a+
A superb natural line that continues above *Telefunken U47*.
FA. Roy Thomas 8.1998

14 I.K.M.E.N.K .... 7a+
Ik kan mijn ei niet kwijt - 'I can't make my point'.
FA. Goi Ashmore 14.9.1998

Dave Henderson moving up the technical wall and open corner of the classic Dinas Rock sport climb *Berlin* (7a+) - *page 189* - one of many superb hard lines to be found on this section of the crag. Photo: Mark Glaister

Inland and Coastal Limestone

Dinas Rock, Taff's Well, Taff's Well West Gilwern, Witches Point, Temple Bay Castle Upon Alun

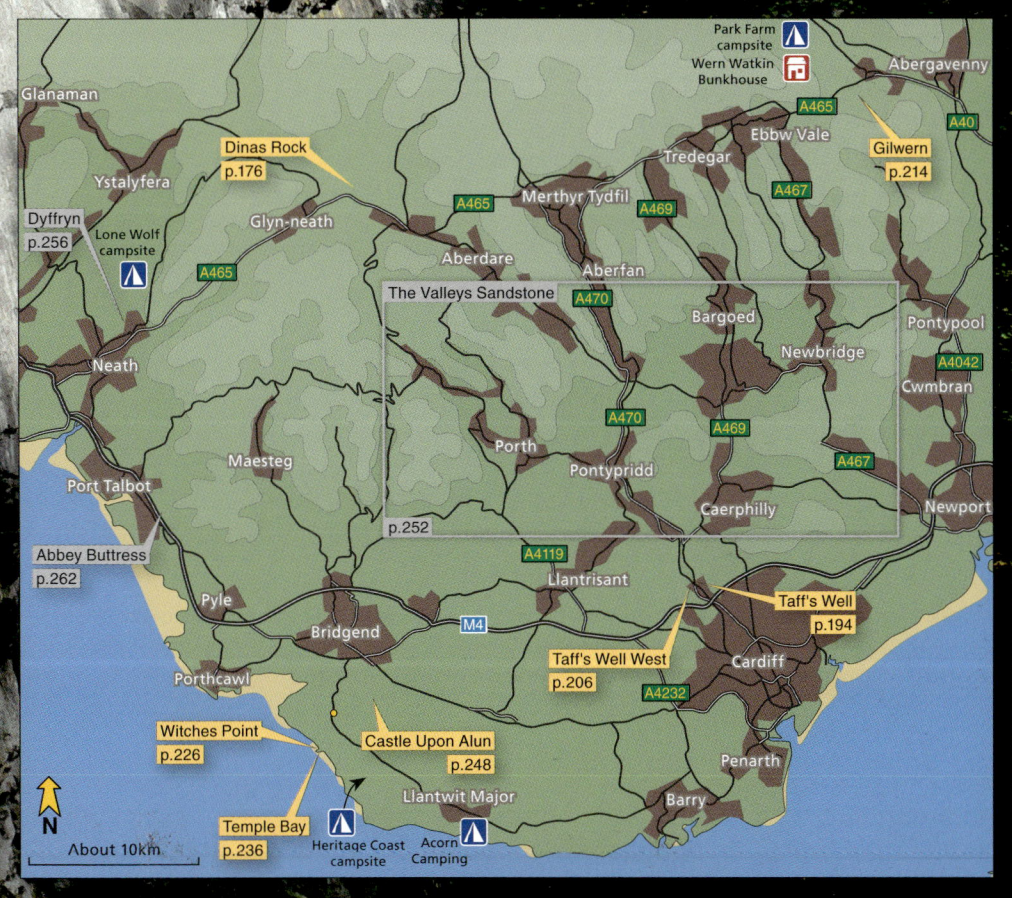

Dinas Rock

	No star	⭐	⭐⭐	⭐⭐⭐
up to 4c	-	2	-	-
5a to 6a+	8	3	-	-
6b to 7a	14	21	8	-
7a+ and up	7	14	16	16

Tucked away in a narrow gorge at the northern end of the Neath Valley, Dinas Rock is one of the best cliffs in South Wales. Its walls of high quality limestone are covered with overlaps, roofs, subtle grooves and water-worn features which combine to give some fine climbing. Technique and perseverance are needed as much as power and guile. Not all of the climbing is in the higher grades and the Roadside crags contain some very accessible routes in the lower and mid-grades.

Approach
Also see map on page 175

Turn off the A465 into Glynneath (this is the second turning signed to Glynneath if approaching from Merthyr Tydfil). Turn right at the traffic lights and take the first turning left in 120m - the B4242, signed 'Pontneddfechan'. Follow this road until just before it begins to rise up a hillside and turn right. This narrow road soon leads through the small village to turn abruptly right over a small bridge with a large car park in the quarry to the left. A small track leads off to the right alongside the river to reach the first area of rocks.

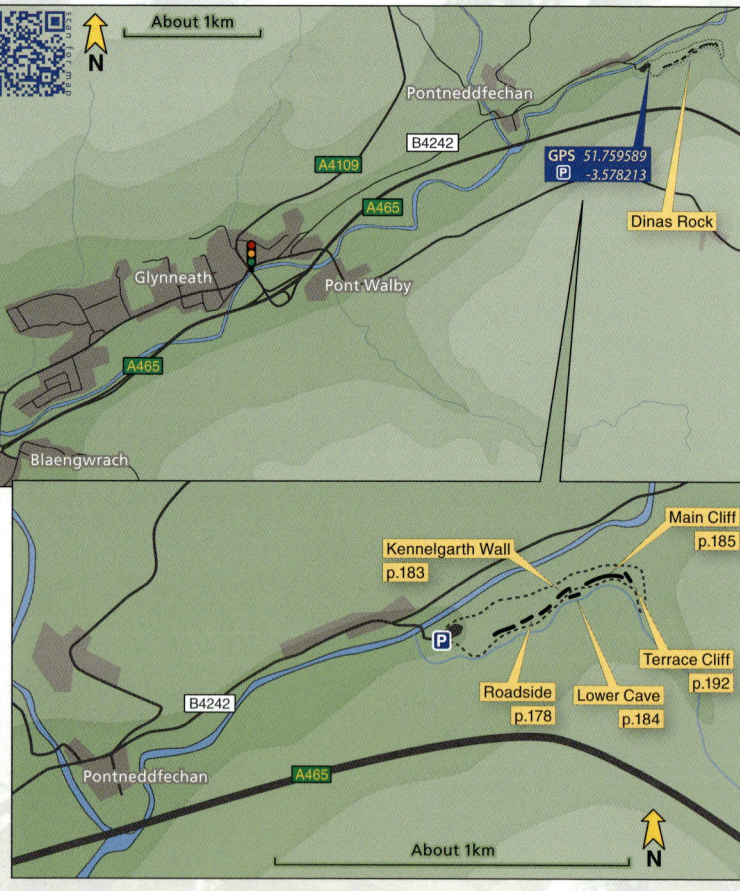

GPS 51.759589 -3.578213

Conditions
Dinas Rock suffers seepage during the winter months and, unless there has been a reasonably dry period, it can take a while to dry out in the spring. Once dry the crags stay dry for long periods and can be climbed on during showery spells, although in humid conditions will feel damp.

Access
The gates on the car park are locked at around 5pm, but it is always possible to exit over the one-way ramps. The Lower Cave is on private land.

Dinas Rock 177

Ben Bransby making the most of some good weather on *The Sharp Cereal Professor* (7b) - *page 190* - on the Main Cliff at Dinas Rock. Photo: Mark Glaister

Dinas Rock — Roadside

Roadside

This is a pleasant spot and a popular destination, only a stone's throw from the parking. The routes cover a good grade range mainly in the 6s with one or two easier routes. It can be used as a destination in itself or as something to get going on before the bigger stuff is tackled to the right.

Approach - Follow the track upstream from the car park and the first section of Roadside is encountered on the left after 100m.

Conditions - The crag faces southeast and gets the morning sun. It dries quickly after rain but it is not steep enough to offer any dry climbing when it is raining. Seepage can be a problem in the winter months, although it receives more sun as the leaves are off the trees.

① Fromage Frais **5c**
An appealing line on the left-hand side of the wall. Move up to left-slanting ledges and follow the wall and right-trending flake/crack to a lower-off.
FA. Roy Thomas, Gary Gibson 1.2.1998

② Rob Roy **7a**
Good climbing up the centre of the wall with a low crux as you move up from the flake. Above the climbing is easier but still tricky until the finish of *Fromage Frais* is joined.
FA. Stephan Doerr 1995

③ Cheesy Rider . . . . **6b+**
A short difficult section leaving the ledge. The opinion on the grade varies - some finding it **6c** and others only **6b**.
FA. Roy Thomas, Gary Gibson 8.6.1995

④ Creme de Roquefort . . . . **6b+**
A series of long moves on generally good holds up the short wall and grey-coloured rock above.
FA. Gary Gibson, Roy Thomas 3.5.2009

⑤ Creme de Rockfall . . . . . **6b+**
A shorter pitch that follows the rib right of *Cheesy Rider*.
FA. Gary Gibson, Roy Thomas 3.5.2009

⑥ Scraping the Barrel . . . . **6a+**
Another short and bouldery line.
FA. Roy Thomas, Gary Gibson 1995

⑦ Tapping the Keg **6c**
The right-hand line is a much tougher proposition that features some very thin climbing.
FA. Roy Thomas 1998

The next walls are just to the right where a wall of rock runs up leftwards from the path.

Dinas Rock

John Warner about to start the hard climbing on the upper section of *The Inflated Roundhead* (7a+) - *page 180* - on the Roadside crag at Dinas Rock. The Roadside crags have lots of quickly accessed lines mainly in the lower and mid-grades Photo: Mark Glaister

Dinas Rock — Roadside

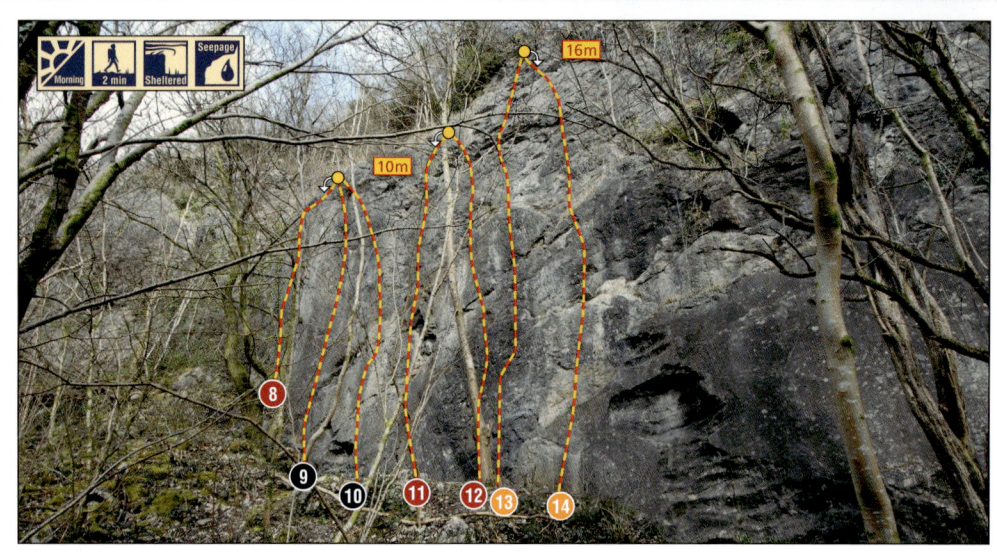

8 Pinheads 6c
The grey wall provides an airy outing just about worth doing. Run out and ivy covered at the time of writing.
FA. Gary Gibson, Roy Thomas 31.1.1998

9 Skin Ed 7c
The smoothest part of the wall provides a stern test of finger strength and adhesive qualities.
FA. Gary Gibson 30.3.1997

10 The Inflated Roundhead .... 7a+
A good face climb, a hard move over a bulge. *Photo page 179*.
FA. Martin Crocker, Roy Thomas 14.4.1988. Direct Gary Gibson 1997

11 Charlie's Rusks 6c
Easier but just as good as *The Inflated Roundhead*.
FA. Gary Gibson 5.1.1997

12 The Deflated Dickhead 6b
A good direct line with a short crux.
FA. Roy Thomas, Gary Gibson 1997

13 Mr Potato Head .... 6a+
Climb the line of staples up the centre of the conglomerate past a flake to a ledge. From the ledge, climb past a niche and roof to moves right into a groove to finish.
FA. Alan Rosier 3.5.2010

Roadside **Dinas Rock** *181*

14 Pothead 5c
Climb just right of the tree.
FA. Roy Thomas 9.5.2009

15 The Dumbfounded Dunderhead
.... 6b
After a hard start, the route is a little less interesting above.
FA. Roy Thomas, Gary Gibson 1997

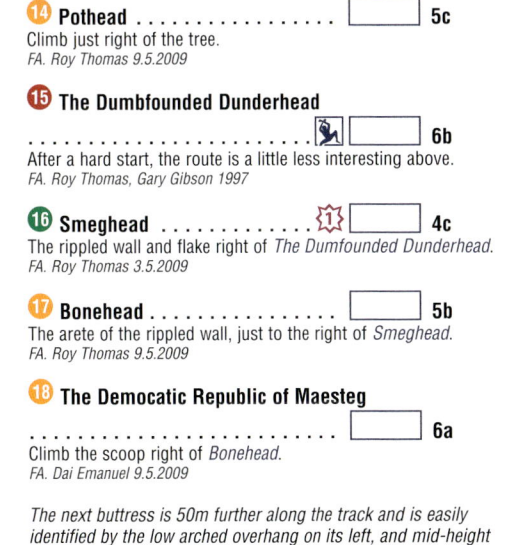

16 Smeghead 4c
The rippled wall and flake right of *The Dumfounded Dunderhead*.
FA. Roy Thomas 3.5.2009

17 Bonehead 5b
The arete of the rippled wall, just to the right of *Smeghead*.
FA. Roy Thomas 9.5.2009

18 The Democatic Republic of Maesteg
.... 6a
Climb the scoop right of *Bonehead*.
FA. Dai Emanuel 9.5.2009

The next buttress is 50m further along the track and is easily identified by the low arched overhang on its left, and mid-height leaning arete in its centre.

19 Connect One 6a
A short problematic bulge. Finish right from the last bolt.
FA. Gary Gibson, Roy Thomas 3.2.1997

20 Southwest Guru 6b
An even more problematic bulge.
FA. Andy Sharp, Pete Lewis 26.4.1988

21 Deadly Nightshade 6c
The compact, technical face gives good clean climbing.
FA. Alan Price 10.1998

22 Screaming Lampshades .... 6c+
A hard boulder problem bulge. Move left to the lower-off.
FA. Gary Gibson, Roy Thomas 3.2.1997

23 Big Ears Takes Flight ...... 6b+
The roof of the cave provides the difficulties but don't underestimate the finishing slab.
FA. Roy Thomas, Gary Gibson 28.3.1997

24 The Wake .... 6b+
Exit the right-hand side of the cave up onto the slab.
FA. Roy Thomas, Gary Gibson 28.3.1997

The next two lines start just to the right of the low arch/cave and are overgrown at the starts, but are good when clean.

25 Bob's Birthday Party 6b
The face just right gives good moves which are over far too quickly.
FA. Bob Powles, Andy Sharp, Pete Lewis 1.10.1988

26 Cujo 6c
After an easy start tackle the smooth face above a flake.
FA. Gary Gibson 3.2.1997

Dinas Rock — Roadside

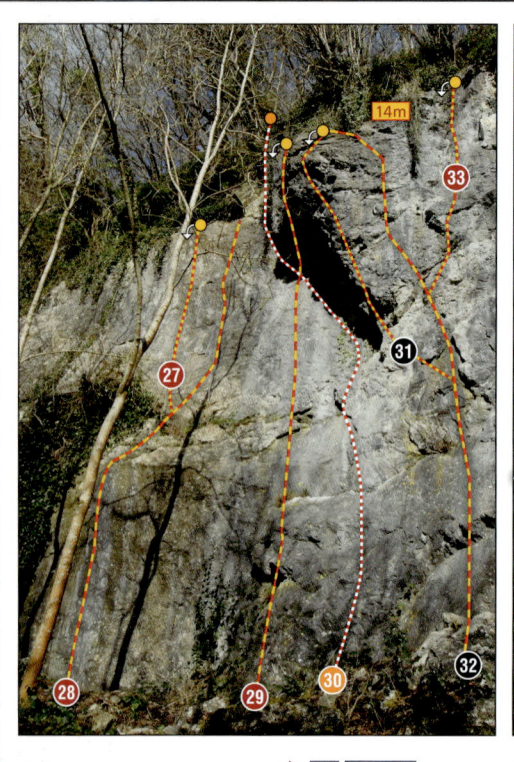

27 Thinner ... 7a
Gaining the slab is straightforward, climbing it proves the meat of the difficulties. The start is overgrown so use the initial thin crack of *The Running Man* to access the base of the slab.
FA. Gary Gibson, Roy Thomas 29.3.1997

28 The Running Man ... 7a?
Technical face climbing above a thin crack. The finish has been altered by rockfall and the lower-off is missing.
FA. Andy Sharp 1.10.1988

29 Miss Alto ... 6b
The pleasant slab and steep hanging corner. This route is not affected by the rockfall.
FA. Gary Gibson, Roy Thomas, Hazel Gibson 28.3.1997

30 For the Love of Ivy ... HVS 5a
The impressive layback corner sometimes choked in ivy. The finish has been altered by rockfall, but still goes at the grade.
FA. Chris Connick, C.Smith 5.1979

31 The Regulators ... 7c
The hanging arete. A short power-packed pitch with an airy finish. It is best to climb up the first two bolts of *The De-Regulators* to miss out a homemade hanger low down - the rest of the bolts are fine.
FA. Gary Gibson 25.5.1997

32 The De-Regulators ... 7a+
A super little route tackling the smooth-looking upper wall just to the right of the hanging arete.
FA. Gary Gibson, Roy Thomas 1.2.1998

33 Beware of Poachers ... 6c+
Start up *The De-Regulators*. Good climbing with a technical move over a bulge to a flake.
FA. Alan Price, Andy Long 1988

34 Open Roads ... 6b+
The slab and short wall, climbing direct through the overlap.
FA. Gary Gibson, Roy Thomas 5.1.1997

35 Squash the Squaddie ... 6b+
A pleasant face starting up a good wall and thin crack.
FA. Alan Price, S.Elias 9.1988

36 Thousand Yard Stare ... 6c+
Start at a very thin seam. An interesting sustained face climb through the left side of the overlap.
FA. Alan Price, S.Thomas 10.1988

37 Pugsley ... 7a
Has a short, sharp crux low down.
FA. Gary Gibson, Roy Thomas 21.4.1995

38 Munsterosity ... 7a+
Surprisingly hard low down and all on awkward flat holds. A similar line to an old trad route *Herman Munster*.
FA. Gary Gibson 27.5.1995
FA. (Herman Munster) Andy Sharp, T.Benjamin, A.Brown 1983

39 Morticia ... 7a
A steep line with good climbing that is run out between the first and second bolts.
FA. Gary Gibson, Roy Thomas 27.5.1995

Kennelgarth Wall — Dinas Rock — 183

Not all lines have lower-offs but bolt belays are in place on the ledge above the wall.

9m

Kennelgarth Wall
A low and severely undercut wall of compact limestone that is a popular bouldering venue and home to a handful of fierce sport pitches. The lower section of the wall has a number of boulder problems that can be linked into the routes for those looking for even tougher challenges.

Approach - Walk to where the track/path ends and the wall is on the left.
Descent - Not all of the lines have lower-offs but bolt belays are in place on the ledge above the wall.
Conditions - The wall gets some sun in the afternoon, and once dry stays dry. The lines might need a brush.

1 Technitis 6c
A short line on the left with a very technical move.
FA. Paul Donnithorne, Tessa Meen 1988

2 By Proxy 7a
The wall just to the right of *Technitis*.
FA. Gary Gibson, Roy Thomas 30.3.1997

3 Out Come The Freaks . . . . 7a+
Climb up past the arched overlap.
FA. Andy Sharp 23.5.1988

4 Fings Ain't What They Used To Be . . . . 2 7b+
Climb the seam and pockets to access a desperate sequence leftwards on the upper wall to finish.
FA. Andy Sharp, Phil Thomas, Pete Lewis 15.5.1988

5 Kennelgarth . . . . 1 7b+
Gain the triangular niche and then climb up left and then back right to finish.
FA. Andy Sharp 1984. FFA. Goi Ashmore 23.7.1994

6 Siberian Husky . . . . 1 7b+
From the triangular niche of *Kennelgarth*, follow the thin line left to join and finish as for *Fings Ain't What They Used To Be*.
FA. Simon Rawlinson 30.4.2010

7 Eugene's High Point . . . . 7b+
The line to the right ends at the final staple - no one has made it to the top.
FA. Eugene Travers-Jones 1995

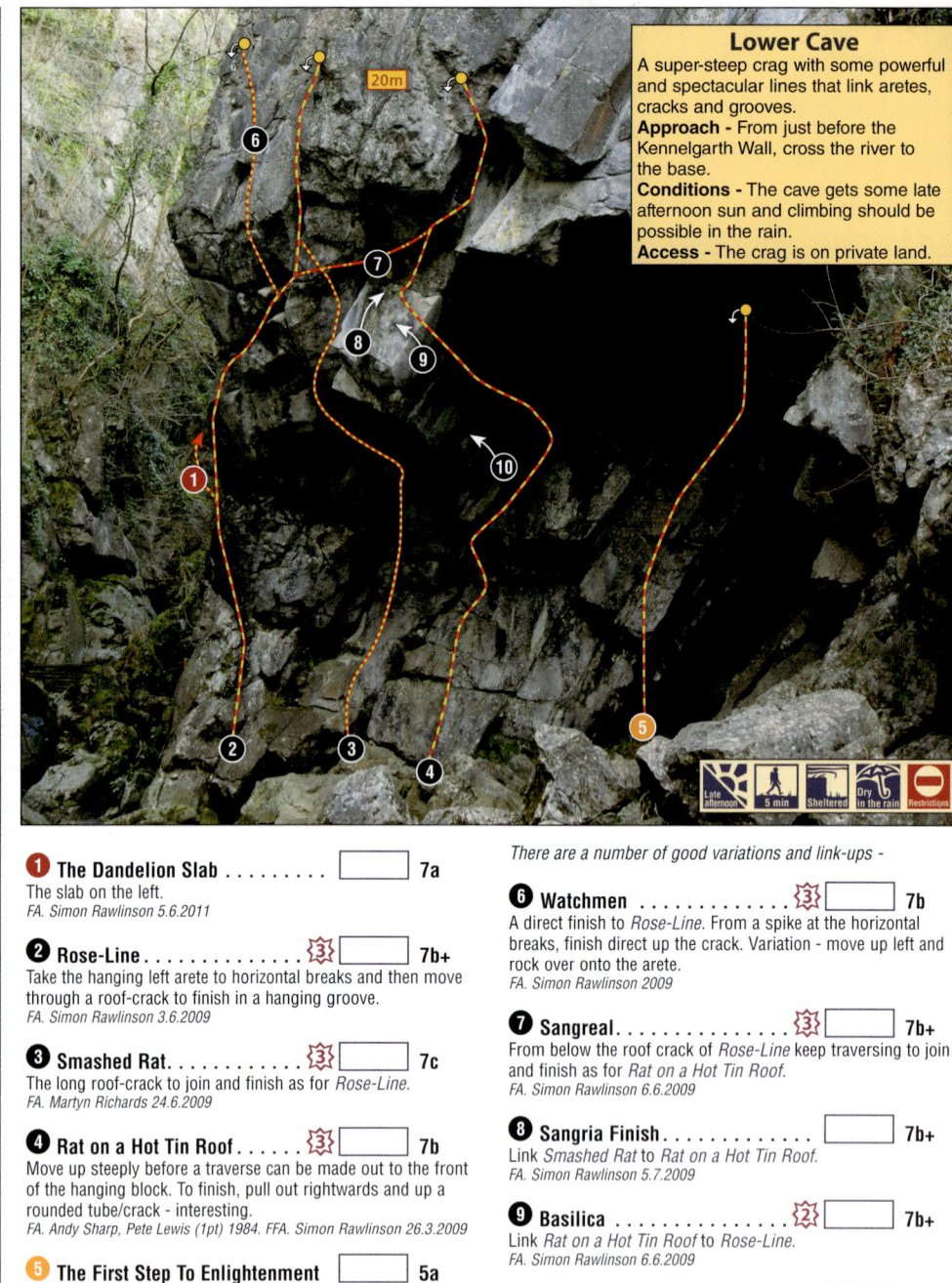

Dinas Rock — Lower Cave

184

Lower Cave
A super-steep crag with some powerful and spectacular lines that link aretes, cracks and grooves.
Approach - From just before the Kennelgarth Wall, cross the river to the base.
Conditions - The cave gets some late afternoon sun and climbing should be possible in the rain.
Access - The crag is on private land.

❶ The Dandelion Slab . . . . ▢ 7a
The slab on the left.
FA. Simon Rawlinson 5.6.2011

❷ Rose-Line . . . . ▢ 7b+
Take the hanging left arete to horizontal breaks and then move through a roof-crack to finish in a hanging groove.
FA. Simon Rawlinson 3.6.2009

❸ Smashed Rat . . . . ▢ 7c
The long roof-crack to join and finish as for *Rose-Line*.
FA. Martyn Richards 24.6.2009

❹ Rat on a Hot Tin Roof . . . . ▢ 7b
Move up steeply before a traverse can be made out to the front of the hanging block. To finish, pull out rightwards and up a rounded tube/crack - interesting.
FA. Andy Sharp, Pete Lewis (1pt) 1984. FFA. Simon Rawlinson 26.3.2009

❺ The First Step To Enlightenment ▢ 5a
A hard start leads to easier ground and a weird trip into the belly of the cave. Worth taking a torch just to look around and beware - the caves that shoot off in all directions go a long way!
FA. Simon Rawlinson 9.6.2011

There are a number of good variations and link-ups -

❻ Watchmen . . . . ▢ 7b
A direct finish to *Rose-Line*. From a spike at the horizontal breaks, finish direct up the crack. Variation - move up left and rock over onto the arete.
FA. Simon Rawlinson 2009

❼ Sangreal . . . . ▢ 7b+
From below the roof crack of *Rose-Line* keep traversing to join and finish as for *Rat on a Hot Tin Roof*.
FA. Simon Rawlinson 6.6.2009

❽ Sangria Finish . . . . ▢ 7b+
Link *Smashed Rat* to *Rat on a Hot Tin Roof*.
FA. Simon Rawlinson 5.7.2009

❾ Basilica . . . . ▢ 7b+
Link *Rat on a Hot Tin Roof* to *Rose-Line*.
FA. Simon Rawlinson 6.6.2009

❿ Tiger Cut . . . . ▢ 7c+
Start up *Rat on a Hot Tin Roof* and flip under the block into *Smashed Rat*. From halfway along the block break left into *Rose-line* and then *The Dandelion Slab*.
FA. Simon Rawlinson 5.7.2009

Chris Shepherd crimps his way up *H1N1* (8a) - *page 189* - on the Main Cliff at Dinas Rock. Photo: Mike Hutton

186 Dinas Rock — Main Cliff

Main Cliff
The showpiece section of Dinas Rock and one of the most important areas for hard sport climbing in South Wales. A series of overlaps and roofs, some of which are very large, guard the contrasting technical upper walls.

Approach - Follow the riverside path past the Kennelgarth Wall and scramble up the left-hand side of the river and the Main Cliff is just a little further on. Alternatively, should the river be in spate, take the path left of the car park. This rises steeply, levels out above the crag, then drops down to the river. Go downstream to the crag.

Conditions - The cliff faces southeast and receives sunshine until about midday. The face can seep after long periods of rain and is not a very good winter venue. When dry it provides a perfect climbing environment.

1 Pis En Lit 6b
Climb direct just to the left of the arete. Stepping in from the right reduces the grade to **6a+**.
FA. Roy Thomas, Gary Gibson 15.2.1998

2 Illegal Congress 6b
Takes on the wall to the right with some good moves.
FA. Roy Thomas, Gary Gibson 15.2.1998

3 Family Values .... 6a+
The right-hand line on the buttress.
FA. Roy Thomas, Gary Gibson 1998

4 Stray Cats 7a
Start in the cave. A long reach over the initial roof gains good holds that lead to a tricky finishing groove.
FA. P.Tilson, M.Danford 1972. FFA. Andy Sharp, John Harwood 9.8.1983

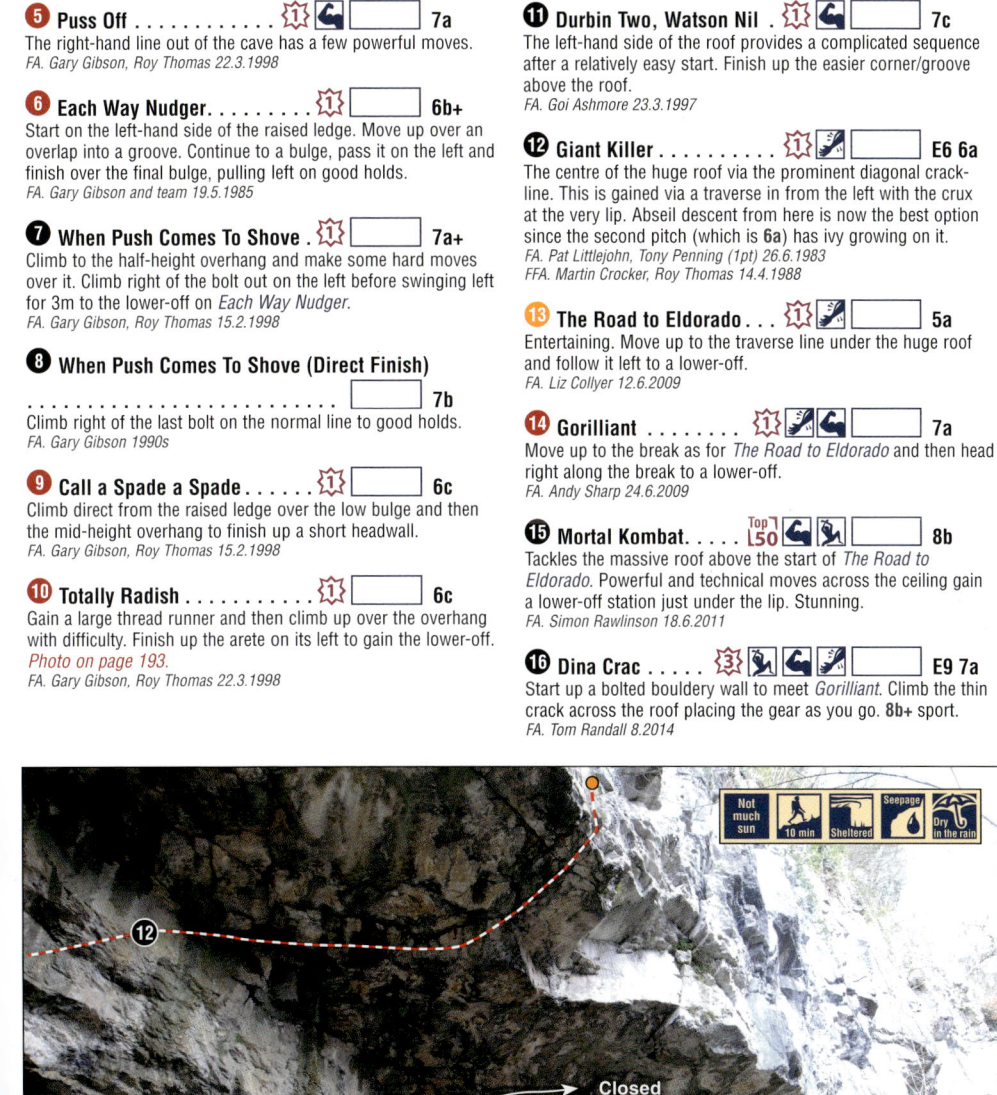

Main Cliff Dinas Rock 187

5 Puss Off 7a
The right-hand line out of the cave has a few powerful moves.
FA. Gary Gibson, Roy Thomas 22.3.1998

6 Each Way Nudger......... 6b+
Start on the left-hand side of the raised ledge. Move up over an overlap into a groove. Continue to a bulge, pass it on the left and finish over the final bulge, pulling left on good holds.
FA. Gary Gibson and team 19.5.1985

7 When Push Comes To Shove . 7a+
Climb to the half-height overhang and make some hard moves over it. Climb right of the bolt out on the left before swinging left for 3m to the lower-off on *Each Way Nudger*.
FA. Gary Gibson, Roy Thomas 15.2.1998

8 When Push Comes To Shove (Direct Finish)
.... 7b
Climb right of the last bolt on the normal line to good holds.
FA. Gary Gibson 1990s

9 Call a Spade a Spade...... 6c
Climb direct from the raised ledge over the low bulge and then the mid-height overhang to finish up a short headwall.
FA. Gary Gibson, Roy Thomas 15.2.1998

10 Totally Radish 6c
Gain a large thread runner and then climb up over the overhang with difficulty. Finish up the arete on its left to gain the lower-off.
Photo on page 193.
FA. Gary Gibson, Roy Thomas 22.3.1998

11 Durbin Two, Watson Nil . 7c
The left-hand side of the roof provides a complicated sequence after a relatively easy start. Finish up the easier corner/groove above the roof.
FA. Goi Ashmore 23.3.1997

12 Giant Killer E6 6a
The centre of the huge roof via the prominent diagonal crack-line. This is gained via a traverse in from the left with the crux at the very lip. Abseil descent from here is now the best option since the second pitch (which is **6a**) has ivy growing on it.
FA. Pat Littlejohn, Tony Penning (1pt) 26.6.1983
FFA. Martin Crocker, Roy Thomas 14.4.1988

13 The Road to Eldorado... 5a
Entertaining. Move up to the traverse line under the huge roof and follow it left to a lower-off.
FA. Liz Collyer 12.6.2009

14 Gorilliant 7a
Move up to the break as for *The Road to Eldorado* and then head right along the break to a lower-off.
FA. Andy Sharp 24.6.2009

15 Mortal Kombat..... 8b
Tackles the massive roof above the start of *The Road to Eldorado*. Powerful and technical moves across the ceiling gain a lower-off station just under the lip. Stunning.
FA. Simon Rawlinson 18.6.2011

16 Dina Crac E9 7a
Start up a bolted bouldery wall to meet *Gorilliant*. Climb the thin crack across the roof placing the gear as you go. **8b+** sport.
FA. Tom Randall 8.2014

188 Dinas Rock Main Cliff

Main Cliff **Dinas Rock** 189

19 Captain Barbarossa 8a
A direct finish to *Sport Wars* up a steep prow.
FA. Simon Rawlinson 9.10.2009

20 H1N1 .... 8a
Follow *Sport Wars* over its roof to a jug. Climb steeply direct to another jug on the right edge of a slab above. Move right into *Bloody Sport Climbers* and finish up *Subversive Body Pumping*. Photo on page 185.
FA. Martyn Richards 26.7.2009

21 The Black Pearl 8a
A good link-up. Climb *H1N1* to the edge of the slab and then finish as for *Captain Barbarossa*.
FA. Simon Rawlinson 10.10.2009

22 Subversive Body Pumping 7b+
Start up *Sport Wars* and then make a hideous contorted entry into the bottomless groove - above things relent only slightly.
FA. Martin Crocker, Roy Thomas 6.3.1988

23 Powers That Be 7c
A rising connection of routes that gives good climbing. From just above the crux of *Subversive Body Pumping* move into *Berlin*, then onto *Still Life* to finish.
FA. Martin Crocker, Roy Thomas 30.4.1988

24 Dinasty 8a
A hard start over the lower overhangs gains the traverse line of *Powers That Be*. Move up to join and finish as for *Hayabusa*.
FA. Martyn Richards 14.6.2009

25 Berlin .... 7a+
A classic landmark route connecting a series of shallow grooves after a bouldery start. Photo on page 1 and 174.
FA. Gary Gibson, Matt Ward, Martin Crocker 18.5.1985

26 Berlin Extension ... 7b
Extends the upper section via a corner to finish as for *Still Life*.
FA. Martyn Richards and Andy Sharp 1.6.2008

27 Hayabusa .... 7c+
A complex but fine climb that features plenty of hard moves. Start up *Berlin* and then head left and up to the beginning of a forearm-draining finale. Finish at the *Subversive Body Pumping* lower-off.
FA. Martyn Richards, Andy Sharp 6.2008

28 Still Life .... 7b+
Technical wizardry throughout, particularly where the line departs *Berlin*. Save something in the tank for the finish.
FA. Gary Gibson, Roy Thomas 30.4.1994

29 Just In Time 7c
A hybrid route, linking up two great lines. Climb *Still Life* until a shattered pocket is reached, then move over to the arete and follow it as for *Outta Time* to finish.
FA. Simon Robinson 29.5.2009

17 Sport Wars 8a
Move up to the roof and execute some powerful moves over it. Traverse leftwards to gain the base of a groove and climb the left-hand wall and arete above.
FA. Gary Gibson (1pt) 27.8.1995. FFA. Goi Ashmore 20.5.1997

18 Bloody Sport Climbers .. 8a
Follow *Sport Wars* to the groove and then pull up right into it. Go right and finish up *Subversive Body Pumping*.
FA. Martin Crocker, Roy Thomas (1pt) 17.4.1988
FFA. Goi Ashmore 20.5.1997

Dinas Rock — Main Cliff

30 Chives of Freedom 7c
Pull through the roof to the base of the groove as for *The Big Time*. Make a desperate sequence through the bulges to reach the base of the central groove on *Still Life* and finish up this. *Photo on page 36*.
FA. (as Angel Heart) Andy Sharp, Pete Lewis (1pt) 24.4.1988
FFA. Goi Ashmore 5.6.1994

31 Outta Time ..... 7c+
A good variation starting up *Chives of Freedom* and then taking the *The Big Time* groove until the arete to its left can be attained. Climb the arete and finish as for *Still Life*.
FA. Martyn Richards, Andy Sharp 21.3.2009

32 The Big Time E6 6c
The long slim corner is the original line of this wall. The groove itself is bold and the direct finish over the roof highly entertaining. The original finish traversed off to the right.
FA. Pat Littlejohn, Tony Penning, John Harwood (1pt) 7.5.1985
FFA. (with direct finish over roof) Gary Gibson, Roy Thomas 8.4.1995

33 Crock of Gold 7c
A pumpy and dynamic roof is combined with a very technical and thin slab up the face to the right of *The Big Time* groove.
FA. Martin Crocker, Roy Thomas 17.4.1988

34 The Sharp Cereal Professor 7b
A brilliant pitch. Climb steeply to the roof and pass it to grasp a good hold over the lip. Move up the slabby wall rightwards passing an overlap with some difficulty. *Photo on page 177*.
FA. Gary Gibson, Roy Thomas 1.5.1994

35 Salem's Lot ..... 7b+
Climb the first section of *Crock of Gold* through the roof and move right to finish as for *The Sharp Cereal Professor*.
FA. Andy Sharp, Pete Lewis (2pts) 1985
FFA. Martin Crocker, Roy Thomas 15.4.1988

36 Muchas Maracas 7c
Climb *The Sharp Cereal Professor* and traverse the sandwiched wall rightwards to breach the overhang as for *Hawaiian Chance*.
FA. Martyn Richards 30.5.2009

37 Harlem ..... 7b+
A classic with plenty of varied moves through the stepped overhangs to finish up a groove in the upper wall.
FA. Andy Sharp, Pete Lewis (2pts) 1985
FFA. Martin Crocker, Roy Thomas 15.4.1988

38 Hawaiian Chance 7c
A direct line with a hard sequence to leave *Spain* at mid-height.
FA. Gary Gibson, Roy Thomas 12.5.1991

39 Spain E4 6a
A traditional classic that incorporates grooves, overlaps and slabs. Plenty of technical moves, a thuggish pull and numerous threads for protection along the way.
FA. Gary Gibson 23.3.1985

40 Groovy Tube Day E2 5c
An unusual climb branching off right from *Spain* into the 'tube'. Quite strenuous low down and technical to gain the tube. Abseil off from a thread belay above.
FA. Chris Connick, D.Hughes 1978

Main Cliff **Dinas Rock** 191

41 Dr Van Steiner .... 7a+
Cross *Groovy Tube Day* to meet and finish up *Spain*. Some gear is needed for the top section and abseil descent.
FA. Gary Gibson 26.5.1991. Start reclimbed after large rockfall by Goi Ashmore 8.8.1999

25m

Closed project

Dinas Rock — Terrace Cliff

Terrace Cliff

Another excellent section of cliff complementing the Main Cliff with a few slightly easier routes and a couple of classics. Most of the routes by the cave have steep starts which prove to be quite awkward because of the shape and nature of the holds. The less well-travelled routes might need a brush up.

Approach - Continue along the path below the Main Cliff and scramble up onto a small terrace by a cave.

Conditions - The walls face southeast and only get morning sunshine. They can suffer from seepage quite badly during the winter but, once dry remain so except in longer periods of rain.

The routes all start from a terrace at 7m that is gained by a diagonal scramble up from the path.

❶ Academy Awards **6c**
The groove at the left end of the terrace. This line used to start from the main footpath and climb over a tough roof to gain the terrace, but is now overgrown.
FA. Roy Thomas, Gary Gibson 9.4.1995

❷ Dream Academy **6c**
A classic slab and face climb with two technical cruxes.
FA. Tony Penning, John Harwood 14.5.1985

❸ El Camino Del Roy . . . . **6c+**
The hanging groove, with some fine and unusual moves to gain entry to it.
FA. Roy Thomas, Gary Gibson 14.5.1995

❹ Danny La Rue . . . . **7a+**
Squeezed in but, not without interest.
FA. Gary Gibson, Roy Thomas 8.4.1995

❺ Incidentally X . . . . **7b+**
A much changed route since the demise of a large flake. This has been resolved by a particularly trying rockover move.
FA. Gary Gibson 23.3.1985 and in 1995 after holds came off.

❻ Tortilla Flats **7b**
Start just to the left of the cave. Unlikely terrain after a grubby start. Lower off the last bolt runner.
FA. Gary Gibson 9.4.1995

❼ Pour Marcel **7b**
Start just to the right of the cave. An unlikely looking pitch on pockets and slopers above the right arete of the cave.
FA. Gary Gibson 14.5.1994

❽ Brazilian Blend . . . . **6c+**
A little gem of a pitch with an airy and unusual crux sequence exiting the bulge.
FA. Gary Gibson 19.5.1985

The next four routes start to the right.

❾ Sverige **7a**
Two very technical sections with a good rest in-between.
FA. Gary Gibson, Tony Penning, Matt Ward 19.5.1985

❿ Ma's Strict . . . . **7a+**
Surprisingly difficult. Long reaches help, as does a sense of direction!
FA. Gary Gibson, Roy Thomas 25.3.1995

⓫ Breakout **6c**
A fine upper section after an easy start.
FA. Andy Sharp, John Harwood 1.9.1983

⓬ Vitamin Z **7a**
A harder right-hand version of *Breakout* on the upper walls.
FA. Andy Sharp, Pete Lewis 1985

Dinas Rock 193

Tom Skelhon tackles the upper section of *Totally Radish* (6c) - *page 187* - at Dinas Rock's Main Cliff, having started up the overhang of *Call a Spade a Spade* (6c). Photo: Mark Glaister

Taff's Well

	No star	★	★★	★★★
up to 4c	7	2	-	-
5a to 6a+	4	8	1	-
6b to 7a	8	20	10	2
7a+ and up	1	1	5	2

Taff's Well has a set of excellent wall climbs that, although close to a major road, are not quite as blighted by noise as might be imagined. Here John Warner inches up the popular *Genghis Khan* (6c+) - *page 199* - on the left-hand side of the Main Wall. Photo: Mark Glaister

Taff's Well

Taff's Well is a roadside crag on the outskirts of Cardiff, close to the M4 corridor. It consists of some big calcite walls mixed with areas of compact grey limestone. The climbs vary in style from short intricate face climbs through to longer routes - up to 35m in some cases - full of atmosphere and technical difficulties. Two other small crags close by have some less intimidating lower-grade lines and are further from the road and consequently quieter.

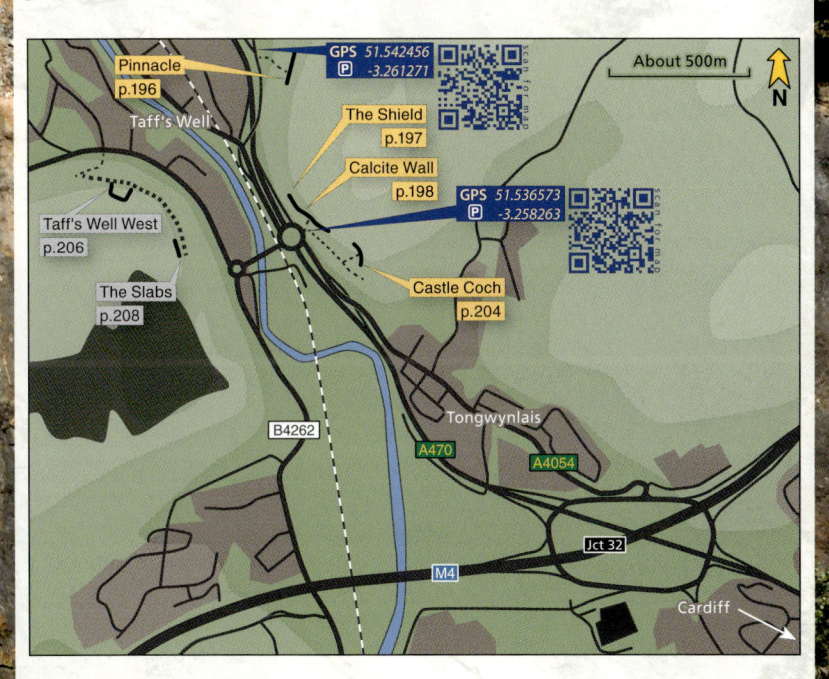

Approach Also see map on page 175

Exit the M4 at junction 32 onto the A470 north for Merthyr Tydfil. Take the first exit signed to Taff's Well and the crag can be seen on the right, immediately above the junction roundabout. Parking is possible in a small pull-off on the roundabout, directly below the cliff.

From Merthyr Tydfil, take the A470 south and take the exit signed for Tongwynlais. Once at the roundabout, the crag is immediately visible on the left above the small parking place. From the parking, a small track leads directly to the main crag in 100m.

For Castle Coch crag continue up the path past some steps on the left, and in 40m head left up a small path. The path goes up the right-hand side of a small valley to the crag which is below the castle.

For the Pinnacle, continue from the roundabout towards Taff's Well. After 300m, turn right, cross over the A470 and, in 350m, turn left onto Forest Road and park. Opposite the junction take a small path to the crag.

Conditions

The crag faces southwest and gets the sun from midday onwards. It dries very quickly and its open aspect gives for a pleasant atmosphere despite the noise from the road below.

Taff's Well — Pinnacle

Pinnacle

A compact crag that has a selection of lower-grade lines on reasonable rock. The crag is easy to reach and gets plenty of sun.

Approach - Continue from the roundabout below Taff's Well Main towards the village of Taff's Well. After 300m, turn right, cross over the A470 and, in 350m, turn left onto Forest Road and park. Opposite the junction, take a small path through the woods to reach the crag in 50m.

Conditions - The wall is open and gets plenty of afternoon sun. Seepage maybe a problem.

Access - Keep noise to a minimum as there are residential houses are close by.

1 Poppin' in the Poop Deck ... 5c
The wall and groove/corner high on the face.
FA. Alan Rosier, Rob McAllister 23.4.2013

2 Megalodon ... 6a
Move out right from the lower wall of *Poppin' on the Poop Deck* and climb the thin flake.
FA. Alan Rosier, Rob McAllister 23.4.2013

3 Kiss the Gunner's Daughter ... 5c
Climb the bulge and tiny overhang before heading left to a shared lower-off with *Megalodon*.
FA. Alan Rosier, Rob McAllister 23.4.2013

4 Angry Pirate ... 5c
Nice climbing up the wall to the left of the dirty central fault.
FA. Alan Rosier, Rob McAllister 25.4.2013

5 Sharktopus vs Megapotamus ... 4c
Features some tricky climbing at the start.
FA. Alan Rosier, Rob McAllister 25.4.2013

6 Yar! ... 5a
Climb the groove direct.
FA. Alan Rosier, Rob McAllister 25.4.2013

7 Jurassic Shark ... 5c
The line on the far right moving left to a shared lower-off.
FA. Alan Rosier, Rob McAllister 25.4.2013

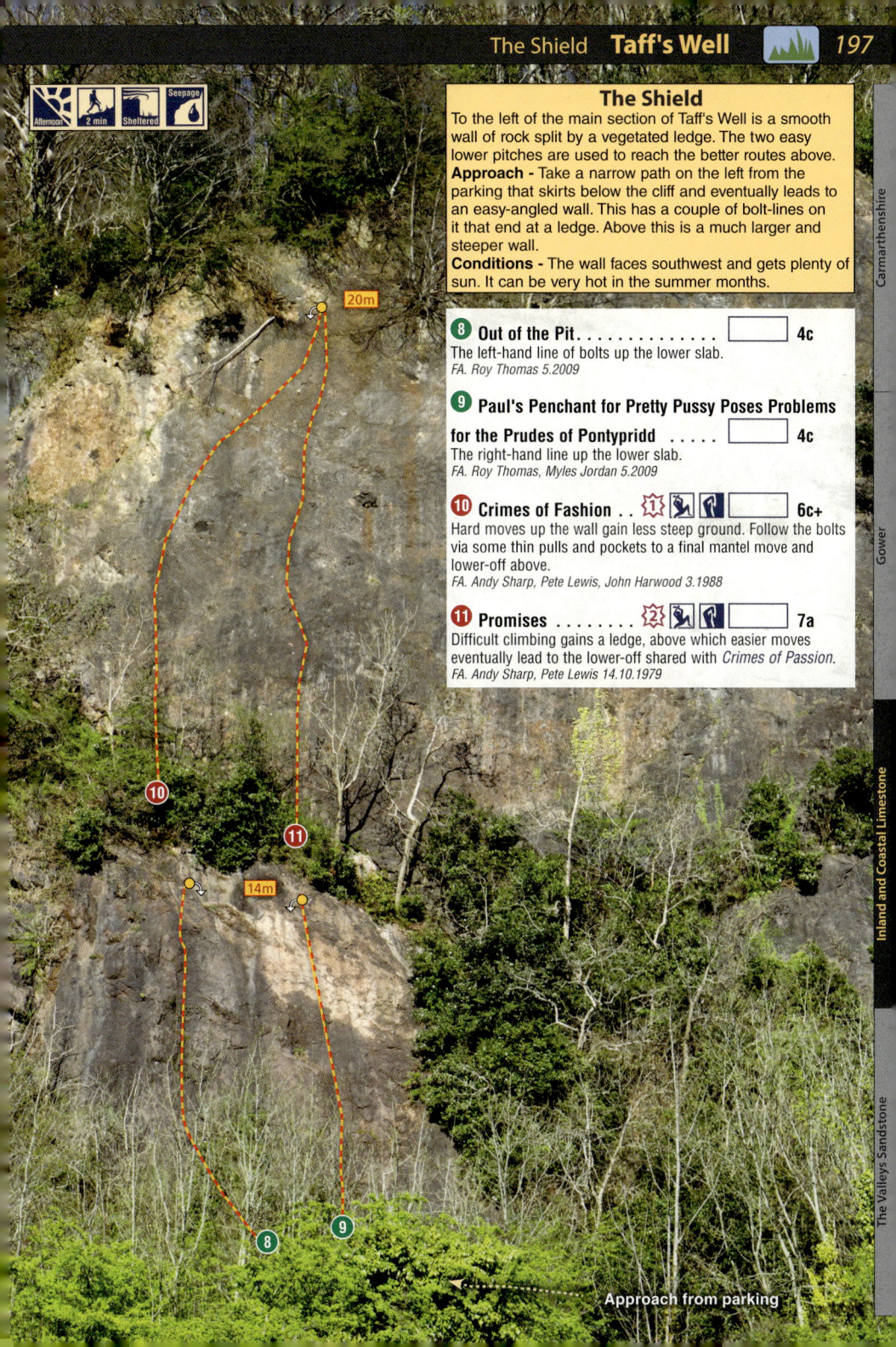

The Shield — Taff's Well — 197

The Shield
To the left of the main section of Taff's Well is a smooth wall of rock split by a vegetated ledge. The two easy lower pitches are used to reach the better routes above.

Approach - Take a narrow path on the left from the parking that skirts below the cliff and eventually leads to an easy-angled wall. This has a couple of bolt-lines on it that end at a ledge. Above this is a much larger and steeper wall.

Conditions - The wall faces southwest and gets plenty of sun. It can be very hot in the summer months.

8 Out of the Pit 4c
The left-hand line of bolts up the lower slab.
FA. Roy Thomas 5.2009

9 Paul's Penchant for Pretty Pussy Poses Problems for the Prudes of Pontypridd 4c
The right-hand line up the lower slab.
FA. Roy Thomas, Myles Jordan 5.2009

10 Crimes of Fashion .. 6c+
Hard moves up the wall gain less steep ground. Follow the bolts via some thin pulls and pockets to a final mantel move and lower-off above.
FA. Andy Sharp, Pete Lewis, John Harwood 3.1988

11 Promises 7a
Difficult climbing gains a ledge, above which easier moves eventually lead to the lower-off shared with *Crimes of Passion*.
FA. Andy Sharp, Pete Lewis 14.10.1979

Approach from parking

Taff's Well — Calcite Wall

Calcite Wall
An impressive and atmospheric wall with a big feel to it and plenty of good routes. Some of the rock is slightly friable. Take a long rope (some of the pitches are over 35m) and plenty of quickdraws (some routes need 18).
Approach - On arriving at the base of the cliff, the wall is on the left.
Conditions - The wall faces southwest and gets plenty of sunshine. The cliffs can be very hot in the summer months.

Calcite Wall — Taff's Well   199

The first three routes share a common initial wall to a ledge and optional intermediate belay (6b).

1 Red Square . . . . 🌟🧗 6b+
The left-hand side of the wall above the intermediate belay with two technical sections.
FA. Andy Sharp, Bob Powles 7.3.1988

2 Organised Chaos . . . 🌟🧗 6c
The central bolted line of the wall is well worth the effort. Sustained with a hard section midway up the wall above the intermediate belay.
FA. Andy Sharp, Pete Lewis, Andy Swann 12.3.1988

3 The Melty Man Cometh . . 🧗 7a
The right-hand of the trio of with three tricky sections all on good rock.
FA. Gary Gibson, Roy Thomas 17.5.2004

The next trio of sport routes take the centre of the huge face starting next to a rib that leads to a tree. There has been a small amount of de-bolting on this section of wall in order to restore the trad lines of Ye Old Campaigner, Painted Bird and Crowman - not described.

4 LA Confidential . . . . 🌟🧗 7a
Climb up just left of a rib to a tree and then go left and up to a two-bolt lower-off (**5a** to here and a bit vegetated). Move up and then right (ignore bolts going left) to a block at the overlap. Continue direct via superb sustained moves.
FA. Gary Gibson, Roy Thomas 8.5.2004

5 Kings of New York 🌟🧗 7a+
Start just right of the rib of *LA Confidential*. A fine pitch with a relatively straightforward (but sometimes dirty) lower section and a fine sustained upper wall. Move right just below double bolts.
FA. Gary Gibson 18.5.2004

6 The Connecticut Connection
. . . . 🌟🧗 7a+
A huge line up the right side of the wall. A superb top half after a dirty start.
FA. Gary Gibson, Roy Thomas 20.3.2009

The next set of lines start on the tall clean wall above where the approach path meets the cliff.

7 Minnesota Nice . . . . ⊖ 7a+
A tremendous route taking the left edge of the wall on positive holds after a technical start. Warning: the very top of this route has been de-bolted but the lower bolts remain.
FA. Gary Gibson, Roy Thomas 21.9.2003

8 Melting Man . . . . . . 🌟🧗 7a
The centre of the face hidden behind the tree. A fine sustained exercise.
FA. Martin Crocker, John Harwood 12.7.1992

9 Genghis Khan . . . . . Top 50 🧗 6c+
A classic pitch with sustained face climbing. A tricky bulge at the start is taken on hidden incuts and pockets. *Photo page 194.*
FA. Andy Sharp, Pete Lewis 1985 - direct start Gary Gibson 9.2003

10 Taurus Bulbous . . . . 🌟🧗 6b+
Excellent face climbing via a tricky bulge low down and a shallow rib above.
FA. Gary Gibson, Roy Thomas 9.6.2003

11 Bulbus Tara . . . . 🌟 4b
The faint groove-line above a prominent tree stump.
FA. Roy Thomas, Gary Gibson 20.9.2003

12 Hirsuit Ulvula . . . . 🌟 6a
The short tricky arete and easy groove above.
FA. Roy Thomas, 9.2003

Taff's Well — Lower Wall

Lower Wall

The Lower Wall runs up diagonally right from the base of the Calcite Wall and has a lot of good pitches that are well shaded. The routes tend to be of a technical and intricate nature.

Approach - The base of the wall is just right of the point where the approach path arrives at the crag.

Conditions - Seepage can be a problem. The routes are well shaded in the summer months by the tree canopy.

❶ Pilgrim **4c**
From the first bolt on *Mega Mix*, head up left to gain the ledge and lower-off at the start of the routes on the Upper Wall (page 202).
FA. Myles Jordan 2016

❷ Mega Mix **5c**
A gentle slab with a tough bulge near the top.
FA. Gary Gibson, Roy Thomas 3.8.2003

❸ Gwest y Gymru 7 Inch Mix
. . . . **6b+**
The grey rib with sloping holds and technical moves.
FA. Gareth Griffiths 2001

❹ The Twelve Inch Version!
. . . . **7a**
A difficult to read, short and bouldery route that features sloping holds and hidden edges.
FA. Gary Gibson, Roy Thomas 17.8.2003

❺ Daggers **6c**
An intricate face route with hidden holds and pleasant moves up a scoop.
FA. Martin Crocker, Roy Thomas 22.1.1989

❻ Look Over Yonder . . . **6c+**
The right-hand companion to *Daggers* is similar in style but a notch harder in difficulty.
FA. Martin Crocker, Roy Thomas 22.1.1989

❼ Wet Afternoon . . **7b+**
Start up *Look Over Yonder* and move right. Highly intricate face climbing with unusual moves and a scary fifth clip.
FA. Gary Gibson, Roy Thomas 28.6.1992

❽ Open Groove **6b**
The lower wall and open groove features some unusual moves.
FA. c.2002

Lower Wall **Taff's Well** 201

Upper Wall p.202

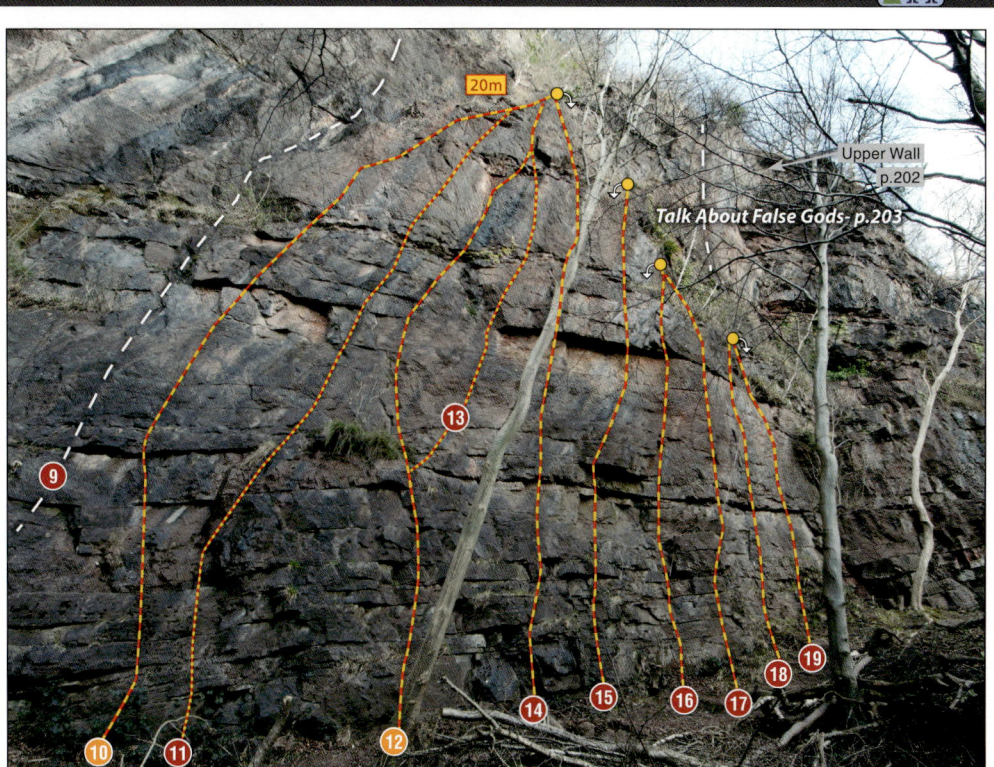

Talk About False Gods- p.203

9 Ulrika Ka Ka Ka .... 6c+
A groove-line leads to an impressive blunt rib on the headwall. 70m rope required.
FA. Gary Gibson, Roy Thomas 16.8.2003

10 D'ya Hear Ma Dear.. 6a+
The blunt, barrel-shaped rib to the right with the hardest moves at the top. Beware of a loose block midway.
FA. Gary Gibson, Roy Thomas 16.8.2003

11 Good Gear, Good Cheer . 6b
The pleasant blunt rib with one short hard section.
FA. Roy Thomas, Nick O'Neill 1.6.2002

12 No Beer, No Fear ...... 6a+
An enjoyable pitch aiming for the groove with a red left wall.
FA. Roy Thomas, Mick Learoyd 1990

13 Not my Fault! .... 6c+
Two boulder problems squeezed onto the wall and rib.
FA. Gary Gibson, Roy Thomas 3.8.2003

14 Id-iot 6b
A technical lower move with fine climbing above.
FA. Roy Thomas 2003

15 CJD 6b
A technical section in the middle is preceded by easier climbing.
FA. Roy Thomas, Gary Gibson 2003

16 Get Down on This 6c
Difficult moves through the upper overlap.
FA. Roy Thomas, Gary Gibson 2003

17 Get Thee Hence .... 6c+
Short but super technical climbing up a blunt rib.
FA. Martin Crocker, Roy Thomas 11.2.1989

18 Matt's Ice Bucket Challenge . 6c
Technical moves up a faint crack.
FA. Matt Hirst 7.2003

19 Tidy as Matt's Toolbox .... 6c+
The blank-looking wall.
FA. Matt Hirst 7.2003

Taff's Well — Upper Wall

Upper Wall

The Upper Wall has some long well-positioned lines that see little action. Some of the rock is still friable in places.
Approach - The first four routes are approached via a scramble (or *Pilgrim* - page 200), the rest are accessed by climbing routes from below on the Lower Wall.
Descent - Lower off or abseil with care.
Conditions - Seepage can be a problem.

The first lines are on the slabby wall just right of the vegetated rake. The belay at the base of the routes is reached by an easy scramble past three trees to a ledge below the left-hand side of the wall.

1 Jesus Wept **6c**
A tricky start to an open slabby face with plenty of interest.
FA. Gary Gibson, Roy Thomas 21.9.2003

2 Christendom **7a**
A long pitch with a delicate crux and easier climbing above.
FA. Martin Crocker, Roy Thomas 3.2.1989
FA. (Direct) Goi Ashmore 26.5.2002

3 Angel of Mons **6c**
A low crux and pleasant climbing above.
FA. Goi Ashmore 28.5.2002

4 Decimus Maximus .. **6b**
Pleasant climbing taking a rib and groove followed by an intricate slab.
FA. Gary Gibson, Roy Thomas 16.8.2003

Upper Wall **Taff's Well** 203

Approach the next routes via Jesus Wept and move left to a belay below a steep wall.

5 Space Cowboys .... 6c+
The left-hand line with a low crux.
FA. Gary Gibson, Roy Thomas 6.9.2003

6 Heavenly 7a
The central line gives a sustained exercise in a great position.
FA. Gary Gibson, Roy Thomas 3.8.2003

7 Celestial Being . 7b
Sustained with technical moves low down and thin ones high up.
FA. Gary Gibson 19.9.2003

8 Maximus Extensicus 6c
The extension above the lower-off of *Decimus Maximus*.
FA. Gary Gibson 9.2003

The next lines are reached via Gwest y Gymru... (page 200).

9 I'm Spartacus .... 7b+
A magnificent route which follows a snaking line up the black-streaked wall. Sustained and high in the grade.
FA. Gary Gibson 8.4.2009

10 Sugar Bullets .. 7b+
An impressive route with an amenable lower half and impressive finale - with the crux being the last move.
FA. Gary Gibson, Roy Thomas 5.6.1993

11 Stray Bullet .... 6c+
The direct version of *Sugar Bullets* gives a fine sustained route.
FA. Gary Gibson, Roy Thomas 9.5.2004

35m

20m to belay

Ulrika Ka Ka Ka - p.201

Lower Wall p.200

Daggers - p.200

12 Scram .... 7a+
Super-sustained face climbing with no single hard move but plenty of them. A bit crumbly but good.
FA. Martin Crocker, Roy Thomas 19.1.1989

13 New Day Today 7a
From the top of *Daggers* (page 200), a hard sequence leads over a bulge then onto a pleasant, easier face.
FA. Gary Gibson, Roy Thomas 11.5.1991

14 Rancho La Cha, Cha, Cha
.... 6c+
An arcing line above *Daggers* (page 200), with sustained climbing on crystalline holds.
FA. Martin Crocker, Roy Thomas 11.2.1989

15 Talk About False Gods ..... 7b+
From above and right of the lower-off of *Get Thee Hence* (page 201), climb the weetabix-like thin wall.
FA. Martin Crocker, Roy Thomas 12.2.1989

Taff's Well — Castle Coch

Castle Coch

A compact section of crag hidden in trees up and to the right of the main cliff. The routes are well bolted and range from powerful steep lines on the left to easier slabs on the right. The area is less noisy than the main areas, being further from the road.

Approach - From the parking, a small track leads up rightwards below the main crag. Continue up the track past some steps on the left, and then 40m further on, head left up a small path. The path goes up the right-hand side of a small valley to the crag which is located just below the castle.

Descent - All routes have lower-offs in place - please do not top out.

Conditions - Sheltered and sunny in the afternoon but seepage can occur.

❶ The Slippery Lip Trip — 6b
Start at the top of the bank on the left side of the crag, level with the narrow undercut slab. Traverse the slab passing a dodgy block (leave well alone) to eventually reach the lower-off of *Games of Ambivalence* - lower off. This pitch is 25m long.
FA. Alan Rosier, Dai Emanuel 16.5.2009

❷ The Crawling Chaos — 7a
Climb up and right over the stepped overhang passing a large rounded blob to a lower-off under the capping roof.
FA. Alan Rosier 21.5.2009

❸ Play The Joker — 6b+
Climb to the low overhang and pull up left past a niche to a shared lower-off with *The Crawling Chaos*.
FA. Roy Thomas 2009

❹ Games of Ambivalence — 6b+
Start up *Play The Joker* but continue up the wall leftwards to a lower-off.
FA. Jamie Maddison, Harry Andrews 5.4.2009

❺ The Warmth of Man — 6a
The line of bolts up the open angle in the back of the bay.
FA. Dai Emanuel, Roy Thomas 5.2009

❻ Ass in the Hole — 6b+
A difficult, steepening line to the left of the corner of *Royal Flush*.
FA. Roy Thomas, Dai Emanuel 2009

❼ Royal Flush — 6b+
The overhanging corner on the right side of the bay.
FA. Roy Thomas, Dai Emanuel 2009

❽ Savant — 6c+
Gain the leaning, rounded edge and use it to pull up and then right onto the slab. Climb easily rightwards to join and finish as for *Stalag Luft*.
FA. Dai Emanuel. 25.5.2009

Castle Coch **Taff's Well** *205*

9 Stalag Luft 5c
Climb the pleasant slab rightwards passing a shothole.
FA. K.Davies, Dai Emanuel 21.2.2009

10 A Ride on the Chocolate Unicorn 5c
Climb the slab to a bulge and lower-off just above it.
FA. Dai Emanuel, K.Davies 21.2.2009

11 The Dark Art of Banana Magic .. 4a
The straightforward slab.
FA. Dai Emanuel, D.Hannam 5.2009

12 R2 Sucking D2 Licking Deep
Inside a Half-Cooked Chicken 4a
The slab to join *The Dark Art of Banana Magic*.
FA. Dai Emanuel 2009

13 For Fonting Friends 4a
The slabby line to the left of the stack of blocks - do not touch!
FA. Jamie Maddison, Harry Andrews 5.4.2009

14 Dissertation Distraction 4a
The steep wall just to the left of the jagged arete.
FA. M.Walter 11.5.2009

Taff's Well West

	No star	★	★★	★★★
up to 4c	1	-	-	-
5a to 6a+	7	8	-	-
6b to 7a	4	8	6	-
7a+ and up	4	3	7	1

Mark Glaister redpoints *Scream for Cream* (7a+) - *page 211* - on the North Wall at Taff's Well West. The pitch is typical of the majority on this section of the cliff, being a combination of powerful undercutting, linked by technical wall climbing - the best being on good rock. Photo: Jen Stephens

Taff's Well West

On the other side of the valley and well hidden from the main crag at Taff's Well is a series of old quarried walls that contain some good sport climbs. The style varies from slabs to slightly overhanging featured walls and all the routes are technical. Although most of the walls apart from the slabs are enclosed and shady, the climbing is well-worth searching out in the right conditions.

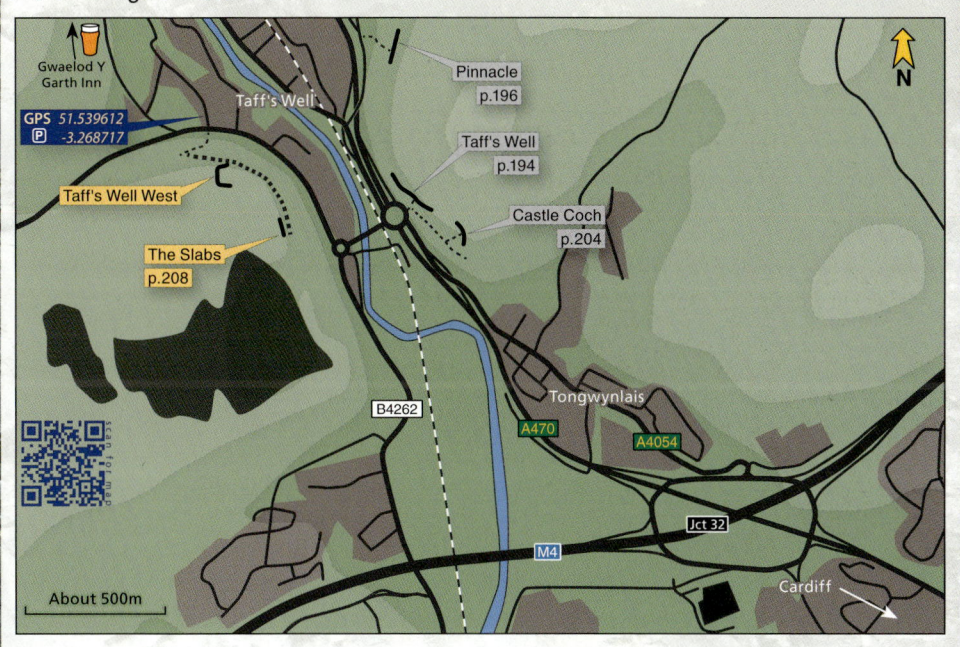

Approach   Also see map on page 175
Exit the M4 at junction 32 onto the A470 north for Merthyr Tydfil. Take the first exit signed to Taff's Well. The main crag can be seen on the right, immediately above the junction roundabout. For Taff's Well West, turn left at the roundabout signed to Radyr. Continue to another roundabout and turn right to Pentyrch. Drive a further 500m to Heol Berry - a minor road on the right - and park here. Cross the road and take a footpath into the woods. Follow the path rightwards until it meets a track. Go left on the track and follow this until Taff's Well West quarry is seen just right of the track. For The Slabs continue along the track until they come into view close to the track on the right.

Conditions
The Slabs are open and not shaded by trees whilst the main quarry is shady and sees little sun. Seepage is often present on the Back Wall. The bases of a number of climbs can gather moss and will need a bit of a clean at times.

Access
The quarry is owned by the adjacent working quarry. Should any problems arise please report details to the BMC and Rockfax.

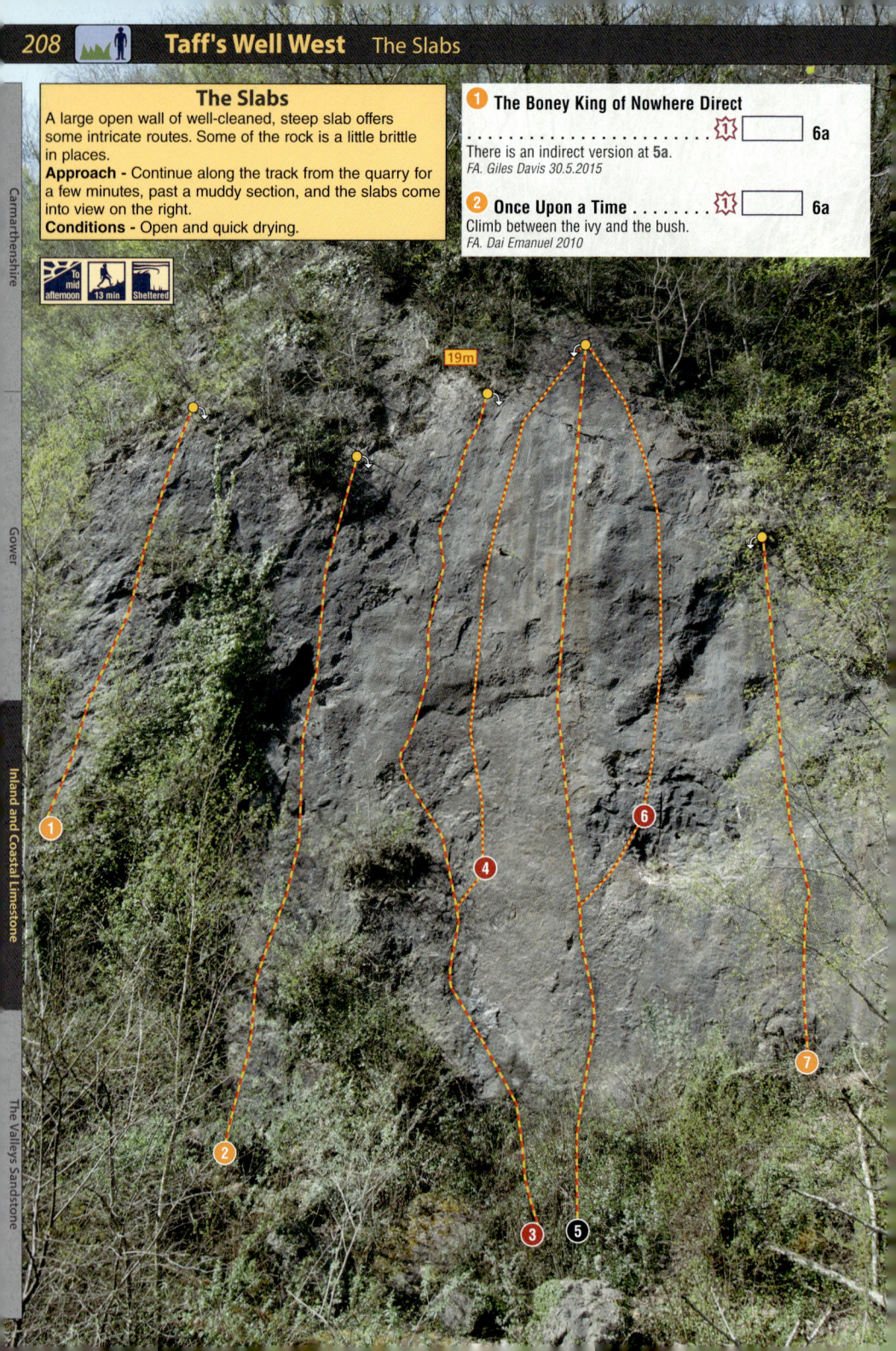

Taff's Well West The Slabs

The Slabs
A large open wall of well-cleaned, steep slab offers some intricate routes. Some of the rock is a little brittle in places.
Approach - Continue along the track from the quarry for a few minutes, past a muddy section, and the slabs come into view on the right.
Conditions - Open and quick drying.

① The Boney King of Nowhere Direct 6a
There is an indirect version at **5a**.
FA. Giles Davis 30.5.2015

② Once Upon a Time 6a
Climb between the ivy and the bush.
FA. Dai Emanuel 2010

The Pinnacle and Diamond Wall — Taff's Well West

❸ Can the Can 6c
Climb leftwards to a point above a bush and finish direct.
FA. Andy Sharp, Pete Lewis 4.1987

❹ Palm 7a
A fine and thin pitch. Start up *Can the Can* before stepping right up the sustained and technical wall.
FA. Andy Sharp, Pete Lewis 10.4.1987

❺ Neil Kinnock's Last Stand 7a+
Climb the slabby wall just left of the mid-height depression. Hard and sustained in its upper reaches.
FA. Goi Ashmore, Richard Lawerence 10.7.1992

❻ Chinese Whispers ..... 6c+
Start up *Neil Kinnock's Last Stand* and move right to a ledge. Climb up over a bulge and tackle the headwall on small holds.
FA. Andy Sharp, Pete Lewis 6.1987

❼ Glenys Encounters Her First Limp Member
.... 6a
The far right-hand line of the slabs.
FA. Roy Thomas, Goi Ashmore 8.2009

The Pinnacle and Diamond Wall
Two narrow buttresses of good rock on the left-hand (south) wall of the main quarried bay. They stay in good condition longer than the North and Back Walls.

❽ Clair de Lune 6a
Follow pockets up the left-hand side of the pinnacle face.
FA. Dai Emanuel, Rich Phillips 21.6.2009

❾ Mare Tranquilis 5a
The short line right of the pockets.
FA. Dai Emanuel, Rich Phillips 21.6.2009

❿ Bristol Beat 7a
Start halfway up the slope on the left-hand side of the wall. Step onto the wall and trend right past a pocket, before difficult moves up the blunt rib reach an easier traverse rightwards.
FA. Andy Sharp, Pete Lewis 3.4.1988

⓫ Streaming Neutrinos 7b+
A hard but excellent line passing through the diamond-shaped niche in the centre of the face.
FA. Martin Crocker, Gary Gibson 13.12.1987

⓬ It's a Black World .... 7a+
Trend rightwards then move up to a borehole and good holds on the left. Move left and pull over a bulge to better holds and continue directly to a ledge.
FA. Gary Gibson, Roy Thomas, Matt Ward 13.12.1987

⓭ Howling Hadrons 6b
Start just right of *It's a Black World* and avoid sloping off right up the slab.
FA. Roy Thomas, Gary Gibson 12.5.2010

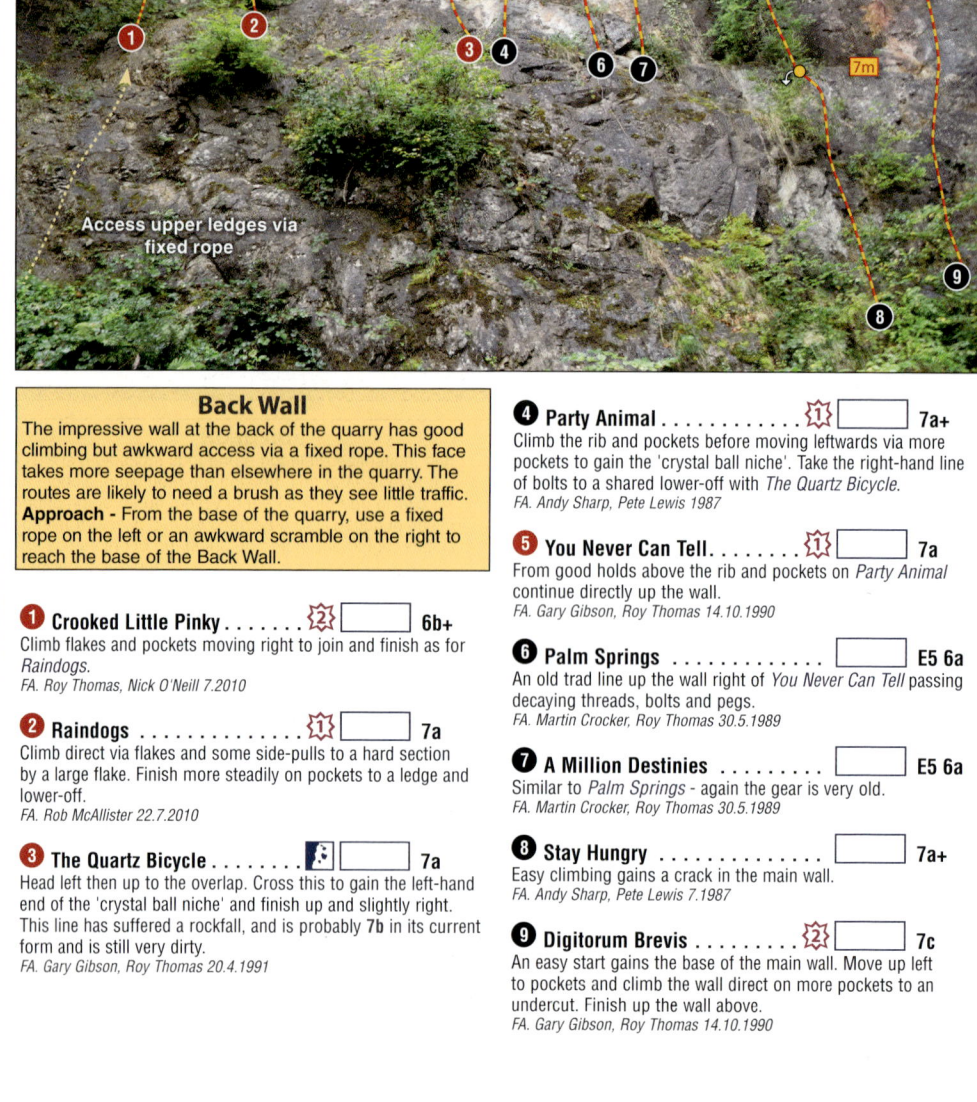

Taff's Well West — Back Wall

Back Wall
The impressive wall at the back of the quarry has good climbing but awkward access via a fixed rope. This face takes more seepage than elsewhere in the quarry. The routes are likely to need a brush as they see little traffic.
Approach - From the base of the quarry, use a fixed rope on the left or an awkward scramble on the right to reach the base of the Back Wall.

1 Crooked Little Pinky . . . . 6b+
Climb flakes and pockets moving right to join and finish as for *Raindogs*.
FA. Roy Thomas, Nick O'Neill 7.2010

2 Raindogs 7a
Climb direct via flakes and some side-pulls to a hard section by a large flake. Finish more steadily on pockets to a ledge and lower-off.
FA. Rob McAllister 22.7.2010

3 The Quartz Bicycle 7a
Head left then up to the overlap. Cross this to gain the left-hand end of the 'crystal ball niche' and finish up and slightly right. This line has suffered a rockfall, and is probably **7b** in its current form and is still very dirty.
FA. Gary Gibson, Roy Thomas 20.4.1991

4 Party Animal . . . . 7a+
Climb the rib and pockets before moving leftwards via more pockets to gain the 'crystal ball niche'. Take the right-hand line of bolts to a shared lower-off with *The Quartz Bicycle*.
FA. Andy Sharp, Pete Lewis 1987

5 You Never Can Tell 7a
From good holds above the rib and pockets on *Party Animal* continue directly up the wall.
FA. Gary Gibson, Roy Thomas 14.10.1990

6 Palm Springs E5 6a
An old trad line up the wall right of *You Never Can Tell* passing decaying threads, bolts and pegs.
FA. Martin Crocker, Roy Thomas 30.5.1989

7 A Million Destinies E5 6a
Similar to *Palm Springs* - again the gear is very old.
FA. Martin Crocker, Roy Thomas 30.5.1989

8 Stay Hungry . . . . 7a+
Easy climbing gains a crack in the main wall.
FA. Andy Sharp, Pete Lewis 7.1987

9 Digitorum Brevis 7c
An easy start gains the base of the main wall. Move up left to pockets and climb the wall direct on more pockets to an undercut. Finish up the wall above.
FA. Gary Gibson, Roy Thomas 14.10.1990

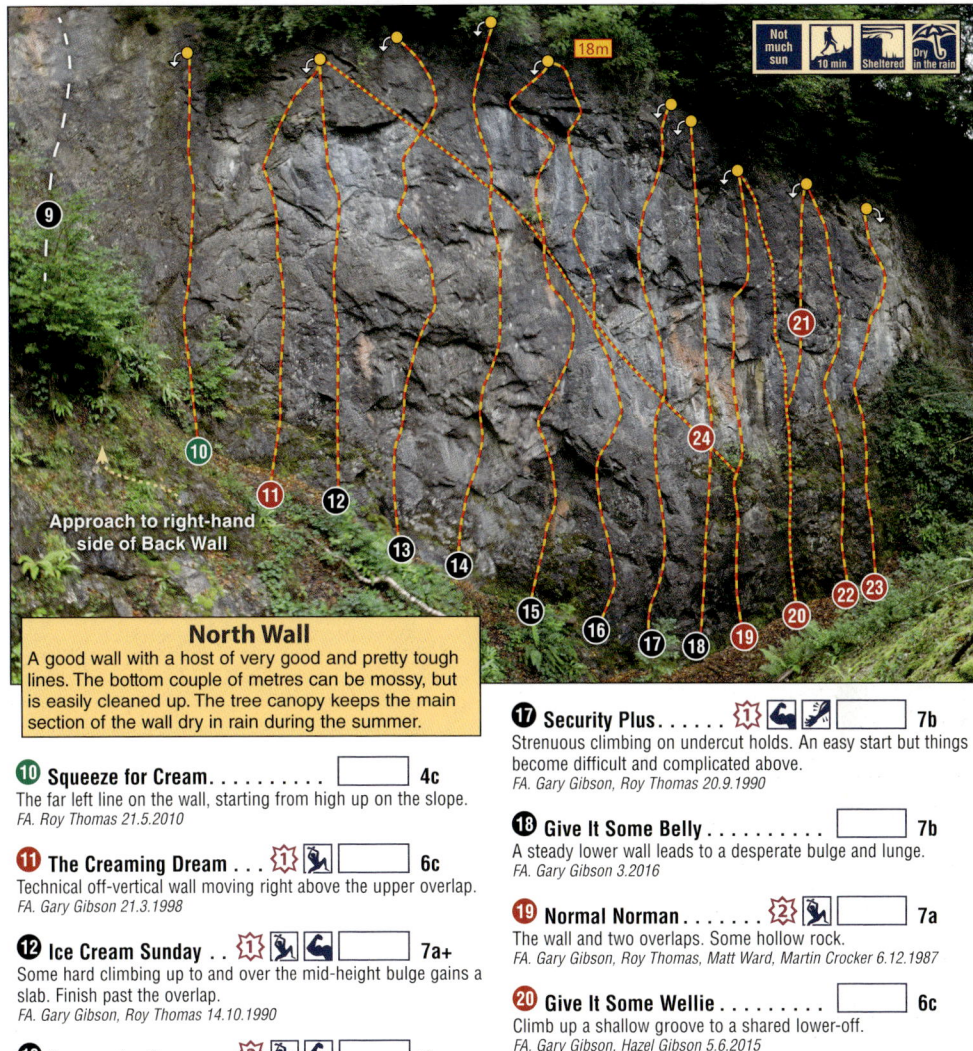

North Wall Taff's Well West

North Wall
A good wall with a host of very good and pretty tough lines. The bottom couple of metres can be mossy, but is easily cleaned up. The tree canopy keeps the main section of the wall dry in rain during the summer.

10 Squeeze for Cream.......... 4c
The far left line on the wall, starting from high up on the slope.
FA. Roy Thomas 21.5.2010

11 The Creaming Dream... 6c
Technical off-vertical wall moving right above the upper overlap.
FA. Gary Gibson 21.3.1998

12 Ice Cream Sunday .. 7a+
Some hard climbing up to and over the mid-height bulge gains a slab. Finish past the overlap.
FA. Gary Gibson, Roy Thomas 14.10.1990

13 Scream for Cream ... 7a+
Move up to the bulge and use undercuts to break through it - hard. Finish direct above the top overlap. Photo on page 206.
FA. Matt Ward, Martin Crocker, Gary Gibson 13.12.1987

14 G.L.C SAF......... 7b
A varied pitch that tackles the bulge, slab and upper wall.
FA. Alan Rosier 15.6.2010

15 Trailblazer 7b
The route of the wall. Sustained and technical with a very difficult finish, first left then right, to reach the lower-off.
FA. Martin Crocker, Matt Ward, Roy Thomas 6.12.1987

16 Sink or Swim...... 7a+
A fine pitch. Sustained and airy climbing with a blind and powerful last few metres. Photo on page 213.
FA. Gary Gibson 21.3.1998

17 Security Plus...... 7b
Strenuous climbing on undercut holds. An easy start but things become difficult and complicated above.
FA. Gary Gibson, Roy Thomas 20.9.1990

18 Give It Some Belly.......... 7b
A steady lower wall leads to a desperate bulge and lunge.
FA. Gary Gibson 3.2016

19 Normal Norman....... 7a
The wall and two overlaps. Some hollow rock.
FA. Gary Gibson, Roy Thomas, Matt Ward, Martin Crocker 6.12.1987

20 Give It Some Wellie......... 6c
Climb up a shallow groove to a shared lower-off.
FA. Gary Gibson, Hazel Gibson 5.6.2015

21 All's Well 6b
Climb the slab. At the overlap move up right to a groove and ledge at its end. Finish up the wall above.
FA. Gary Gibson, Roy Thomas, Matt Ward, Martin Crocker 6.12.1987

22 Bitter End 6c
Climb up to a flake (sometimes dirty). Above it, move rightwards and up a slab to finish.
FA. Roy Thomas 2000s

23 Adam Hussein's Nan 6b
The moss-covered slab and wall right of Bitter End.
FA. Roy Thomas, Goi Ashmore 27.6.2010

24 Taffy Duck........ 6c
A rising diagonal line that uses bolts on other lines.
FA. Gary Gibson 28.4.1991

Taff's Well West   The Outer Pit

The Outer Pit
A gloomy wall, but it does have some decent pitches and offers the possibility of climbing in the rain.
Conditions - Mossy on its margins, but clean and sheltered from rain in its central section where the best lines are to be found. Will take some time to dry once it has got wet.

1 Affluenza **5c**
Can be dirty. Best to start as for *Honeybucket Supreme* and then head left past a tree stump. Originally climbed direct.
FA. Dai Emanuel, Roy Thomas 11.6.2010

2 Honeybucket Supreme **5b**
A dirty line past a mix of small and large bolts.
FA. Dai Emanuel 6.6.2010

3 Faster! Pussycat **5c**
Dirty at the start. Continue to join *Tinkers Dog* near the top.
FA. Dai Emanuel, Roy Thomas 6.6.2010

4 Tinkers Dog **6a**
Sometimes mossy at the start.
FA. Roy Thomas 9.2009

5 Full Metal Jacket . . . . . . **6a+**
The wall and bulge to a lower-off at the upper diagonal break.
FA. Gary Gibson, Roy Thomas 5.2010

6 Any Old Iron **6c**
A worthwhile route on the final section of clean rock.
FA. Roy Thomas and team 13.12.1987

7 Rag and Bone . . . . **6b+**
The best on the wall, but no giveaway. The lower-wall has some good climbing, but the upper wall is both leaning and powerful.
FA. Roy Thomas 7.10.1998

8 Wreckers ball **6a**
Make a hard starting sequence that leads to another tricky section just before the break and lower-off.
FA. Roy Thomas 21.5.2010

9 Knackers Yard . . . . **6a+**
A line of two halves. The upper wall is steep but has good holds.
FA. Roy Thomas 1998

10 Landfill Tax **6a**
Climb to the midway break and then make some steep moves on good holds to the lower-off.
FA. Roy Thomas, Dai Emanuel 6.2010

The Outer Pit **Taff's Well West**

11 Sustainable Development 5c
The tricky lower wall leads to the break before a couple of steep pulls gain the lower-off. Quite tough.
FA. Roy Thomas 2.10.2009

12 Industrial Salvage 5c
The short line up the blank open groove. It is just off of the topo.
FA. Roy Thomas, Dai Emanuel 6.2010

Jen Stephens on the redpoint of the excellent *Sink or Swim* (7a+) - *page 211* - on the North Wall at Taff's Well West. Photo: Mark Glaister

Gilwern

Gilwern is an old limestone quarry working, set high up on the edge of moorland overlooking the Black Mountains to the north. The quarries are not very high but have some good little pitches that are well bolted and very popular. The grades span the 5s and 6s, the highlights being the lines on Gilwern Main Wall's covering of flowstone and the compact technicalities on offer at Gilwern East. The quarries are both exposed to wind and rain, but are good spots in warm weather, having pleasant bases and expansive outlooks over the Usk valley and the Black Mountains.

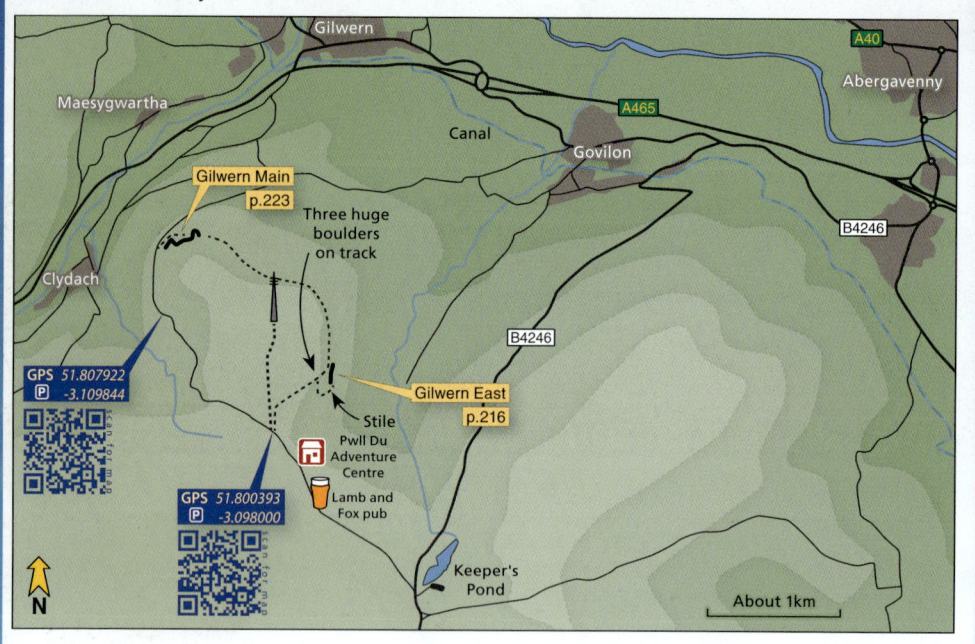

	No star	☆	☆☆	☆☆☆
up to 4c	3	2	-	-
5a to 6a+	8	14	3	-
6b to 7a	16	14	6	2
7a+ and up	1	1	-	-

Approach   Also see map on page 175

From the A465 turn off at the Abergavenny junction and head south on the B4246 following signs to Blaenavon. Continue up the hill to Keeper's Pond, then turn right onto a minor road and follow it past the Lamb and Fox pub.

For Gilwern East, park where two tracks head off to the right. Take the right-hand track for 700m to where the track is blocked by three huge boulders. Head back right and down along the top of the cliff until you can walk back left and over a stile to the base of the cliff.

For Gilwern Main, continue driving past the parking for Gilwern East to parking on the right by a row of stone blocks - this is just before the road makes a right turn above a quarry. Walk along the road for 400m and, just after the road passes through a small cutting, take a path up the hill and then left to the quarry (100m from the road).

Conditions

The quarries are high on the edge of moorland and very exposed, however they are set back into the slope. Gilwern East receives the sun in the morning and Gilwern Main gets the sun in the late afternoon in the summer months.

Gilwern 215

Bridget Collier heading up the steep flowstone on *Pwll Du Crack* (5c) - *page 223* - on the Main Wall at Gilwern. Photo: Mark Glaister

Gilwern Gilwern East

Gilwern East
A series of good walls composed of excellent compact limestone that give some intense and fingery pitches. The cliff has a peaceful setting, beautiful outlook and a very pleasant grassy base. The lines have been well thought out and bolted, and, although close together, are generally independent of each other.

Approach - From the three huge boulders on the approach track, walk down right and back left over a stile.
Conditions - The wall faces east and gets morning sun. Seepage can be a problem in the central section.

1 Bring out the Crimp .... 6a+
The arete and groove with a tricky start.
FA. Pete Blackburn 2012

2 All the Pies Arete .... 6b+
Climb the short steep arete with difficulty. Good moves.
FA. Pete Blackburn, Paul Tucker 2012

3 Cheapskate .... 6b+
Use the bolts of *Black Night's Rein*. Head left from the corner past a small overhang and finish direct.
FA. Pete Blackburn, Paul Tucker 2013

4 Black Night's Rein 6a
Short but with good moves. Climb the groove before making a nifty pull rightwards and up onto a ledge. Finish more easily up the crozzly wall and then leftwards to gain the lower-off.
FA. Paul Tucker, Pete Blackburn 2012

5 Direct Start (Black Night's Rein)
.... 6b
Use the bolts on *Black Nights Rein*. Pull blindly and strenuously up to the ledge on *Black Night's Rein*. Finish via that route.
FA. Pete Blackburn 2012

6 The Slytherin 7a
Technical moves up the wall and overlap with the aid of vague side-pulls. Using the large hold out left on the arete reduces the grade to **6c**.
FA. Pete Blackburn 2014

7 Microwaves 6c
Reachy and thin climbing directly up the wall and delicate groove above.
FA. Paul Tucker 2012

8 Fergie's Folly 6b
Thuggish moves lead to easier climbing and then a steep and stretchy finish.
FA. Pete Blackburn, Paul Tucker 2012

9 Thorn in my Side E2 5b
A trad climb. Steep bold moves lead to steadier climbing where the rock needs care.
FA. Paul Tucker, Pete Blackburn 2012

10 Quakering 6c
The direct start to *Mr Softy* requires a long reach.
FA. Pete Blackburn, Paul Tucker 2013

11 Mr Softy .... 6a+
Climb the tricky corner and wall to a ledge on the left. Steep climbing on good holds leads to the lower-off.
FA. Pete Blackburn, Paul Tucker 2012

12 Pearlescence .... 6b+
Perplexing climbing up the wall and groove.
FA. Paul Tucker, Pete Blackburn, Adrian Ledley 2012

Gilwern East Gilwern 217

13 Tallulah Dream .... 6b+
Small edges lead up the wall to a crucial hold in the groove on the right. Finish steeply up the wall above.
FA. Adrian Ledley, Paul Tucker, Pete Blackburn 2012

14 In the Groove 6c
Intricate climbing leads to a good hold in the groove. Continue steeply to ledges. Finish more easily up the wall.
FA. Pete Blackburn, Michael Marder 2014

15 One Step Beyond 6b
Delicate and slightly bold moves up and leftwards across the slabby wall lead to an easier finish.
FA. Pete Blackburn, Paul Tucker 2012

16 Reach for a Peach .... 6b+
Start via the water-worn feature to a stiff pull up the mini-pillar to halfway ledges. Balancy moves lead in turn to a stretch to a small flake which unlocks the finish
FA. Pete Blackburn, Paul Tucker 2013

17 What's the Craic E2 5b
A trad climb. Ascend the chimney and crack. Difficult to protect until the crux, where a good nut placement protects the steep pull up the finishing crack.
FA. Pete Blackburn, Paul Tucker 2012

Rosy Klinkenberg enjoying the good holds that furnish the excellent line of *The Plumb* (5b) - page 220 - at Gilwern East. Photo: Mark Glaister

Gilwern — Gilwern East

18 Petering Out — 6b
Climb the crack-line just right of the off-width of *What's the Craic* to a steep finish. Use the first three bolts of *The Golden Tower* and avoid bridging into *What's the Craic*.
FA. Pete Blackburn, Paul Tucker 2012

19 The Golden Tower — 6c
A difficult and sequency climb that wends its way up the indefinite pillar. A sharp tufa 'ear' proves crucial to accessing the final moves.
FA. Pete Blackburn, Paul Tucker 2012

20 Half Pipe Dream — 6c
A quality line. Climb the water-worn tube via some wide bridging. Continue steeply up and leftwards to finish as for *The Golden Tower*.
FA. Paul Tucker, Pete Blackburn 2012

Gilwern East **Gilwern** 219

㉑ Magic Carpet. 6b
An improbable but rewarding climb that transports you magically and steeply through an area of hanging rock while still giving solid support. Step right near the top. *Photo this page.*
FA. Pete Blackburn, Paul Tucker 2012

**㉒ Original Start (Life on Planet Earth)
. . . .** 6c
A sequence of steep and sketchy moves lead up and right into *Life on Planet Earth*. Unfortunately can suffer from seepage.
FA. Paul Tucker 2012

㉓ Life on Planet Earth . . . . 6b+
Ascend the corner to a taxing move which accesses the steep upper section that is best climbed with care. Stay left of the large holds on *The Plumb*.
FA. Paul Tucker, Pete Blackburn 2012

Jay Astbury starting up the steep section of the pumpy *Magic Carpet* (6b) - *this page* - on the central section at Gilwern East. This section of the crag has some of Gilwern's best routes, all on fine rock. Photo: Mark Glaister

Gilwern — Gilwern East

24 The Plumb — 5b
The longest route at the crag heads directly up a pillar on large spaced jugs and stuck-on holds. A fun pitch. *Photo on page 217.*
FA. Pete Blackburn, Paul Tucker 2012

25 Asteroids — 5a
Climb on good holds past some large conglomerate blocks and up the final wall.
FA. Paul Tucker, Pete Blackburn 2012

26 Scorpion — 6a+
A stiff pull directly past the overhang leads to engaging climbing up the groove to the ledge. All that awaits is the sting in the tail!
FA. Pete Blackburn, Paul Tucker 2013

27 Thug Life — 6c
Start right at the back of the cave on the left and make some reachy moves out to the lip - high first bolt. Thug your way around the lip until under a bolt, then finish straight up, joining *Garden of Eden* at its third bolt.
FA. Jason Jones 30.8.2016

Gilwern East **Gilwern** 221

28 Garden of Eden .... 6a+
An athletic pull onto the slab below the groove leads to more delicate climbing up the open groove and another slab above.
FA. Paul Tucker Pete Blackburn 2012

29 Superposition .. 7a
Packs a lot of climbing into a short distance. Using a complex series of moves on edges and pinches, gain the midway break via a long reach. Finish more easily. Difficult to on-sight.
FA. Paul Tucker 2012

30 Sidewinder ...... 6b+
A classic pitch on superb rock. Climb the steep wall and groove using a sharp fin of rock. Delicate climbing awaits.
FA. Pete Blackburn, Paul Tucker 2012

31 Firepower .... 7a+
A steep and powerful sequence using an edge on the right, a small pocket and a series of rounded holds, will hopefully propel you to the top.
FA. Paul Tucker 2013

32 Crackatoa E2 5c
A trad route. Climb the twin cracks with adequate protection to a hard move or two to reach a ledge.
FA. Pete Blackburn, Paul Tucker 2012

33 Talking Hands .... 6b+
Harder than it looks with confusing moves to the large ledge. The key is to make the rounded side-pull work somehow. Difficult to on-sight but very worthwhile.
FA. Pete Blackburn, Henry Brown, Caroline Gill 2014

34 Hand in Pocket 6b
Steady climbing to the pocket before steep blind pulls transport you to the top. A nice pitch.
FA. Pete Blackburn, Paul Tucker 2012

35 Inch Pinch .... 6b+
Good steep climbing requiring the right sequence. Ascend sharp pockets to a good finger slot in the overhang. Swing right on small footholds and then levitate up the hanging groove. It can get a little dirty.
FA. Pete Blackburn, Paul Tucker 2012

36 The Imp 7b
Takes a direct line up the middle of the blank wall, technical and fingery. Finish as for *Dolphin Snoggin'*.
FA. Jason Jones 30.8.2016

37 Dolphin Snoggin' 6a
The corner is best lay-backed before steep climbing leads leftwards to the lower-off.
FA. Pete Blackburn, Paul Tucker 2013

38 Periscope .... HVS 5a
A trad route. Climb the wall 5m to the right of the bolts of *Dolphin Snoggin'* and finish up some suspect rock to belay at the large tree.
FA. Paul Tucker 2013

Gilwern — Pear Buttress

Pear Buttress
A compact buttress further on from the Main Wall that might prove to be useful if the crag is busy.
Approach - Walk past the main wall for 100m.
Conditions - Shady but quick drying. Seepage may occur but the rock does dry quickly after rainfall.

1 Wayne Fell in Do Do 4a
The narrow rib.
FA. Paul Tucker, Howell Jones 3.2012

2 Jetison Bilge 5a
The crack.
FA. Paul Tucker, Pete Blackburn 3.2012

3 Fruitless Pair . . . . 6b+
Climb smooth rock to the right of the crack.
FA. Paul Tucker, Pete Blackburn 3.2012

4 La Poire 6b
Start up a tiny right-facing corner and then take the face above rightward to finish.
FA. Pete Blackburn, Paul Tucker 3.2012

5 Posh and Becs. 6c
The wall passing a tiny orange niche.
FA. Paul Tucker, Pete Blackburn 3.2012

6 Apples and Pairs 6a
Follow a series of blind corners staying clear of poor rock to the right.
FA. Pete Blackburn, Paul Tucker 3.2012

7 Jug Fest 4b
An enjoyable little line that starts on the far left of the wall and heads up and right and then back left on good flowstone.
FA. Bill Gregory, Paul Bowen 4.2007

8 Black Tide. 5b
Climb stuck-on holds onto a black slab. Move left at the top.
FA. Peter Blackburn 4.10.2016

9 Porcellena 5c
The groove. A steady start leads to a tricky move up the corner.
FA. Peter Blackburn 2.10.2016

Main Wall
The left-hand side of the main area is composed of a fine wall of flowstone which, although not very tall, offers some sustained and enjoyable pitches. The right-hand side is less appealing but the climbs are a bit more challenging than first appearances might suggest.
Approach - This section is 200m further along from the Hindu Kush Area.
Conditions - The area is high up and exposed to the elements. Seepage may occur but the rock does dry quickly after rainfall.

Main Wall **Gilwern** 223

10 Destination Brynmawr 6a
Climb up and right into a steep right-leaning corner. Make a strenuous pull to gain a flake and finish on sometimes dirty holds to a lower-off on the right.
FA. Bill Gregory 2005

11 Tea Leaves 6b
The left-hand arete of the flowstone face has some testing moves in its upper half where a couple of pulls up right gain better holds. Climbing the line direct is closer to **6c**.
FA. Bill Gregory, Bob Brewer 2.2007

12 Battle of the Bulge 6c
The direct line up the smooth face and bulge to a lower-off.
FA. Bill Gregory, Bob Brewer 2000s

13 Nose Job .... 6c+
Climb the steep calcite wall with a hidden pocket high up.
FA. Pete Blackburn 6.2016

14 Flow Job........... 6b
An excellent piece of flowstone face climbing from start to finish.
FA. Paul Tucker, Paul Bowen 2000s

15 Christian Broke My Flake .... 6a+
Climb up before making a hard sequence rightwards to more reasonable holds. Continue on still interesting ground to the top. At the upper end of the grade.
FA. Paul Tucker, Paul Bowen 2000s

16 Diagnosis Made Easy ..... 6c+
Climb directly up to and over the bulge onto the thin wall. It may have lost holds making the route harder.
FA. Bill Gregory, Bob Brewer 2000s

17 Pwll Du Crack 5c
Good climbing up the steepening line of weakness on some excellent holds. *Photo on page 215.*
FA. Paul Bowen 2000s

18 Go With The Flow 6a
A worthwhile line with flowing moves up the slight rib between *Pwll Du Crack* and *There's No Business Like Flow Business*.
FA. Paul Tucker, Paul Bowen 2000s

19 There's No Business Like Flow Business
.... 5c
Climb the fine drape of flowstone to the left of the short corner in the middle of the crag. Slightly escapable.
FA. Paul Tucker, Paul Bowen 2000s

A low-level bouldering traverse of the wall starting to the left of Jug Fest and finishing at All Aboard my Dingy is **f5**.

Gilwern — Main Wall

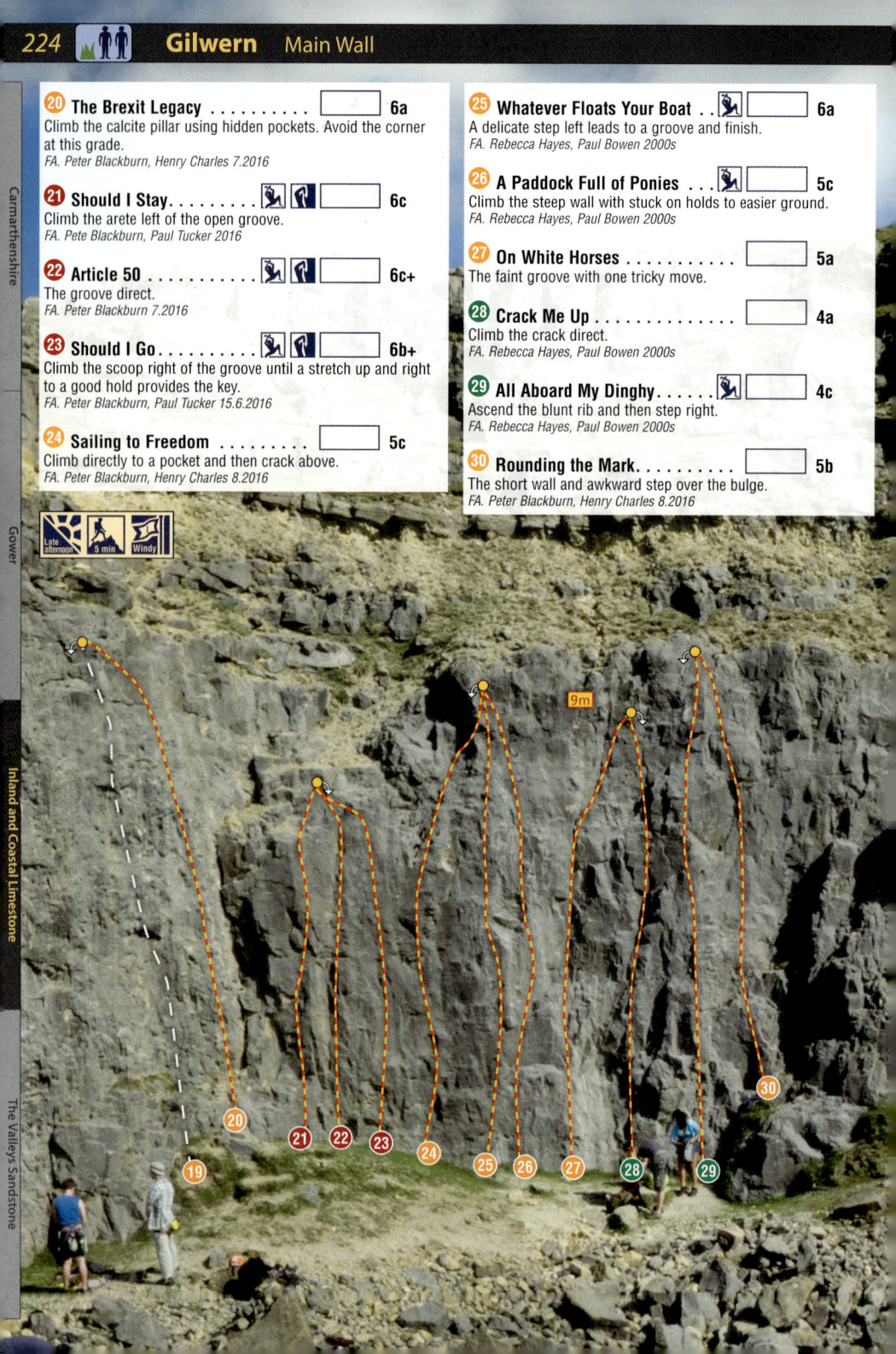

20 The Brexit Legacy 6a
Climb the calcite pillar using hidden pockets. Avoid the corner at this grade.
FA. Peter Blackburn, Henry Charles 7.2016

21 Should I Stay 6c
Climb the arete left of the open groove.
FA. Pete Blackburn, Paul Tucker 2016

22 Article 50 .... 6c+
The groove direct.
FA. Peter Blackburn 7.2016

23 Should I Go .... 6b+
Climb the scoop right of the groove until a stretch up and right to a good hold provides the key.
FA. Peter Blackburn, Paul Tucker 15.6.2016

24 Sailing to Freedom 5c
Climb directly to a pocket and then crack above.
FA. Peter Blackburn, Henry Charles 8.2016

25 Whatever Floats Your Boat 6a
A delicate step left leads to a groove and finish.
FA. Rebecca Hayes, Paul Bowen 2000s

26 A Paddock Full of Ponies 5c
Climb the steep wall with stuck on holds to easier ground.
FA. Rebecca Hayes, Paul Bowen 2000s

27 On White Horses 5a
The faint groove with one tricky move.

28 Crack Me Up 4a
Climb the crack direct.
FA. Rebecca Hayes, Paul Bowen 2000s

29 All Aboard My Dinghy 4c
Ascend the blunt rib and then step right.
FA. Rebecca Hayes, Paul Bowen 2000s

30 Rounding the Mark 5b
The short wall and awkward step over the bulge.
FA. Peter Blackburn, Henry Charles 8.2016

Hindu Kush Area **Gilwern** 225

Hindu Kush Area
A long low crag that has a number of good little pitches that are technical and sustained. This makes for more of an experience than might first be anticipated. The rock is good and the crag base is flat and grassy.
Approach - This is the first wall encountered on the approach from the road.
Conditions - Exposed to wind and rain but the face is quick drying. It gets the sun from mid-afternoon onwards.

❶ Cod Liver Oil 6b
Make some intricate moves up left before heading back rightwards to a lower-off. More involved than it first appears.
FA. Bill Gregory, Paul Bowen 2000s

❷ Glucosamine and Chondroitin
. . . . 6c
Climb directly up the wall to the bulge and pull through it on crimps. Short but intense climbing.
FA. Bill Gregory, Paul Bowen 2000s

The wall between has been climbed sharing bolts at **7a+**.

❸ Fuelled by Pies . . . . 7a+
Thin and complex pulling and undercutting up the wall just right of *Glucosamine & Chondroitin*.
FA. Bill Gregory 2000s

❹ Johnny Takes a Tumble . . 6a
Climb the crack and traverse left to shared lower-off. Can be muddy on the finishing holds.
FA. Bill Gregory, Paul Bowen 2000s

❺ Snap Crackle 'n' Pop . . . 6a
A good pitch that has a difficult start. Above things gradually ease.
FA. Laura Jones, Becky Hayes 8.9.2007

❻ White Noise 5a
Follow the faint thin crack on good holds to a shared lower-off with *Snap Crackle 'n' Pop*.
FA. Julien Steer, Becky Hayes 8.9.2007

❼ Back, Crack and Sack 5a
Follow the crack-line to the overlap and then move up rightwards to a lower-off.
FA. Julien Steer, Becky Hayes 8.9.2007

❽ Take me up the Hindu Kush . . 5c
An easy start leads to a hard move to finish.
FA. Becky Hayes, Julien Steer 8.9.2007

❾ To Dai or not to Dai 5c
Relatively easy climbing leads to one hardish move.
FA. Paul Bowen, Dai Williams 8.9.2007

❿ Brittle Biscuit 4c
Avoiding the crack pushes the grade up to **5c**.
FA. David Williams, Paul Bowen 8.9.2007

⓫ Under a Blood Red Sky 5c
Thoughtful climbing requiring delicate footwork.
FA. Becky Hayes, Julien Steer 8.9.2007

Witches Point

226

	No star	✦	✦✦	✦✦✦
up to 4c	3	-	-	-
5a to 6a+	7	3	-	-
6b to 7a	6	11	11	1
7a+ and up	3	6	7	6

Carmarthenshire

Gower

Inland and Coastal Limestone

The Valleys Sandstone

Martyn Richards making the most of some crisp evening conditions on the Top 50 line *This God is Mine* (7b+) - *page 228* - on the Stone Wings Cliff at Witches Point. Photo: Mark Glaister

Witches Point 227

Witches Point is one of the jewels in the crown of hard sport climbing in South Wales. The setting is stunning - an idyllic position above a magnificent 'blue flag' sandy surf beach; in the summer months it takes on a holiday atmosphere. All of the cliffs have good rock and the variety of climbing style ranges from powerful to technical and sustained. The only drawbacks are that it is tidal and conditions can be frustrating in humid warm weather.

Approach   Also see map on page 175
From the A48 Bridgend bypass, take the B4265 southwards to St. Brides Major. Drive through the village and turn right towards Southerndown (ignore earlier signs for Southerndown). Turn left by the Three Golden Cups pub and follow the road down a steep hill to Dunraven Bay car park (fee). The cliff is on the left-hand side of the beach. A walk across the beach reaches the crag in 5 minutes.

Tides
The crag is partially tidal though apart from those on Witches Cave, most of the routes are accessible at high tide. The approach to the cliff is cut-off for around two hours at high water but the base of the cliff stays dry in calm sea conditions. Witches Cave is accessible for 2 hours on either side of low water.

Conditions
The cliff is northwest-facing, keeping it out of the sun for most of the day. This provides welcome shelter in a hot summer but also makes it a good evening venue at other times. Seepage can occur in the winter months and early spring, but once dry, it remains so for long periods of time. Conditions can be frustrating in humid warm weather before any sun comes onto the faces.

Access
Dogs are not allowed on the beach in the summer.

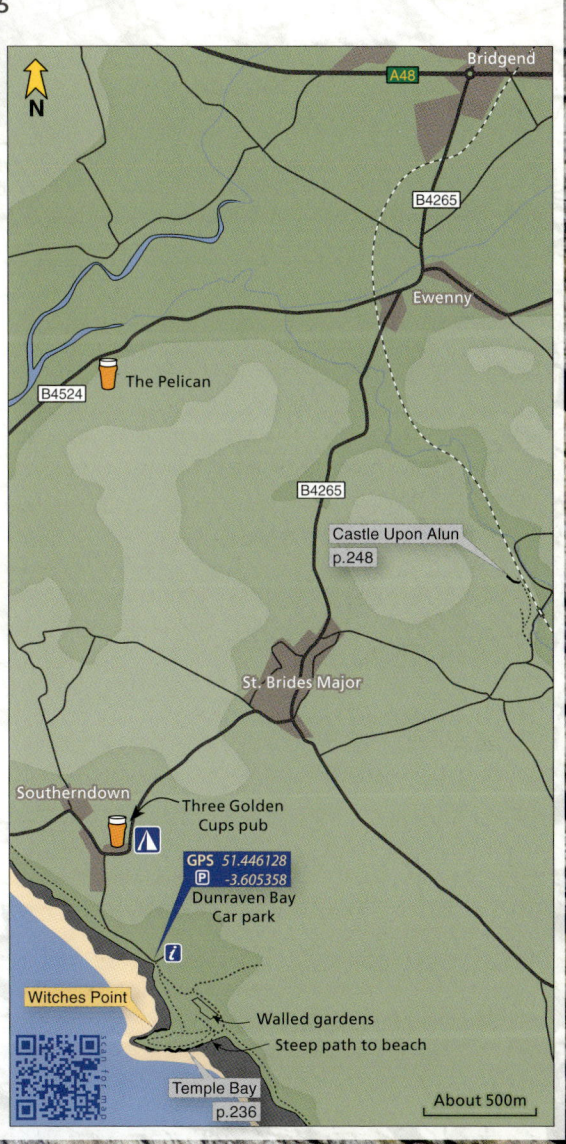

Witches Point — Stone Wings Cliff

Stone Wings Cliff
A superb wall which is overhanging on the left-hand side with sustained and pumpy routes to match. Further right it gives some delicate face routes at easier grades. The rock is of the highest quality but can suffer seepage in its central section well into the warmer months.

Approach - Walk across the beach when the tide is out.
Conditions - The walls face northwest and get late afternoon/early evening sun. This is not a good venue if it is humid.

1 Liassic Lark 7a
A super little jamming crack with a tough bulge. It can be greasy early in the season. Above the bulge step right to a lower-off.
FA. Roy Thomas 8.1994

2 In Search of Bedrock . . . 7a+
The natural continuation to *Liassic Lark* that moves left from its lower-off to climb a steep groove system and headwall.
FA. Roy Thomas, Gary Gibson 16.7.1994

3 Help, Help Me Rhondda
. . . . 7c
A steady start leads to a desperate, fingery sequence through the mean-looking bulge.
FA. Eugene Travers-Jones 8.1993

4 The Dai Vinci Coed . . . 7c
From the first jug on *Help, Help Me Rhondda* move right slightly then up to the overlap on undercuts and side-pulls. From a good undercut, move right to a pod and make a hard fingery traverse back left before moving up to the lower-off.
FA. Rob Lamey 26.6.2013

5 Methuselah 8a
Follow *The Dai Vinci Coed* and move right into *This God Is Mine*. Instead of pulling over the bulge to easy ground, make a wild series of moves right across a sloping rail into *Masada*. Finish up this.
FA. Dave Pickford, 7.8.2016

6 This God is Mine . . . . . Top 50 7b+
A classic of its type. Sustained climbing up the thin crack-line which proves to be tough all of the way to the lower-off.
Photo on page 226.
FA. Gary Gibson Roy Thomas 6.8.1994

7 Masada . . . . 8a+
The ascent of the smooth-looking wall requires imagination, ability and endurance. The wall beneath the first overlap is climbed direct, not by stepping out of the crack.
FA. Eugene Travers-Jones 1995

8 Stone Wings E5 6a
The antithesis of its neighbours. Brutal jamming combined with hard-earned gear placements.
FA. Pat Littlejohn, S.Robinson (1pt) 27.7.1979
FFA. Gary Gibson, Roy Thomas 19.6.1994

Stone Wings Cliff Witches Point 229

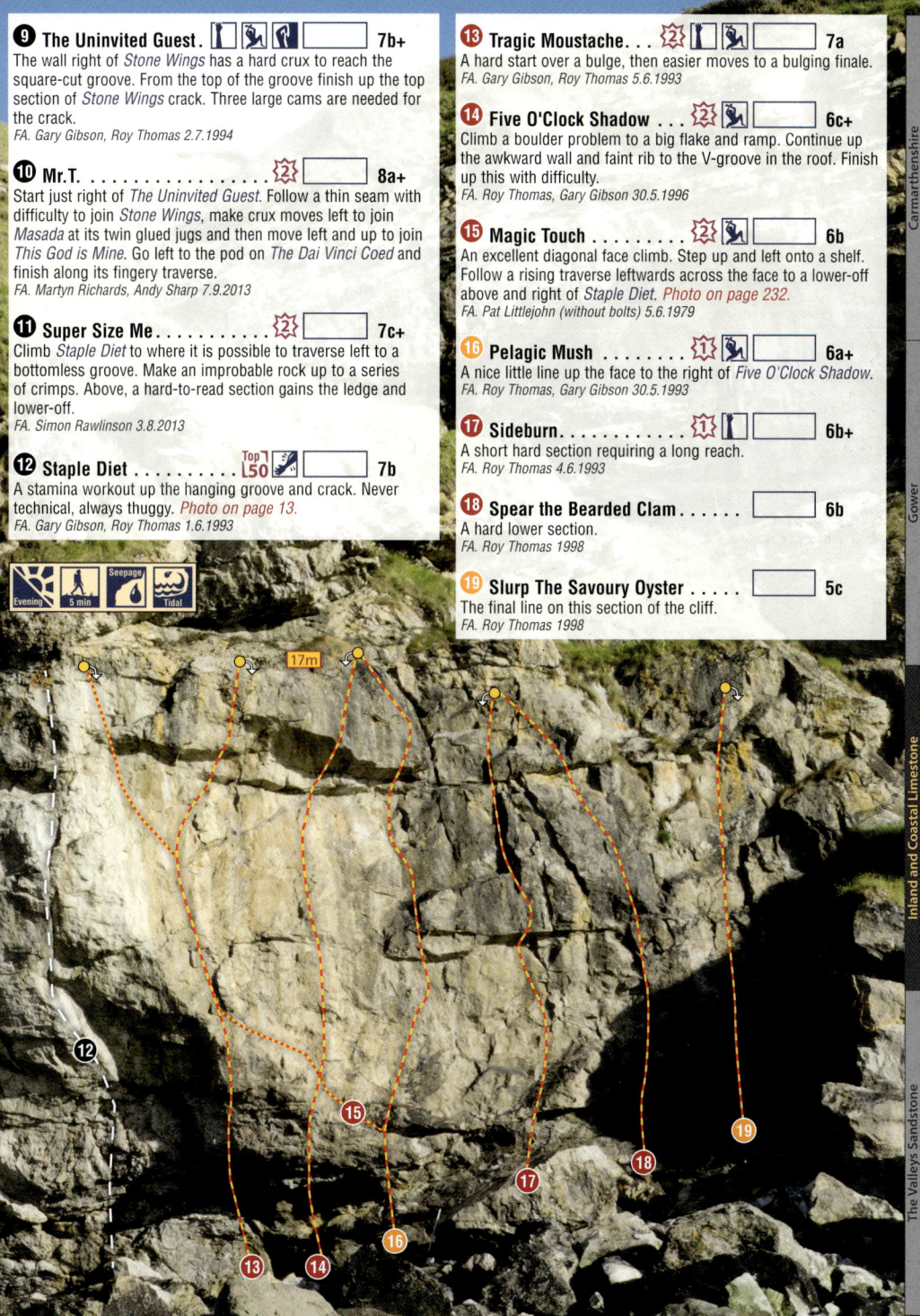

9 The Uninvited Guest. 7b+
The wall right of *Stone Wings* has a hard crux to reach the square-cut groove. From the top of the groove finish up the top section of *Stone Wings* crack. Three large cams are needed for the crack.
FA. Gary Gibson, Roy Thomas 2.7.1994

10 Mr.T. 8a+
Start just right of *The Uninvited Guest*. Follow a thin seam with difficulty to join *Stone Wings*, make crux moves left to join *Masada* at its twin glued jugs and then move left and up to join *This God is Mine*. Go left to the pod on *The Dai Vinci Coed* and finish along its fingery traverse.
FA. Martyn Richards, Andy Sharp 7.9.2013

11 Super Size Me 7c+
Climb *Staple Diet* to where it is possible to traverse left to a bottomless groove. Make an improbable rock up to a series of crimps. Above, a hard-to-read section gains the ledge and lower-off.
FA. Simon Rawlinson 3.8.2013

12 Staple Diet 7b
A stamina workout up the hanging groove and crack. Never technical, always thuggy. *Photo on page 13.*
FA. Gary Gibson, Roy Thomas 1.6.1993

13 Tragic Moustache... 7a
A hard start over a bulge, then easier moves to a bulging finale.
FA. Gary Gibson, Roy Thomas 5.6.1993

14 Five O'Clock Shadow 6c+
Climb a boulder problem to a big flake and ramp. Continue up the awkward wall and faint rib to the V-groove in the roof. Finish up this with difficulty.
FA. Roy Thomas, Gary Gibson 30.5.1996

15 Magic Touch 6b
An excellent diagonal face climb. Step up and left onto a shelf. Follow a rising traverse leftwards across the face to a lower-off above and right of *Staple Diet*. *Photo on page 232.*
FA. Pat Littlejohn (without bolts) 5.6.1979

16 Pelagic Mush 6a+
A nice little line up the face to the right of *Five O'Clock Shadow*.
FA. Roy Thomas, Gary Gibson 30.5.1993

17 Sideburn 6b+
A short hard section requiring a long reach.
FA. Roy Thomas 4.6.1993

18 Spear the Bearded Clam 6b
A hard lower section.
FA. Roy Thomas 1998

19 Slurp The Savoury Oyster 5c
The final line on this section of the cliff.
FA. Roy Thomas 1998

Witches Point — Dunraven Cliff

Dunraven Cliff

A large section of the cliff that has an impressive central wall cut by ramps and grooves in its upper reaches. On either side are shorter and steeper sections of crag - The Tufa Terrace and The Gantry (which are tricky to reach).

Approach - When the tide is out, make an easy stroll across the beach to the central section of the cliff. To reach the Tufa Terrace, scramble carefully up rungs and grass. To access The Gantry climb one of the lower lines. Tufa Terrace and The Gantry can be accessed from above but the approach down steep grass slopes is insecure and dangerous in the wet.

Conditions - The walls face northwest and get late afternoon/early evening sun. This is not a good venue in humid weather. Seepage can be a problem.

1 Tufa Joy 7a
A hard start is followed by a powerful finish rightwards.
FA. Gary Gibson, Roy Thomas 5.7.1993

2 Tufa at the Top 7a
A gem of a route taking the 'sexual' tufa. Harder than it looks.
FA. Roy Thomas, Gary Gibson 6.6.1993

3 Its Tufa at the Bottom ... 7a+
Appropriately named and not all over until the belay.
FA. Gary Gibson, Roy Thomas 3.7.1993

4 Tufa Tennis 6c
A pleasant companion route on the 'bobbles' to the right,
FA. Roy Thomas, Gary Gibson 3.7.1993

5 PCB 6a
The first line on the left of the lower main wall is short and starts halfway up the grassy gully leading to Tufa Terrace.
FA. Dai Emanuel 2009

6 Croeso I Gymru .... 6b+
Pleasant climbing and tricky in its top half.
FA. Martin Crocker, Roy Thomas 23.8.1986

7 The World-v-Gibson . 7a
A worthwhile pitch with a technical crux low down and sustained climbing above.
FA. Martin Crocker, Roy Thomas 23.8.1986

8 Straining at The Leash .. 7b
A hard bouldery crux that packs a punch.
FA. Gary Gibson, Roy Thomas 15.5.1993

9 Leave it to The Dogs ... 7a+
A sustained climb up a groove and arete.
FA. Gary Gibson, Roy Thomas 4.7.1993

Dunraven Cliff **Witches Point** 231

10 There's Life in the Old Dog Yet .... 6c+
A short, sharp crux in a fine position gains easier climbing above.
FA. Roy Thomas, Gary Gibson 16.5.1993

11 Plus ça Change 7b
The centre of the wall via a prominent flake with a trying crux.
FA. Gary Gibson Eugene Travers-Jones 30.5.1993

12 Hanging by a Thread ... Top 50 6c
One of the classics of the grade in South Wales. Superb and sustained climbing.
FA. Roy Thomas, Mick Learoyd 8.1986

13 Edge-More 7c
A short, hard and fingery crux that includes a bolt-on hold.
FA. Gary Gibson, Roy Thomas 3.7.1994

14 Edge-Hog .... 7b+
The leaning arete and powerful bulge in a fine position.
FA. Gary Gibson, Roy Thomas 11.7.1993

15 Grow-Up! 7c
A steep line through the centre of the bulges and roofs.
FA. Martin Crocker 14.5.1994

16 Pasty = Man Boobs 4a
The left-hand bolted line on the slab below The Gantry.
FA. Dai Emanuel 2009

17 Young Gifted and Beige 4a
The right-hand bolted line on the slab below The Gantry.
FA. Dai Emanuel, Roy Thomas 2009

18 The Overlook ...... 7b+
A very powerful series of heel-hooks and rotations. Tape your hands up for this one!
FA. Gary Gibson 15.5.1994

19 Anchors Away .... 6b+
A tricky bulge in a good position.
FA. Roy Thomas, Gary Gibson 15.5.1994

20 Cast Adrift 6c
Technical climbing on 'dinks'.
FA. Roy Thomas, Gary Gibson 11.7.1994

21 Broken on the Rocks 6b
A short pleasant wall.
FA. Roy Thomas, Gary Gibson 11.7.1994

22 Marooned 6b
A single hard move on the right-hand side of the wall.
FA. Roy Thomas, Gary Gibson 11.7.1994

Witches Point

Andy Sharp on the smart little rising traverse of *Magic Touch* (6b) - *page 229* - on the Stone Wings Cliff at Witches Point. The steeper classics of the crag *Staple Diet* (7b) and *This God is Mine* (7b+) take the bulging rock to his left. The cliff comes into its best condition with a bit of evening sunshine on it; at other times it needs a breeze to dry out. Photo: Mark Glaister

Witches Point Witches Cave

Witches Cave

Just before the tip of Witches Point is a wide shallow cave topped by a vertical white and black wall. Either side are shorter overhanging walls. There are lots of pitches here but they see far less attention than elsewhere on Witches Point due to the tidal restrictions and the difficulty in finding good conditions, nevertheless the better lines are worth tracking down.

Approach and Tides - An easy stroll across the beach, when the tide is out, gains the ledges below the crag. The crag is accessible for around 2 hours on either side of low water. However the ledges below the crag are exposed for plenty of time in calm seas and it is possible to climb out from one of the far right-hand lines and walk over the top of the headland back to the car park.

Conditions - The crag faces northwest and gets late afternoon/early evening sun. Not a good venue in humid weather and seepage can be a problem.

❶ **Fatman and Nob In** 3c
The wall just right of the corner.
FA. Roy Thomas 2010

❷ **Gay Batman** 5a
A gently leaning wall to a shared lower-off.
FA. Dai Emanuel 2009

❸ **Robin's Yoghurt Supper** 5a
Climb the wall to the left of the corner and capping overhang to a shared lower-off.
FA. Dai Emanuel, Roy Thomas, Rich Philips 28.6.2009

❹ **Abra-Ker-Fucking-Dabra** 5c
Interesting climbing. Climb up to the hanging corner and move out right to clear the capping roof.
FA. Dai Emanuel 2009

❺ **Sorcerer's Assistant** . 6a+
Follow the undercut nose and roof stack to the right of the corner on big holds.
FA. Roy Thomas 2009

❻ **Magic Circle** 6b
Powerful pulling through the large double overhangs.
FA. Roy Thomas, Rich Phillips, Gavin Leyshon 2009

❼ **Smoke and Mirrors** . 6b
A wild route taking in some very steep ground.
FA. Roy Thomas, Rich Phillips 2009

❽ **Great Expectorations** ... 6b
Take the multiple roof stack to meet and finish up a groove in the upper wall.
FA. Roy Thomas, Eugene Travers Jones 18.6.2013

❾ **Phlegmatic Solution** . 6c
Take the roof stack just left of the rockfall and then swing right onto the upper wall - and a difficult finish awaits.
FA. Roy Thomas, Eugene Travers-Jones, Myles Jordan 20.7.2013

Witches Cave **Witches Point** 235

There has been a small rockfall below the roof.

10 Evil Ways 7b
Climb up to the roof and, utilising a footlock, pull onto the upper wall. Finish up the technical wall.
FA. Martin Crocker 19.7.1986

11 Evil K'nee Full ..... 7a+
Impressive. Move up to the overhang and reach for a good hold at the lip. Pull onto the upper wall and climb up a faint rib to a hard move up for a sharp edge. Finish at a lower-off above.
FA. Roy Thomas, Goi Ashmore 2.9.1996

12 Willie The Pimp. .... 6c+
Follow *Thin LIzzy* until above the lip of the cave and then foot traverse left across the roof. Move up into a niche and climb diagonally left to a lower-off.
FA. Eugene Travers-Jones 18.8.2014

13 White Witch E5 6b
Continue the traverse of *Willie The Pimp* to finish up *Evil K'nee Full*. The old fixed gear is no more, but some of the bolts on the face may suffice?
FA. Martin Crocker, Roy Thomas 19.7.1986

14 Thin Lizzy ..... 6c+
Make powerful moves past the low roof to below a corner. Take the technical crack leftwards to the roof, then move left to a 'V' groove. Finish up the groove taking care with some flakes.
FA. Roy Thomas, Graham Royle 19.7.1986

15 Wrasse Wipe 6c
Start up *Thin Lizzy* and then continue up the corner.
FA. Roy Thomas 24.6.2009

16 Wrasseputin's Hypodermic Typewriter
.... 6c
Make some steep moves on sharp holds, then finish up the wall above to a shared lower-off with *Thin Lizzy*. Staple bolts.
FA. Dai Emanuel, Rich Phillips 28.6.2009

17 Didymo Clogs Yer Tackle
.... 6b
Start with a big reach to the first good hold - easier above.
FA. Roy Thomas, Nick.O'Neill 2007

18 Fishermen Pump Their Rods . 6a+
Similar sharp pulling on steep ground.
FA. Roy Thomas, Matt Hirst 2007

19 Wrasse Bandit........... 6b+
Tough stuff through the overhang and bulge.
FA. Roy Thomas, Goi Ashmore 2006

20 Sore Wrasse 6c
The hardest of the shorter steep lines hereabouts.
FA. Goi Ashmore, Roy Thomas 2006

21 Wrassetafarian .... 6b+
The short overhanging wall where the overhangs start to fade.
FA. Goi Ashmore 13.7.2009

22 Little Wrasse Cull 6a
A boulder problem start leads to easy ground.
FA. Roy Thomas, Myles Jordan 7.2013

23 The Bedraggled Trousered Misogynist
.... 5c
Knob pulling at its finest!
FA. Roy Thomas, Nick O'Neill 8.2013

Temple Bay

	No star	☆	☆☆	☆☆☆
up to 4c	2	2	-	-
5a to 6a+	23	17	-	-
6b to 7a	3	13	3	-
7a+ and up	-	-	-	-

On the other side of the headland at Witches Point is a collection of tidal low walls. These contain a number of short sport routes in a pleasant seaside environment. The style of climbing varies from thin technical walls to overhanging faces and juggy roof stacks. Although not in the same class as the best on offer at Witches Point, there is plenty here to keep those after a bit of mileage busy, the grade range is friendly and the beach is superb.

Approach   Also see map on page 175

From the car park at Dunraven Bay, walk through the gates in the wall and along the track for 650m, past some unusual walled gardens on the right, until the cliff top is reached. Go right on a path and in a short distance go through a gate on the left. Follow a path up and then down to a stone wall. A path goes left steeply down to the beach from where the Temple Bay crags are easily reached. This is the best approach to use on a first visit. At low tide the crags can be accessed by walking around the headland. Also a ramp between the First and Second Inlet allows easy access up and down from the fisherman's ledges on the top of the headland, but it is not easy to locate from above on first acquaintance.

Tides
The Temple Bay sport crags are tidal but most are accessible for around 6 hours at low water. With careful planning a long day of climbing is possible by working along the cliff line toward the headland as the tide falls, and then as the tide comes in work your way back again.

Conditions
The crags face due south and get lots of sun. They are sheltered from a northwesterly wind. The bases of the routes dry quickly once the tide has retreated although the caves can be damp if there is no breeze.

Temple Bay 237

Jay Astbury on the pumpy *Reverted Revisionist* (6a+) - *page 243* - typical of many of the steeper lines to be found at Temple Bay. With careful planning a long day of climbing is possible by working along the cliff line toward the headland as the tide falls, and then as the tide comes in work your way back again. Photo: Mark Glaister

Temple Bay — First Inlet

238 | Carmarthenshire | Gower | Inland and Coastal Limestone | The Valleys Sandstone

To mid afternoon — 15 min — Tidal

16m

First Inlet
A compact wall of excellent rock with a number of tough little lines, most of them having very fingery starts.
Approach - The inlet is tidal and can be climbed on for around 6 hours at low water. The inlet is the furthest wall of bolted lines towards the headland, just beyond an easy-angled ramp that leads to the fisherman's ledges above the cliff.
Conditions - The base of the cliff takes a little time to dry once the tide has gone out.

1 Long Awaited **6c**
The wall left of the right-leaning arete with the crux low down on some super sharp holds.
FA. Roy Thomas, Graham Royle 1988

2 Fools Rush In . . **6c+**
The wall and right-leaning arete starting up *Long Awaited*.
FA. Roy Thomas, Graham Royle 10.1988

3 Lasting Impressions **E3 5c**
The leaning corner.
FA. Mick Learoyd, Roy Thomas, Stuart Robinson, Dave Meek 21.9.1986

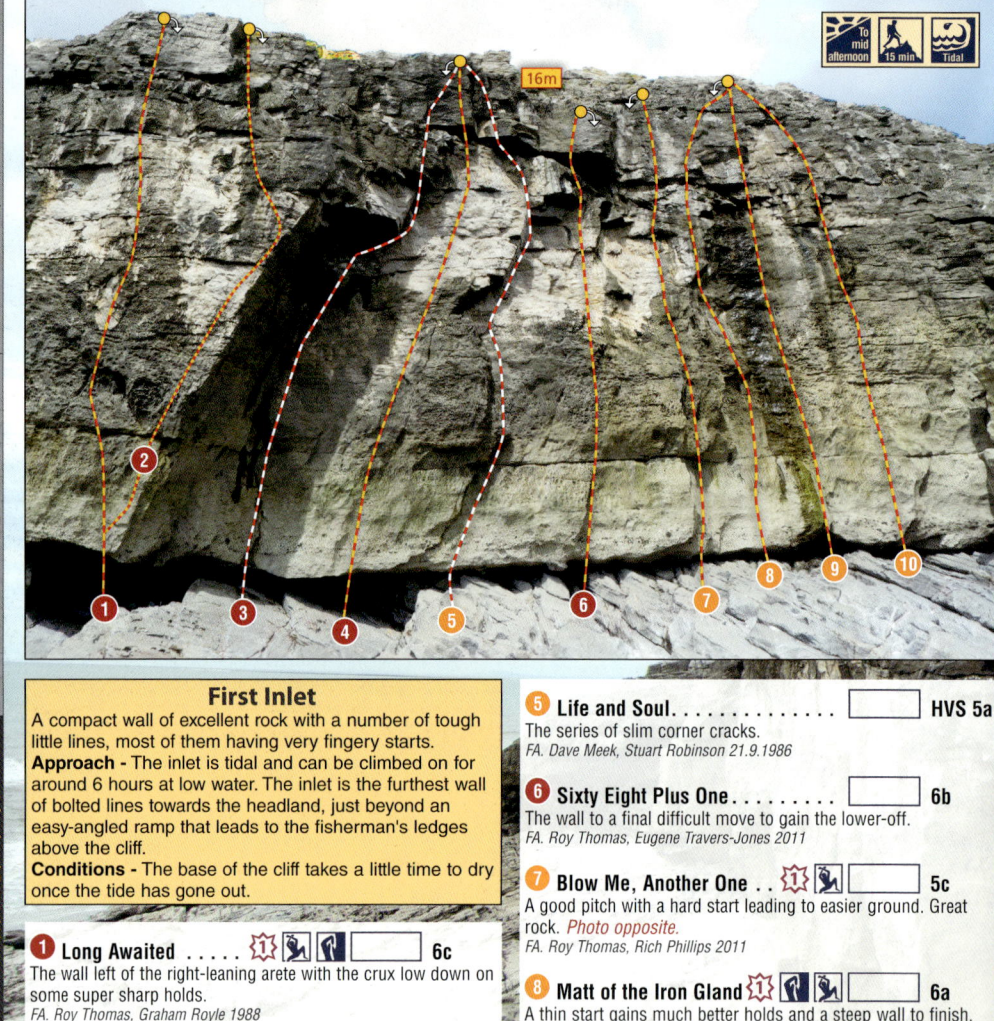

4 Dross of 86 . . . . **6b**
A perplexing start to pass the lower bulge gains good holds on the upper wall.
FA. Roy Thomas, Rich Phillips 2010

5 Life and Soul . . . . **HVS 5a**
The series of slim corner cracks.
FA. Dave Meek, Stuart Robinson 21.9.1986

6 Sixty Eight Plus One **6b**
The wall to a final difficult move to gain the lower-off.
FA. Roy Thomas, Eugene Travers-Jones 2011

7 Blow Me, Another One . . **5c**
A good pitch with a hard start leading to easier ground. Great rock. *Photo opposite.*
FA. Roy Thomas, Rich Phillips 2011

8 Matt of the Iron Gland **6a**
A thin start gains much better holds and a steep wall to finish.
FA. Roy Thomas, Rich Phillips 2010

9 Wreckers Bay . . . . **6a+**
The gold-coloured wall on comforting pockets heads up to a steep finish.
FA. Roy Thomas, Goi Ashmore 2010

10 Surly Temple . . . . . . **6a+**
The wall left of the ledge on the right, again with a hard start.
FA. Roy Thomas 1986

First Inlet **Temple Bay** 239

Bridget Collier on the golden-coloured rock of *Blow Me, Another One* (5c) - *opposite* - at the First Inlet, Temple Bay. The Inlet is home to some enticing lines on superb rock. Photo: Mark Glaister

Temple Bay — Second Inlet

Second Inlet

A series of short, but punchy and sharp pitches. The rock is very good but will take its toll on soft skin.

Approach - Walk along the beach until the wall is seen next to a big boulder that sits on the rock platform. The easy ramp that leads up to the fisherman's ledges above the cliff is just to the left.

Descent - Routes 1 to 10 and 14 and 15 have belay bolts set back from the edge - use a long sling to set up a lower-off. This can be set up and retrieved by an easy scramble up to the fisherman's ledges on the left. The other routes have lower-offs in place.

Conditions - The base of the cliff takes a little time to dry out once the tide has gone out. The routes on the left-hand side of the wall get less sun.

❶ Themis is Out of Order . . . . **6a+**
The leftmost bolt-line of the wall is a tricky number.
FA. Roy Thomas, Eugene Travers-Jones 23.11.2014

❷ Alchemy of Error **6a**
Climb the leaning wall to a big jug and less steep face above.
FA. Roy Thomas, Rich Phillips 25.3.2015

❸ OW! **7a**
As the name implies a very sharp experience, with the hardest moves between the first and second bolts.
FA. Eugene Travers-Jones, Roy Thomas 23.11.2014

❹ 300 Spartans **6b**
Climb the compact prow on its left-hand side.
FA. Roy Thomas, Goi Ashmore 5.2013

❺ Sliced Up at Thermopylae **6a**
The right-facing groove is very sharp.
FA. Roy Thomas, Eugene Travers-Jones 23.9.2014

❻ Minsir **6c**
Climb the awkward groove and burly bulge to a lower-off on the ledge above - sharp and steep.
FA. Eugene Travers-Jones, Goi Ashmore 12.10.2014

❼ Leonidas' Last Breakfast . . . . . **6a+**
The wall just to the right of the groove of *Minsir*.
FA. Roy Thomas, Eugene Travers-Jones 16.9.2014

❽ Tip Ripper **6c**
A hard bouldery start. Undercut, bridge, crimp and lurch to a shared lower-off with *Achilles Hasn't A Foot to Stand On*.
FA. Roy Thomas 2013

❾ Achilles Hasn't a Foot to Stand On
. . . . **6b+**
Opposite the boulder is a shallow arete with a tiny 'tooth' of rock at the base. Follow the arete and face above.
FA. Roy Thomas, Eugene Travers-Jones 2011

❿ Euclid's Theorem **6a**
Climb the wall to the right of the shallow arete of *Achilles Hasn't a Foot to Stand On*. Shared lower-off.
FA. Roy Thomas 2011

Second Inlet Temple Bay   241

11 Gift of the Gods . . . . 🧗 ☐ **6b+**
The fingery wall with just one bolt. Walk off.
FA. Goi Ashmore 4.8.2011

12 Gods of Long Ashton . . . . ☐ **6a**
The left-hand thin crack. Shares bolts with the next line.
FA. Roy Thomas 2011

13 The Dark Force of Glamorgan . . ☐ **6a**
The right-hand crack. Shares bolts with the previous line.
FA. Roy Thomas 2011

14 It's all Greek to me . . . . ☐ **5c**
Juggy barnacle-encrusted pulling. Use a long sling on bolts on the ledge for a lower-off.
FA. Roy Thomas 2011

15 One Less for the Spoiler . . . . . ☐ **4c**
The arete. Use a long sling on bolts on the ledge for a lower-off.
FA. Roy Thomas 1987

The next set of routes are on the wall just to the right of the huge boulder.

16 Medusa Spares No Head . . . . . ☐ **6a+**
The left-hand line has a tricky finish.
FA. Roy Thomas, Eugene Travers-Jones, Goi Ashmore 12.10.2014

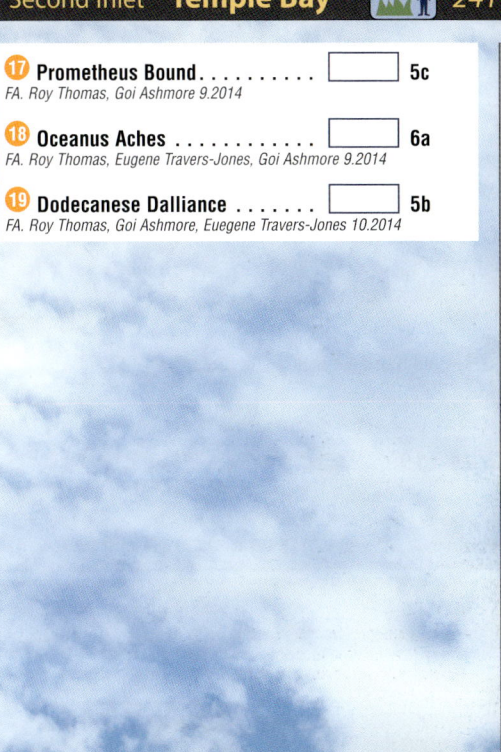

17 Prometheus Bound . . . . ☐ **5c**
FA. Roy Thomas, Goi Ashmore 9.2014

18 Oceanus Aches . . . . ☐ **6a**
FA. Roy Thomas, Eugene Travers-Jones, Goi Ashmore 9.2014

19 Dodecanese Dalliance . . . . ☐ **5b**
FA. Roy Thomas, Goi Ashmore, Euegene Travers-Jones 10.2014

Temple Bay — Cave Inlet

Cave Inlet

These two good sections of cliff are dotted with caves and offer well-bolted routes with some exhilarating lines. Many of the routes take reasonably steep ground with good juggy rails that favour long arms and short legs.

Descent - Most of the routes have lower-offs. Routes 1 and 2 and 10 to 12 have belay bolts set back from the edge - use a long sling to set up a lower-off. This can be set-up and retrieved by an easy scramble up to the fisherman's ledges on the left.

Conditions - The caves can be damp if the sun has not been out or the weather is humid.

1 The Barnacle Bill 6b
The steep, short and crusty hanging arete. Long sling needed for lower-off.
FA. Roy Thomas, Rich Phillips 30.9.2014

2 Canaan Grunts .... HVS 4c
The barnacle-encrusted chimney is trad. Walk off or use a long sling on the lower-off of *The Barnacle Bill*.
FA. Roy Thomas, Nick O'Neill 4.7.2014

3 Hundred Years of Reflection
.... 6b+
Upside down barnacle pulling leading to the ledge of *Zacchaeus Repents* - finish up direct to a chain lower-off.
FA. Roy Thomas, Nick O'Neill 8.2014

4 Dulce Et Decorum Est ... 6b+
Make very steep moves from the right-hand side of the cave around and onto the wall before joining and finishing as for *Hundred Years of Reflection*.
FA. Eugene Travers-Jones, Roy Thomas 23.9.2014

5 Zacchaeus Repents .... 6b+
Move up and then out left to steep rib and ledge. Head up and back right to a shared lower-off with *Chargeable Event*.
FA. Roy Thomas 2011

6 Chargeable Event 6a
Up the barnacles to some fun steep moves and a lower-off in the corner.
FA. Roy Thomas 2011

7 Lips Off My Shofarot 6a+
Climb easily up the lower wall and make a powerful pull up into the hanging corner. Finish up the corner by some technical bridging. *Photo on page 247.*
FA. Roy Thomas, Rich Phillips, Rich Leyshon 2011

8 Lane Discipline .... 6a+
Head up the easy lower wall, from where steep and committing moves are needed to pass the overhang.
FA. Roy Thomas, Rich Phillips, Rich Leyshon 26.4.2014

Up and right is another cave that is less tidal.

9 Hogging the Mid Lane .. 6b
Good juggy climbing taking the line just left of the upper cave, with one long move.
FA. Roy Thomas, Eugene Travers-Jones 8.3.2014

10 Life in the Slow Lane ... 6b+
Steep stuff up the left-hand overhanging arete.
FA. Roy Thomas, Goi Ashmore 12.4.2012

Cave Inlet **Temple Bay** 243

11 Quiet Flows The Jordan . . . . . . ☐ 5b
Steep climbing up the right-hand side of the cave.
FA. Roy Thomas 2011

12 Sultan's Spring . . . . ☐ 5c
The wall just right of the cave needs a leg-up or jump for the first holds.
FA. Roy Thomas 1987

13 Blowing The Ram's Horn. . . . . . ☐ VS 4c
The slim corner is trad.
FA. Roy Thomas, Graham Royle 1986

14 Climb a Sycamore Tree. . . . . . . ☐ HVS 5a
Move easily up to a hanging arete and then steeply up this to finish via ledges.
FA. Roy Thomas 1987

15 Tumbledown . . . . ☐ HS 4b
Start up *Climb a Sycamore Tree* and then take the ramp right.
FA. Roy Thomas 1986

16 Consequentialist Perfectionism . ☐ HVS 5a
Make some steep but juggy pulls to ledges.
FA. Roy Thomas 1987

17 Nietzche's Niche . . . . . . ☐ 5c
Spectacular climbing. Short and pumpy moves passing a couple of overhangs.
FA. Roy Thomas, Rich Phillips 8.2012

18 Reverted Revisionist ☐ 6a+
Similar in style and quality to *Nietzche's Niche*.
Photo on page 237.
FA. Roy Thomas, Eugene Travers-Jones 28.7.2012

19 Cartesian Dualism . . . . . ☐ 5b
Climb just left of the leaning prow and right of the cave.
FA. Roy Thomas 2012

20 Descartes' Dithers . . ☐ 5c
The leaning prow is a good outing. *Photo on page 244.*
FA. Roy Thomas 2012

21 Archimedes Screws . . . . ☐ 6a+
Wild moves over the big overhangs.
FA. Roy Thomas 2012

22 The Burning Glass . . . . . ☐ 6b
Move up *Siege of Syracuse* and then power up direct after the first overhang.
FA. Roy Thomas, Eugene Travers-Jones 10.2012

23 Siege of Syracuse . . . . . ☐ 6b
Very steep pitch taking a series of rails and overhangs on good but spaced holds. A fine climb.
FA. Roy Thomas, Goi Ashmore 23.8.2012

Temple Bay

Temple Bay 245

Rosy Klinkenberg on *Descarte's Dithers* (5c) - *page 243* - at the Cave Inlet, Temple Bay. Temple Bay presents a long line of low tidal crags that offer plenty of sport climbs which vary in style from thin fingery walls to strenuous stacked overhangs as pictured here. Photo: Mark Glaister

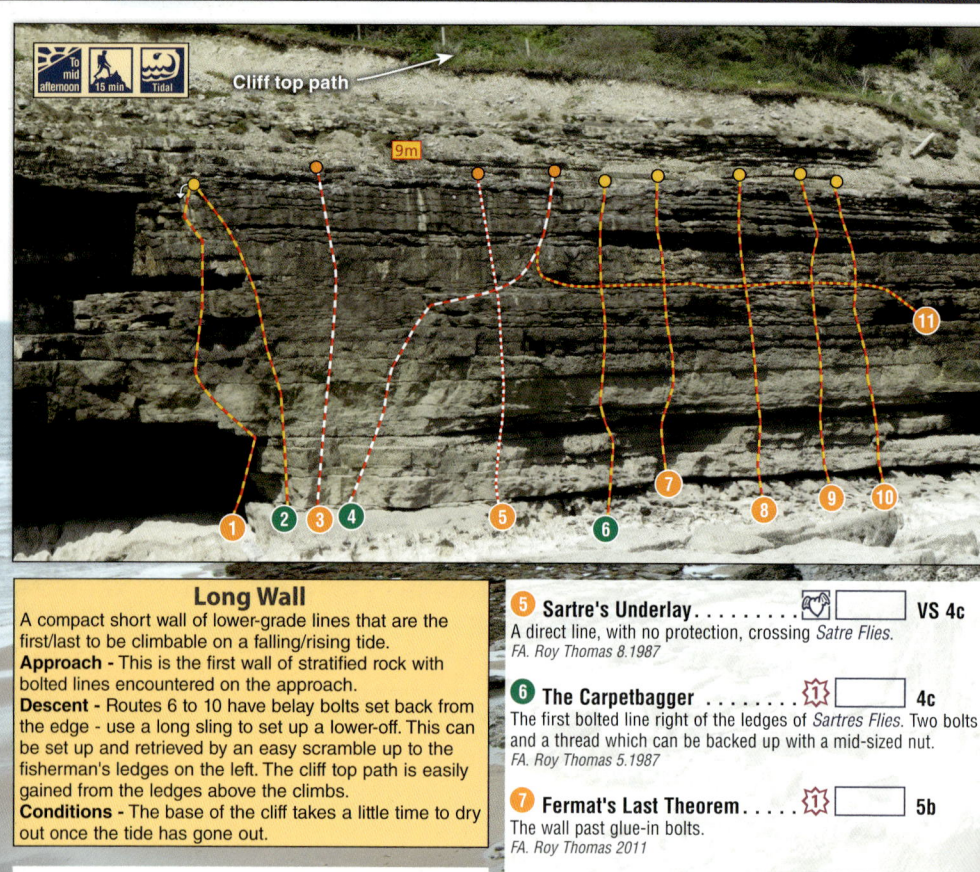

Temple Bay Long Wall

Long Wall

A compact short wall of lower-grade lines that are the first/last to be climbable on a falling/rising tide.

Approach - This is the first wall of stratified rock with bolted lines encountered on the approach.

Descent - Routes 6 to 10 have belay bolts set back from the edge - use a long sling to set up a lower-off. This can be set up and retrieved by an easy scramble up to the fisherman's ledges on the left. The cliff top path is easily gained from the ledges above the climbs.

Conditions - The base of the cliff takes a little time to dry out once the tide has gone out.

1 Socrates Sucks 5c
Climb the left-hand side of the arete avoiding the ledges on the left. The roof at the start is tough.
FA. Roy Thomas 2011

2 Kant Hooks 4c
Not as easy as it looks, better (and a bit harder) if done direct without reaching out to the right. Nice climbing.
FA. Roy Thomas 2011

3 Rude Buoys . . . . HS 4a
Climb straight up the wall avoiding easy ground on the right.
FA. Joe Gallacher, Matt Moore 23.6.2015

4 Sartre Flies . . . . Mod
The right-leading line of ledges is an easy way to get to the top.
FA. Roy Thomas 2011

5 Sartre's Underlay . . . . VS 4c
A direct line, with no protection, crossing *Satre Flies*.
FA. Roy Thomas 8.1987

6 The Carpetbagger 4c
The first bolted line right of the ledges of *Sartres Flies*. Two bolts and a thread which can be backed up with a mid-sized nut.
FA. Roy Thomas 5.1987

7 Fermat's Last Theorem 5b
The wall past glue-in bolts.
FA. Roy Thomas 2011

8 Orestes' Suffering . . . . 6a+
A sharp and hard starting sequence.
FA. Roy Thomas 2011

9 Electra's Revenge 5c
Past some threads high up.
FA. Roy Thomas 2011

10 Probing Proctologist 6a
The final line on the right. Climb left of the bolts at the grade.
FA. Roy Thomas, Rich Phillips 8.2012

11 Heading for a Sea of Tears 5c
A right-to-left girdle finishing as for *Sartre Flies*. A good outing when the tide is in.
FA. Nick O'Neill, Roy Thomas 2012

Temple Bay 247

John Warner in the finishing corner of *Lips Off My Shofarot* (6a+) - *page 242* - at The Cave Inlet, Temple Bay. Photo: Mark Glaister

Castle Upon Alun

	No star	⭐	⭐⭐	⭐⭐⭐
up to 4c	2	-	-	-
5a to 6a+	3	2	-	-
6b to 7a	4	5	4	-
7a+ and up	-	-	-	-

An old quarry located in a tranquil setting that has a number of its walls developed. The majority of the well established climbing is on a steep slab of excellent well-bolted limestone and offers some hard, thin and fingery routes. If the wall has not been climbed on regularly some of the climbs become dirty and will probably need a brush.

Approach   Also see map on page 175

Approaching from Bridgend, turn left off of the B4265 into the village of Ewenny (signed Corntown). Follow the road past a shop and go right at a fork towards Wick. Follow the road keeping right at another fork to a small junction by a house. Turn right here and go down the lane to a parking spot on the right just before a ford. Cross the ford and walk along the road to a viaduct. 200m beyond the viaduct a cobbled track on the right leads uphill to a gate. 30m beyond the gate take a vague path on the right. The path contours around the wooded hillside below a small escarpment, and passes a fence to arrive at the top of the wall. Walk down rightwards to gain the base of the quarry.

GPS 51.469648 -3.571808

Conditions

The walls faces northwest and see little sun, but dry fairly quickly as the quarry is sheltered and takes little seepage. Some of the climbs may need a clean unless they have seen regular traffic.

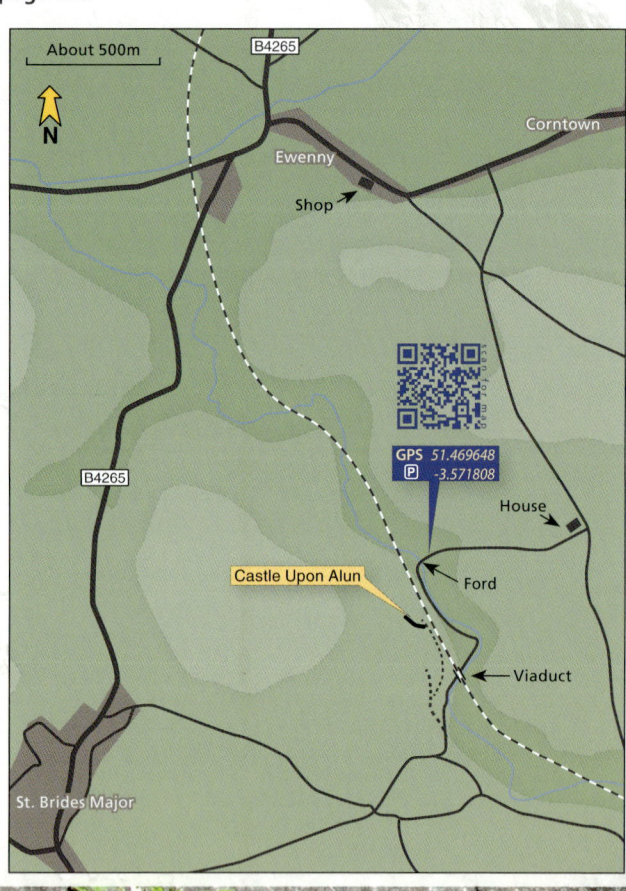

Castle Upon Alun 249

Jay Astbury on the testing *A Freem of White Horses* (6b) - *page 250* - at Castle Upon Alun. The crag is a steep slab of excellent rock that is home to some fine technical climbs. Photo: Mark Glaister

Castle Upon Alun

Castle Upon Alun
A steep slab that has some worthwhile and fingery lines, plus a newer set of walls with easier lines on the right.
Approach - The approach path is down the right-hand side (looking out) of the crag.
Conditions - The walls have a shady aspect and see little sun. Humidity can be a problem.

1 Jump on the Gravy Train 4c
The first short bolted line on the left.
FA. Roy Thomas 8.2016

2 Off the Rails 4c
Stay on the line to avoid a small amount of shattered rock.
FA. Roy Thomas 2005

3 The Fat Controller 5c
Climb the wall just left of an arete directly behind the tree.
FA. Roy Thomas 2005

4 Scrape the Bottom of the Barrel . 5c
The blocky corner moving right over the roof.
FA. Roy Thomas, Eugene Travers-Jones 28.7.2016

5 Eugene Genie 7a
Follow the initial line of bolts with a thin start and hard finish.
FA. Eugene Travers-Jones 1995

6 Cordoba Express 6c+
Start up *Eugene Genie* and, at its first bolt, move up and right to a jug. From the jug finish direct on still tricky ground.
FA. Roy Thomas 1995

7 Matalanafesto 6c
A direct start to *Cordoba Express* past two bolts.
FA. Goi Ashmore 29.5.2005

8 Barry Freight ... 6b+
A thin initial sequence gains some better holds that allow a fairly direct line to be followed on the upper wall.
FA. Roy Thomas 1995

9 A Freem of White Horses 6b
A good pitch when clean. Move up to a shallow hole and then make fingery pulls up the wall on edges and pockets.
Photo on page 248.
FA. Andy Freem pre -1991

10 California Freeming . 6b
An excellent exercise. Reasonable holds lead to a well-defined slot. Reach for a crack and finish direct to a lower-off.
FA. Andy Freem pre-1991

11 Pubic Enema ...... 6b+
Climb direct to a poor crack that leads to a square-cut groove.
FA. Roy Thomas 1995

12 Freeming of Jeannie ... HVS 5a
Climb the right-leaning thin crack and finish by moving into the bolt line of *Branch Line*.
FA. Andy Freem pre-1991

13 Branch Line 6a
Thin climbing at the start. Unfortunately this line gets dirty.
FA. Roy Thomas 1995

There are three moss covered projects to the right.

14 Anal Retention 6c
Up and right of the alcove at the base of the crag is a white section of rock. Climb this by technical moves.
FA. Roy Thomas 1995

15 Banal Pretention 6c
Gain a slot by a technical sequence and continue with difficulty.
FA. Roy Thomas 1995

16 The Trainspotter 6b
A tricky start, but easier above.
FA. Roy Thomas 1995

17 Trolley Service Suspended .. 6b
Make a difficult mantleshelf move to gain widely spaced holds.
FA. Roy Thomas, Matt Hurst 13.8.2016

18 Weak Lemon Drink .... 6b+
A difficult start is followed by a dyno for a big triangular pocket.
FA. Roy Thomas 1995

Castle Upon Alun — 251

19 In The Sidings .... ☐ **6a**
The last vertical line on the wall at the top of the bank.
FA. Roy Thomas, Giles Davies 26.7.2016

20 Top Rail .... ☐ **6b**
Start as for *In The Sidings* and then make a rising hand traverse left, finishing at a lower-off in a small corner.
FA. Roy Thomas, Eugene Travers-Jones 8.2016

On the far side of the quarry are more lines.

21 Harris's List .... ☐ **4b**
A stepped series of walls and ledges leads to a high lower-off.
FA. Dai Emanuel 24.9.2016

22 Freeming at the Gusset .... ☐ **6a**
The left side of the wall, passing some large orange scars.
FA. Roy Thomas 9.2016

23 Freempie .... ☐ **5c**
Takes the short wall, ledge and final layback of *Freeming at the Gusset*.
FA. Roy Thomas, Ed Chapman 15.9.2016

24 Galena Puts Lead In Your Pencil
.... ②☐ **5c**
The rib and crack to a lower-off right of a high roof.
FA. Roy Thomas, Goi Ashmore 31.8.2016

25 Plum Bob .... ①☐ **5b**
An easy start leads to a short groove.
FA. Roy Thomas, Goi Ashmore 31.8.2016

26 Burton Line .... ①☐ **5b**
The groove to the right of *Plum Bob*, starting direct via a rail.
FA. Roy Thomas, Ed Chapman, Jon Wollacot 1.9.2016

27 Quadcam of Solice ...... ①☐ **5b**
Follow the left-trending crack-line.
FA. Roy Thomas, Dai Emanuel 17.9 2016

28 Crack Liqour .... ①☐ **6b+**
The crack in the short wall just right of *Quadcam of Solice*.
FA. Roy Thomas, Rich Phillips Gavin Leysham 23.9.2016

29 The Freem Team .... ☐ **5b**
Gain and climb the right arete of the pillar.
FA. Roy Thomas, Rich Phillips Gavin Leysham 23.9.2016

The next lines are on the wall to the right.

30 Sticky Fingers .... ☐ **4c**
Start as for the following then step left to a layback crack.
FA. Roy Thomas, Nick O'Neill, Rich Phillips 9.9.2016

31 Fickle Finger of Fate ...... ☐ **4c**
The groove to a tree/sling lower-off on the right.
FA. Roy Thomas, Nick O'Neill 7.9.2016

32 Knuckle Down .... ☐ **4a**
The groove to a lower-off on the right shared with *Ring Finger*.
FA. Roy Thomas, Nick O'Neill 4.10.2016

33 Ring Finger .... ☐ **4c**
Climb a shattered groove, avoiding a loose block at the top.
FA. Roy Thomas, Nick O'Neill 4.10.2016

34 Finger Flicking Good ...... ☐ **5c**
The layback crack to a shared belay with *Fingertip Mistress*.
FA. Roy Thomas, Rich Phillips 4.10.2016

35 Fingertip Mistress .... ①☐ **6a**
Gain and climb the crack left of the roof of *Knee Trembler*.
FA. Roy Thomas, Rich Phillips 4.10.2016

36 Knee Trembler .... ①☐ **6b**
Start up *Bush Trimmer's Corner* and then take the overhangs to its left.
FA. Roy Thomas, Eugene Travers-Jones 25.9.2016

37 Bush Trimmer's Corner .... ①☐ **5c**
FA. Roy Thomas, Rich Phillips Gavin Leyshon 23.9.2016

The Valleys Sandstone

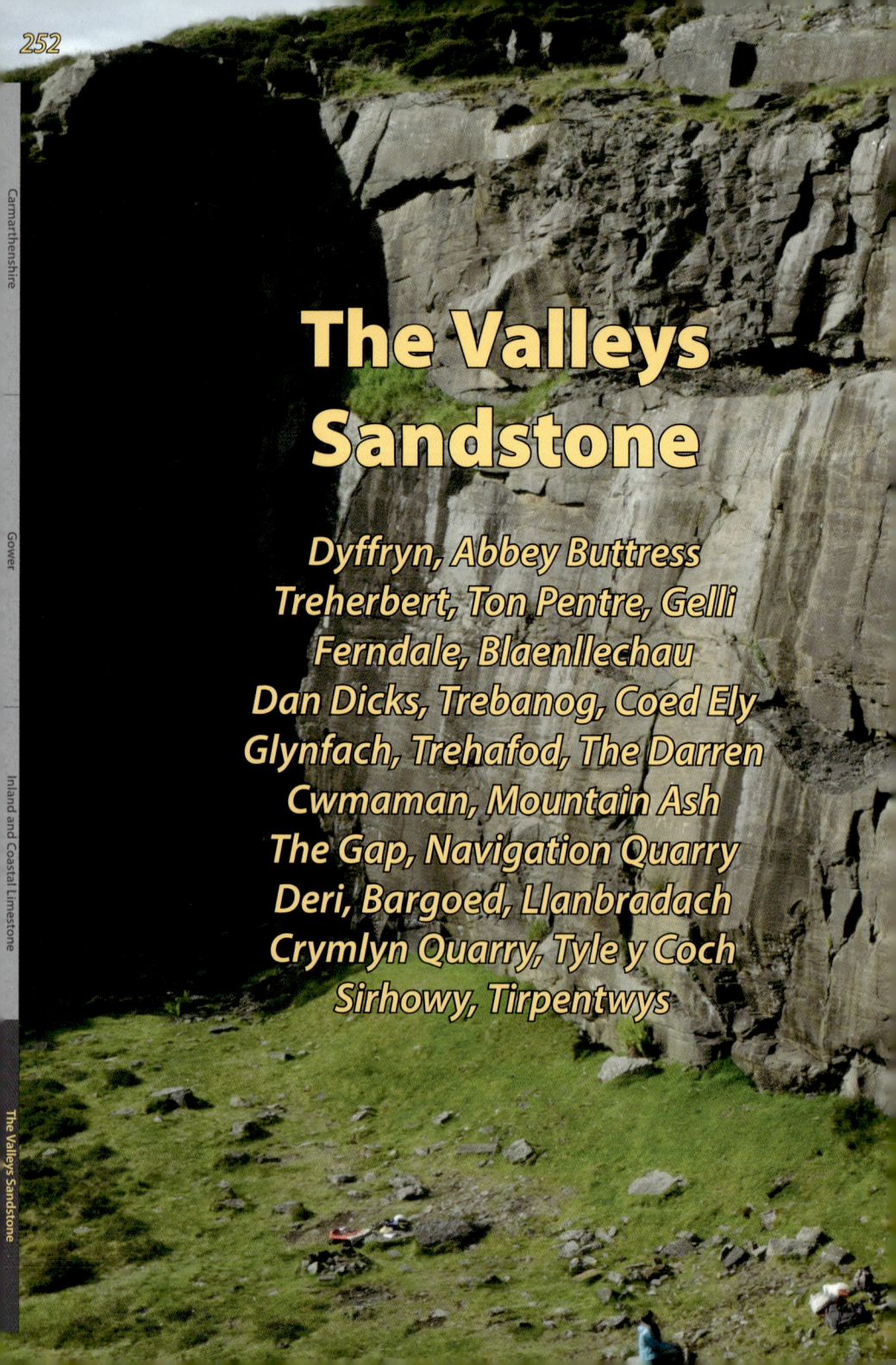

Dyffryn, Abbey Buttress
Treherbert, Ton Pentre, Gelli
Ferndale, Blaenllechau
Dan Dicks, Trebanog, Coed Ely
Glynfach, Trehafod, The Darren
Cwmaman, Mountain Ash
The Gap, Navigation Quarry
Deri, Bargoed, Llanbradach
Crymlyn Quarry, Tyle y Coch
Sirhowy, Tirpentwys

John Warner mid-crux on one of the Valleys' classic sandstone lines *Western Front Direct* (7a) - *page 332* - at Navigation Quarry. Photo: Mark Glaister

254 The Valleys Sandstone — Area Map

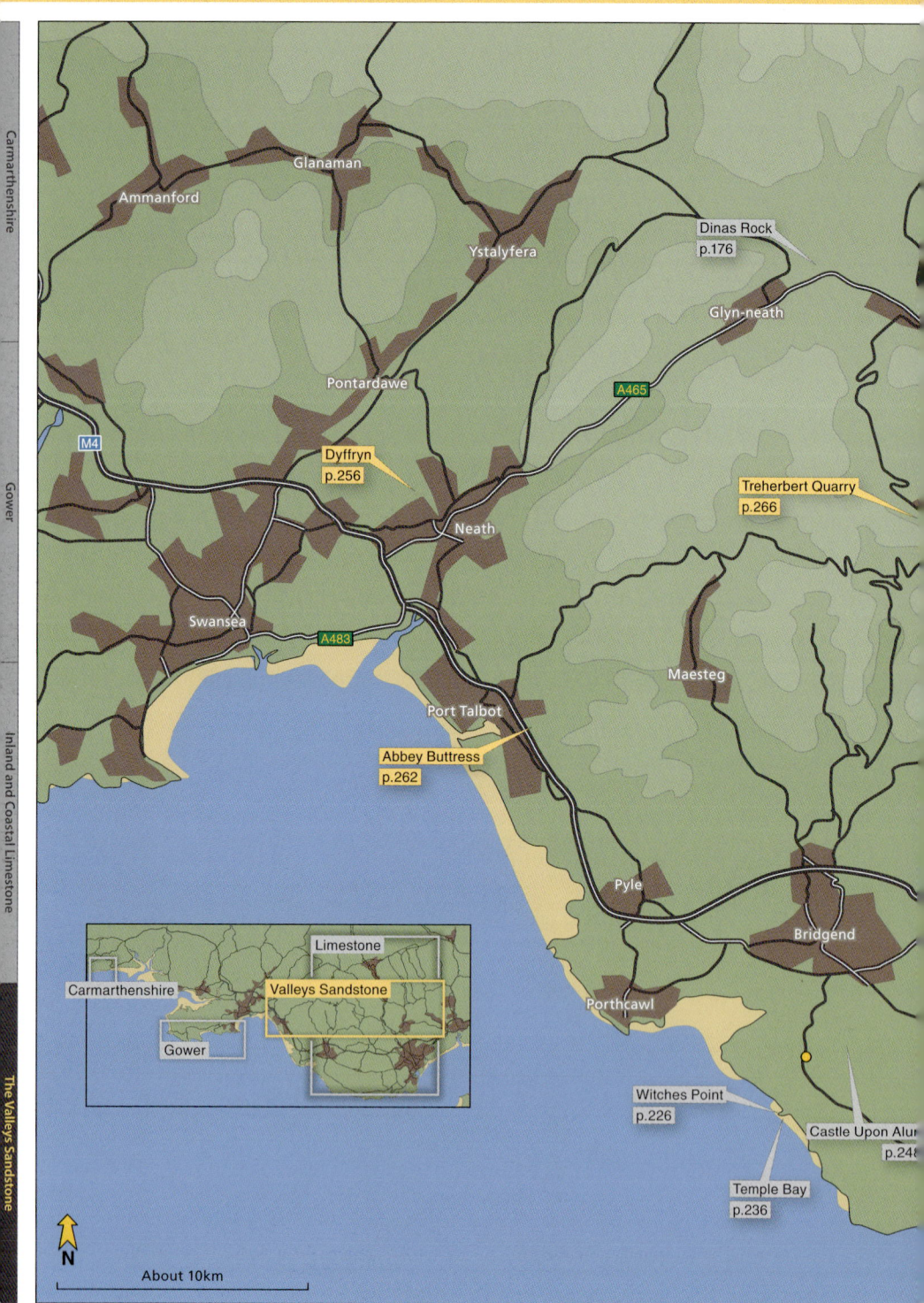

Area Map: The Valleys Sandstone

- Abergavenny
- Gilwern p.214
- Ebbw Vale
- Tredegar
- Merthyr Tydfil
- Mountain Ash p.312
- Aberdare
- Aberfan
- Cwmaman p.306
- herbert Quarry p.266
- Deri p.334
- Blaenllechau p.286
- The Gap p.320
- Bargoed p.336
- Crymlyn Quarry p.352
- Tirpentwys p.368
- Ferndale p.284
- Navigation Quarry p.328
- Pontypool
- Newbridge
- Tyle y Coch p.354
- Cwmbran
- Cwmcarn Forest camping
- Dan Dicks p.288
- Ton Pentre p.274
- Porth
- The Darren p.302
- Llanbradach p.340
- Gelli p.278
- Pontypridd
- Trehafod p.298
- Sirhowy p.358
- Trebanog p.290
- Glynfach p.296
- Caerphilly
- Newport
- Coed Ely p.292
- Llantrisant
- Taff's Well p.194
- Taff's Well West p.206
- Cardiff
- Penarth
- Barry
- Llantwit Major
- Sully Island — Bouldering - not described

Carmarthenshire · Gower · Inland and Coastal Limestone · The Valleys Sandstone

256 Dyffryn

	No star	⍟	⍟⍟	⍟⍟⍟
up to 4c	1	-	-	-
5a to 6a+	19	7	1	-
6b to 7a	6	10	1	-
7a+ and up	-	-	-	-

Matt Woodfield making some shapes on *Porno Text King* (6b) - *page 259* - one of many short but intense pitches to be found at Dyffryn. Photo: Stuart Llewellyn

Dyffryn

A quiet crag set high above the Neath valley that has a number of short climbs on generally good rock. The routes are almost exclusively fingery and technical, and what they lack in length, they make up for in intensity. This is a great place to brush up on technique and build up finger strength.

Approach   Also see map on page 254

From the M4 at Junction 43, drive northbound on the A465. Turn off after 3km, signposted to Neath, and take the first exit. At the next roundabout take the second left (the first is to Tesco) and continue to a double mini-roundabout. Go right up the hill and continue past two more mini roundabouts, some speed humps and the Clydach Hotel on the right. Just after a church, make a very sharp turn left onto a narrow lane. Drive down the lane which makes a sharp right - 300m after the sharp turn. Park just beyond a footpath sign on the left. Do not park further up this road. Walk up the road passing a gas installation on the left and stables on the right to enter Dyffryn Woods. At a junction of tracks go left and continue to another junction. Go straight on and in a few hundred metres, the crag will appear next to the track.

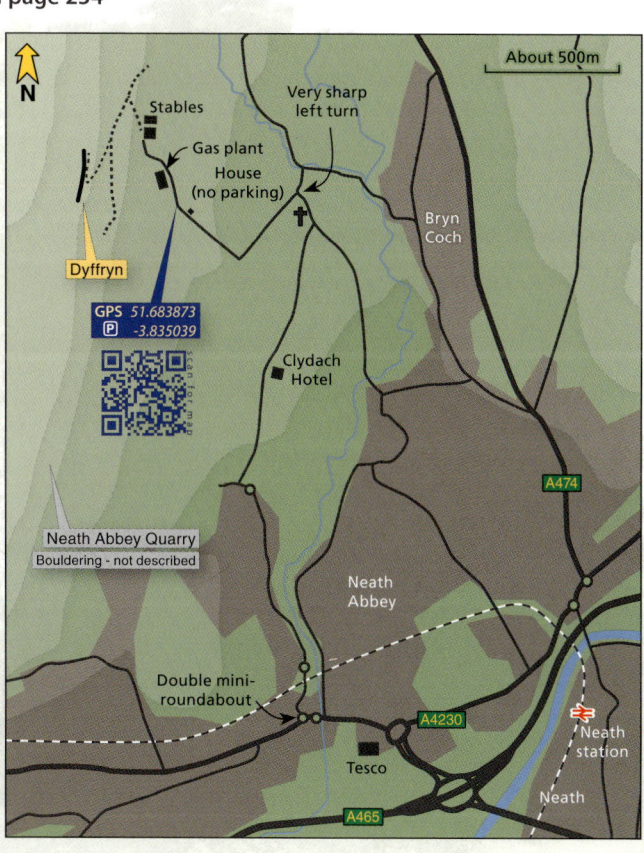

Conditions

The crag is sheltered from westerly winds and dries quickly. Nettles on the right-hand side of the crag can be a problem and a stick to bash them down might prove useful. It gets the sun until midday.

Access

Please park carefully as described - **no access is allowed by vehicle to the crag**. No camping or fires at the crag.

Dyffryn — Left

Left

The left-hand section of the quarry has a number of smart little lines that are both fingery and tricky to read - especially if not chalked up. The rock on the whole is solid and clean. A good place to give the fingers a workout.

Approach - The first wall and shady bay.
Conditions - Sunny in the morning but the left wall of the corner rarely gets any sun.
Access - Do not drive up to the crag. Absolutely no camping or fires.

The first route is 50m to the left of the quarry.

1 Sub Prime Market 4b
The small slabby wall to a single bolt lower-off.
FA. Roy Thomas, Goi Ashmore 2008

The front face of the jutting buttress gives five worthwhile routes on good rock.

2 Serendipity 5c
Follow the line marked out by a bolt and pegs.
FA. Roy Thomas 2007

3 Enigma 6b
The crimpy rippled wall to the left of a crack is good.
FA. Roy Thomas 2007

4 Who Dunnit 6a
The crack and niche is an awkward exercise.
FA. Roy Thomas 2007

5 You Dunnit 6b
The compact walls and bulges to the right of the crack are tackled via some positive horizontal slots.
FA. Gary Gibson 2007

6 Pocket Battleship ... 5c
A fine pitch up the rounded rib on positive but hard to see edges and a pocket.
FA. Roy Thomas 2007

7 Light Cruiser ...... 6a+
Take the wall and steep thin headwall just to the right of the arete of *Pocket Battleship*.
FA. Roy Thomas 2007

8 Dirty Deeds 5c
Climb the wall and headwall just to the left of the blocky crack. There is a low peg, but the line is fully bolted.
FA. Roy Thomas 2008

9 Get Your Fist In 5c
Climb the wall and then the wide crack.
FA. Roy Thomas 2008

Left Dyffryn 259

10 Leave it to me 7a
Follow the arching groove and wall above it.
FA. Matt Hirst 2007

11 Flue Liner 6a
When dry the rounded chimney corner gives a good exercise in three-dimensional movement.
FA. Roy Thomas 2007

12 Pot Black .... 6b+
A nice thin wall climbing just to the right of the *Flue Liner* chimney.
FA. Roy Thomas 2007

13 Slab Happy 6b
The slabby wall to the right of *Pot Black*.
FA. Roy Thomas 2007

14 Repetitive Strain Inquiry . 6a+
Climb to and up the arete right of *Slab Happy*.
FA. Roy Thomas 2007

15 Porno Text King 6b
Follow the wall and right-hand side of the pillar.
Photo on page 256.
FA. Roy Thomas 2007

16 Silent Mode 6a
The low overlap and short wall.
FA. Roy Thomas 2007

17 Rotters Club 5c
Start below a very strange looking initial bolt. Climb the small right-facing corner to a lower-off under the upper overhang.
FA. Roy Thomas 2007

18 Bad Bad Boy 6b
Start below another strange looking first bolt. Climb the wall to the overhang and pull up left onto the steep wall to finish.
FA. Roy Thomas 2007

19 Down the Drain 5b
The left-hand crack-line.
FA. Roy Thomas 2008

20 Our Man From Hyder 5b
The right-hand crack.
FA. Roy Thomas 2008

21 Mind like a Sewer .... HVS 5a
The rightward-curving crack at the end of the wall is trad.
FA. Myles Jordan, Nicola Ruddock 2007

Dyffryn — Right

Right

The right-hand side of the quarry continues the theme of short intense pitches, but these see less traffic due to the dense carpet of nettles that crop up in the summer. A nettle whacker would be a good addition to the equipment list.

Approach - The right-hand side of the quarry (often guarded by nettles).
Conditions - Sunny in the morning.
Access - Do not drive up to the crag. Absolutely no camping or fires.

1 Off to Oz 5b
The slabby wall on the far left past two pegs - old lower-off.
FA. Rich Phillips 2007

2 Ed's Triumph 5c
Climb straight up to the old lower-off shared with *Off to Oz*.
FA. Ed Rees 2007

3 Nick's Dilemma 6a
The thin crimpy wall to a final bulge.
FA. Roy Thomas 2007

4 Playing Away .... 6a+
Climb the seamed wall of blind cracks and grooves.
FA. Roy Thomas 2007

5 A Bit of Nokia on the Side 6b
Follow the curving grooves to a bulge and headwall. Big staples.
FA. Roy Thomas 2007

6 Barbara 6b
The broken looking line to a short upper groove.
FA. Gary Gibson 2007

7 Milky White 6a
The parallel seams sometimes hold grass.
FA. Roy Thomas 2007

8 Why Did I Bother .... 6b+
Inch up the slightly rounded rib.
FA. Roy Thomas 2007

9 Predictive Text 6b
The wall just right of *Why Did I Bother* is a good pitch.
FA. Roy Thomas 2007

10 Baggle Brook Affair 5b
A pleasant little slab, passing a pocket leads to a short corner.
FA. Roy Thomas 2007

11 Nifty Fingers 6a
The slabby wall to a break and then the leaning red wall above to finish.
FA. Roy Thomas 2007

12 Lip Service 6a
Climb over broken overlaps and ledges to the upper red wall.
FA. Roy Thomas 2007

13 Family Day 6b
The low overhang and grooves up the red wall to a lower-off above a grassy ledge.
FA. Roy Thomas 2007

14 Affairs of Man 6b
The wall/corner to a bulge and steep headwall above.
FA. Roy Thomas 2007

15 Supply on Demand 6b
Take a steep wall to a notch in a bulge that is passed on pockets.
FA. Roy Thomas 2007

Right **Dyffryn** 261

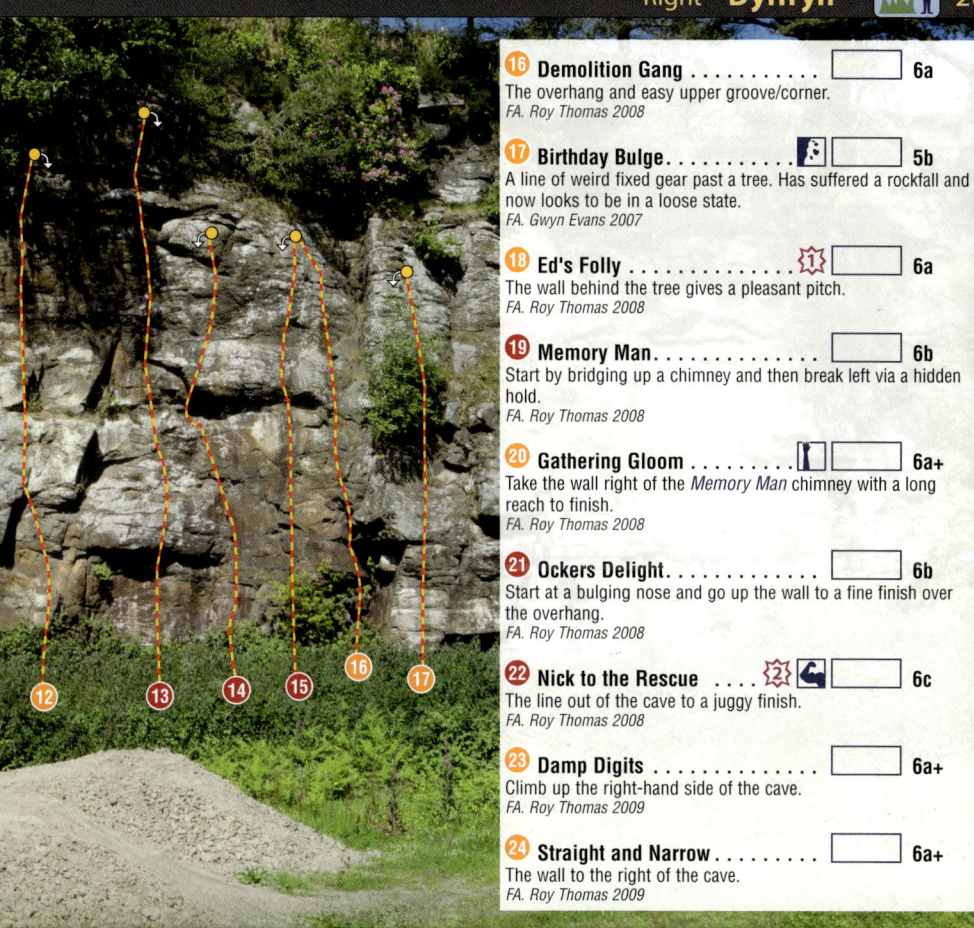

16 Demolition Gang .... ☐ 6a
The overhang and easy upper groove/corner.
FA. Roy Thomas 2008

17 Birthday Bulge .... ☐ 5b
A line of weird fixed gear past a tree. Has suffered a rockfall and now looks to be in a loose state.
FA. Gwyn Evans 2007

18 Ed's Folly .... ☐ 6a
The wall behind the tree gives a pleasant pitch.
FA. Roy Thomas 2008

19 Memory Man .... ☐ 6b
Start by bridging up a chimney and then break left via a hidden hold.
FA. Roy Thomas 2008

20 Gathering Gloom .... ☐ 6a+
Take the wall right of the *Memory Man* chimney with a long reach to finish.
FA. Roy Thomas 2008

21 Ockers Delight .... ☐ 6b
Start at a bulging nose and go up the wall to a fine finish over the overhang.
FA. Roy Thomas 2008

22 Nick to the Rescue .... ☐ 6c
The line out of the cave to a juggy finish.
FA. Roy Thomas 2008

23 Damp Digits .... ☐ 6a+
Climb up the right-hand side of the cave.
FA. Roy Thomas 2009

24 Straight and Narrow .... ☐ 6a+
The wall to the right of the cave.
FA. Roy Thomas 2009

Abbey Buttress

	No star	☆	☆☆	☆☆☆
Mod to S / 4c	-	-	-	-
HS-HVS / 5a-6a+	6	-	-	-
E1-E3 / 6b-7a	4	9	2	1
E4 / 7a+ and up	1	1	1	-

An interesting spot that is set high above the vast industrial complex of Port Talbot and the M4. Despite this, it is actually a pleasant place to climb and the restored routes are well worth a look. The cliff was guarded by huge banks of gorse for many years, but a good path has now been cut and the routes cleaned and re-equipped. A visit could easily be combined with one of the other crags in the area for an evening's climbing, or a perfect stopping off point on the way to or back, from Pembroke.

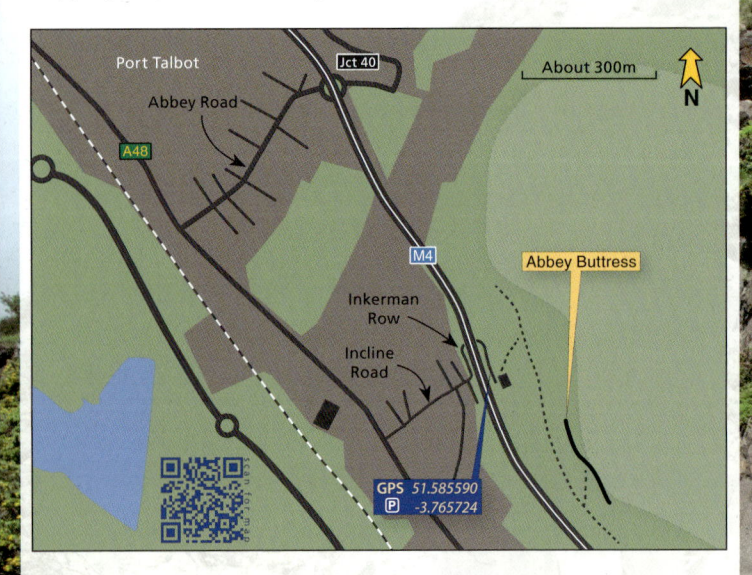

GPS 51.585590 -3.765724

Approach   Also see map on page 254
Leave the M4 at junction 40 and follow the signs for Port Talbot. At a T-junction, turn left onto the A48 and follow it for 700m and turn left onto Incline Road (this changes to Inkerman Row). Pass under the motorway bridge and park on the right before the bungalow and dog grooming business. Take the track just left of the bungalow and, after 100m, go right on a path that contours the slope. After 300m a path heads steeply up left through dense gorse to the quarry.

Conditions
The cliff is extremely open and exposed to any westerly or southwesterly winds. This does mean it dries quickly. The crag receives sun on its walls in the afternoon.

Access
Do not park in front of the bungalow or dog grooming business.

Abbey Buttress

Marti Hallett making the break on one of Abbey Buttresses best lines *Sign of the Times* (7a) - *page 264*. Abbey Buttress sits high above the M4 and looks out over the huge Abbey Steel Works complex. Despite this industrial outlook, it is a much more pleasant spot than might be imagined. Photo: Mark Glaister

Abbey Buttress

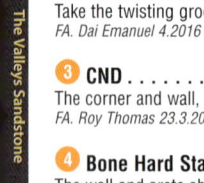

Abbey Buttress
A good vertical wall seamed with cracks and grooves. Some of the rock needs careful handling.

Approach - A path has been cut through the gorse bushes below and aids a quick but steep walk from the footpath.

Conditions - The wall faces west and is a perfect afternoon and evening venue. The crag dries quickly after rain, but can take seepage during the winter months and long periods of bad weather.

1 Community Spirit 5c
Move up the technical lower wall passing a ledge to gain the upper corner.
FA. Roy Thomas, Goi Ashmore 23.3.2016

2 Ta-Ta Tata 5c
Take the twisting groove and arete past a muddy ledge.
FA. Dai Emanuel 4.2016

3 CND 5c
The corner and wall, joining and finishing as for *Ta-Ta Tata*.
FA. Roy Thomas 23.3.2016

4 Bone Hard Start 6a
The wall and arete above the 'Bone and Anne' graffiti.
FA. Nick O'Neill, Roy Thomas 10.3.2016

5 Anne's Stiff Entry 6a
The right-hand finish to *Bone Hard Start*.
FA. Roy Thomas, Nick O'Neill 10.3.2016

6 Closed Shop .... 6b+
The left-leading ramp gains a series of cracks on the upper wall.
FA. Roy Thomas, John Bullock, Gwyn Evans, L.Moran 26.10.1986

7 Restrictive Practices E3 5c
Start up *Closed Shop* and take a thin crack and wall on the right.
FA. Roy Thomas, Graham Royle 30.9.1986

8 Gaz 316 .... 6b+
The wall past the mid-height break above the GAZ graffiti.
FA. Roy Thomas, Dai Emanuel 13.3.2016

9 Crack Basher E3 5c
The long snaking crack-line provides superb climbing.
FA. Roy Thomas, Graham Royle 28.9.1986

10 Sign of the Times 7a
The crack, flake and another crack on the left at the top.
Photo on page 263.
FA. Roy Thomas (1pt) 9.1986. FFA. Martin Crocker 18.10.1986

11 PR Job 7a
The line of hollow flakes and cracks.
FA. Martin Crocker, Roy Thomas 18.10.1986

Abbey Buttress

265

⑫ Urban Development 7a
The wall and finger-crack to a thin pull left to join *PR Job*.
FA. Roy Thomas, Graham Royle (1pt) 1986. FFA Martin Crocker 18.10.1986

⑬ Fe 500 . . . . 7a+
The continuation above the finger-crack of *Urban Development*.
FA. Eugene Travers-Jones 15.3.2016

⑭ Writings on the Wall . . . . 6b+
The hanging groove and leaf of rock.
FA. Graham Royle, Roy Thomas 9.1986

⑮ Stump Stroker . . . . 6c+
The steep hanging corner and leaning final wall passing a stump.
FA. Roy Thomas, Nick O'Neill 28.4.2016

⑯ Split the Equity . . . . 6b+
The steep flake-line and corner above a small cave.
FA. Roy Thomas, Graham Royle, John Bullock 4.1988

⑰ Hot Mill 7b
A tough testpiece via a very shallow leaning groove.
FA. Roy Thomas, John Bullock 1995

⑱ Pig Iron . . . . 6c+
The hard-to-read pillar right of *Hot Mill* to a shared lower-off.
FA. Roy Thomas, Nick O'Neill 2009

⑲ High Jinx 6b
Start as for *Pig Iron* then move right to the crack and a sting in the tail on the final arete.
FA. Roy Thomas, Eugene Travers-Jones 15.3.2016

⑳ Mud Lark Crack 6a
The line of bolts below *High Jinx*. Can be a bit dirty.
FA. Roy Thomas, Dai Emanuel 19.3.2016

㉑ Schmisse . . . . 6c+
Move up to a bolt and swing onto the arete. Climb the groove above via some technical moves.
FA. Dai Emanuel 19.3.2016

㉒ Industrial Relations E1 5b
The corner and crack-line in the tower.
FA. Graham Royle, Roy Thomas 9.1986

㉓ Chain Reaction 6b
The slab, gnarly groove and final arete.
FA. Roy Thomas, Goi Ashmore 17.3.2016

㉔ Cold Rolled . . . . 6c+
The isolated steep slab on the right. Delectable technicalities.
FA. Roy Thomas 1995

㉕ Nether Edge 7b
Not in Sheffield! The short arete with a desperate rockover.
FA. Eugene Travers-Jones 1997

Treherbert Quarry

	No star	☆1	☆2	☆3
Mod to S / 4c	1	1	-	-
HS-HVS / 5a-6a+	16	5	-	-
E1-E3 / 6b-7a	7	2	2	2
E4 / 7a+ and up	1	1	-	1

High above the small town of Treherbert, at the head of the Rhondda Valley, lies an excellent little quarry. The quarry is nicely situated with some fine climbing on good quality rock with routes mainly in the range from 5c to 7a+.

Approach   Also see map on page 254

From the main road - A4061 - that runs thorough Treherbert turn onto Station Road and park at the railway station. Cross over the railway line and go left for 100m to where a stream flows down from the right. Walk up to another track just above, cross the stream and then go right, up a gradually steepening track to a bench. Take a path on the left up through woods and when the edge of the quarry is reached, take a faint path left to below the first walls.

Conditions

The altitude and aspect of the quarry means that this is really only a warm weather venue, but the walls dry quickly and don't suffer from seepage. It gets limited sun from mid-afternoon onwards, except the Back Crag which sees the sun until mid-afternoon. It catches the wind and as such can be a good spot if the midges at other venues are out and about.

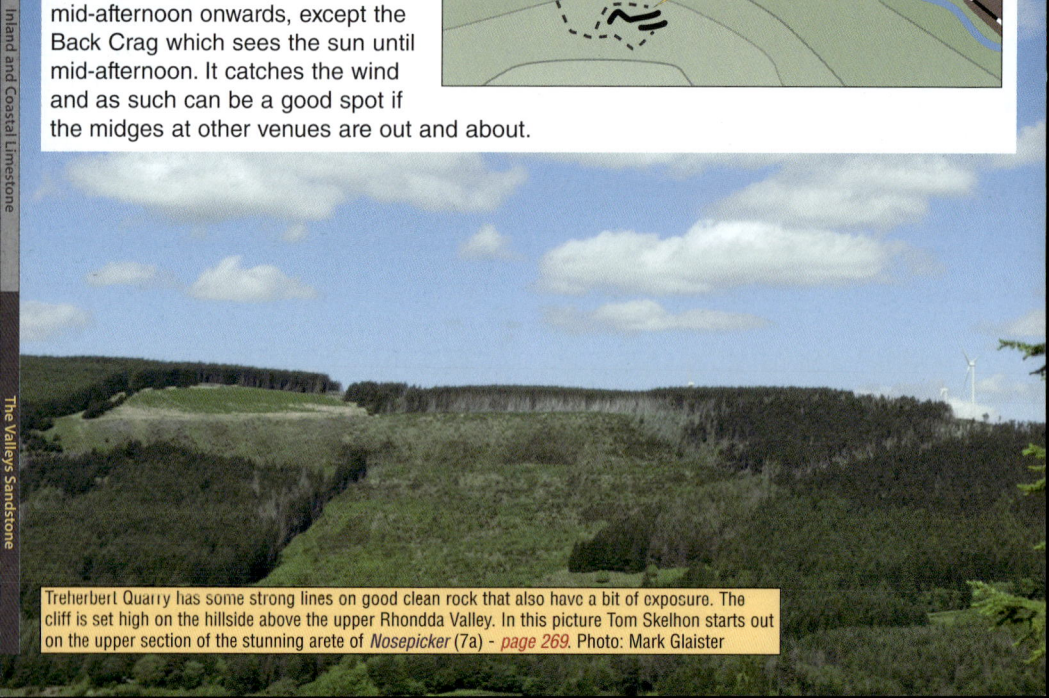

Treherbert Quarry has some strong lines on good clean rock that also have a bit of exposure. The cliff is set high on the hillside above the upper Rhondda Valley. In this picture Tom Skelhon starts out on the upper section of the stunning arete of *Nosepicker* (7a) - *page 269*. Photo: Mark Glaister

Treherbert Quarry   267

Treherbert Quarry — Main Wall

Main Wall
A long and indistinct section of cliff that has some reasonable pitches. and is worth tracking down once the best elsewhere has been sampled.
Approach - The first lines are at the far left end of the quarried wall, whilst the others require a short scramble up to the base of the crag.
Conditions - Fairly shady but the ribs get the sun earlier.

1 Spoilt Bastard 6a
The tall arete on the far left is a good line and has some fine positions.
FA. Roy Thomas, Goi Ashmore 22.6.2014

2 Uncle Eddie Meets the Modern Parents
. . . . 6a+
Move over the low bulge with some difficulty and continue up the front of the narrow wall to a hard ending.
FA. Roy Thomas 8.6.2014

3 Norman's Knob 6b
The face starting to the left of a chimney. A good first half.
FA. Roy Thomas 2014

4 Tally Whore! 5c
Climb the chimney formed by the huge boulder next to the main wall before moving left onto the face.
FA. Dai Emmanuel 2014

5 Student Grant 6a
Climb the wall and arete to the left of a thin crack. Move rightwards at the top to a lower-off.
FA. Roy Thomas, Rich Phillips 20.8.2014

6 Little Big EGO E2 6a
From the top of the huge boulder, step onto the wall and climb it to finish at the lower-off of *Student Grant*.
FA. Roy Thomas 20.8.2014

7 Biffa Bacon . . . . 6b+
The jamming crack, chimney and arete.
FA. Roy Thomas, Goi Ashmore 8.6.2014

8 Johnny Fartpants 6b
Avoiding the block, follow the wall left of the fist-crack into the chimney then bridge up the right wall to a lower-off.
FA. Roy Thomas, Eugene Travers-Jones 28.9.2014

9 Submerged by Blubber E2 5b
A trad crack and roof.

10 Scrotal Scratch Mix 6a
The bolted crack and roof.
FA. Roy Thomas, Rich Phillips 7.8.2014

Rhondda Pillar **Treherbert Quarry** 269

Rhondda Pillar

This fine buttress juts out from the main bulk of the crag and provides a small number of good pitches. One of the best bits of rock in the valley.

Approach - The prominent square-cut buttress as the cliff line bends around to the main quarried basin.

Conditions - Very exposed to the elements. The routes on the right get the sun in the afternoon but the rest only get evening sun.

11 Rowan Jelly 5c
The arete gives a fine line that is steep to get going.
FA. Roy Thomas, Rich Phillips 7.10.2013

12 Mint Sauce Dressing ... 6a+
The alternative start to the arete of *Rowan Jelly* is short but intense with hard-to-spot holds.
FA. Roy Thomas, Rich Phillips 7.10.2013

13 Lamb Leer Disease . E2 5c
The very appealing left-trending thin crack to a lower-off gets technical near the finish.
FA. Matt Ward, Martin Crocker 31.12.1988

14 Bizarre Geetar E3 6a
The left side of the arete past various bits of fixed gear. Lower-off in place on the right.
FA. Martin Crocker, Matt Ward 31.12.1988

15 Nosepicker 7a
The well-defined arete is tricky to get going on but eases after half-height. *Photo on page 267.*
FA. Martin Crocker, Roy Thomas 2.7.1989

16 Thumbsucker E5 6a
The finger-crack doesn't quite make it to the floor but is one of the best trad lines on the sandstone.
FA. Martin Crocker, Matt Ward 31.12.1988

17 Nailbiter 7a
The wall to the right of *Thumbsucker*.
FA. Martin Crocker, Roy Thomas 2.7.1989

Charlotte Macdonald taking on the pumpy leaning wall and cracks of the popular *Terry Forkwit* (6b) - *page 272* - at Treherbert Quarry. Photo: Mark Glaister

Treherbert Quarry 271

Treherbert Quarry — The Leaning Towers

① Drinks at 'The Dog and Hammer' — 5c
The wall left of the wide chimney.
FA. Roy Thomas 2014

② Billy the Fish — HVS 4c
The wide corner chimney.

③ Clock Sucker — 4c
Take the arete on the right of the chimney.
FA. Roy Thomas, Goi Ashmore 10.2013

④ Crock Licker — 6b+
The main arete of the tower is a cracking outing that maintains its interest to the final holds.
FA. Roy Thomas, Goi Ashmore 10.2013

⑤ Terry Forkwit — Top 50 — 6b
The centre of the leaning face is climbed on generally good but slightly spaced holds. *Photo on page 270.*
FA. Roy Thomas, Goi Ashmore 24.3.2014

⑥ Norbert Colon Meets The Fat Slags — 6a
The right-hand arete of the tower to finish at the *Terry Forkwit* lower-off.
FA. Roy Thomas, Dai Emanuel 18.5.2014

⑦ Buster Gonads — 5c
The first of the shorter bolted lines on the walls to the right of the leaning tower.
FA. Roy Thomas, Dai Emanuel 18.5.2014

⑧ A Fish Called Rhondda — 5c
The line of bolts left of the break. Named after a chip shop down in the valley.
FA. Roy Thomas, Goi Ashmore 26.6.2014

The Leaning Towers
These are the series of tower-like buttresses first encountered on the approach. The routes, although not of any great height, are pretty steep and pack in the moves.
Approach - The first buttress is just off of the main approach - a low wall that is actually a detached block.
Descent - Walking off is easy. Some of the shorter routes have bolts on top of the crag that can be used as a belay or to set up lower-offs.
Conditions - The routes are exposed to the elements, but get the afternoon sun.

Belay bolts on top of the crag. Lower-offs best arranged with long slings.

Back Crag Treherbert Quarry 273

9 Crescent Wanker 5c
The first line of bolts right of the break.
FA. Roy Thomas, Rich Phillips 7.10.2013

10 OMG She's a Squirter 5c
The centre of the wall via some good moves and rock.
FA. Roy Thomas, Rich Phillips 7.10.2013

11 The Day The Drill Conked Out . . 5b
The arete is one of the better shorter routes hereabouts.
FA. Roy Thomas 25.9.2013

12 Burning Brush . . . . 6b+
Takes the wall just to the right of the arete.
FA. Roy Thomas 25.9.2013

Back Crag
Tucked away from the main quarry is this steep wall which is worth a look and gets the morning sun.
Approach - Continue up the approach path behind the main quarry and then go left on a small path that leads down to the base of the wall.
Conditions - Back Crag gets the sun from first thing and is sheltered from the wind.

13 The Thin Drum. 4c
The long rib to the left of the main section of the crag.
FA. Roy Thomas 14.4.2014

14 Gallow's Step 5c
Start on a block and move up and out right to climb the arete.
FA. Roy Thomas, Eugene Jones 23.4.2014

15 Grunter Ass. . . . . 6b+
Climb direct up the wall to join and finish as for *Gallow's Step*.
FA. Roy Thomas, Gavin Leyshon 21.5.2014

16 Lynch 'Em. E5 6a
The slightly impending slim groove-line with little gear.
FA. Martin Crocker, Roy Thomas 2.7.1989

17 Exterminate All Bolt Thieves . . E4 6a
Climb past one high peg above a bad landing.
FA. Martin Crocker, Roy Thomas 2.7.1989

18 String 'Em Up 5a
The arete before moving left to a lower-off.
FA. Roy Thomas, Goi Ashmore 14.4.2014

19 Seb Eats Shite. . . . . 6a+
Care needed with the rock at the start.
FA. Roy Thomas, Goi Ashmore 14.4.2014

20 Coprophagic Canine. . . . . . . 6a+
Again take care with the rock at the start.
FA. FA. Roy Thomas, Goi Ashmore 21.4.2014

21 The Faecal Finger of Fate . . . . . 6a+
The wall direct on pockets.
FA. FA. Roy Thomas, Goi Ashmore 21.4.2014

22 Double or Squits . . . . 6a+
Move off of a block and ascend the blunt rib without deviation.
FA. FA. Roy Thomas, Goi Ashmore 21.4.2014

Ton Pentre

	No star	☆	☆☆	☆☆☆
up to 4c	-	-	-	-
5a to 6a+	5	1	-	-
6b to 7a	1	5	2	-
7a+ and up	-	-	-	-

Ton Pentre is a leaning wall of quarried rock that has a line-up of testing routes in a small bay. The crag is well bolted and gets plenty of sun from early in the day. It is easily combined with a visit to Gelli, which is just across the valley and similar in style.

Approach   Also see map on page 254

Follow the A4058 to Gelli Primary School (on the left) and then take the second right onto Green Hill. At its top turn left onto Uplands and then right onto Meadow Walk and park. Where Meadow Walk meets Oaklands Drive, take a path between houses and then go left. Walk along the level path, passing a gate after 350m, and the quarry entrance is 100m further on the right.

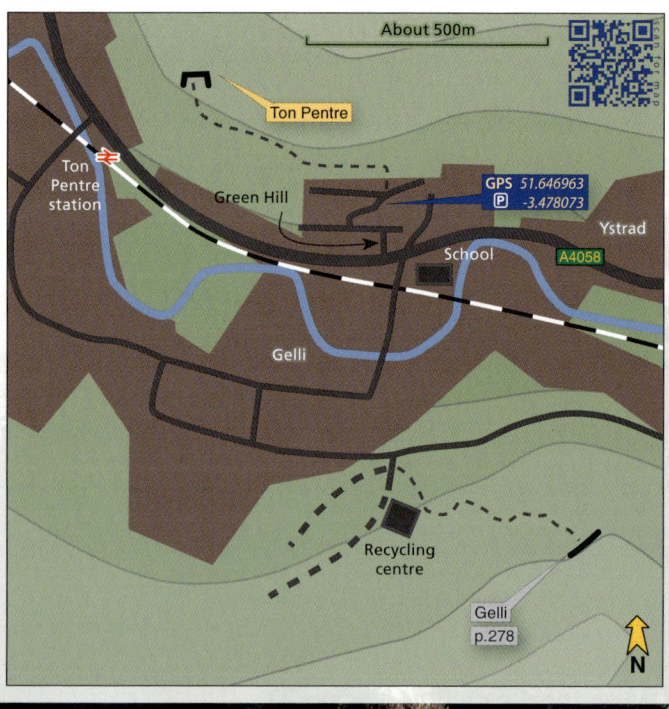

Conditions

The crag is sunny and sheltered but does seep after rain, although a couple of the routes might stay dry in light rain.

GPS 51.646963 / -3.478073

Ton Pentre 275

Nik Goile on *The Road to Nowhere* (6b) - *page 276* - on the leaning back wall at Ton Pentre. Photo: Stuart Llewellyn

Ton Pentre

Ton Pentre
Ton Pentre quarry is a quiet spot that gets plenty of sun and is easily accessed. The climbs on the main section of leaning wall are sustained and pumpy.
Approach - Walk along the footpath and the quarried bay is set back on the right.
Conditions - The main wall gets sun in the morning and is fairly sheltered from the wind. Once the sun goes off of Ton Pentre, Gelli is just coming into the sun.

1 Bland Of Four 6a
The first line on the far left of the crag.
FA. Roy Thomas, Eugene Travers-Jones 15.7.2013

2 Solihull Calling 6b
The steep wall has some very good climbing.
FA. Roy Thomas, Eugene Travers-Jones 2013

3 Alone and Blue .... 6b+
Good steep wall climbing.
FA. Roy Thomas, Graham Royle 1990

4 Help the Aged E1 5b
The crack is not bolted. It can easily be top-roped from the lower-off of *Alone and Blue*.
FA. Roy Thomas, Mick Learoyd 1990

5 Too Posh to Brush 6b
Climb a narrow pillar of rock between two cracks. There is a hard section close to the finish.
FA. Roy Thomas, Mick Learoyd 1990

6 The Road To Nowhere .. 6b
Follow a crack to hard moves on the upper section above the break.
Photo on page 275.
FA. Roy Thomas, Mick Learoyd 1990

Ton Pentre 277

7 April Fool 6c
Follow a crack-line up the lower wall and over an overhang at mid-height to a sloping shelf. Move left and up the stiff wall to finish.
FA. Mick Learoyd, Roy Thomas, Lyndsey Foulkes 1990

8 Spirt of Ystrad 7a
Start up the wall to the right of the crack-line of *April Fool* and make hard moves up onto the shelf at mid-height. Move up and slightly right to a lower-off.
FA. Mick Learoyd, Roy Thomas 1990

9 Tibial Plates Extension 5c
Take the left-hand side of the narrow slab and continue directly up the steep headwall.
FA. Roy Thomas 6.2013

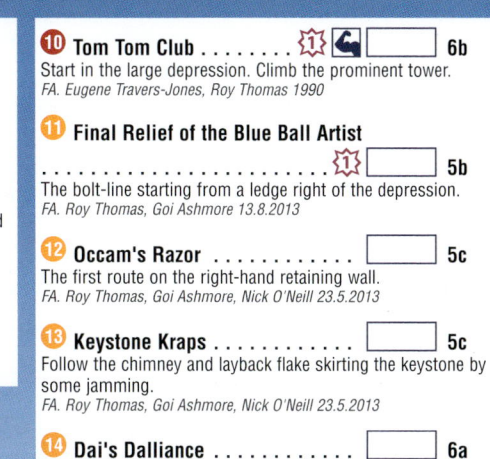

10 Tom Tom Club 6b
Start in the large depression. Climb the prominent tower.
FA. Eugene Travers-Jones, Roy Thomas 1990

11 Final Relief of the Blue Ball Artist
.... 5b
The bolt-line starting from a ledge right of the depression.
FA. Roy Thomas, Goi Ashmore 13.8.2013

12 Occam's Razor 5c
The first route on the right-hand retaining wall.
FA. Roy Thomas, Goi Ashmore, Nick O'Neill 23.5.2013

13 Keystone Kraps 5c
Follow the chimney and layback flake skirting the keystone by some jamming.
FA. Roy Thomas, Goi Ashmore, Nick O'Neill 23.5.2013

14 Dai's Dalliance 6a
The line to the left of the arete.
FA. Dai Emanuel, Roy Thomas 2013

Gelli

	No star	☐	☐	☐
Mod to S / 4c	8	1	-	-
HS-HVS / 5a-6a+	16	10	1	-
E1-E3 / 6b-7a	5	8	1	-
E4 / 7a+ and up	-	-	-	-

Above the town of Gelli is a long quarried crag on the upper level of a series of bays. This provides lots of pitches in the 5th and 6th grades. The outlook is excellent and the base of the crag clean and pleasant, although the start of the approach is a bit unpleasant, being up a dirty track next to some dilapidated sheds and stables. The routes are well bolted, clean and the rock is reasonable - a good spot on a summer afternoon, or a day combined with Ton Pentre.

Approach   Also see map on page 254
From Tonypandy on the A4058, drive past ASDA and turn left at the traffic lights onto the B4223 signed to Gelli. Take the road to the entrance of the Recycling Centre on the left and park just before or after it, where the road widens. Walk up a track just left of the recycling compound, past dilapidated sheds, and then on steep paths leftwards to the top quarry level where the climbing is located.

Conditions
The quarry is very exposed and is shady for much of the time, although it does get the late afternoon and evening sun in summer. There is no chance of climbing if it is raining.

Gelli 279

Nik Goile on *Ladyboy's Cage* (6a) - *page 282* - at Gelli. Photo: Stuart Llewellyn.

Gelli

Gelli
The climbing at Gelli is located on a long quarried level that sits at the top of the workings. The climbs are well bolted, but care is required with the rock on the less well travelled lines.

Approach - Walk to the very top level of the quarry workings and the developed walls are to the left.

Conditions - It is very exposed and only gets late afternoon sun in summer. There is no shelter from rain.

1 Jockey Club 6a
The first line on the left-hand side of the crag to a lower-off.
FA. Roy Thomas, Goi Ashmore, Eugene Travers-Jones 5.6.2013

2 Horses Bolted 6b
The wall and overlap to a shared lower-off with *Jockey Club*.
FA. Roy Thomas, Nick O'Neill 4.7.2013

3 Fools on Horses .... 6a+
The short steep black wall.
FA. Roy Thomas, Goi Ashmore 8.2012

4 Free Lunch 6c
A technical and bouldery start gains steadier ground above. Glue-in bolts.
FA. Ollie Burrows, Hazel Watchorn 22.5.2013

5 Stable Boy's Breakfast 6b
The short wall right of *Free Lunch* is a brief but worthwhile exercise.
FA. Roy Thomas, Goi Ashmore, Eugene Travers-Jones 5.6.2013

6 Green Arete .... HS 4a
The arete has a loose finish.
FA. Gary Lewis 1989

7 KES .... VS 4c
The wall to the right. Finish up *Green Arete*.
FA. Mick Learoyd 1989

8 Kestrel for a Knave 4a
Climb the easy-angled wall to the right of *KES*.
FA. Roy Thomas 17.6.2013

9 Joey's Full Pint .... S
The grubby corner.
FA. Gareth Tucker 2003

10 Mr Farthing .... S
The crack right of *Joey's Full Pint* behind the rowan tree.
FA. Roy Thomas 17.6.2013

11 Miss Halfpenny 4a
The red tower to the same belay as *Mr Farthing*.
FA. Roy Thomas 17.6.2013

12 Feeling Lucky 6a
The short arete left of the Y-crack of *Wot No Metal*. Take care with a large rectangular flake.
FA. Roy Thomas, Ed Rees 29.5.2012

13 What No Metal E1 5c
The Y-crack to the right of the arete is not bolted but there is a shared lower-off on the ledge that it finishes on.
FA. Roy Thomas, Graham Royle 1989

Gelli

14 **Little Treasure** . . . . 6a+
The concave wall to the right of the Y-crack of *Wot No Metal*.
FA. Mick Learoyd, Roy Thomas 1989

15 **Toil** . . . . HVS 5a
The thin crack-line just left of the larger grassier crack. Do not use the larger crack at this grade.
FA. Gary Lewis 1989

16 **My Little Pony's on the Job** . . . 5c
Climb the wall just right of the large grassy crack.
FA. Roy Thomas, Rich Phillips, Gavin Leyshon 5.2012

17 **Galvanised** . . . . 6a+
The flake-crack gives a good pitch.
FA. Roy Thomas, Mick Learoyd, Graham Royle 1989

18 **Long Forgotten** . . . . 6b+
A very hard initial section. The holds on *Galvanised* are out of bounds.
FA. Roy Thomas, Graham Royle 1989

19 **Hoarse Trader** 4c
The arete right of a pine tree in a crack.
FA. Roy Thomas, Ed Rees 29.5.2012

20 **Marinated Goat Cheese** 4a
Climb just right of *Hoarse Trader*.
FA. Roy Thomas, Ed Rees 29.5.2012

21 **Squeezing the Curd** 5a
Short pitch below *Marinated Goat Cheese*. Either continue up *Marinated Goat Cheese* or walk off.
FA. Roy Thomas, Nick O'Neill 2012

22 **The Babcock Test** 6b
A short thin climb between the cracks.
FA. Roy Thomas, Nick O'Neill 2012

23 **Titanium Man** E1 5b
The crack right of the chimney.
FA. Graham Royle, Roy Thomas 1989

24 **Cigarillo** 6b
Another crack.
FA. Mick Learoyd 1989

25 **Tobacco King** . . . . 6c+
The wall right of the cracks of *Cigarillo*. Stay off the flake to the right at this grade.
FA. Mick Learoyd, Lyndsey Foulkes, Roy Thomas 1990

26 **Down Under** 4c
The good looking slab is a pleasant climb with spaced bolts.
FA. Roy Thomas, Mick Learoyd, Lyndsey Foulkes, Graham Royle 1989

Gelli

27 Working to a Budget . . . . □ 4c
The two short stepped walls.
FA. Roy Thomas 26.5.2013

28 Hung Like a Donkey . . . . □ 6a
Climb the pleasing wall starting just to the right of a tree stump.
FA. Roy Thomas Goi Ashmore 22.5.2013

29 All Talk . . . . □ 6a+
A difficult route with a tricky move off a finger jam. Finish by moving left to a shared lower-off with *Hung Like a Donkey*.
FA. Roy Thomas, Dai Emanuel 5.2012

30 Talking Hoarse . . . . □ 5c
The shallow groove has a difficult start.
FA. Roy Thomas, Dai Emanuel 15.5.2012

31 Little Taff . . . . ⟨1⟩ □ 6a+
Follow the thin crack-line.
FA. Roy Thomas, Mick Learoyd, Lyndsey Foulkes, Graham Royle 1989

32 Stubborn as a Mule . . . . □ 5a
Climb the steepish crack to the right of *Little Taff*.
FA. Roy Thomas, Gavin Leyshon, Rich Phillips 3.6.2013

33 Hoarse Whisperer . . . . . . ⟨1⟩ □ 6b
The wall right of the crack of *Stubborn as a Mule*.
FA. Roy Thomas 2012

34 A Little Something I Prepared Earlier
. . . . ⟨2⟩ □ 6b
A good and sustained wall pitch left of the corner.
FA. Roy Thomas, Mick Learoyd, Lyndsey Foulkes 1989

35 Something That Came Up Much Later
. . . . □ 4a
The corner.
FA. Roy Thomas, Ed Rees, Dai Emanuel 29.5.2012

36 Unearthed . . . . □ HS 4b
The slab and crack moving left to a lower-off.
FA. Roy Thomas 1989

37 Ladyboy's Cage . . . . □ 6a
The large unstable flake right of the arete. *Photo on page 279.*
FA. Dai Emanuel, Ed Rees 29.5.2012

38 Worzel Budgie Spunker . . ⟨1⟩ □ 6b+
Thin crack climbing to a shared lower-off.
FA. Dai Emanuel 2012

39 Talking Shop . . . . □ 6a
Climb the crumbly arete to a shared lower-off with *Hoarse Breather*. Keep away from very loose ground to the left.
FA. Roy Thomas, Gavin Leyshon 6.2012

Gelli

40 Snorting Horse E1 5a
The left-to-right ascending crack. Clipping the surrounding sea of bolts is not allowed if you are tradding!
FA. Roy Thomas, Mick Learoyd, Graham Royle 1989

41 Hoarse Breather 5c
The wall above the ledge on good holds.
FA. Roy Thomas, Gavin Leyshon 6.2012

42 Worzel Cloaca Sniffer . . . 6a+
Good pumpy climbing to a lower-off at the top of the flared chimney, or head out right to a lower-off (on *Empty Talk*) which ups the grade to **6b**.
FA. Roy Thomas, Gavin Leyshon 24.7.2012

43 Empty Talk 6a
A worthwhile steepish little number.
FA. Roy Thomas, Nick O'Neill 20.5.2012

44 Gilding the Lily 6a
From the right-hand side of the raised ledge, move up to a small block roof and gain pockets in the wall above.
FA. Roy Thomas, Goi Ashmore 24.4.2013

45 Polishing the Turd 5a
Climb direct to a shared lower-off with *Gilding the Lily*.
FA. Roy Thomas, Goi Ashmore 15.5.2013

46 Ice Station Gelli . . . . 6a+
The crack that can be a little floral at times.
FA. Mick Learoyd 1989

47 One in Her Eye . . . . . . 6b+
The wall passing a hard section above the second bolt - pumpy above.
FA. Roy Thomas, Nick O'Neill 8.2012

48 Send in the Specials . . . . 6a+
Move left from the higher grassy ledge.
FA. Roy Thomas, Graham Royle, Mick Learoyd 1989

49 Hole in One 5c
A poor line on the far right starting from a high grassy ledge.
FA. Gary Lewis 1989

Following the track up and right to a bay gains an isolated line.

50 Donkey Work . . . . 6a+
The short wall on staple bolts.
FA. Roy Thomas, Rich Phillips, Ritchie Leyshan 22.5.2012

Ferndale

Ferndale quarry is located high above the valley that heads north from Porth. The crag has some reasonable faces that are well bolted, in pleasant surroundings and with an open outlook. The climbing is worthwhile, if little travelled. Ferndale faces east and gets the morning sun whilst across the valley Blaenllechau is west facing and picks up plenty of sun later in the day - combining a visit to both crags is easy.

	No star	★	★★	★★★
up to 4c	-	-	-	-
5a to 6a+	-	1	-	-
6b to 7a	1	3	2	-
7a+ and up	-	1	1	-

Approach   Also see map on page 254

From Porth, take the A4233 to Ferndale. In the middle of Ferndale the road dog-legs. At the dog-leg turn left and go up the road, past a couple of clubs, to a footpath sign on the left, just past the last house on the left. Park just beyond on the roadside and walk back to the footpath. Follow this uphill to a metal gate on the left. Go through the gate and take the right-hand path for 60m before breaking right up a faint path. Follow this up the hillside to the quarry floor - the main climbing area is 100m on the left.

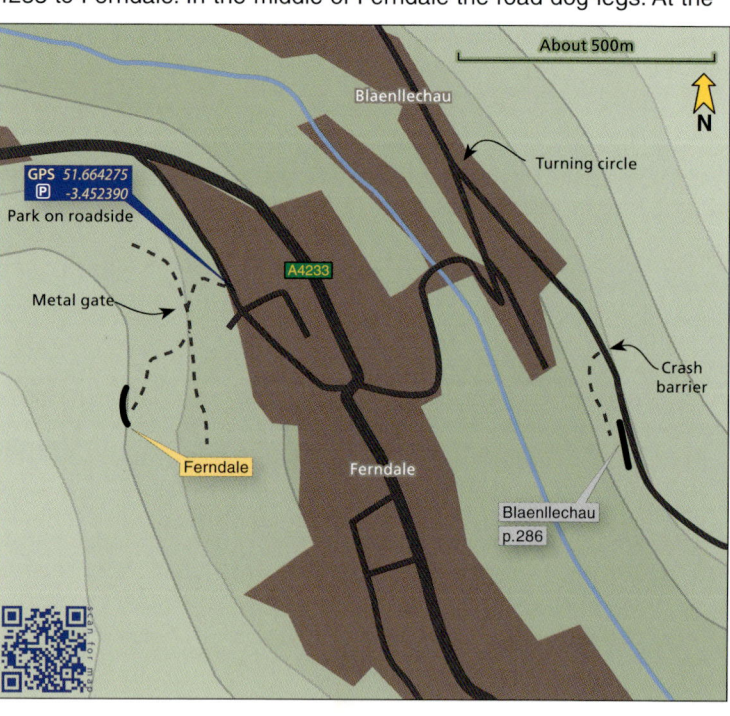

GPS 51.664275 -3.452390

Conditions

The quarry faces east, and gets the sun in the morning and is fairly sheltered from a westerly wind. Seepage is a problem after rain and during the winter months.

---

❶ Culture Vulture . . . . ★ ☐ 6b
Start up the rounded arete (high initial bolt) and make hard moves right before finishing up the wall. The route is slightly harder if started direct.
FA. Andy Sharp, Pete Lewis 15.4.1989

❷ Bucket of KFC and Two One Armers
. . . . ☐ 6b
The bolted line to the right of *Culture Vulture* sports a rattly hold at mid-height.
FA. Andy Sharp 2010

The next trio of lines (two sport and one trad) start from a higher ledge/terrace.

❸ Race You Up The Wallbars
. . . . ★ ☐ 7a+
A thin sequence up the central line on this wall. Start up just left of the initial bolt.
FA. Andy Sharp, Pete Lewis 8.4.1989

❹ Rhondda Ranger . . . ★ ☐ 7a
Climb the slabby wall just to the left of the thin trad crack of *Silent Movies*.
FA. Martyn Richards, Andy Sharp 26.5.2010

Ferndale 285

5 Silent Movies .... HVS 5a
The striking finger-crack in the centre of the wall to belay a at a tree. Abseil descent from the belay tree.
FA. Andy Sharp, Pete Lewis 1.4.1989

The next routes are around 50m to the right, past a tall triangular buttress.

6 Physical Presents 7b
Start up *By Appointment Only*, and at a big staple bolt, take the wall on the left via difficult moves to a shared lower-off.
FA. Andy Sharp, Pete Lewis 8.1.1989

7 By Appointment Only ...... 6c+
Start underneath a niche below a small roof midway up the wall. Climb up to the roof and move over it and up the wall direct to the top.
FA. Andy Sharp, Pete Lewis 1.4.1989

8 Nine Green Bottles......... 6c
The right-hand side of the wall to a shared lower-off. Start by coming in from the right.
FA. Pete Lewis, Andy Sharp 8.4.1989

The next sport line is 20m to the right.

9 La Digue............... 6c
The wall left of a crack.
FA. Martin Crocker, Roy Thomas 15.1.1989

Blaenllechau

Blaenllechau is a compact quarry that has some good lower-grade routes. The rock is solid, well bolted and the base of the crag pleasant and quiet. Take care following the approach description as the path from the road is easily missed.

	No star	☆	☆☆	☆☆☆
up to 4c	3	4	-	-
5a to 6a+	2	1	1	-
6b to 7a	-	5	1	-
7a+ and up	-	-	-	-

Approach   Also see map on page 254

From Porth, take the A4233 to Ferndale. In the centre of Ferndale the road dog-legs. At the dog-leg, turn right to Blaenllechau. Go up into the village and, at the shops, use a turning circle to make an extremely tight right turn onto Blaenllechau Road. Go up the road and park near the last houses. Walk up the road to the first (small) crash barrier and, 10m further on, go down a faint vegetated path onto the top of the grassy spoil heaps. Walk along these to the quarry.

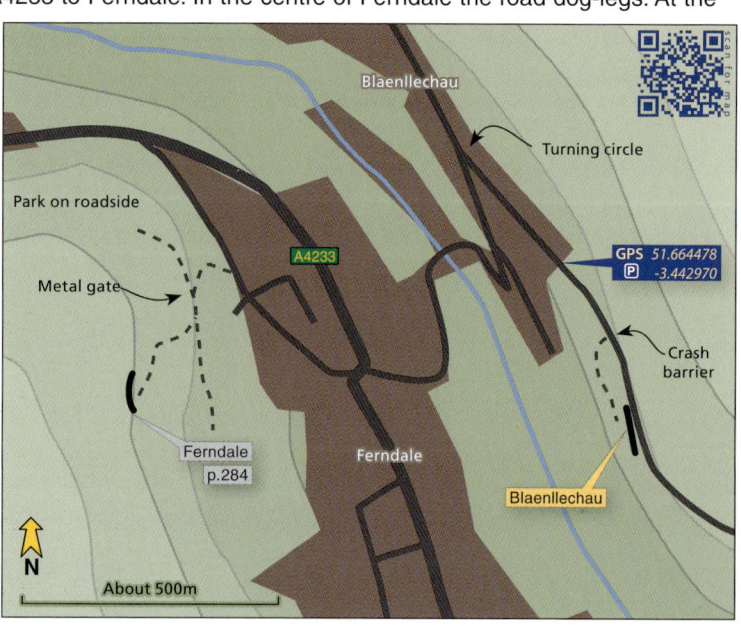

Conditions

The quarry faces west and gets the sun from midday onwards. However, the hillside is high above the valley floor and exposed to westerly winds. The faces dry quickly and seepage is not too much of a problem.

On entering the quarry, the first routes are found on a tall buttress on the left.

1 Dirtbag Arete ☆ **6b**
The wall left of the arete finishing on the left-hand side of the arete itself.
FA. Roy Thomas, Eugene Travers-Jones 6.2011

2 Electrolux .... **HVS 4c**
Climb the groove and wall to a shared lower-off.
FA. Simon Coles 8.2.1992

3 Dicky Dyson ☆☆ **5c**
The striking arete to the right of the *Electrolux* groove.
FA. Roy Thomas, Rich Phillips 6.2011

4 Dust Devil **5a**
The wide groove and right edge of the wall above.
FA. Roy Thomas, Ed Rees, Nick O'Neill 6.2011

5 Suction Power **4a**
The grassy and run-out staircase leading to the tree.
FA. Goi Ashmore 6.2011

The next set of routes are a little further on, the first lines being on a short rounded slab.

6 Raspberry Ripple ☆ **4c**
Climb the left edge of slab via a blunt arete.
FA. Roy Thomas, Ed Rees, Nick O'Neill 6.2011

7 Ripple Slab ☆ **3a**
As the name says. A nice little exercise.
FA. Ed Rees, Roy Thomas, Nick O'Neill 6.2011

8 Fairy Godmother ☆ **4c**
The far left line on this bit of the crag.
FA. Roy Thomas, Goi Ashmore 5.2011

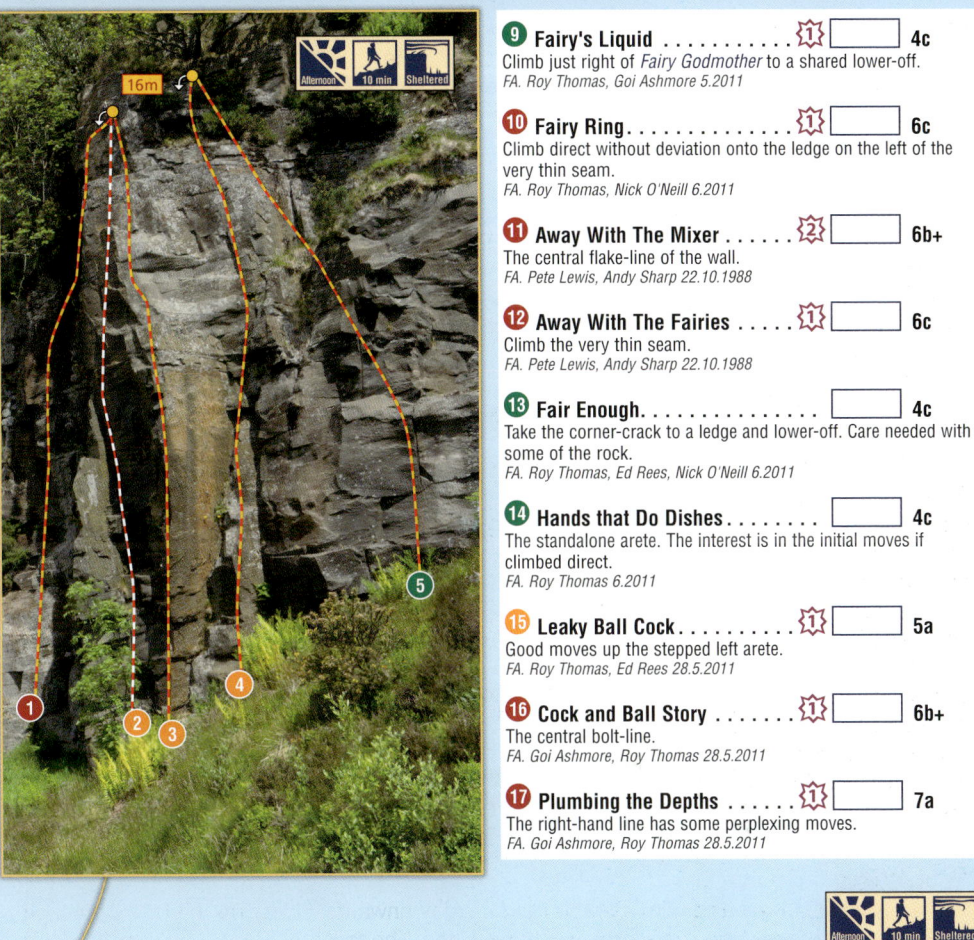

Blaenllechau 287

9 Fairy's Liquid 4c
Climb just right of *Fairy Godmother* to a shared lower-off.
FA. Roy Thomas, Goi Ashmore 5.2011

10 Fairy Ring 6c
Climb direct without deviation onto the ledge on the left of the very thin seam.
FA. Roy Thomas, Nick O'Neill 6.2011

11 Away With The Mixer ...... 6b+
The central flake-line of the wall.
FA. Pete Lewis, Andy Sharp 22.10.1988

12 Away With The Fairies 6c
Climb the very thin seam.
FA. Pete Lewis, Andy Sharp 22.10.1988

13 Fair Enough 4c
Take the corner-crack to a ledge and lower-off. Care needed with some of the rock.
FA. Roy Thomas, Ed Rees, Nick O'Neill 6.2011

14 Hands that Do Dishes 4c
The standalone arete. The interest is in the initial moves if climbed direct.
FA. Roy Thomas 6.2011

15 Leaky Ball Cock 5a
Good moves up the stepped left arete.
FA. Roy Thomas, Ed Rees 28.5.2011

16 Cock and Ball Story .... 6b+
The central bolt-line.
FA. Goi Ashmore, Roy Thomas 28.5.2011

17 Plumbing the Depths 7a
The right-hand line has some perplexing moves.
FA. Goi Ashmore, Roy Thomas 28.5.2011

Dan Dicks

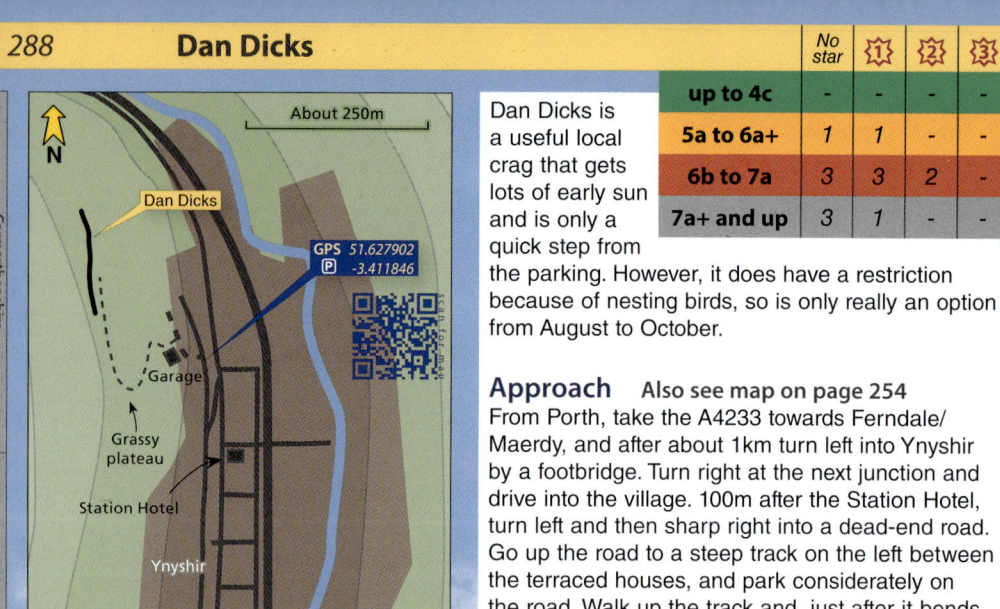

	No star	⭐1	⭐2	⭐3
up to 4c	-	-	-	-
5a to 6a+	1	1	-	-
6b to 7a	3	3	2	-
7a+ and up	3	1	-	-

Dan Dicks is a useful local crag that gets lots of early sun and is only a quick step from the parking. However, it does have a restriction because of nesting birds, so is only really an option from August to October.

Approach   Also see map on page 254
From Porth, take the A4233 towards Ferndale/Maerdy, and after about 1km turn left into Ynyshir by a footbridge. Turn right at the next junction and drive into the village. 100m after the Station Hotel, turn left and then sharp right into a dead-end road. Go up the road to a steep track on the left between the terraced houses, and park considerately on the road. Walk up the track and, just after it bends right, take a path that begins on the right of a padlocked garage. Follow the path behind the garage and then leftward to reach a grassy plateau. Head right and the quarry is quickly reached.

Conditions
The quarry is low lying and faces southeast, receiving plenty of sun until early afternoon.

GPS 51.627902 -3.411846

Dan Dicks   289

❶ **Steely Dan** . . . . 🧗 **7b**
The wall and slab with some very thin moves midway.
FA. Martyn Richards, Andy Sharp 9.2009

❷ **Rhod Above the Bridge** **6b**
The long corner groove finishing on the left - move right to gain the lower-off.
FA. Dai Morris, Andy Sharp 9.2009

❸ **Road Whore** **7a**
Climb the groove of *Rhod Above the Bridge* and finish direct.
FA. Andy Sharp 9.2009

❹ **Banjo Versus The Pigeon** . . . **6b**
Climb *Rhod Above the Bridge* and finish on the right.
FA. Dai Morris 9.2009

❺ **Catch The Pigeon** **6b**
Follow the arete just right of *Rhod Above The Bridge*.
FA. Dai Morris, Andy Sharp, Pete Lewis 9.2009

❻ **Tricky Dickie Takes a Sickie**
. . . . 🧗 **7b+**
At the first bolt of *Catch the Pigeon*, step right and climb the blank wall without drifting back into *Catch the Pigeon*.
FA. Martyn Richards, Andy Sharp 10.2009

❼ **The Corner** . . . . **HVS 5a**
The full-height corner holds plenty of vegetation.
FA. John Harwood, Andy Sharp 4.1991

❽ **Dan'ds-Inferno** **6b**
Climb the arete to the right of *The Corner*.
FA. Andy Sharp, Pete Lewis 9.2009

❾ **Sweet Whistling Geronimo** . . **7a**
Start up the narrow corner and finish up the fine arete.
FA. Andy Sharp, Dai Morris 7.2009

❿ **Dixienormous** . . . . **7a+**
Climb the wall to the right of *Sweet Whistling Geronimo* and finish up the arete as for *Sweet Whistling Geronimo*.
FA. Martyn Richards, Andy Sharp 9.2009

⓫ **Dan Dix** **6a**
The wall 16m to the right of *Dixienormous*.
FA. Andy Sharp, Pete Lewis 4.1991

Just to the right is a bay with some routes on both walls.

⓬ **Whistle Dixie** . . . . **7a+**
The bolted line up the left side-wall.
FA. Andy Sharp 9.2009

⓭ **Speechless** **6c**
The thin crack in the right wall.
FA. Andy Sharp, Dai Morris 8.2009

⓮ **Pre Nups** . . . . **6b+**
Climb the right arete, moving left to a shared lower-off with *Speechless*.
FA. Martyn Richards, Andy Sharp 8.8.2009

Access - No climbing 1st March to 31st July because of nesting birds.

Trebanog

	No star	★	★★	★★★
up to 4c	-	-	-	-
5a to 6a+	-	-	-	-
6b to 7a	2	4	1	-
7a+ and up	-	1	-	-

Trebanog is a small edge of partially quarried rock that sits close to the village in an exposed position. The rock is excellent and has both trad and sport pitches, all of which are relatively popular given their moderate height. The rock is good, well-weathered sandstone that dries out very quickly. There are lots of lower-grade trad lines here, but the sport pitches described here are well worth a quick visit.

Approach   Also see map on page 254

From the A4058 in Porth, turn towards Trebanog at some traffic lights. Continue for about 1.5km to the traffic lights on the A4233 in the middle of Trebanog. Turn right towards Edmondstown and the crag is on the right after 200m, just above the road. Park on the street and walk up the short grass slope to the base. The sport routes are to the left.

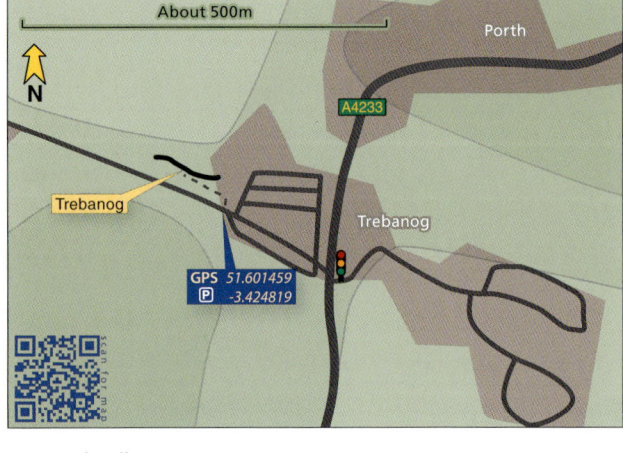

Conditions

The edge is open and exposed to the elements, but gets plenty of sun, dries quickly and does not seep badly.

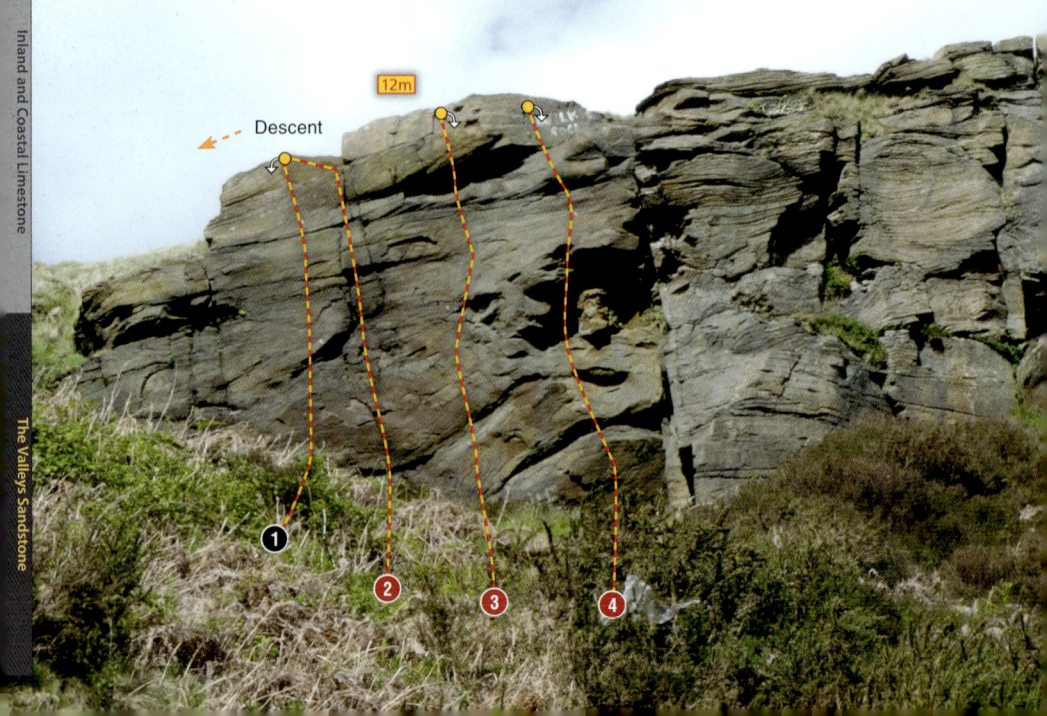

Trebanog   291

❶ March Of Progress . . 🔲🪝🧗 ▭ **7b**
The featureless wall left of the *For Your Hands Only* crack has a tough crux sequence. Using holds in *For Your Hands Only* reduces the grade.
FA. Andy Sharp, Pete Lewis 1990

❷ For Your Hands Only 🔲🪝🧗 ▭ **6c**
The central crack-line is an excellent little route. It shares the bolts of other lines.
FA. Andy Sharp 1984

❸ Banog's Barmy Army . . . 🔲🧗 ▭ **7a**
A very good pitch. Start right of the crack of *For Your Hands Only*. Stand up on a low ledge, move right and climb to the upper overhang. Swing left past the overhang to jugs.
FA. Andy Sharp, Pete Lewis 1990

From mid morning | 1 min | Windy

❹ Grab Some Tree and Follow Me
. . . . 🔲🪝🧗 ▭ **7a**
Start just to the left of the corner. No bridging across to the corner at this grade. Make difficult moves to the break and then continue over the overhang and up the wall direct to finish.
FA. Andy Sharp 1991

❺ Firewater . . . . 🔲🪝🧗 ▭ **6b**
The blank looking wall to the left of a niche in the centre of the wall is a popular pitch.
FA. Andy Sharp 1984

❻ Hair of the Dog . . . . 🔲 ▭ **6c+**
Climb direct up from the central niche to finish at the same lower-off as *Firewater*.
FA. Andy Sharp 1983

❼ Blagdon . . . . ▭ **6c**
Climb the wall and move left to the lower-off of *Hair of the Dog*.
FA. Andy Sharp 1984

❽ Blagdon Direct Finish . . . . . . 🧗 ▭ **6c+**
Climb *Blagdon* to its second bolt then head straight up (instead of traversing left) via a thin layaway to the top.
FA. Andy Sharp 1984

Coed Ely

	No star	⭐	⭐⭐	⭐⭐⭐
up to 4c	1	-	-	-
5a to 6a+	1	-	-	1
6b to 7a	-	2	4	-
7a+ and up	-	-	-	-

Coed Ely is a fine little venue that is easily reached and has a sunny and sheltered aspect. The main wall at the back of a tiny quarry is composed of good sandstone that is deceptively steep and gives the routes some punch given their modest length.

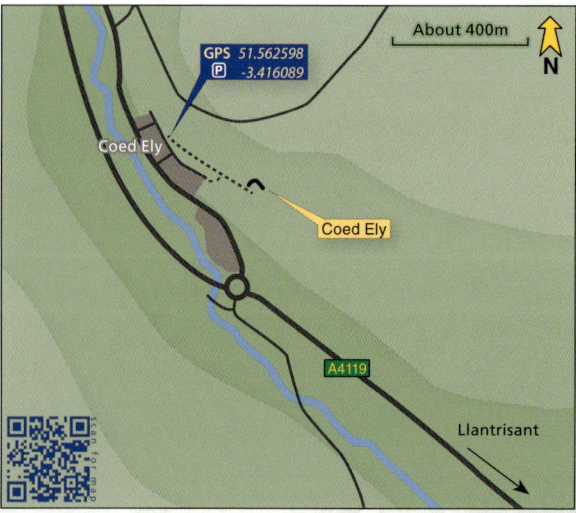

Approach   Also see map on page 254

Approach from Llantrisant on the A4119 and turn off for Coed Ely at a roundabout (this is the second roundabout signed for Coed Ely if travelling south on the A4119). Drive towards Coed Ely and take the first right up a short steep road. At its top, turn left and park (this is where most spaces are - away from the parking in front of houses). Walk back south to the end of the terrace, go through a gap in the fence and pick up a rising track on the left that quickly leads to the quarry.

Conditions

The crag is sheltered, sunny and quick drying.

Access

Occasionally climbers have been asked to leave, although the identity of the landowner is not known. If requested to leave, please do so politely and forward details of the owner to the BMC and Rockfax so that any issues with regard to climbing access can be resolved.

Coed Ely 293

Mark Glaister sussing out the final thin moves on the excellent wall climbing of *Behind the Lines* (6c) - *page 295* - at Coed Ely. The lines on this section all have a little sting in the tail that can be puzzling to work out at first. Photo: Mark Glaister collection

Coed Ely

Coed Ely
An interesting and reliable little quarry that has a small selection of testing pitches on good quality sandstone.
Approach - From the parking, walk south to the end of the terraces and go through a gap in the fence. Pick up a track on the left that leads quickly to the quarry.
Conditions - Sunny, sheltered and quick drying.
Access - Occasionally climbers have been asked to leave, although the identity of the landowner is not known. If requested to leave, please do so politely.

① Lager Lout 4c
The wall between two short vertical cracks, passing a couple of red bolts.
FA. Dave Viggers, Emma Alsford, Paul Donnithorne 15.6.1991

② Alements 5c
The wall when climbed direct, has some pressing moves.
FA. Paul Donnithorne, Emma Alsford 1991

③ Scandal (in the bin) . 6c
The clean vertical wall is a worthwhile line and fairly popular.
FA. Andy Sharp, John Harwood 1989
FA. (Direct finish) Andy Sharp, Pete Lewis 10.2008

The fractured crack-line to the right is **Bush Whacker's Crack, HVS 4c** - it is loose. Right again is **My JCB's Exploded, VS 4c**.

Coed Ely 295

4 Tall Dark and Handsome .... 6c+
Climb direct without using the arete. There is an indirect variation that is **6b+**.
FA. Andy Sharp 1989

5 Campaign For See-through Bikinis
.... 6a+
A superb line with good moves make this one of the better mid 6s in the area. Execute some hard moves to a ledge, then tackle the steepening thin crack-line to an awkward step up onto the finishing ledge and lower-off. *Photo on page 40.*
FA. Gary Lewis 4.3.1989

6 Young Free and Single
.... 7a
The continuously leaning wall is sustained and has a hard thin initial section.
FA. Andy Sharp 4.3.1989

7 The Uninvited 7a
Fine climbing up the centre of the wall. Make a series of hard moves to reach and get established on the shallow ledge between the first and second bolts. Finish up the wall and crack to a lower-off on the ledge above.
FA. Andy Sharp 19.2.1989

8 Behind the Lines ... 6c
An excellent pitch of escalating difficulty. Traverse a finger-rail and climb the wall past a pocket to a final thin pull that gains the top of the wall. Grovel onto the ledge and lower-off above.
Photo on page 293.
FA. Andy Sharp 21.2.1989

9 Uninvited Lines 6b
Start as for *Behind the Lines* and move left to join and finish as for *The Uninvited*'s final crack - a really good pitch.

Glynfach

	No star	✹	✹✹	✹✹✹
up to 4c	-	-	-	-
5a to 6a+	2	3	-	-
6b to 7a	-	4	-	1
7a+ and up	-	-	1	-

A small quarried crag set high above the valley with good views. The quarry is quiet and has good rock, with some worthwhile climbs which are intense and well bolted.

Approach *Also see map on page 254*
Follow the A4058 out of Pontypridd towards Porth. At the Rhondda Heritage Park and Hotel roundabout, continue in the direction of Porth and take the third right (signed to Porth Town Centre). Take the third left by a Chinese take-away onto River Terrace, and continue uphill over a metal railed bridge and bear immediately left onto Cross Street. Follow this until it bends right and park. A path leads up onto the hillside - where various paths lead steeply to the quarry.

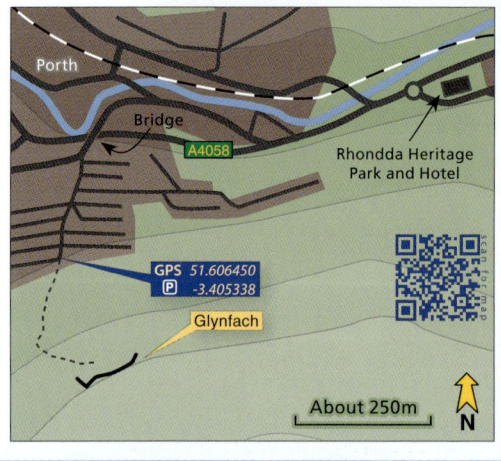

Conditions
The crag is high up and exposed, but gets plenty of sun and dries out fairly quickly.

GPS 51.606450 / -3.405338

Glynfach 297

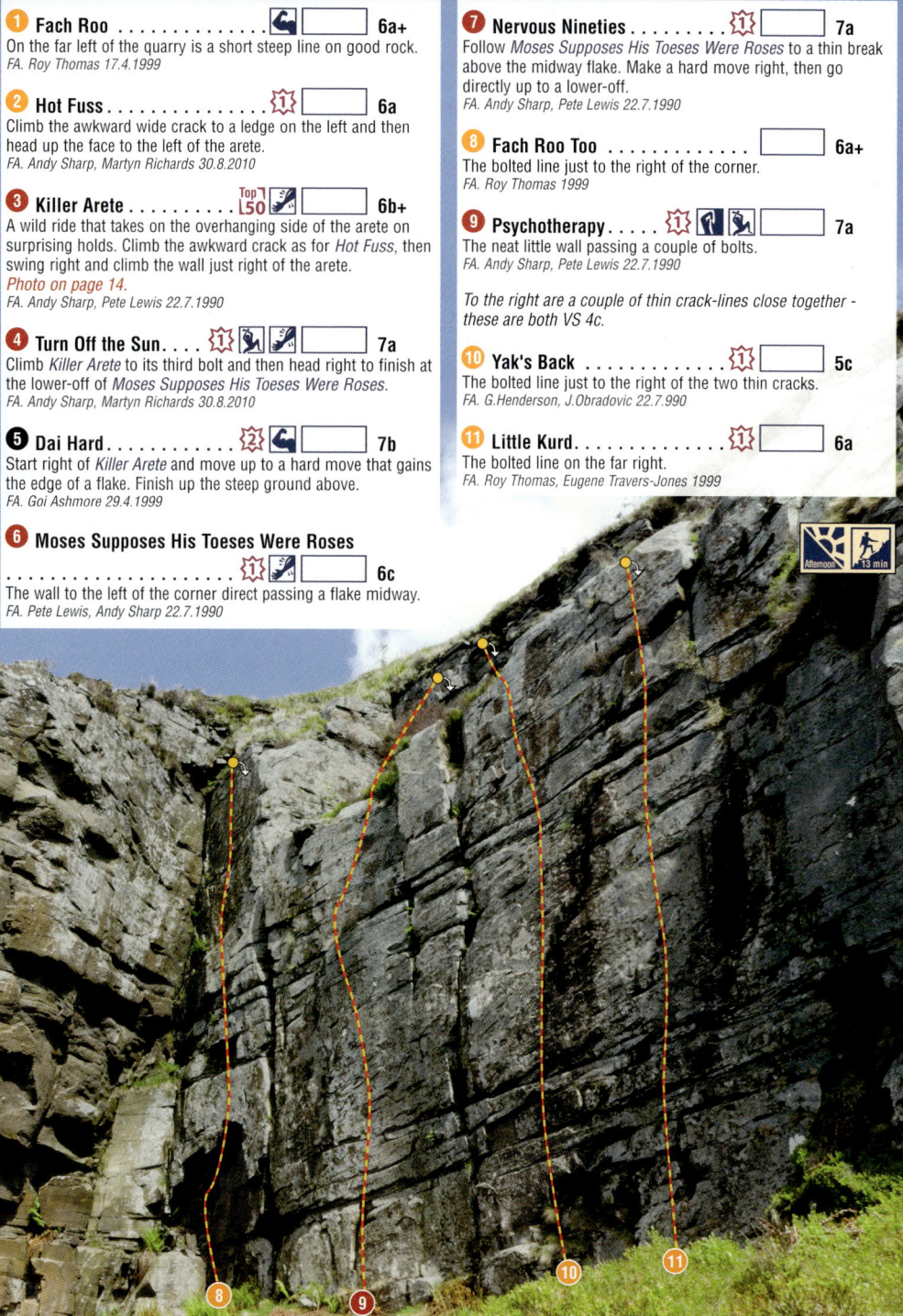

1 Fach Roo .... 6a+
On the far left of the quarry is a short steep line on good rock.
FA. Roy Thomas 17.4.1999

2 Hot Fuss 6a
Climb the awkward wide crack to a ledge on the left and then head up the face to the left of the arete.
FA. Andy Sharp, Martyn Richards 30.8.1990

3 Killer Arete .... Top 50 6b+
A wild ride that takes on the overhanging side of the arete on surprising holds. Climb the awkward crack as for *Hot Fuss*, then swing right and climb the wall just right of the arete.
Photo on page 14.
FA. Andy Sharp, Pete Lewis 22.7.1990

4 Turn Off the Sun 7a
Climb *Killer Arete* to its third bolt and then head right to finish at the lower-off of *Moses Supposes His Toeses Were Roses*.
FA. Andy Sharp, Martyn Richards 30.8.2010

5 Dai Hard 7b
Start right of *Killer Arete* and move up to a hard move that gains the edge of a flake. Finish up the steep ground above.
FA. Goi Ashmore 29.4.1999

6 Moses Supposes His Toeses Were Roses
.... 6c
The wall to the left of the corner direct passing a flake midway.
FA. Pete Lewis, Andy Sharp 22.7.1990

7 Nervous Nineties 7a
Follow *Moses Supposes His Toeses Were Roses* to a thin break above the midway flake. Make a hard move right, then go directly up to a lower-off.
FA. Andy Sharp, Pete Lewis 22.7.1990

8 Fach Roo Too .... 6a+
The bolted line just to the right of the corner.
FA. Roy Thomas 1999

9 Psychotherapy 7a
The neat little wall passing a couple of bolts.
FA. Andy Sharp, Pete Lewis 22.7.1990

To the right are a couple of thin crack-lines close together - these are both VS 4c.

10 Yak's Back 5c
The bolted line just to the right of the two thin cracks.
FA. G.Henderson, J.Obradovic 22.7.990

11 Little Kurd 6a
The bolted line on the far right.
FA. Roy Thomas, Eugene Travers-Jones 1999

Trehafod

	No star	★	★★	★★★
Mod to S / 4c	-	-	-	-
HS-HVS / 5a-6a+	5	2	1	-
E1-E3 / 6b-7a	4	7	-	-
E4 / 7a+ and up	-	-	-	-

Trehafod is a small crag with a limited number of short but fairly good lines. It is handy for a quick hit if passing, or an evening workout for the fingers. Its sunny aspect and quiet roadside location (coupled with the possibility of dry climbing in light rain) makes it a useful standby if all other crags nearby are out of condition.

Approach   Also see map on page 254

From the A4058 Pontypridd to Porth road, exit for Trehafod at a roundabout next to the Rhondda Heritage Park and Hotel. Drive into the village and, just after crossing a large metal bridge, turn left opposite the Funeral Directors (about 100m from the railway station parking). Go under a bridge and park immediately on the left. The crag is just up the road on the right.

GPS 51.610791 -3.383051

Conditions

A sunny aspect and quick drying. In light rainfall, there is a possibility of climbing here as the dense vegetation on top of the cliff gives some shelter.

Paul Cox on the final crimpy wall of the sustained *Discount Included in the Price* (6a+) - *page 301* - at Trehafod. Photo: Mark Glaister

Trehafod

299

Trehafod

Trehafod

A series of walls that are worth a local visit or a quick stop-off if passing. The climbs look a bit innocuous but are sustained and more often than not fingery.
Approach - Scramble up the short earth bank to the wall from the road.
Conditions - Sunny and often dry. The walls are also fairly sheltered from rain by the trees at the top.

1 Roaches Revisited .... HVS 5b
The off-width crack on the left-hand side of the wall.
FA. Chris Evans 1992

2 Beauty School Drop-out . 7a
The wall right of the off-width climbed direct is thin and sustained. Using the crack edge reduces the grade to **6c**.
FA. Andy Sharp, Pete Lewis 2.1992

3 Earl of Porth .... 6a+
The wall just right of *Beauty School Drop-out* is a good little outing and well travelled.
FA. Andy Sharp, Pete Lewis 12.2008

4 Guto Nythbran 6b
A bouldery thin pull past the small overlap gives the crux.
FA. Andy Sharp, Pete Lewis 1.2009

The next buttress is 20m to the right.

5 Elf and Safety 6c
Pull over the low overhang at a crack.
FA. Andy Sharp, Pete Lewis 27.12.2008

6 Rhubarb Lets Fly ... 7a
Make a dyno to pass the low overhang and take the wall above via more hard climbing.
FA. Chris Evans, Andy Sharp 1992

7 Meg (a) Skater Girl from Gelli .. 6a
The right side of the overhang past a groove and wall.
FA. Andy Sharp, Pete Lewis 27.12.2008

The next buttress is 30m to the right.

8 Missing Link .... 6b+
The wall past pockets. Shares the first bolt with *Demi Moore*.
FA. Chris Evans 1992

9 Demi Moore 7a
Nice wall climbing past a pocket.
FA. Andy Sharp, Pete Lewis 1992

10 Gorki's Zygotic Mynci 6c+
Very good and feels longer than it appears.
FA. Chris Evans 1992

Trehafod   301

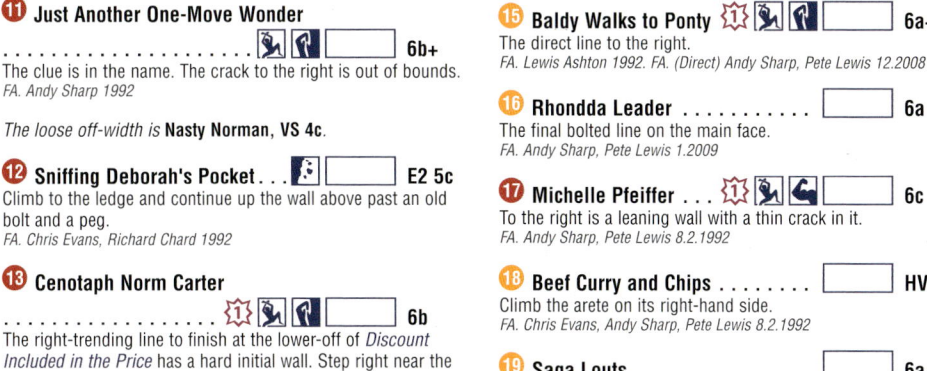

⓫ Just Another One-Move Wonder
. . . . 6b+
The clue is in the name. The crack to the right is out of bounds.
FA. Andy Sharp 1992

The loose off-width is **Nasty Norman, VS 4c**.

⓬ Sniffing Deborah's Pocket . . . E2 5c
Climb to the ledge and continue up the wall above past an old bolt and a peg.
FA. Chris Evans, Richard Chard 1992

⓭ Cenotaph Norm Carter
. . . . 6b
The right-trending line to finish at the lower-off of *Discount Included in the Price* has a hard initial wall. Step right near the top to avoid poor rock.
FA. Chris Evans, Richard Chard 1992

⓮ Discount Included in the Price
. . . . 6a+
Worth stopping by for. It has plenty of climbing and is no pushover. Finish direct on thin crimps. *Photo on page 299.*
FA. Chris Evans 1992. FA. (New finish) Andy Sharp, Pete Lewis 12.2008

⓯ Baldy Walks to Ponty   6a+
The direct line to the right.
FA. Lewis Ashton 1992. FA. (Direct) Andy Sharp, Pete Lewis 12.2008

⓰ Rhondda Leader 6a
The final bolted line on the main face.
FA. Andy Sharp, Pete Lewis 1.2009

⓱ Michelle Pfeiffer . . .   6c
To the right is a leaning wall with a thin crack in it.
FA. Andy Sharp, Pete Lewis 8.2.1992

⓲ Beef Curry and Chips . . . . HVS 5b
Climb the arete on its right-hand side.
FA. Chris Evans, Andy Sharp, Pete Lewis 8.2.1992

⓳ Saga Louts . . . . 6a+
The wall direct.
FA. Andy Sharp, Pete Lewis 1.2009

The low-level traverse starting from Meg (a) Skater Girl from Gelli is **Sir Kit, f6A+**.

The Darren

	No star	⭐	⭐⭐	⭐⭐⭐
up to 4c	-	-	-	-
5a to 6a+	1	1	-	-
6b to 7a	5	4	1	-
7a+ and up	2	1	4	2

Hidden away in some woods high above Pontypridd is this compact quarry which has some good strenuous pitches which are well equipped and on good rock. The walls see little in the way of sunlight and are heavily shaded by tree cover, and as a consequence take time to come into condition. Once dry the Terminal Overhanging Wall stays dry in light rain. A rockfall altered the starts of a number of the lines but these have now been cleaned up, rebolted and reclimbed.

Approach   Also see map on page 254

The approach through Pontypridd is quite complicated. From the large roundabout in the centre, take the exit signed to the town centre. Follow this road and turn left towards Graigwen just after a pedestrian crossing. Follow the road as in winds gently uphill and eventually round to the left dropping down to a T-junction. Turn right and follow the road steeply up the hill for 1km to a right into Whiterock Avenue. Follow this then take the first left into Whiterock Close and then left again into Lanwood Road. Park 50m down this road, next to a path between two bungalows on the left. Follow the path rightwards behind the bungalows and, at a 'keep out' sign, contour left on a smaller path to the quarry.

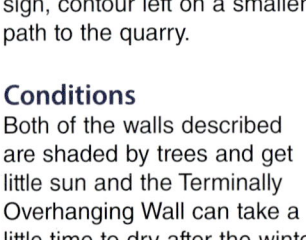

Conditions

Both of the walls described are shaded by trees and get little sun and the Terminally Overhanging Wall can take a little time to dry after the winter months. However, once dry it can be climbed on in light rain. The B.A.T. Wall takes little seepage and dries much more quickly, but does not stay dry in the rain.

The Darren   303

Martyn Richards on the steep ground of *Capstan* (7b+) - page 305 - typical of the lines to be found on the Terminally Overhanging Wall at The Darren. Photo: Ian Parnell

The Darren — The Terminally Overhanging Wall

The Terminally Overhanging Wall
The Terminally Overhanging Wall is a tall overhanging wall, covered in vertical cracks and overlaps. A well-regarded training venue. To the right is another lesser wall (The B.A.T. Wall) which is at a gentler angle and has some slightly easier lines.

Approach - The wall is just beyond the first bay.

Conditions - The Terminally Overhanging Wall gives shelter from light rain, and is a good venue in warm weather. The B.A.T. Wall gets some morning sun, but dries quickly and takes little seepage.

The first quarried bay has a couple of short bolted wall/slab climbs - not shown on a topo.

1 Striking Twelve 6c
The thin wall on the left-hand side of the small quarry.
FA. Andy Sharp, P.Harding, Tony Foster 23.4.1989

2 My New House .... 6b+
A line of old bolts up the steep slab on the right-hand side of the quarry bay.
FA. Goi Ashmore, Rich Lawrence 2.5.1992

The Terminally Overhanging Wall — The Darren 305

The first two lines are just to the left of the edge of the wall.

3 The Short Sharp Manic Depressive 6c
The left arete of the inset corner.
FA. Andy Sharp, Martyn Richards, Jon Williams 1994

4 Smack 6c
The right-hand arete of the inset corner.
FA. Andy Sharp 1989

5 Arizona Stan ...... 7a+
The left arete of the wall, taken on its right-hand side, exiting left to a lower-off at mid-height.
FA. Andy Sharp, Pete Lewis 9.6.1990

6 Capstan .... 7b+
The logical extension improves the previous route considerably.
Photo on page 303.
FA. Andy Sharp 1997

7 The Basildon Slapper ... 7b+
A big pump. Head up between the arete and the cracks via a series of small overlaps. Starts up the rockfall scar.
FA. Andy Sharp 5.1997. FA. (After a rockfall) Martyn Richards 9.2014

The start of the old trad line of **Alive and Kicking, E5 6a** *has been lost in the rockfall.*

8 Round Are Way ..... 7a+
Start just right of the rock scar and move up to the overhang. Head left and then up steep ground right of the crack/niche.
FA. Andy Sharp, Pete Lewis, John Harwood 8.5.1997

9 Rise 7b
Start up *Round Are Way* and follow the discontinuous thin crack-line, oblong niche and layaway with hard moves just above half-height and big moves above.
FA. Tony Forster, P.Harding 1990

10 Sharpy Unplugged .. 7b+
The classic of the wall with brilliant climbing all the way to the lower-off.
FA. Andy Sharp 10.5.1997

11 Enter the Darren .... 6c+
Climb up the tricky slab to gain and follow the crack past a couple of overhangs to a lower-off
FA. Pete Lewis, Andy Sharp 24.6.1989

This is a popular training venue and a number of good link-ups are as follows.

12 Night Train .... 7b+
At the fourth bolt of *The Basildon Slapper*, traverse to *Round Are Way* and at the hanging flake move right to the niche of *Rise*. Go right into and finish as for *Sharpy Unplugged*.
FA. Martyn Richards 21.8.2014

13 Niart Thgin .... 7a+
Start up *Sharpy Unplugged* and finish as for *Arizona Stan*.

14 Kosovo 7a
Start up *Rise* and finish up *Arizona Stan*.
FA. Martyn Richards 1999

B.A.T. Wall

An old trad line **Autumn Leaves, E3 6a** *took the overgrown wall to the tree.*

15 Gutted 6b
Slabby and pleasant with a few good moves.
FA. Andy Sharp, 1999

16 Sorry Lorry Morry 6b
A good pitch up the flared corner/groove and thin crack.
FA. Andy Sharp, Pete Lewis 8.1.1989

17 Juvenile Justice .... 7a+
A bald slab with tiny holds at the crux and a very trying sequence to match.
FA. Andy Sharp, Pete Lewis 7.1.1989

18 Boulevard De Alfred Turner (1926) .... VS 4b
The deep-set groove, moving right at the tree to a thin crack.
FA. Gary Lewis, Haydn Griffiths 1981

19 Andrew the Zebra ... 6a+
Take the bulge and crack to a lower-off.
FA. Gary Lewis, Charlie Heard, Steve Robinson 1981

20 Shaken not Stirred ..... 6c+
Short and to the point. Climb the wall right of a large flake-crack.
FA. Andy Sharp, John Harwood, Pete Lewis 15.1.1989

21 Madame-X 7a
The arete at the right-hand end of the wall.
FA. Andy Sharp, John Harwood, Pete Lewis 15.1.1989

Cwmaman

	No star	⭐	⭐⭐	⭐⭐⭐
up to 4c	-	-	-	-
5a to 6a+	9	5	-	-
6b to 7a	4	4	1	-
7a+ and up	-	1	3	2

The Main Wall at Cwmaman is not that big, but it does have a great set of sustained and fingery pitches. Mark Glaister is on the start of *A Clear Head and a Blow Lamp* (6c) - *page 308*. Photo: John Warner (Glaister Collection)

Cwmaman

Cwmaman is hidden in the back of one of the valleys, high in the Dare Valley. It is a fine little quarry in a decent setting and with some good routes. There are two sections of crag, both of which receive the sun for some of the day. The Main Wall is a clean sheet of almost perfect sandstone and has some of the area's best sport routes. The Right-hand wall has a gentler atmosphere with routes in the lower grades.

Approach   Also see map on page 254

From the A470, take the A4059 through Mountain Ash towards Aberdare. Turn left at a roundabout towards Aberaman and at a T-junction turn right (again signed to Aberaman). Follow the road and take the first left, (almost back on yourself) for Cwmaman. Follow this road to a T-junction and turn left into Jubilee Road. Follow this road for 1 mile and just after the Shepherd's Arms take the third left. Take the next left which goes down a short steep hill and around a left-hand bend. Continue up this for 100m and park. Take a small road on the left (signed footpath) to twin cottages. From here follow the upper of two paths on the left for 100m to a telegraph pole. Continue for 15m and take a small path on the right steeply uphill to the quarry.

Conditions

The Main Wall sees the sun for most of the day whilst the other walls get sun in the afternoon. The Main Wall dries quickly, but can suffer some seepage towards its right-hand side well into early summer and for this reason a couple of its routes can remain a little dirty.

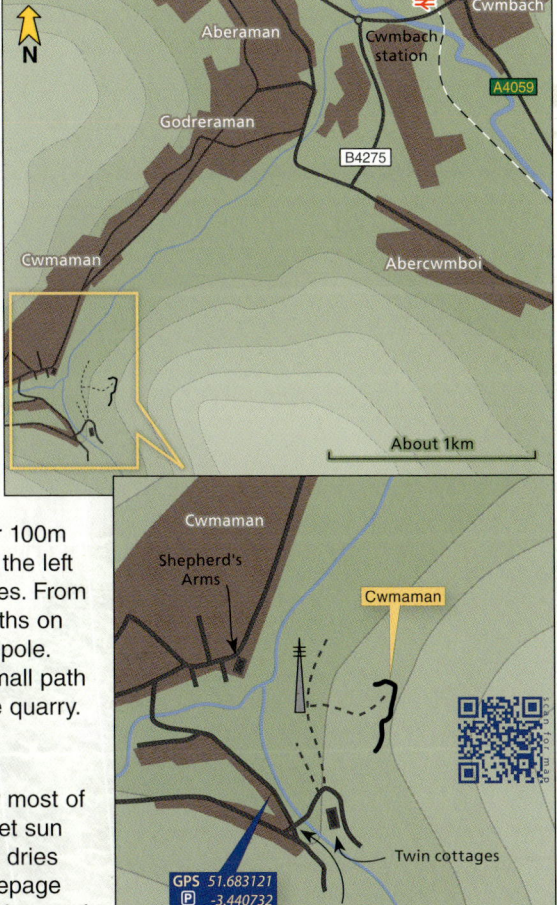

Cwmaman — Main Wall

Main Wall

A fine south-facing wall of compact vertical sandstone that has a handful of good fingery pitches. The setting is very pleasant, being both quiet and away from any roads.

Approach - The Main Wall is on the left when entering the quarry.

Conditions - The wall gets plenty of sun and is sheltered from westerly winds. It gets hot in summer but does get some shade in the evening. There is some seepage at the very base of the wall that affects a number of the starts.

❶ 30' is the new 20' 6c
The crimpy wall just to the right of the corner.
FA. Steven Delaney, Gareth Jones 26.4.2010

❷ Good Tradition 6b
The left-hand side of the wall gives a pleasant pitch.
FA. Andy Sharp, Pete Lewis 5.11.1988

❸ A Clear Head and a Blow Lamp
.... 6c
The crack-line is stern. Boulder out the initial move and continue up still tough ground to the top. Move left to the lower-off.
Photo on page 306.
FA. Andy Sharp, Pete Lewis 5.11.1988

❹ A Clear Conscience and a Blow Job
.... 6c+
A good extension to *A Clear Head and a Blow Lamp*. Move right on edges and then on up to a lower-off on the right.
FA. Andy Sharp, Pete Lewis 5.11.1988

❺ Maybe Tomorrow ... 7b
The direct start to *A Clear Conscience and a Blow Job*.
FA. Andy Sharp 1995

❻ Mother of Pearl . 7a+
The centre of the wall gives one of the original classics of the area. The mid-section is particularly thin.
FA. Andy Sharp, Pete Lewis 5.11.1988

❼ Two for Tuesday .... 6c+
The crack-line is much better than it looks, but can be dirty.
FA. Andy Sharp, Pete Lewis, John Harwood 8.5.1989

Main Wall **Cwmaman** 309

8 The World is my Lobster .... 6c+
The left-hand side of the higher wall via a small overlap low down.
FA. Andy Sharp, Pete Lewis, John Harwood 8.5.1989

9 Propaganda .... 7a+
Classic climbing of its genre left of centre on the main wall.
FA. Andy Sharp, Pete Lewis 7.11.1988

10 Science Friction. 7a+
A fine route up the centre of the wall. Similar to *Propaganda* but with a harder start.
FA. Andy Sharp, Pete Lewis 5.11.1988

11 La Rage ... 7b
The wall just right of centre suffers seepage and has one very hard move.
FA. Andy Sharp, Pete Lewis 16.5.1989

12 Innuendo 7b
The right-hand line is rarely dry and is very hard when it is.
FA. Martin Crocker, Roy Thomas 18.5.1989

13 The Numbers Game 7a
A traverse of the wall. Start up *Good Tradition* and traverse the high break to the mid-way broken corner, then move up to the next horizontal break. Follow the break right to meet and finish up *Innuendo*.
FA. Andy Sharp, Pete Lewis 16.5.1989

Cwmaman   Zoo Time Wall

Zoo Time Wall
A small wall just to the right of the Main Wall with four fairly popular easier lines.
Conditions - The wall gets the sun in the afternoon and is fairly sheltered.

1 Looking for Leather 5b
The first line on the left-hand side of the wall.
FA. Myles Jordan, Nicola Jordan 12.6.2010

2 Instead of This 5c
The wall past the prominent ledge. A pig-tail lower-off.
FA. Gary Gibson, Roy Thomas 16.6.1990

3 Circus Clowns 6a
Climb the central line of the trio that end at the pig-tail lower-off.
FA. Roy Thomas, Gavin Leyshon 6.2010

4 Zoo Time 5c
The clean section of the wall to the right gives good climbing.
FA. Roy Thomas, Gary Gibson 16.6.1990

Right-hand Wall
A good wall with a handful of quality pitches on its far right. Some of the rock is suspect so care is required.
Approach - The Right-hand Wall is the first area encountered on the approach.
Conditions - The wall gets afternoon sun and is fairly sheltered.

5 Cilly Arete 6a
The lone arete with a vegetated slope leading up to it.
FA. Gary Lewis, Steve Delaney 20.4.2010

6 Sam Sparrow 5c
The left-hand bolt-line up the broken looking wall.
FA. Gary Lewis, Steve Delaney 3.2010

Dirty north-facing wall

Right-hand Wall Cwmaman 311

7 Alys Rook .... ☐ 5b
The right-hand line of bolts moving out of *Sam Sparrow*. The direct start goes at **6c**.
FA. Gary Lewis, Steve Delaney 3.2010

8 Spam Javelin .... ☐ 5b
The wall to the left of the prominent arete of *Pork Sword* is very dirty but does have one sport line on it.
FA. Roy Thomas, Eugene Travers-Jones 1990

9 Pork Sword .... ☐ 6b
The arete taken on its right-hand side has very hollow rock.
FA. Roy Thomas 15.3.1998

10 Turkey Twizzler .... ☐ 6a+
The line just right of the arete of *Pork Sword* passing through the loose niche has hollow rock above.
FA. Roy Thomas, Nicola Jordan, Myles Jordan 2010

11 Anniversary Walk ... ☐ 5c
The wall right of the low niche of *Turkey Twizzler* is a good introduction to this section of the face. Good moves.
FA. Roy Thomas, Martin Crocker 13.11.1988

12 The Forgotten Route ...... ☐ 5c
Climb direct to a lower-off below a grassy niche close to the top.
FA. Gary Lewis, Steve Delaney 1.9.2009

13 Hey Mister .... ☐ 6a
A good wall pitch that finishes just right of a grassy niche.
FA. Roy Thomas, Martin Crocker 13.11.1988

14 Buff the Happy Lamp ☐ 6b
A strange line but with decent climbing. The original started more directly but now a tree is in the way. Climb *Yank the Plank* and make thin moves up left to join *Hey Mister* before following a rising line to finish at the lower-off of *Anniversary Walk*.
FA. Roy Thomas, Paul Hadley 8.1999

15 Yank the Plank .... ☐ 6a
A pleasing little pitch.
FA. Roy Thomas, Paul Hadley 8.1999

16 Evil Ways .... ☐ 6a
The right-most line on the wall has a tough move near the finish.
FA. Paul Hadley, Roy Thomas 8.1999

Mountain Ash

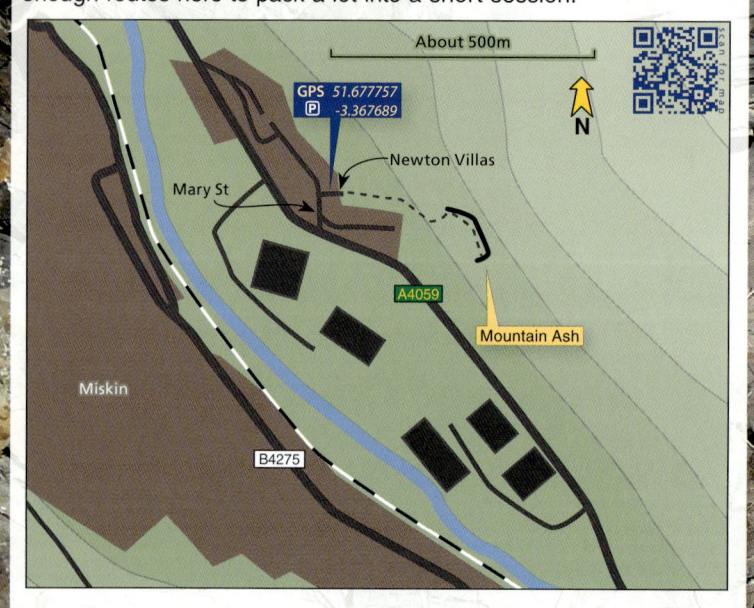

	No star	★	★★	★★★
Mod to S / 4c	-	-	-	-
HS-HVS / 5a-6a+	14	4	1	-
E1-E3 / 6b-7a	10	11	3	-
E4 / 7a+ and up	1	6	5	1

Mountain Ash quarry is in the shape of a bowl and provides a welcome retreat from any harsh weather. There is a good mixture of climbing styles and grades ranging from short and desperate fingery testpieces through to some long and slabbier walls. There are enough routes here to pack a lot into a short session.

Approach   Also see map on page 254

When approaching from the south on the A470, take a left turn at the main roundabout at Abercynon. Follow the A4059, signposted Aberdare, until you come into the town of Mountain Ash, 2km after the Cynon Business Park. Take the first right by a prominent red telephone box into Mary Street, and after 100m go right into Newton Villas. Either park here or continue up the dirt track directly ahead to park alongside an old bonfire site. A short track zig-zags up and slightly to the left into the secluded quarry entrance.

Conditions

This is a very sheltered venue with walls that face in all directions. The right-hand wall does suffer a bit of dampness after rain and through the winter months, but there is plenty to do here in dry weather. The cliff takes little in the way of seepage.

Access

Take care when parking not to block any access.

Carrie Hill midway up the long single-pitch line of *Weeping Stump* (5b) - *page 317* - at the Sap Rising Area, Mountain Ash. Photo: Mark Glaister

Mountain Ash — Cointreau Area

1 What's The Arc De Triomphe For Then? 6a
The slab on the left has a single tough move.
FA. Jon Williams 1992

2 The Old Firm 6c
The centre of the wide rib and upper wall. Big glue-in bolts.
FA. Chris Evans 1992

3 Coggars Lane .... 6b+
Climb up the pillar and through the overhang.
FA. Chris Evans, P.Green 1992

4 Outspan .... 7a+
Quality climbing with a bold start and fingery climbing above.
FA. Martin Crocker, Roy Thomas 25.9.1988

5 Hot Cross Guns . 7b+
Sustained climbing that links the start of *Outspan* to the upper section of *Ripe and Ready*.
FA. Martyn Richards, Andy Sharp 14.4.2009

6 Ripe 'n Ready ..... 7b+
A 'fingernail' desperate up the centre of the wall, or just a pure dyno - you choose.
FA. Martin Crocker, Roy Thomas 27.10.1988

7 Pastis on Ice ...... 7a+
The prominent arete gives a test of finger strength and ingenuity.
FA. Martin Crocker, Roy Thomas 25.9.1988
FA. (Direct) Eugene Travers-Jones 23.5.1995

8 Cointreau .... Top 50 7a+
The orange wall gives a sandstone classic. *Photo on page 26.*
FA. Martin Crocker, John Harwood 17.4.1994

9 Choice Cut E2 5c
The thin crack from ledges high on the right.
FA. Paul Donnithorne, Alan Price 7.11.1988

10 Blacker than Black .... 6c+
A desperate problem. Jump down onto the last bolt to lower-off.
FA. Martin Crocker, John Harwood 17.4.1994

11 Branch Manager .... 6c+
Typical of these walls, more of an extended boulder problem.
FA. Roy Thomas 31.3.1996

12 Totally Stumped 6c
Desperate moves via a vague scoop.
FA. Roy Thomas 21.3.1995

13 Molybdenum Man 6c
The excellent little arete. Surprisingly hard.
FA. Martin Crocker, Roy Thomas 27.10.1988

14 Ferndale Revisited .. 7b
Another desperate boulder problem from bottom to top.
FA. Andy Sharp, Pete Lewis 22.4.1989

15 Dusk .... 7a+
Marginally easier than its left-hand neighbour.
FA. Eugene Travers-Jones 21.3.1995

16 I Came .... 6a+
Finally something easier angled. The left side of the slab and the short headwall.
FA. Roy Thomas 22.3.1995

Cointreau Area
Three walls that are the first encountered on entering the quarry. The high orange-coloured wall of smooth rock with the route *Cointreau* is the best here. Below it is a low wall of compact sandstone with some short but testing little lines. All three sections are clean and dry quickly.
Approach - The first climbable wall on entering the quarry.

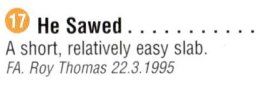

Cointreau Area **Mountain Ash** 315

17 He Sawed 5a
A short, relatively easy slab.
FA. Roy Thomas 22.3.1995

18 I Conkered .... 6a+
Further right of a chimney.
FA. Roy Thomas 22.3.1995

Mountain Ash Sap Rising Area

Sap Rising Area
A good couple of walls with three longer routes and some worthwhile shorter pitches. An open aspect means that the walls get plenty of sun, although seepage can be a problem on the bottom walls of the longer lines.
Approach - The walls are easily identified a short distance on from the Cointreau Area.

1 Bring Back the Birch 5b
A pleasant slab that has a single hard move.
FA. Roy Thomas 22.3.1995

2 Under the Axe 6b
A short blunt rib and sharp V-groove.
FA. Roy Thomas 22.3.1995

3 No Barking up this Tree 5b
A single hard move.
FA. Roy Thomas, Paul Donnithorne 23.3.1995

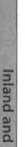

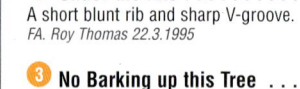

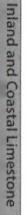

4 A Sight for Saw Eyes . . . . 6a+
The dyno is at the start. The rest is easier.
FA. Roy Thomas, Paul Donnithorne 23.3.1995

5 Tragedy E1 5a
The splendid unprotected arete to the right.
FA. Martin Crocker, Mick Learoyd, Roy Thomas, Pete Lewis 9.10.1988

6 More than a Feeling 6b
Layback up the right-hand side of the arete.
FA. Alan Rosier 17.7.2014

Mountain Ash

7 The Future Holds **7b**
A complicated sequence with a trying finish.
FA. Martin Crocker, 16.10.1988

8 Narcissi **E1 5b**
A long and pleasant route taking the blunt rib of the slab via a shallow groove high up.
FA. Gary Lewis, J Boyle 1987

9 Rising Sap . . . . **6a+**
A super route. A long pitch finishing up a flying arete.
FA. Roy Thomas 1995

10 Weeping Stump **5a**
Follow the groove, exit left and continue to the right arete.
Photo on page 313.
FA. Roy Thomas, Gareth Tucker, Nick Goile, Alan Rosier 3.07.2008

The walls now fizzle out for about 50m. There is no worthwhile climbing on this section of cliff until a sharp arete is reached. Just right of this is a shady, right-facing wall where the routes begin again (the following lines are not featured on a topo).

11 Attrocities . . . . **6b+**
The bolted line on the left-hand side of the wall.
FA. Al Rosier, Rob McAllister 9.7.2014

12 No Chips Round Here **7b**
The steep wall moving rightwards to finish direct. The original route, **A Clip Round the Ear, 7a+** finished leftwards.
FA. Goi Ashmore 12.7.1995
FA. (A Clip Round the Ear) Andy Sharp, Pete Lewis 3.3.1991

13 Constantinople **5c**
The corner to the right of *No Chips Round Here*.
FA. Gary Lewis 2016

14 Helmet Man's Day Off **5a**
The left-hand line on the slab.
FA. Matt Hirst 13.7.1995

15 Ant Frenzy **5b**
The centre of the slab.
FA. Matt Hirst 13.7.1995

16 Homebase **5c**
Just before the start of the terrace at the left end of the Main Bay is an arete. Climb this to a shared lower-off.
FA. Gary Lewis, Giles Barker 1989

17 Cymru Euro **5a**
The shallow corner right of *Homebase*.
FA. Gary Lewis, L.Elgar 2016

Mark Tomlinson setting up for the crux of *A Certain Peace* (6b) - *page 318* - at the Main Bay, Mountain Ash. Photo: Mark Glaister

Mountain Ash — Main Bay

Main Bay
The final area in the quarry is an impressive right-angled corner which is home to some excellent routes. Once dry these walls stay in good condition, but get less sun than the other parts of Mountain Ash.

The first routes start on a raised ledge on the left.

1 Little Polvier 5a
The corner on the left side of the terrace.
FA. Gary Lewis, A.Keward 1989

2 Double Bore .... 6b+
The groove and wall left of *Slap Happy's* left-trending thin crack.
FA. Andy Sharp, Pete Lewis 28.3.2009

3 Slap Happy .... 6c+
The left-trending crack moving right at the top.
FA. Andy Sharp, Pete Lewis 11.4.1991

4 Sport for All ...... 7b+
The very blank-looking face to the right is not all it appears.
FA. Andy Sharp, Pete Lewis 31.3.1991

5 Sporting Supplement ... 6b
Fine climbing via the shallow scoop.
FA. Pete Lewis, Andy Sharp 13.4.1991

6 Sunday Sport E3 5c
The flake-line with an old peg.
FA. Andy Sharp, Pete Lewis 16.4.1991

7 The Abdominal Showman ... 7a+
The flake-line just left of the corner. Desperate if climbed direct.
FA. Andy Sharp, Pete Lewis 13.4.1991

8 A Certain Peace 6b
The short wall and arete is a lovely route. *Photo on page 317.*
FA. Roy Thomas, Martin Crocker 27.10.1988

9 Misadventure 7a
The fine wall to the right gives a pitch worth seeking out.
FA. Roy Thomas 12.7.1995

10 Mountin' Ass Crack .... 6b+
The narrow crack-line just right of *Misadventure*.
FA. Alan Rosier 15.7.2014

11 A Far Cry from Squamish ... E4 6a
The diagonal crack-line has been cleaned up. Can be linked into *The Theory and Practice of Glue Sniffing*.
FA. Martin Crocker 22.7.1990 (Link - Roy Thomas, Paul Hadley 1999)

12 The Theory and Practice of Glue Sniffing
.... 6c+
Branch out left from *Jet Lagged* at 5m via a rib and corner.
FA. Goi Ashmore 12.7.1995

Main Bay **Mountain Ash** 319

13 Jet Lagged 6c
The wall above a bouldery crux start.
FA. Martin Crocker 22.7.1990

14 Sennapod Corner .... HVS 5a
Speaks for itself really. Gets a star if it is clean.
FA. Phill Thomas 1970

15 Whiter than White Wall . 7a+
The clean-looking wall has a particularly trying crux.
FA. Martin Crocker, Matt Ward 21.5.1988

16 A Load of Rubbish E2 5b
The first series of cracks gives a worthwhile pitch.
FA. Alan Richardson 1984

17 Valleys Initiative ... 7a
One of the better routes in the vicinity. A climactic finale.
FA. Andy Sharp, John Harwood 4.10.1991

18 Ain't as Effical E3 5c
The next to last crack-line is often a little dirty.
FA. Martin Crocker, Matt Ward, Gordon Jenkin 21.5.1988

19 Grave Concern .... 6a+
The crack-line.
FA. Roy Thomas, Ed Rees 1998

20 Final Plot .... 6a+
Climb the wall to crux moves that access the small ramp.
FA. Roy Thomas, Ed Rees 1998

21 Parabola .... 6a+
The slab and roof over to the right..
FA. Al Rosier, Nik Goile 4.7.2015

The Gap

	No star	✧	✧✧	✧✧✧
up to 4c	1	-	-	-
5a to 6a+	6	10	4	-
6b to 7a	3	13	8	-
7a+ and up	-	1	8	1

The Gap is one of the original and best known of the sandstone climbing areas in South Wales, although nowadays others have overtaken it in popularity. Sitting high on a hill overlooking the A470 Cardiff to Merthyr Tydfil road, it has a nice open aspect and plenty of routes at all grades that are well equipped. The majority of the routes are wall climbs, with the hardest featuring sustained sequences on thin edges. There are plenty of routes in the lower 6s including a few smart crack-lines.

GPS 51.657952 -3.330310

Approach   Also see map on page 254
At the large roundabout on the A470 when travelling from Cardiff, turn right, signposted Ystrad Mynach (A4059), or left when approaching from Merthyr Tydfil. At the next roundabout, turn left (A4054) towards Quakers Yard. Upon entering the village, and just before a pelican crossing, take the first left over a narrow bridge across the river. From here the road ascends steeply through a built-up area until the A470 is recrossed on a bridge. Take the first right immediately after the bridge and after 1km the cliff will be seen on the left. Parking is readily available below the quarries.

Conditions
The cliff is very open and dries relatively quickly, although it does take seepage in the winter. Due to its exposed nature it is best avoided in windy or cold conditions. The crag gets very little sun except first thing in the morning, which makes it the ideal venue in hot weather. Midges can be a problem in very humid and calm weather.

The Gap 321

Dave Henderson tackling the puzzling moves on *Pleasant Valley Sunday* (7a+) - *page 325* - at The Gap. The Gap is one of the most developed of all the South Wales sandstone sport crags and has numerous technical and fingery routes in the mid-grades. Photo: Mark Glaister

The Gap — Left Wall

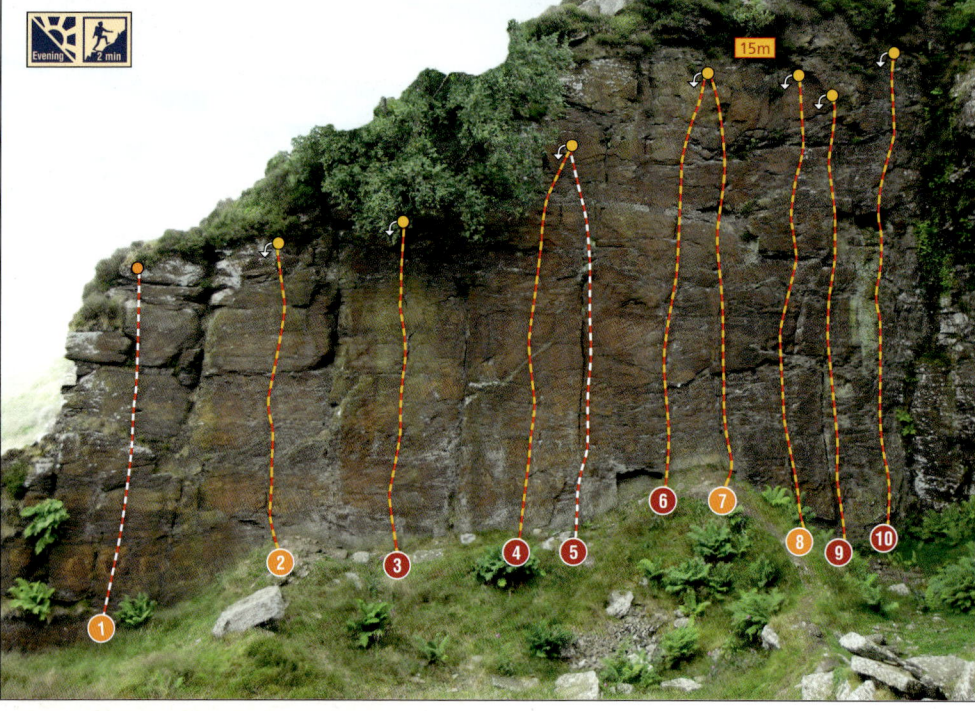

Left Wall

A pleasant section of the crag that looks a little uninspiring at first, but actually has a number of intense sport routes with pleasant fingery climbing on good rock.
Approach - A quick stroll up the hill from the parking area and the wall is on the left of the bay.
Conditions - The wall faces north and only receives evening sunshine in mid-summer. It dries relatively quickly, but suffers from a little seepage towards its right-hand side.

1 As it Was .... VS 4c
The short wall just to the right of the arete.
FA. Roy Thomas 1994

2 Kabuto Mushi .... 6a+
Tough thin crimping up the short narrow wall.
FA. Roy Thomas, Eugene Travers-Jones 1993

3 Yikes .... 6b+
A problematic wall on small holds. Thankfully the difficulties are short lived.
FA. Martin Crocker, Roy Thomas, Mick Learoyd 25.3.1990

4 So Uncool 6c
A fingery start leads to balancy and sustained moves up the ramp above. Clip-stick the first bolt.
FA. Gary Gibson, Roy Thomas 6.2.1993

5 Just Hanging Around ... E1 5b
The fine traditional crack-line is well worth the effort, or it can be handily top-roped from the lower-off of *So Uncool*.
FA. Roy Thomas, Graham Royle 1990

6 Bluster 6b
Start on top of the mound and follow the left-hand line of bolts to a shared lower-off. The start keeps getting harder due to wear and tear.
FA. Roy Thomas 1993

7 Fluster .... 6a+
The right-hand line of bolts starting on top of the mound is similar to *Bluster*, though not as tricky at the start.
Photo opposite.
FA. Roy Thomas 1993

8 Marlin on the Wall ..... 6a+
The 'marlin' adds a new dimension to the word protection - the old hook was once used as a piece of protection. Good climbing.
FA. Roy Thomas 1993

9 Don't Blame Me 6b
A pleasant line which tackles the wall on edges and incuts. Can be damp.
FA. Matt Hirst 2005

10 Sumo no Shiro .... 6b+
The green streak. Climb the wall to a shallow small cave and pull out of it onto the headwall.
FA. Roy Thomas, Eugene Travers-Jones 1993

Left Wall **The Gap** 323

Bridget Collier sampling The Gap's typically fingery wall climbing on *Fluster* (6a+) - *opposite* - on the Left Wall. Photo: Mark Glaister

The Gap — Main Wall

Main Wall
A good wall of excellent sandstone. It is seamed with grooves and small overlaps towards its left. To the right, it forms a gently leaning wall of compact rock split by long cracks and covered in matchstick-edge crimps.

Conditions - The wall faces northeast and gets early morning sun, making it an ideal summer venue. It dries very quickly and only suffers seepage problems towards its left-hand side.

Approach - A quick stroll up the hill from the parking area and the wall is directly ahead.

1 Canine League — 6a+
Through the roof right of the corner. Good climbing when dry.
FA. Roy Thomas, Simon Coles 22.9.1994

2 Sleeping Dogs Lie — 6b+
A classic of its type through the centre of the roofs.
FA. Roy Thomas 1993

3 Don't Bark Yet — 7a
The bulge and wall finishing over the overlap.
FA. Matt Hirst 2004

4 Smack My Bitch Up — 6b+
The right-hand side wall of the corner has good moves.
FA. Roy Thomas, Matt Hirst 2004

5 Generation Bitch — 6b
Start up Generation Gap and climb direct.
FA. Roy Thomas 2004

6 Generation Gap — 5c
A pleasant pitch starting up the left-hand edge of the pillar and taking the right-hand line of bolts.
FA. Graham Royle, Roy Thomas 1993

7 Mister Faraday — 6a
A stubborn start leads to the upper section of Generation Gap.
FA. Roy Thomas 1993

8 Poker in the Eye — 6a+
Take the roof and storm the walls above.
FA. Roy Thomas 1993

9 Grout Expectations — 6a
An easier line past an overlap and up a groove.
FA. Roy Thomas 1993

10 Shackles of Love — 6a+
Climb the crack, wall and shallow groove.
FA. Roy Thomas 1993

11 Ring of Confidence — 6b
The low-level flakes and wall on the right to the top.
FA. Roy Thomas 1993

12 Get Flossed — 7a+
A tough start to the last route. Keep direct for the tick.
FA. Gary Gibson, Roy Thomas 18.6.1994

Main Wall **The Gap** 325

13 Loctite 7b+
Desperate fingery climbing on thin edges. Eases off above, just!
FA. Andy Sharp, Pete Lewis 15.7.1989

14 Land of the Dinosaurs 6b
The crack-line gives a sport route with a traditional feel.
Variation, 6c - Move up left from the lower-off to the finish of Loctite.
FA. Roy Thomas, Gareth Davies, Mick Learoyd 1990

15 A Momentary Lapse of Reason 7b+
A stern test of fingertip strength. Climb straight up the wall between the cracks. The belay is the last staple, not the belay above. It can be started from the right.
FA. Tony Forster, P.Harding 6.1989

16 Rattle Those Tusks 6b
The long crack and upper roof gives some classic crack climbing - with bolts.
FA. Roy Thomas, Mick Learoyd 1990

17 Mad at the Sun 7c
Still one of the hardest routes on sandstone more than 25 years after the first ascent. Start up *Leave it to Me* and make a technical traverse left out onto the face. Finish over the roof.
FA. Martin Crocker, Roy Thomas 8.4.1990

18 Leave it to Me 6c
The shallow groove and short headwall above the start of *Mad at the Sun* is a worthwhile and varied line.
FA. Matt Hirst 2007

19 Salmon Running, Bear Cunning 7b
The right-hand side of the arete to a slab and a cruxy finale.
FA. Pete Lewis, Andy Sharp 17.6.1990.
Extended by Eugene Travers-Jones 1992

20 Anything You Can Do 7b
The excellent open wall has a clearly defined crux sequence through the tiny overlap.
FA. Andy Sharp, Pete Lewis 17.4.1990
FA. (Finish) Gary Gibson, Roy Thomas 28.6.1992

21 Encore Magnifique 7b+
The sandstone classic slap bang up the centre of the wall. Continuously interesting moves on excellent sandstone.
FA. Martin Crocker, Roy Thomas 25.3.1990

22 Pleasant Valley Sunday 7a+
Typical of the wall with an unusual crossover crux. Linking into *Encore Magnifique* gives a quality **7b**. *Photo on page 321.*
FA. Andy Sharp, Pete Lewis 18.7.1989. Direct start by Gary Gibson 1992.

The Gap — Right Wall

326

Right Wall
The right-hand side of the quarry is a little more open with a small selection of routes.
Approach - A quick stroll up the hill from the parking area and the wall is up on the right.
Conditions - The wall dries quickly after rain.

1 One Track Mind 7a
The fine arete is one of the best on the sandstone.
FA. Andy Sharp, Pete Lewis 11.7.1989

2 Greased Balls 6b
The left wall of the corner is popular when in condition.
FA. Roy Thomas 1994

3 Controlled Emission 6c
A gem of a pitch that features some intricate face moves.
FA. Paul Donnithorne, Emma Alsford 1993

4 Sperm Wail .... 7a+
The smooth-looking wall with a testing middle section. Watch out for the worrying fourth clip.
FA. Martin Crocker, Roy Thomas 11.4.1990

5 Scrotum Oil 6c
The fine wall with good moves between positive holds.
FA. Roy Thomas 1994

6 Has the Fat Lady Sung? 6b
Climb the short wall and face above the ledge to a lower-off. Take care with a block close to the top.
FA. Roy Thomas 8.2009

7 Pick up the Pieces .... 6a+
The slim wall proves better than it looks.
FA. Roy Thomas 1991

8 Perfect Scoundrels .. 6c
The alcove, roof and rib gives a good varied mix of moves.
FA. Tony Penning, Pete Lewis, Andy Sharp 1990
FA. (Direct) Gary Gibson 18.6.1994

9 Butt Out 5c
Start on the right-hand side of the cave. Climb past some dubious rock onto a grassy ledge, then up the headwall.
FA. Roy Thomas, Matt Hirst 2004

10 Per Rectum 5b
The rib on the right-hand side of the cave and the wall above the ledge. Shares staple bolts with those on *Stool Sample*.
FA. Roy Thomas, Matt Hirst 2004

11 Stool Sample 5c
The short pillar. Shares staple bolts with *Per Rectum*.
FA. Nick O'Neill, Roy Thomas 2005

12 As it is 5c
The blunt arete.
FA. Roy Thomas 1994

13 Turd Strangler 6c
The short fingery wall.
FA. Matt Hirst, Roy Thomas 2004

14 Dai Horrea 6b
Start a little higher up the slope. Steep moves to gain the belay.
FA. Roy Thomas, Matt Hirst 2004

Upper Quarry **The Gap** 327

Upper Quarry
A smaller quarry with some bolted lines between the older trad lines which (mainly) follow the cracks.
Approach - From the parking, walk up the dirt track on the right and the quarry is on the left as it levels out.
Conditions - The quarry faces northeast and gets only limited early morning sunshine. The walls dry quickly after rain, but it is a little more exposed than the Main Quarry.

15 Newton's Apple 5c
A nice little pitch up the wall between the big cracks. A sling and large hex are needed for the lower-off around a large boulder on top.
FA. Roy Thomas, Graham Royle 1990

16 It's A Sine . . . . 6a+
The slabby wall to the left of the nasty looking corner on good rock.
FA. Roy Thomas 5.5.1995

17 Scared Seal Banter . . . . . . 7a+
A good route that has some hard and complex sequences.
FA. Martin Crocker, Roy Thomas, Mick Learoyd 4.3.1990

18 The Mastic Mick 6c
The overlap, large hole and wall above to the left of the big off-width crack.
FA. Martin Crocker, Mick Learoyd 4.3.1990

19 The Grout Of San Romano . . . 6c
The wall to the right of the big off-width crack is hard at the start and only slightly less pressing above.
FA. Martin Crocker 4.3.1990

20 The Godfather . . . . 6a+
Climb the good looking arete with some balancy moves, to pass a smooth ledge and make steeper moves to finish.
FA. Gary Lewis, Hadyn Griffiths 1990

21 Up Yours 6a
The juggy rib on less quarried rock.
FA. Roy Thomas, Mick Learoyd 1990

22 Mortar Life 6a
A short wall to the right. Top out as there is no lower-off.
FA. Roy Thomas 1992

23 Shorter Life 5a
The wall to the right of *Mortar Life*. Top-out as there is no lower-off.
FA. Roy Thomas 2005

Navigation Quarry

Navigation Quarry offers some fine long sport routes on its main face. Here Mark Glaister is approaching the finish of the thin and fingery *Deus Ex Machina* (6c) - *page 331*. Photo: Jon Warner (Glaister Collection)

Navigation Quarry

	No star	★	★★	★★★
Mod to S / 4c	-	-	-	-
HS-HVS / 5a-6a+	4	4	-	-
E1-E3 / 6b-7a	5	8	7	2
E4 / 7a+ and up	1	2	1	-

Navigation Quarry is a pleasant climbing venue located on moorland high above the valley. This is one of the older cragging spots developed on the sandstone and consequently some of the routes are not full clip-up sport routes. Bolts have been kept off of the established trad lines, but there are still plenty of excellent fully bolted sport climbs for those up to them. Not all of the established traditional lines are included here and only fully bolted sport pitches are given sport grades.

Approach   Also see map on page 254

If travelling north on the A470 from Pontypridd, turn off towards Abercynon on the B4275. Continue straight on at the roundabout and at the traffic lights. Continue for 100m to parking on the right, just before the Navigation Inn, or down the road opposite the pub.

If travelling south on the A470 from Merthyr Tydfil, go east on the A472 from the large roundabout just north of Abercynon to another roundabout, and then south on the A4054 towards Cilfynydd. At the first set of traffic lights go right across the A470 then right again at the next lights to the parking by the Navigation Inn.

Walk back up to the traffic lights and turn left over the A470. At the next lights cross the main road and go through a gate to a path. Follow this for 300m to where another path cuts back left. Follow this path uphill for 100m to where another path branches back right, and follow this path for 500m until the quarry can be seen on the left.

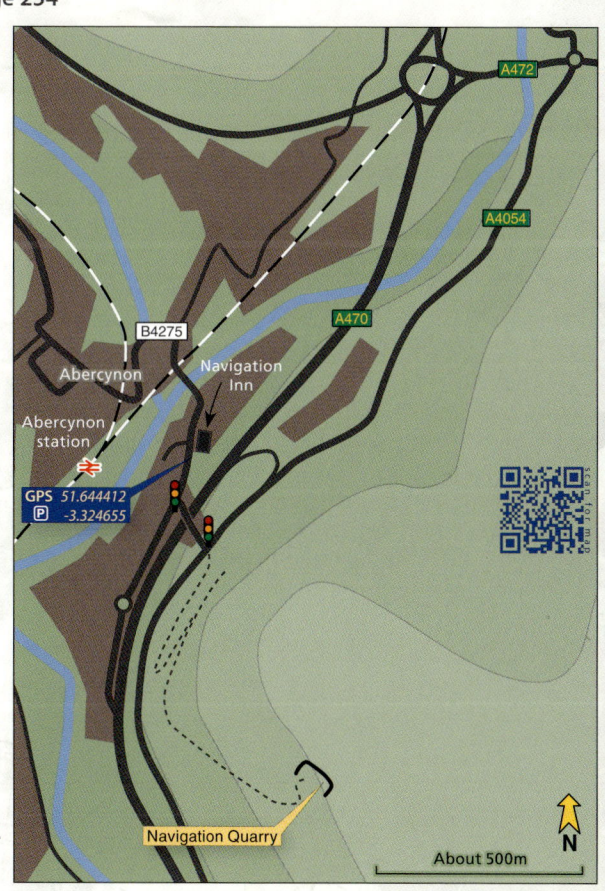

GPS 51.644412, -3.324655

Conditions
The quarry faces southwest, gets plenty of sun and is fairly sheltered, making it a possible year-round venue. Seepage does occur, but the rock dries quickly after rainfall.

Access
There is a restriction due to nesting birds from March 1st to August 1st. This is a variable restriction and applies only to a small section of the crag - see UKClimbing or BMC RAD.

Navigation Quarry

Navigation Quarry
Those sport lines without lower-offs in place require a belay from large staples in the back wall.

⛔ **Access** - No climbing 1st March to 1st August due to nesting birds. This restriction only applies to routes near where the bird nests. See BMC RAD for details.

The first two lines are on the unattractive left wall.

1 Leftover 5a
The left-hand side of the left wall past a loose and vegetated section.
FA. Gary Lewis 2000s

2 Gold Block 5c
Climb just to the left of the corner with two possible finishes.
FA. Gary Lewis, Mick Learoyd 1984

3 Half Man, Half Machine . 6b
The black groove - often dirty - and the right-leading line above the bulge to a lower-off on the grassy ledge.
FA. Alan Rosier 18.3.2012

4 The Elastic Retreat .. E4 6b
From a belay on a high ledge (reached via routes below), climb the wall and overhang past a bolt.
FA. Giles Barker 7.1989

5 Rockover Beethoven 5c
Climb the thin black slab to the grassy ledge and lower-off on the left. Alternatively finish up *Squash Match* - harder.
FA. Bob Brewer 1988

6 The Bolt Fund Blues .... 6b+
Climb the slab and high notch to the right of *Rockover Beethoven* (clip its first two bolts) and then make a difficult rockover above and finish direct.
FA. Alan Rosier, R.Giles 27.9.2007

7 Where Did You Get That Bolt . 7a
The wall via a slot to join *Squash Match* past an old bolt. Finish up *The Bolt Fund Blues*.
FA. Andy Sharp, Pete Lewis 11.2.1989

8 Squash Match ... 6a
Follow a left-trending line to gain the grassy ledge. Go left and then follow the right-trending ramp up the final wall - airy.
FA. Gary Lewis, Mick Learoyd, Lyndsey Foulkes 1983

Descent

Good large staples in back wall of quarry for belays

25m

Navigation Quarry

9 Blood Sweat and Beers ... 6b
A good route up the slab, fingery overlap and juggy headwall.
FA. Alan Rosier 27.9.2007

10 Death Wish E2 5b
The bold shallow arete right of a corner. Finish up the headwall.
FA. Mick Learoyd 1984

11 Fly Me to the Moon .... VS 5a
The cracks and headwall.
FA. Gary Lewis, Steve Blackman 1982

12 A Blank Abstract E3 6b
The thin slab with bolt protection on the crux.
FA. Goi Ashmore, Rich Lawrence 10.1.1992

13 Man or Mouse 7b
The tricky blank slab.
FA. Andy Sharp, Pete Lewis 11.2.1989

14 Let Me Play Among the Stars E2 5c
Climb to and up the right-hand crack (two bolts). Finish up the wall above.
FA. Gary Lewis, Steve Blackman, Charlie Heard 1982

15 Deus Ex Machina ... 6c
Good climbing. A tough start above the low overlap gains easier but interesting ground. *Photo on page 328.*
FA. Alan Rosier 24.3.2012

16 Black Magic 6b
Start up the thin crack. A fine climb with continual interest.
Photo on page 3.
FA. Tony Foster 1988

17 The Relaxed Ladybird 6c
A good route with a steep finish.
FA. Alan Rosier 13.8.2007

18 Great Expectations .. 6c+
Hard moves interspersed with good rests up the blank face.
FA. Mick Learoyd, Gary Lewis 4.11.1988

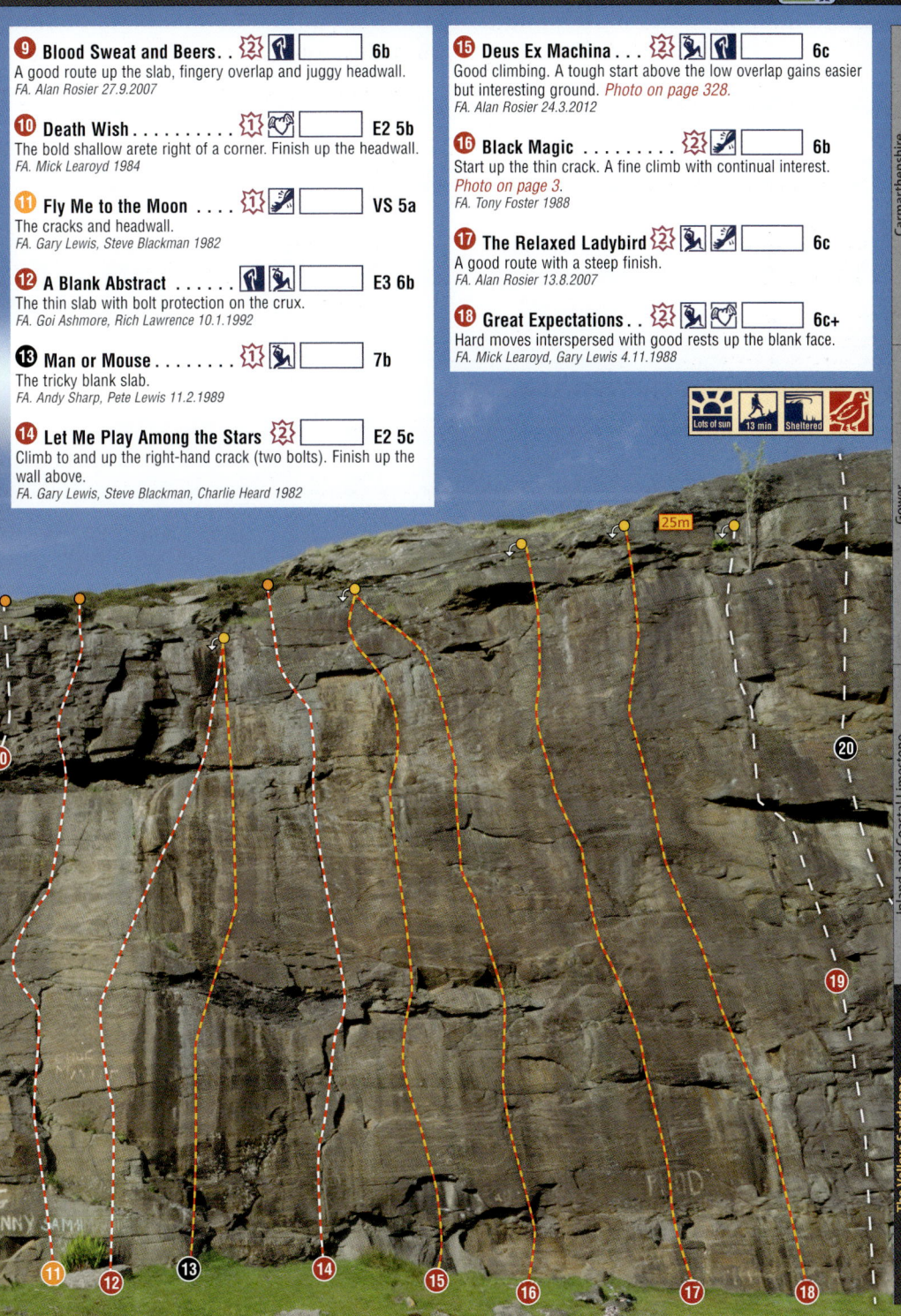

332 Navigation Quarry

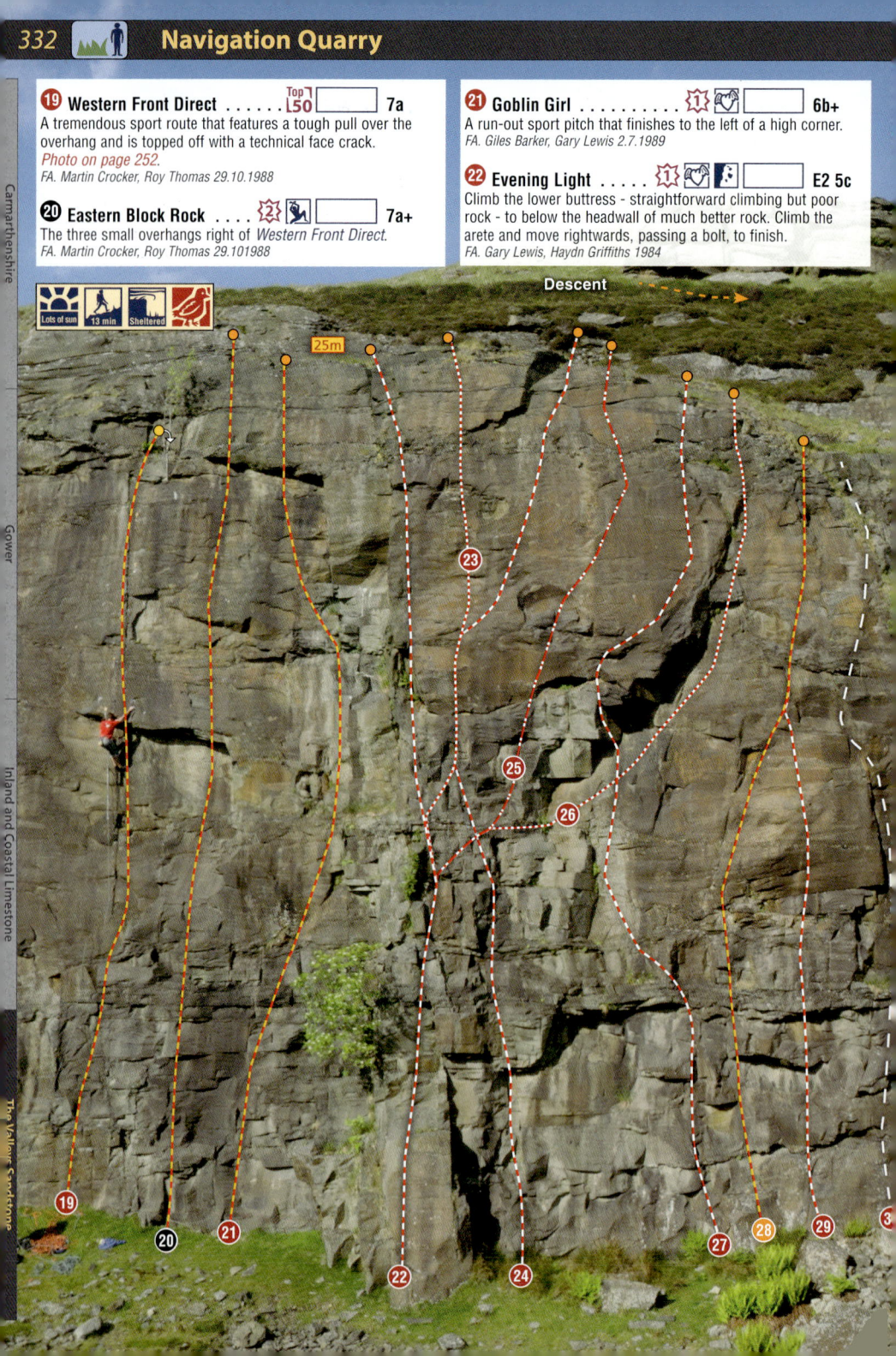

19 Western Front Direct ..... Top 50 — 7a
A tremendous sport route that features a tough pull over the overhang and is topped off with a technical face crack.
Photo on page 252.
FA. Martin Crocker, Roy Thomas 29.10.1988

20 Eastern Block Rock .... — 7a+
The three small overhangs right of *Western Front Direct*.
FA. Martin Crocker, Roy Thomas 29.101988

21 Goblin Girl .... — 6b+
A run-out sport pitch that finishes to the left of a high corner.
FA. Giles Barker, Gary Lewis 2.7.1989

22 Evening Light ..... — E2 5c
Climb the lower buttress - straightforward climbing but poor rock - to below the headwall of much better rock. Climb the arete and move rightwards, passing a bolt, to finish.
FA. Gary Lewis, Haydn Griffiths 1984

Navigation Quarry

23 Save a Mouse Eat A Pussy E3 6a
Climb easily to the upper slab and, from a borehole, climb up onto the slab and follow the scoop past an old bolt to the top.
FA. Gary Lewis, Giles Barker 6.1989

24 Mouse Trap E3 5c
The hardest climbing is on the upper slab and is bolted. Start up a small corner and then climb (no bolts) to a line of bolts on the upper slab that are followed rightwards to the top.
FA. Gary Lewis, P.Jones 15.8.1992

Access - No climbing 1st March to 1st August due to nesting birds. This restriction only applies to routes near where the bird nests. See BMC RAD for details.

25 The Owl and the Antelope E2 5c
Climb to an overhung ledge at the start of the right-trending line of overhangs. Move up to a niche and climb the wall above rightwards to the top, passing two horizontal cracks.
FA. Gary Lewis, Charlie Heard, Mick Learoyd 1983

26 On Jupiter and Mars E1 5b
A fine feature of the buttress that follows the right-trending line of overhangs. Care with the rock needed at the start.
FA. Gary Lewis, Steve Blackman 1982

27 Over the Moon E3 5c
Follow a leftward-slanting line that gains *On Jupiter and Mars*. Move right and pull over the overhang to get established on the headwall. Move right and finish up the exposed arete.
FA. Alan Rosier, Gary Lewis 3.4.2008

28 Crash Landing 6a
The slab and right-leading groove right of *On Jupiter and Mars*. The bolts are spaced and the finish needs care with the rock.
FA. Gary Lewis, Dick Renshaw 1983

29 Ol' Blue Eyes E3 6b
Climb to and over a prominent bulge past a single bolt.
FA. Giles Barker, M.Kidd 6.1989

30 Heart Throb E1 5c
Climb up to a corner and follow it (passing two bolts) to its end. Move left onto slabby ground to finish.
FA. Gary Lewis, Dave Hart 15.1.1989

31 Sheepbone Wall .... HVS 4c
The loose groove below a tree.
FA. Gary Lewis, Mick Learoyd 1983

32 Feeling Sheep 7b
A very brief bouldery crux on the right of the wall. Tree belay.
FA. Goi Ashmore 18.10.1997

To the right is a buttress with two bolted lines.

33 Alco-Troll 6a
The bolt-line up the left-hand side of arete.
FA. Alan Rosier, R.Giles 1.3.2008

34 Principles of Rock Mechanics, Part 1
.... 7a
Takes the right-hand side of the arete.
FA. Alan Rosier 5.3.2008

Deri

Deri is a steep wall of compact rock, tucked away in the hills above the town of the same name. It is not too far from Bargoed Quarry and a visit to both on the same day could be easily combined, if finger strength is not depleted! The main attraction at Deri is the steep wall of grade 7s which, once clean, gives some excellent sustained pitches. The crag has been de-bolted in the past, but most of the routes have been restored. It can be dirty, but once back in regular use should remain clean.

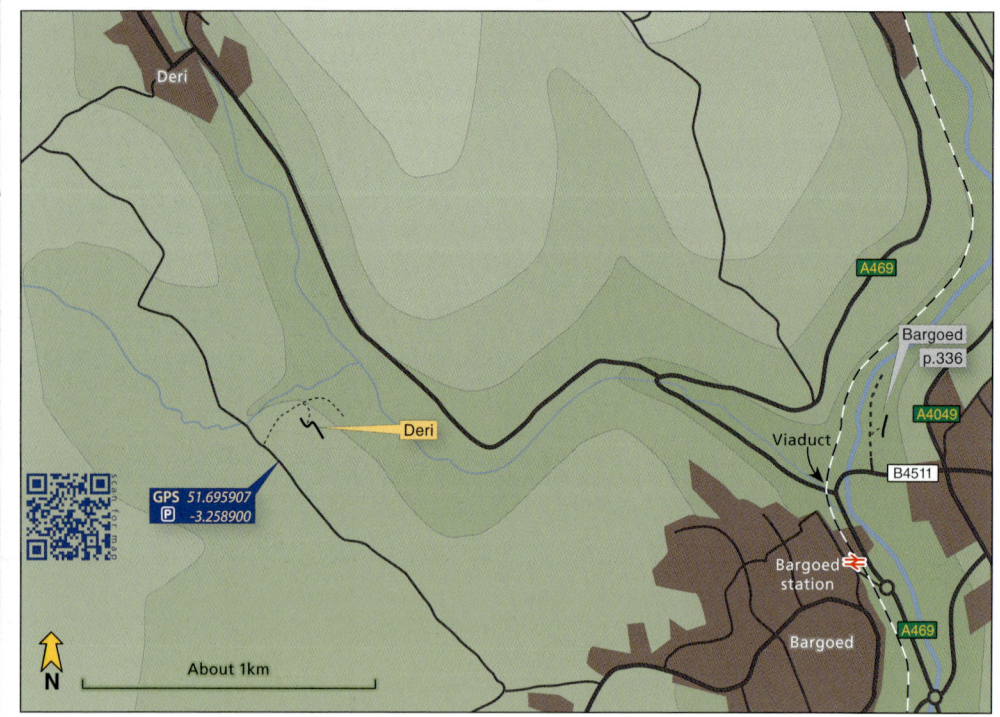

	No star	☆	☆☆	☆☆☆
up to 4c	-	-	-	-
5a to 6a+	1	-	-	-
6b to 7a	2	5	2	-
7a+ and up	2	2	-	1

Approach   Also see map on page 254

Take the A469 to Bargoed and drive past the station to a junction below a big viaduct. Turn left (signed to Deri) and continue to another left turn (also signed Deri). Once in the village, turn left over the river and, just beyond at a sharp right-hand bend, head straight on up a steep road. Go up this narrow road for 600m and turn left at a cattle grid. Follow the single track road for 1500m, past a farm, and down into a wooded dip. A little way up the road is some limited space to pull off and park. Walk back down to the wooded dip and go over a stile at a signpost. Walk downstream and, after 200m, a faint path contours off right to a fence. Step over and pick up another faint path that quickly leads to the quarry.

Conditions

The crag is shady and fairly high up, but well sheltered from the wind. The main wall is steep enough to allow climbing in light rain. Seepage does occur after prolonged rainfall.

Access

A restriction because of nesting birds is in place from 1st March to 30th June.

Deri

1 Ace in the Hole . . . . ☐ 5c
The short wall on the left of the crag, finishing through some overhangs. Needs cleaning and re-gearing.
FA. Roy Thomas, Gary Gibson 4.9.1994

2 Two of a Kind . . . . ☐ 7a+
The short wall with a scoop above a starting overhang. Climb this either by a hit and miss jump, or a stylish heelhook and rockover. The wall above is straightforward.
FA. Gary Gibson 4.9.1994

3 Mine's a Pair. . . . . ☐ 6b+
A steep start to the corner/groove.
FA. Gary Gibson 8.10.1994

4 Joker in the Pack . . . . ☐ 6c
The wall to the left of the arete of *House of Cards*.
FA. Roy Thomas, Gary Gibson 4.9.1994

5 House of Cards . . . . ☐ 7a
The left-hand side of the main arete. To be rebolted.
FA. Gary Gibson, Roy Thomas 1.9.1994

6 Kicking Ass and Taking Names
. . . . ☐ 7a
The main arete on its right-hand side is a fine line and climb.
FA. Andy Sharp, Pete Lewis, Tom Foster, P.Harding 27.3.1989

7 Chattery Teeth . . . . . ☐ 7a+
Excellent moves up the blank wall to a shared lower-off.
FA. Gary Gibson, Roy Thomas 8.10.1994

8 Olympic Doctor . . . . ☐ 7a+
Hard sequences at the start and finish.
FA. Andy Sharp, Pete Lewis 1993

9 Deri Made. . . . . ☐ 6c
Start up the flared crack. Move onto the wall and up to a break and sapling (don't touch the big wedge block). Continue up a crack to a final hard move.
FA. Roy Thomas, Gary Gibson 1.9.1994

10 Steroid John . . . . ☐ 6c+
A pumpy pitch up the wall to the right.
FA. Pete Lewis, Andy Sharp 1993

11 Coffee Shop . . . . ☐ 7a
Hard to start and a blind finish. There is a lone bolt to the right.
FA. Gary Gibson 1.9.1994

12 Full Dog . . . . ☐ 7b
The blunt arete is loose at the start. Still to be re-equipped.
FA. Gary Gibson, Roy Thomas 1.9.1994

13 Menage a Chien . . . . . . ☐ 7a+
Link *Mister Foothold* into *Full Dog*. Good climbing.
FA. Martin Crocker, Roy Thomas 13.5.1989

14 Mister Foothold . . . . ☐ 7a
The wall, groove and slot to a pumpy headwall on hidden jugs.
FA. Andy Sharp, Pete Lewis 1993

15 Troilism Trouble. . . . . ☐ E2 5c
The jamming crack left of the dirty corner. Good when clean.
FA. Roy Thomas, Martin Crocker 13.5.1989

Access - No climbing 1st March to 30th June because of nesting birds. See UKC and BMC RAD.

Bargoed

	No star	★	★★	★★★
up to 4c	-	-	-	-
5a to 6a+	4	1	1	1
6b to 7a	5	12	1	-
7a+ and up	-	1	1	-

Bargoed is a compact quarried wall with some worthwhile wall climbs which are of a fingery and technical nature. The routes are well equipped, and the rock is generally reliable and clean. This is a good spot for those looking for some good grade 6s with extremely quick and easy access.

Approach   Also see map on page 254

Follow the A469 past Bargoed railway station and downhill to a large viaduct on the left. Don't go under the viaduct but continue up the hill for 100m and turn left into a small lane - Quarry Row. Drive past the row of houses and continue for 100m to parking spaces on the right. The crag is just a short walk through the trees on the right. Do not park in sight of the houses.

GPS 51.696657 -3.229297

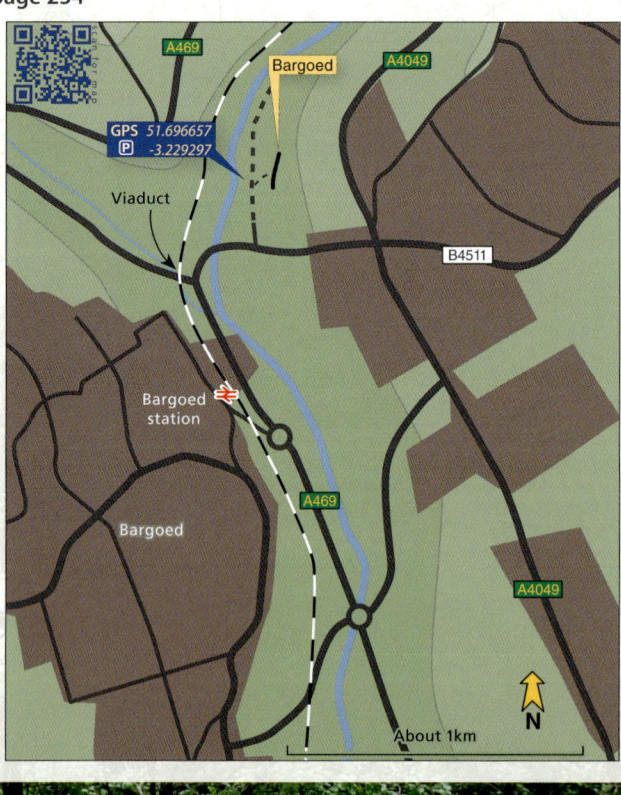

Conditions

The cliff is set amongst trees, west facing and sheltered. The rock is clean and dries fairly quickly, although some sections do seep.

Access

Park considerately - do not park in sight of the houses. No camping or fires.

Bargoed 337

Charlotte Macdonald making the final moves on Bargoed's most striking line - *Groping for Jugs* (6a) - *page 339*. Bargoed quarry is not extensive but has plenty of fingery and technical lines that are action packed from start to finish. Photo: John Warner

Bargoed

Bargoed
A quarried wall of good rock with a wide selection of well-equipped lines that are mostly technical and fingery.
Approach - Walk a short way through the wood.
Conditions - Sunny in the afternoon and quick to dry in the warmer months.

1 Gift Wrapped at Bargoed. 5c
The awkward slab on the far left.
FA. Liam Jay 2011

2 Ianto's Bargoed Bumblers Blind Spot
. . . . 6a+
Climb past staples and a bolt.
FA. Roy Thomas, Goi Ashmore, Eugene Travers-Jones 14.9.2013

3 Bargoed Bushwhacker . . 6b
Technical moves up the pockets and flakes to a shared lower-off.
FA. Roy Thomas, Goi Ashmore 13.10.2011

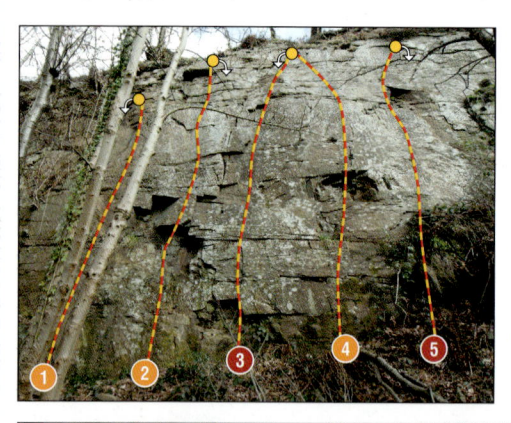

4 Bargoed Sideshow 6a
Move up ledges and continue past a red niche.
FA. Roy Thomas, Dai Emanuel 7.10.2011

5 Meat Seeking Missile 6b
The right-trending line above some ledges.
FA. Dai Emanuel 2012

6 Simply Simian 6b
A sneaky undercut at the coal break helps gain good footholds.
FA. Roy Thomas, Dai Emanuel 9.2011

7 Mr. Gorrilla's Got a Big Nose . . . E3 6b
Hard wall climbing passing a slot at mid-height.
FA. Martin Crocker, Roy Thomas 4.3.1989

8 Super Strung Direct . . . . 6b+
The left-hand start to the original line joins it near the top.
FA. Roy Thomas, Alan Rosier 11.9.2011

9 Super Strung Out at Bargoed
. . . . 6b
Climb up to a hole near the top and a lower-off just above.
FA. Roy Thomas, Dai Emanuel 2011

10 Bringing The Brane Theory To Bargoed
. . . . 6b
Climb the wall right of the high scoop passing a ledge.
FA. Roy Thomas, Goi Ashmore 1.9.2011

11 Bargoed Blow Job 6b
Aim for an undercut flake before moving left to a lower-off.
FA. Roy Thomas, Eugene Travers-Jones 4.9.2011

12 Beavers at Bargoed . 6a+
A hard start on pockets and edges gains the final overhang.
FA. Roy Thomas, Goi Ashmore 8.2011

Bargoed

13 Balthazaar's Ball Sac Bulges Beholding Bouncing Bargoed Booties 6b
The slab has a thin and difficult initial sequence.
FA. Roy Thomas, Alan Rosier 9.2011

14 House Training Catwoman 6b
Hollow flakes left of the corner. Finish over the overhang.
FA. Dai Emanuel, Roy Thomas 10.2011

15 Pepperatzi 6b
The corner, overhang and groove is a good line.
FA. Lyndsey Foulkes, Mick Learoyd 1989

16 Twenty One Ounces Of Blow . 6b+
Pull out left over the overlap. Follow the left arete to an awkward swing left at a pocket and finish up the *Pepperatzi* groove.
FA. Goi Ashmore 1.9.2011

17 Blowing For Tugs ...... 7a+
Direct up the front of the pillar via a hard bouldery rockover.
FA. Andy Sharp, Pete Lewis, John Harwood 29.1.1989

18 Groping For Jugs 6a
The superb central arete moving onto the left side at the top.
Photo on page 337.
FA. Goi Ashmore, Roy Thomas 1.9.2011

19 Hawk's Cheep .... 6a+
The corner to the right of *Groping for Jugs* has good moves.
FA. Pete Lewis, Andy Sharp, John Harwood 29.1.1989

20 Brittania 6b
The wall just right of the corner passing a small square niche via a very thin pull.
FA. Alan Rosier, Roy Thomas 26.9.2011

21 Beware the Burly Butcher of Bargoed .... 6b+
A left-trending line with a long undercut move and thin cracks.
FA. Roy Thomas, Goi Ashmore 8.8.2011

22 Our Man In Bargoed . 6c+
Climb direct above the start of *Beware the Burly Butcher*...
FA. Andy Sharp, Pete Lewis, John Harwood 29.01.1989

23 Lyddite .... 7a+
Thin fingery wall to a well positioned upper arete.
FA. Goi Ashmore 4.9.2011

24 Black Dog .... 6b+
Gain the ramp, move up a few metres and then step left. Climb the groove and crack above to finish.
FA. Andy Sharp, Pete Lewis, John Harwood 29.1.1989

25 Up For Grabs .... 6b+
From the ramp of *Black Dog*, move right and up past overhangs to a lower-off on the ledge.
FA. Mick Learoyd, Lyndsey Foulkes 1989

26 Bored of Brackla Becomes Benefactor of Bargoed 6c
The wall right of the *Black Dog* corner has a hard start.
FA. Goi Ashmore 6.8.2011

27 Bargain Basement Bargoed 6a
The final bolted line up the wall to a shared lower-off.
FA. Roy Thomas, Goi Ashmore 8.2011

Llanbradach

	No star	☆	☆☆	☆☆☆
up to 4c	3	-	-	-
5a to 6a+	6	1	-	-
6b to 7a	24	29	9	-
7a+ and up	2	5	5	3

Llanbradach quarry is the second largest sandstone quarry in southeast Wales and has the number of routes to match. It also has the biggest routes on sandstone to date - two-pitch routes up to a height of 50m. However, Llanbradach is not a place for those of an unadventurous nature as the wooded lower quarry is a bit of a jungle and the walls are dominated by vegetation, apart from the Expansionist Wall which penetrates the tree canopy. The Upper Tier has some good routes but they have seen little attention in recent years, and many will need a good clean before an ascent. All the routes have good fixed gear and lower-offs - they just need some TLC.

Approach   Also see map on page 254

From a large roundabout on the Caerphilly ring road, head north on the A469 signed to Llanbradach. Turn left at the next roundabout (this is the southern roundabout signed to Llanbradach if approaching from the north). Around 300m from the roundabout, a quarry track can be seen leading off to the left and under a railway bridge. Park at the roadside 150m further on, just beyond the traffic calming installation on the edge of the village. Go back to the quarry track and walk up it under the railway. Turn left onto a flat, wide path alongside the railway. Walk along the track for 100m to a narrow path on the right that leads through trees to a pond on the right-hand side of the quarry, from where all of the areas apart from the Western Wall and Upper Tier can be reached. To reach the Western Wall, walk a little further and take a vague path on the right which leads quickly to the crag. To reach the Upper Tier, continue along the wide track next to the railway line to some gateposts. Walk a further 230m along the track and pick up a gentle quarry incline that cuts back right. Follow a path up this and on to the bottom of the Upper Tier.

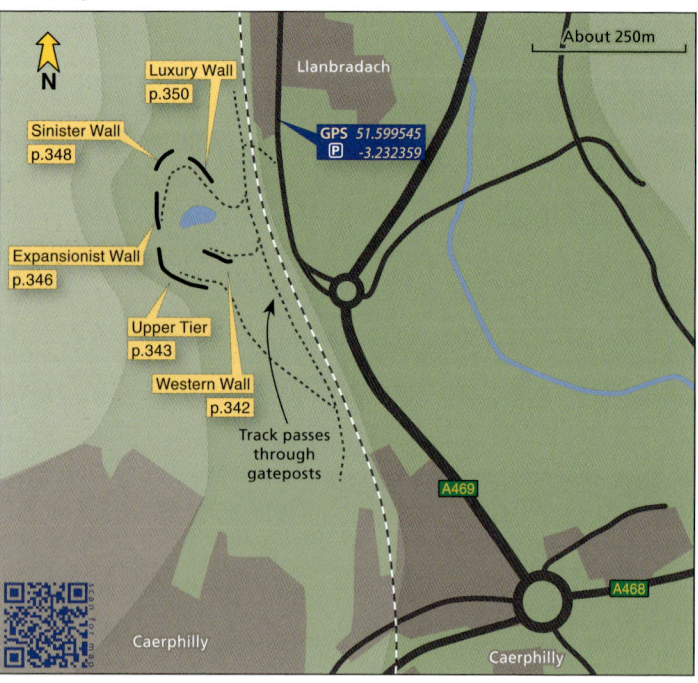

Conditions
The lower quarry is heavily vegetated and will be humid in warm weather and takes time to dry after wet weather, it is very sheltered, although this means it can be midgy. The Upper Tier is more open but the base is heavily vegetated and takes a bit of negotiating.

Llanbradach

Mark Tomlinson crimping his way up the leaning wall of *Slip Into Something Sexy* (7a+) - *page 350* - at Llanbradach Quarry. When clean and in prime condition Llanbradach offers some excellent routes. Photo: Mark Glaister

342 Llanbradach Western Wall

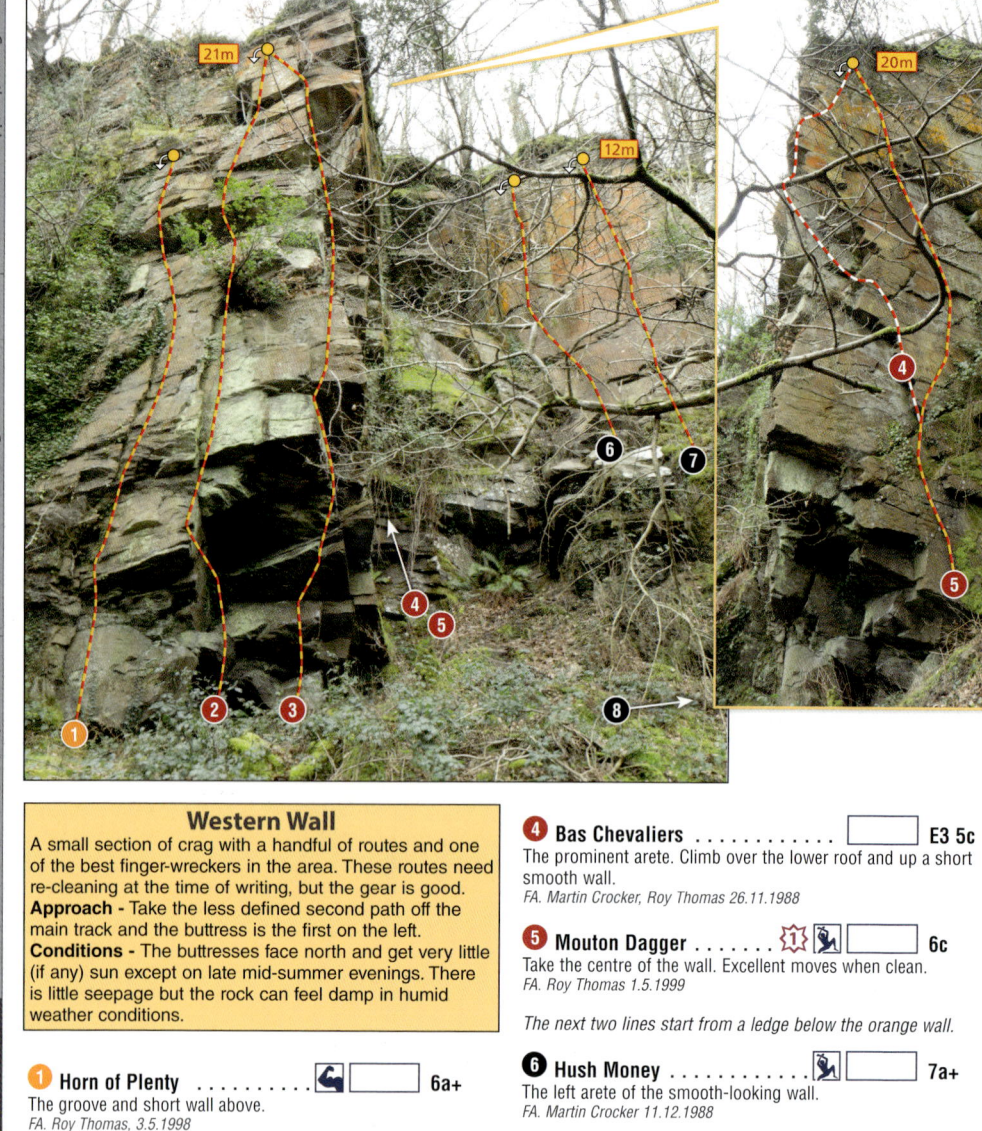

Western Wall

A small section of crag with a handful of routes and one of the best finger-wreckers in the area. These routes need re-cleaning at the time of writing, but the gear is good.
Approach - Take the less defined second path off the main track and the buttress is the first on the left.
Conditions - The buttresses face north and get very little (if any) sun except on late mid-summer evenings. There is little seepage but the rock can feel damp in humid weather conditions.

① Horn of Plenty .... 6a+
The groove and short wall above.
FA. Roy Thomas, 3.5.1998

② Magellan's Straight .... 6b+
The short overhang, groove and centre of the tower above.
FA. Roy Thomas 7.5.1998

③ Maurice Chevalier 7a
Pull right under the overlap to climb the groove and face above.
FA. Goi Ashmore 5.4.1999

④ Bas Chevaliers E3 5c
The prominent arete. Climb over the lower roof and up a short smooth wall.
FA. Martin Crocker, Roy Thomas 26.11.1988

⑤ Mouton Dagger 6c
Take the centre of the wall. Excellent moves when clean.
FA. Roy Thomas 1.5.1999

The next two lines start from a ledge below the orange wall.

⑥ Hush Money .... 7a+
The left arete of the smooth-looking wall.
FA. Martin Crocker 11.12.1988

⑦ Contraband 7c
Brilliant technical face climbing up the centre of the wall.
FA. Martin Crocker, Matt Ward, Roy Thomas 11.12.1988

The next line is on an isolated face 100m to the right.

⑧ Boston Strangler ... 7b
The narrow rectangular face.
FA. Martin Crocker 1990

Upper Tier **Llanbradach** *343*

Upper Tier

The upper tier of Llanbradach offers well equipped lines in a variety of styles in the mid-grades.
Warning - most of these routes need extensive re-cleaning at the time of writing.
Approach - Follow the track past the lower quarry entrance to gate posts. Walk another 230m and cut back up rightwards via an old angled quarry track to the left-hand end of the tier.
Conditions - The wall faces east and gets the sun until just after midday.

The first routes on the Upper Tier are on a smaller section of wall to the left and not on the topo.

❾ Roraima **6c**
The centre of the isolated tower.
FA. Roy Thomas, Gary Gibson 23.3.1997

❿ Three Men in a Goat **6c**
The left-hand of three routes from a small terrace keeping out of the crack on the left.
FA. Roy Thomas, Matt Hirst, Goi Ashmore 2.4.1997

⓫ Once Bitten **6b**
The centre of wall. Pleasant after the crux start from the ledge.
FA. Roy Thomas, Martin Crocker 1991

⓬ Twice Shy **6a**
The easier right-hand line of the wall. Pleasant.
FA. Roy Thomas, Gary Gibson 23.3.1997

⓭ Hollow Feeling **6b**
The short arete gives a gem of a route.
FA. Mick Learoyd, Roy Thomas 1991

⓮ Practice What You Preach **E3 5b**
A bold traditional route up the centre of the wall.
FA. Martin Crocker, Roy Thomas 1991

The following lines are shown on the topo.

⓯ Pampered **6b**
The left arete of the slabby wall.
FA. Roy Thomas 14.4.1997

⓰ You Change Me . . . . **6c+**
The centre of the slabby wall direct, swinging right from the arete to the belay.
FA. Martin Crocker 1991

⓱ Nappy Rush **6b**
An exciting route on positive holds but with poor rock low down.
FA. Roy Thomas 1997

⓲ Torch the Earth . . . . **7b+**
Fierce technical face climbing.
FA. Martin Crocker, Roy Thomas 27.1.1991

⓳ Dirty as a Dog **6b**
The impressive crack-line.
FA. Roy Thomas, Graham Royle, Mick Learoyd 27.1.1991

⓴ Desert Storm . . . . **7a+**
Sustained with one tricky move near the top.
FA. Martin Crocker, Roy Thomas 27.1.1991

344 Llanbradach Upper Tier

Many of these routes need re-cleaning at the time of writing, but the gear is in good shape.

㉑ Twenty Second Chance .... 7a+
A desperate start up the rounded arete.
FA. Martin Crocker, Roy Thomas 26.1.1991

㉒ Sixty Seconds Go See 7a
More hard starting moves with fine face climbing above.
FA. Martin Crocker, Roy Thomas 26.1.1991

㉓ Roaring Forties .... 6b+
Good wall climbing finishing via a crack and shallow groove.
FA. Roy Thomas, John Bullock 1989

㉔ Between the Lines .... 6b+
The right-hand line on the wall.
FA. Roy Thomas, Graham Royle 1991

㉕ The Missing Quarter .... 6b+
The blunt rib. Take care with a large flake and watch out for the top section.
FA. Roy Thomas, Ed Rees 1998

㉖ Saboo 6c
The shallow groove system is a little fragile and has a hard move to leave the ledge at the top.
FA. Mick Learoyd, Roy Thomas 1989

㉗ Dandelion 6b
A pleasant shallow groove system and the wall above. Can suffer from seepage.
FA. Matt Hirst 8.4.1997

㉘ Burdock 6b
The wall just left of the main angle of the bay.
FA. Matt Hirst 6.6.1997

㉙ Blinded by Love .... 6b+
A superb sustained outing on the stepped arete.
FA. Roy Thomas, Graham Royle, Mick Learoyd 1991

㉚ The Laughing Policeman .... 6b+
The crack and groove system starting up a difficult rib. It suffers from seepage low down, hence the line is on the rib on the right at the start.
FA. Roy Thomas 13.7.1997

㉛ Fair Cop .... 6b+
The crack, wall and flying arete. A long sustained pitch with an 'out there' finish.
FA. Roy Thomas, Gary Gibson 24.5.1997

㉜ Aptitude Test 7a
The blunt and desperately technical low-level arete.
FA. Martin Crocker 1991

㉝ The Merthyr Infill 6c
A short, technical and worthwhile wall.
FA. Gary Gibson 23.3.1997

㉞ My Blue Bell .... 6a+
The shallow groove with an awkward bulge.
FA. Gary Gibson, Roy Thomas 18.5.1997

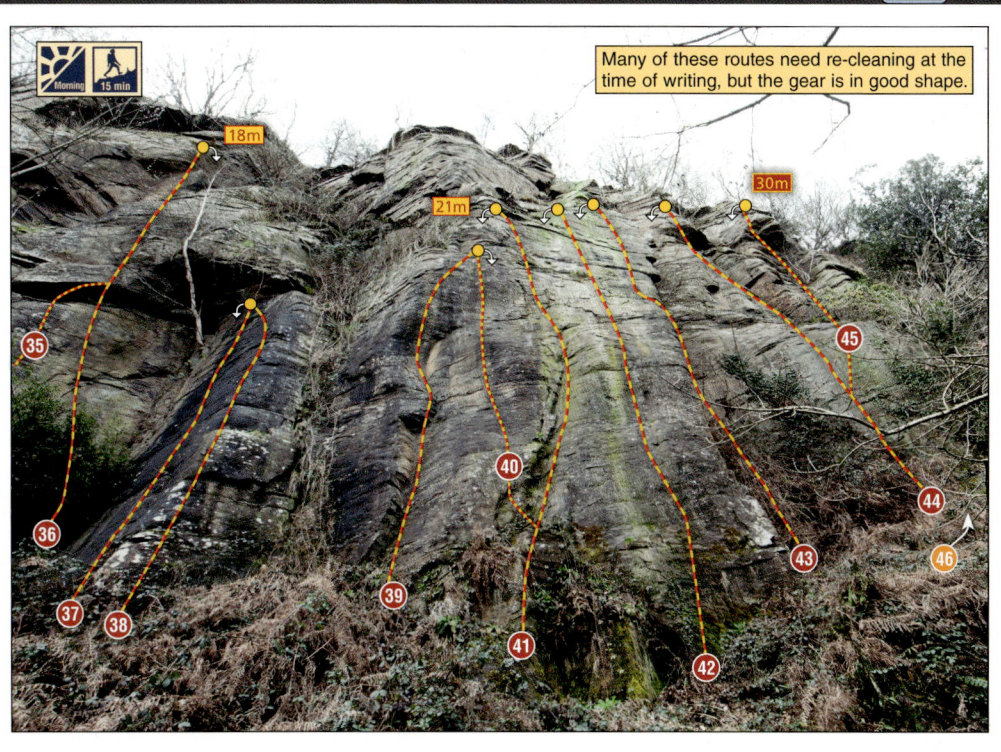

Upper Tier Llanbradach   345

Many of these routes need re-cleaning at the time of writing, but the gear is in good shape.

35 All Sand Together .... 6c+
A blunt rib with a short steep section. Move right at the third bolt into *Red 'erring*.
FA. Gary Gibson 18.5.1997

36 Red 'erring .... 6b+
The steep pink wall, bulge and bold rounded finale.
FA. Gary Gibson, Roy Thomas 18.5.1997

37 Plaque Attack .... 6b+
Technical climbing up the angled face.
FA. Gary Gibson, Roy Thomas 23.3.1997

38 Incidentally .... 6b+
The arete of the wall moving left to the belay.
FA. Gary Gibson, Roy Thomas 23.3.1997

39 Cop the Lot 7a
The blunt rib on the other side of the dirty groove has a hard finish.
FA. Gary Gibson 24.5.1997

40 The Caerphilly Cop Out ..... 6c+
The blunt rib via a long reach and short difficult face.
FA. Gary Gibson 24.5.1997

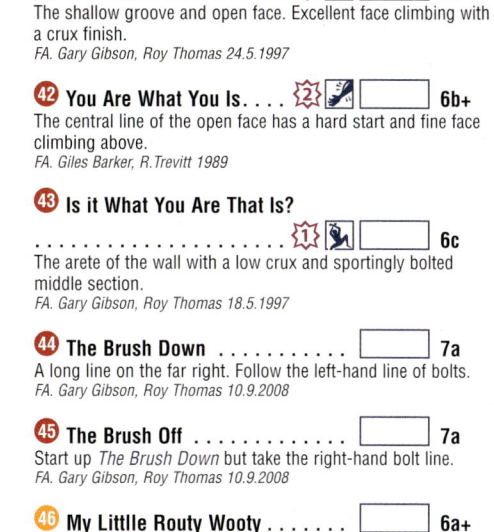

41 I Am What I Am 6b
The shallow groove and open face. Excellent face climbing with a crux finish.
FA. Gary Gibson, Roy Thomas 24.5.1997

42 You Are What You Is .... 6b+
The central line of the open face has a hard start and fine face climbing above.
FA. Giles Barker, R.Trevitt 1989

43 Is it What You Are That Is?
.... 6c
The arete of the wall with a low crux and sportingly bolted middle section.
FA. Gary Gibson, Roy Thomas 18.5.1997

44 The Brush Down 7a
A long line on the far right. Follow the left-hand line of bolts.
FA. Gary Gibson, Roy Thomas 10.9.2008

45 The Brush Off 7a
Start up *The Brush Down* but take the right-hand bolt line.
FA. Gary Gibson, Roy Thomas 10.9.2008

46 My Littlle Routy Wooty .... 6a+
A line on the far right.
FA. Gary Gibson, Roy Thomas 10.9.2008

Llanbradach — Expansionist Wall

Expansionist Wall

In the centre of the quarry lies its largest section of cliff. The lower walls provide a series of pitches with a friendly feel to them, whilst the upper section has a handful of routes with a significantly bigger feel to them. The upper wall is difficult of access but the best approaches are via the routes on the lower walls below or by an abseil in.

Approach - Take the path into the lower quarry and skirt around the base of the wall past the Sinister Wall. The first three routes are on the left, up a steep slope. The routes on the impressive upper wall are reached by pitches on the lower section, plus one of two connecting pitches.

Conditions - The wall faces east, is sheltered and receives the sunshine until about 1pm. It dries quickly and, apart from a little seepage in its lower half (most of which can be avoided), provides an ideal venue in many weather conditions.

This is the tall vertical wall on the left reached via a steep slope below the main crag.

❶ Amnesia 7a
The first line on the left of the wall to the right of a tree growing out of a crack high on the wall.
FA. Gary Gibson 5.5.1996

❷ Insomnia 6c
The central line of the wall that features a hard move to gain a ledge. Go careful with the final flake-crack.
FA. Gary Gibson 5.5.1996

❸ Acatalepsia .... 6a+
The wall just left of the right-facing flake/crack.
FA. Roy Thomas 3.6.1996

❹ Sub-Contraction 7a
The left arete of the wall has a single desperate move.
FA. Gary Gibson 7.4.1996

❺ Simple Addition 6c
A flat wall peppered with pockets.
FA. Roy Thomas, Gary Gibson 5.4.1996

❻ Post Expressionist 6b
A good pitch up the centre of the wall via a prominent flake. Can be used to reach *The Caerphilly Contract* and *Little White Lies*.
FA. Roy Thomas, Gary Gibson 31.3.1996

❼ Too Keynes by Half 6c
A fine little route up the right edge of the wall. Care is needed with the initial holds. Can be used to reach *Caerphilly Contract* and *Little White Lies*.
FA. Roy Thomas, Gary Gibson 5.4.1996

❽ Falling Freely .... 7a+
A left-trending pitch up the prominent red wall. Fingery and on good rock. Any wetness at the start can be avoided.
FA. Gary Gibson 17.3.1996

❾ Splashdown .... 6c+
The prominent left-slanting groove exiting right to a lower-off. Take care at the start.
FA. Gary Gibson, Goi Ashmore 16.3.1996

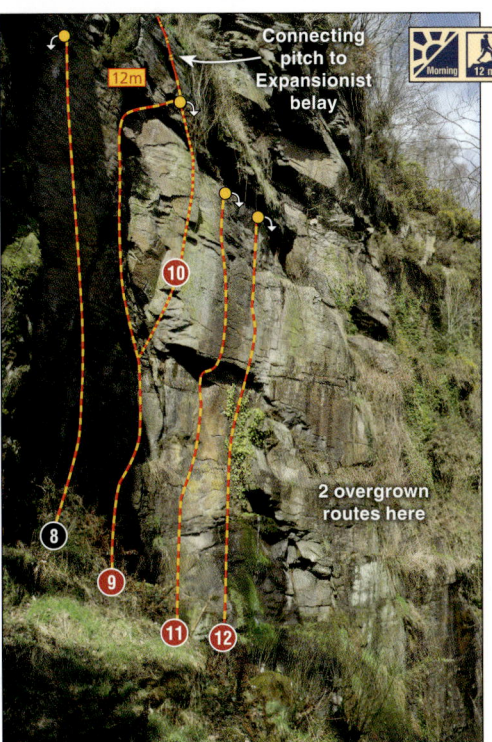

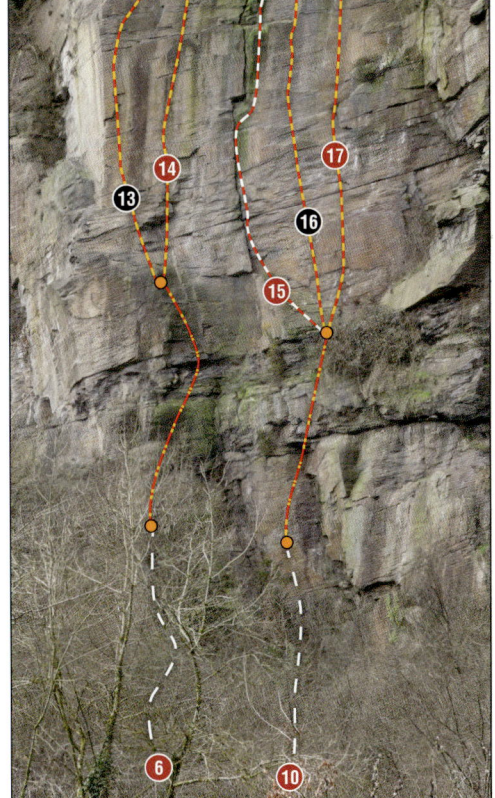

Expansionist Wall **Llanbradach** 347

⑩ Total Recoil. .... 6b+
A varied route with a short crux wall. There is a link pitch from this to the *The Expansionist* and routes to the right.
FA. Gary Gibson, Roy Thomas 16.3.1996

⑪ Cascade .... 6c+
A technical sequence leads through the overlap.
FA. Gary Gibson 3.2.1996

⑫ Sphagnum 45 .... 6b
The groove and wall above the spring.
FA. Gary Gibson 5.4.1996

There are two routes to the right, **Splash it on all Over**, 6c and **Bathtime**, 6b but these have become completely overgrown.

This upper wall has a number of routes in an impressive and quite intimidating position. They are best reached by Post Expressionist or Total Recoil and a connecting pitch.

⑬ The Caerphilly Contract
.... 7b+
The magnificent upper arete provides a classic route with a well defined crux section. Easier for the tall.
FA. Martin Crocker, Roy Thomas, Matt Ward 6.11.1988

⑭ Little White Lies ...... 6c+
The easier wall to the right of *The Caerphilly Contract* is not quite so fine but still worth the effort.
FA. Martin Crocker, Roy Thomas 27.11.1988

⑮ The Expansionist E3 5b
The striking central crack-line gives a brilliant pitch. The first pitch fell down so start up *Total Recoil*.
FA. Pat Littlejohn, John Harwood, Clive Horsfield 25.5.1978

⑯ Grit Box .... 7a+
One of the finest wall pitches in the area. The crux is at the start - the rest just majestic cranking.
FA. Gary Gibson 5.4.1996

⑰ Giant Sand 7a
The right-hand line on this wall is worth doing if you have made the effort to get up here in the first place.
FA. Gary Gibson, Roy Thomas 31.4.1996

Llanbradach Sinister Wall

Sinister Wall
A compact wall split into two sections, the right-hand being more overhanging than the left. Both walls give some nice routes mostly on small edges and pockets and all with a fingery feel to them.

Approach - From the Luxury Wall, continue on the path and bear right after 50m to the wall that can be seen amongst the trees.

Conditions - The wall faces southeast and gets sunshine until mid-afternoon. Unfortunately it does suffer seepage during the winter months.

❶ Bringeth yon Leach . . . . **7a+**
The first line on the wall involves some extreme crimping.
FA. Gary Gibson 2009

❷ Food for Parasites . . . . **7a+**
The hardest on this section of wall and a true test of finger strength and technique.
FA. Roy Thomas, Graham Royle 12.1996

❸ The Host **6c**
Climb just left of the central streak utilising a few flaky holds. Finish on the left.
FA. Roy Thomas 1.7.1996

❹ Giving it all Up **7a**
The centre of the wall has a crux at half-height.
FA. Roy Thomas, Gary Gibson 5.5.1996

❺ Dreaming in Colour **7a**
A superb sustained and fingery sequence is needed to solve the problem posed by the wall to the left of the arete.
FA. Roy Thomas, Gary Gibson 28.4.1996

❻ Letters of Life **6c**
The left-hand side of the blunt arete with one difficult move.
FA. Roy Thomas, Gary Gibson 28.4.1996

Sinister Wall **Llanbradach** *349*

7 The Evil Eye 7a
The cracks and wall past the 'eye' to a difficult slab. Climbable when it is raining.
FA. Gary Gibson 28.4.1996

8 In Blood, of Life, of Sin?
.... 7a+
An excellent fingery wall climb, with a dynamic crux.
FA. Gary Gibson 28.4.1996

9 Abbattoir and Costello
.... 7b+
The centre of the black wall. Intricate, sustained and steep.
FA. Gary Gibson 29.6.1996

10 Sinister 7b
The final route of the wall has a low crux and a finger stamina test above.
FA. Gary Gibson, Roy Thomas 4.5.1996

The wall above has two routes.

11 Overleaf 6b
The wall above the ledge gained from *Dreaming in Colour* with a wobbly 'leaf'.
FA. Roy Thomas, Gary Gibson 19.6.1996

12 Snapper 6c
From the top of *The Evil Eye*, straightforward climbing leads upwards in a superb position.
FA. Gary Gibson 29.6.1996

350 Llanbradach   The Luxury Wall

The Luxury Wall
This is the wall next to the pond, and the first encountered on the main approach. It has a handful of pitches with two in particular that are worth seeking out.
Approach - Take the path off the main track and the wall is situated directly above the murky pond.
Conditions - The wall faces southwest and gets the sun from mid-morning. It takes a little seepage but dries relatively quickly. Midges can be a problem in humid weather due to the closeness of the pond.

1 Shadow of the Sun . . 7a
A super little route on the isolated wall to the left.
FA. Roy Thomas, Gary Gibson 29.6.1996

2 Slip into Something Sexy
. . . . 7a+
The fine wall gives an excellent exercise in fingery wall climbing.
Photo on page 341.
FA. Martin Crocker, Roy Thomas 12.11.1988

3 Slipped. . . . . 6c+
The corner, utilising the right wall.
FA. Alan Rosier 2009

The Luxury Wall Llanbradach 351

4 Slipping into Luxury . 6b+
Technical face climbing on 'dinks' and pockets up the wall between the corner and arete gains a mid-height ledge on the rib. Finish up the rib. Very pleasant.
FA. Matt Ward, Gordon Jenkin, Martin Crocker 6.11.1988

5 The Slap of Luxury . . 7a
The right-hand side of arete and wall has a butch start and a technical finish.
FA. Roy Thomas, Gary Gibson 30.3.1996

6 The Luxury Gap 7a
The centre of the wall above a ledge. Surprisingly technical.
FA. Gary Gibson 30.3.1996

7 Internal Reflection 6a
A decent easier route.
FA. Roy Thomas, Gary Gibson 30.3.1996

8 Gladness 4c
The groove has some poor rock.
FA. Roy Thomas, Gary Gibson, Dai Emanuel 2009

9 Madness. 6b
The bulge and poorer upper wall.
FA. Roy Thomas, Gary Gibson 2009

10 Sadness 5a
The groove system.
FA. Gordon Jenkin, Roy Thomas 6.11.1988

11 Blandess. 4c
Climb past some unreliable rock.
FA. Gary Gibson, Roy Thomas, Dai Emanuel 2009

12 Badness 4a
Climb on poor rock up sloping ledges.
FA. Gary Gibson 2009

Crymlyn Quarry

	No star	⭐	⭐⭐	⭐⭐⭐
up to 4c	-	-	-	-
5a to 6a+	6	-	-	-
6b to 7a	4	5	1	-
7a+ and up	1	1	-	-

Crymlyn Quarry is a local venue made up of a series of walls that are extensive but heavily vegetated. Only the routes on the Main Wall and Viaduct Quarry are included here - for details on all of the routes see SWMC website.

Approach   Also see map on page 254
On the A467 north of Newbridge, at the traffic lights at the junction with the B4251, continue for 100m and turn right on a minor road. Follow the road left for 50m and park at a pull-in.
Main Wall - On the other side of the road is a path leading up behind houses. Follow this for 450m (past garages and below a retaining wall) to a stile and tarmac path. Cross the path and head up the slope to the quarry and the Main Wall is on the left.
Viaduct Quarry - Walk along the road past a barrier for a couple of hundred metres and the wall is on the right amongst the trees.

Conditions
A rather sombre spot that is best visited on a sunny evening. There is lots of vegetation although the Main Wall is relatively clean. Seepage occurs and the walls take time to dry. Viaduct Quarry may offer dry climbing in the rain in summer as the dense tree canopy shelters the crag to some degree.

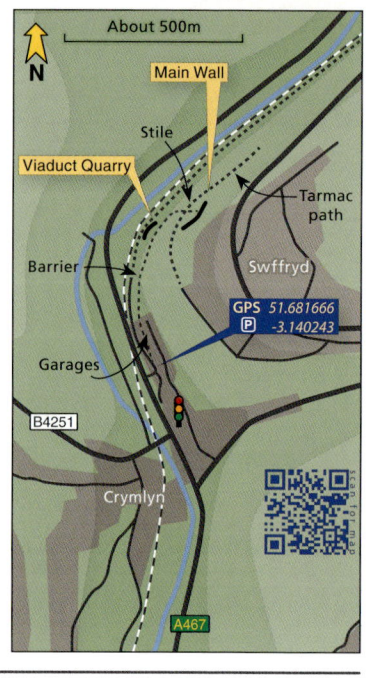

GPS 51.681666 / -3.140243

Viaduct Quarry
A very compact vertical wall of reasonable rock that has a number of face routes that may stay dry during rain in the summer months. The tree canopy is very dense and as a result once wet the face does take time to dry. Some of the lines on the margins are dirty but the central lines do stay clean.

1 Night Watchman **6a**
Move up the short wall left of a crack and then traverse right to a lower-off. Often vegetated.
FA. Roy Thomas 8.2010

2 Sticky Wicket . . . . **6a+**
Climb the thin short wall to a lower-off shared with *Night Watchman*.
FA. Roy Thomas, Dai Emanuel 4.8.2010

3 Opening Batman **6a**
The first of the longer lines.
FA. Roy Thomas 19.5.2010

4 Amber Leaf . . . . **6a+**
The curving thin crack-line.
FA. Alan Rosier 9.11.2009

5 Arabesque **E5 6a**
Takes a short thin wall to join *Malice*.
FA. Martyn Crocker 3.6.2010

6 Malice . . . . ⭐ **6c**
Follow pockets to the break and then make hard moves above.
FA. Alan Rosier 9.11.2009

7 Green Ginger Wine **6a**
Climb the wall past a round pocket to the break, and then take the ramp above to finish.
FA. Alan Rosier 9.11.2009

8 Tikka-tikka Kiss-kiss . . . . **6b+**
The wall to the right of *Green Ginger Wine*.
FA. Alan Rosier 18.6.2010

9 Chubby Rambo **6b**
The fingery wall is hard. The lower wall may need a brush.
FA. Alan Rosier 27.6.2010

10 I Wish My Wife Was This Dirty **6b**
Often mossy. The upper wall is climbed direct, past a pocket.
FA. Alan Rosier 12.9.2010

To the right is a bolted line in the sidewall that has been reclaimed by the vegetation.

Crymlyn Quarry

Main Wall

The Main Wall at Crymlyn has the best routes of the various walls hereabouts. The wall was extensively cleaned when it was first developed, but is prone to becoming dirty and also takes time to dry out. Only venture here during good weather and expect to have to do some cleaning.

11 The Clart Mountain Project 7b
The roof crack up and left of the main wall is a fierce undertaking - best to tape up.
FA. Simon Rawlinson 27.5.2011

12 A Star Too Far .... 6a+
The series of cracks and ledges on the left to an exposed leftwards finish up the final wall.
FA. Chris Wyatt 5.5.2010

13 Piano Dentist .... 6b+
Climb to a rest below the roof, then pull over it at a crack using jams and a wedged block. Finish up the crack in the wall.
FA. Rob McAllister 18.7.2009

14 Birth Canal .... 6c+
A slim corner and rib lead to the break and roof. Pull over with difficulty and finish up the still tricky upper wall.
FA. Rob McAllister 28.7.2009

15 Jalapeno Desperado 7a
Climb the intricate lower wall to the break (lower-off here - 6b to this point). Make a long reach over the roof to holds, pull over and climb the contrasting wall above to a lower-off.
FA. Alan Rosier 18.7.2010

16 Brown Eyed Girl 6c
Climb directly up to the break and niche in the roof just above. Pull over the roof past the niche and finish up a thin flake-line.
FA. Alan Rosier 22.8.2010

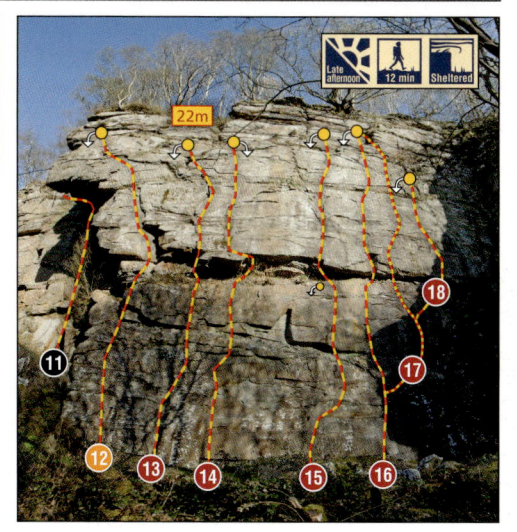

17 The Inscrutable Umberto Manteca .... 6c+
Start up *Brown Eyed Girl* and, at its second bolt, move right and climb to the break. Pull over the roof right of the niche and finish up the wall above to a shared lower-off with *Brown Eyed Girl*.
FA. Alan Rosier 22.8.2009

18 Blackberry Crumble 6c
From the fourth bolt on *The Inscrutable Umberto Manteca*, climb to the break. Pull over and climb the face above.
FA. Alan Rosier 16.10.2009

Tyle y Coch

	No star	★	★★	★★★
up to 4c	8	-	-	-
5a to 6a+	-	2	-	-
6b to 7a	-	4	5	-
7a+ and up	-	1	1	-

Tyle y Coch quarry is set in a pleasant quiet dell on the hillside between Abercarn and Newbridge. It has a sheer main wall of quality sandstone plus another wall with some pleasant easier offerings.

Approach   Also see map on page 254
From the A467 turn off towards West End and follow the road into the village and past The Crown pub. Continue out of the village and, after around 500m, park in a large lay-by on the left. Walk back 20m and, at a telegraph pole, nip up the steep bank and follow a path left to a low tunnel under the disused railway line. The quarry is on the other side of the tunnel.

Conditions
The quarry gets some morning sun but there is a dense tree canopy. Seepage does occur and the Main Wall takes time to dry out; once dry the Main Wall is steep enough to allow climbing in the rain.

Access
The cliff is on private land and a notice is posted stating that climbing is prohibited, although no reports of climbing being prevented have been reported. The issue is to do with civil liability - please leave if asked and report any information to the BMC and Rockfax. The inclusion of the quarry in this book implies no right of access to climb there.

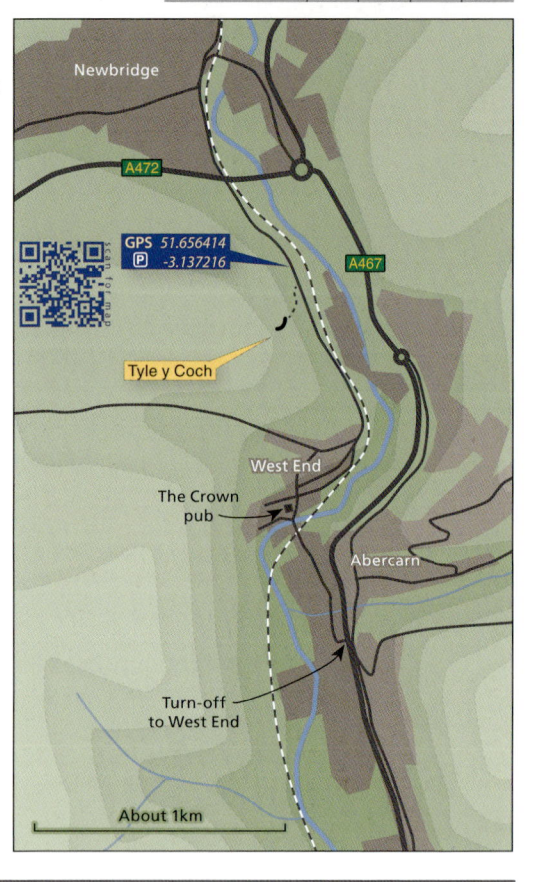

GPS 51.656414 -3.137216

Main Wall
The Main Wall is a tall and compact sheet of quarried sandstone split vertically by lots of thin cracks and crossed by some overlaps. This is a good spot for those after some tough lines in the mid-grades.
Conditions - Very shady due to the dense tree canopy in summer and suffers quite badly from seepage - best to have a plan B as it can be wet when least expected. However, once dry it gives sheltered climbing in the rain.
Access - The crag is on private land and climbing is not allowed by the landowners.

❶ **Y Caled Caled** 7c
Steep new line 20m to the left of the main wall.
FA. Mathew Wright 20.9.2016

❷ **Rump and Scoop** 6a
The arete to the left of the large corner is worthwhile.
FA. John James, Steve Abbott, Wayne Gladwin 8.10.2000

❸ **Root Canal** .... 6a+
The large corner is a bit of a struggle right until the end.
FA. John James, T.Williams 23.7.2000

❹ **Belly Up** 7b
The vague crack-line via a hole and a difficult and fingery finale on the headwall.
FA. Gordon Jenkin 16.9.2001

Main Wall **Tyle y Coch** 355

⑤ A Cleft Stick 7a
Climb the left fork of the thin Y-crack in the lower wall and then continue via an overlap and tricky sequence on the headwall.
FA. Gary Gibson, Roy Thomas 23.9.2001

⑥ The Pink Lady 6c+
Take on the centre of the wall trending rightwards via an incipient crack-line that forms the right fork of the Y-crack in the lower wall.
FA. Gordon Jenkin, Gary Gibson 16.9.2001

⑦ Paradise Row 7a
An excellent wall climb both sustained and technical. The finish provides the crux.
FA. Gary Gibson, Roy Thomas 23.9.2001

⑧ Fairies Wear Boots 6c+
The long thin snaking crack gives a great outing. The lower-off is just above the second overlap. *Photo on page 357.*
FA. Alan Rosier, Bill Gregory, Rob McAllister 16.8.2013

⑨ The Four Minute Tyle 7b
A direct line with a hard start and finish.
FA. Guy Percival 17.9.2014

⑩ Peachy 6b+
The wall past a jutting hold and a borehole. The overlap above provides the main difficulties.
FA. John James, Wayne Gladwyn 14.7.2000

⑪ Mislivings 7a
A peculiar left-trending line to a final bulging finish. Start up *Peachy* and go left with feet under the overlap initially.
FA. John James, Wayne Gladwyn 22.6.2001

⑫ The Big Tissue 6b+
The overlap to the left of the arete, starting with a tough mantle move and finishing up a thin wall.
FA. John James, Wayne Gladwyn, D.Jones 13.5.2001

⑬ Cheeky Arete S
The arete with a single peg in place.
FA. Steve Abbott, John James, Wayne Gladwyn 14.5.2000

Tyle y Coch — Minor Wall

356

Minor Wall

The Minor Wall is the first wall seen on entering the quarry. It is a little off-putting but has some easier lines that do get traffic.

Conditions - Very shady due to the dense tree canopy in summer and suffers quite badly from seepage. If planning a visit it is best to have a plan B as it can be wet when least expected. Once dry is gives sheltered climbing in the rain.

⛔ **Access** - The crag is on private land and climbing is not allowed by the landowners.

1 Bore Hole 3c
Climb the line of borehole strikes on the left of the wall.
FA. Wayne Gladwyn, John James 16.7.2000

2 The Ring 3c
Climb the tiny corner line and go direct above.
FA. Wayne Gladwyn, John James 16.7.2000

3 Mal Culo 4c
Head out right from *The Ring* to a slab and finish over an overhang.
FA. Wayne Gladwyn, John James, J.Keyhole 7.5.2000

4 Buen Culo 4b
Climb a steep wall to easier angled ground above.
FA. Wayne Gladwyn, Steve Abbott, John James 13.5.2000

5 Suppose a Tree 4c
Start up the corner and move left before climbing to a lower-off that is just above a small roof.
FA. Wayne Gladwyn, John James 8.7.2000

6 High Moon 6b
A good little pitch up the face sandwiched between the arete and the corner.
FA. John James, Wayne Gladwyn 12.1999

7 Enema of the Affair .... 6c+
The arete via some perplexing manoeuvres.
FA. John James, Wayne Gladwyn 14.5.2000

8 Jumping Jack Flash 4c
The short orange wall. To be bolted.
FA. Steve Abbott, John James, Wayne Gladwyn 14.5.2000

9 Lily of The Valleys 3c
The final easier-angled line. To be bolted.
FA. Steve Abbott, John James, Wayne Gladwyn, D.Jones 4.2.2001

Al Rosier on *Fairies Wear Boots* (6c+) - *page 355* - at Tyle y Coch. Photo: Rob McAllister

Sirhowy

	No star	⭐	⭐⭐	⭐⭐⭐
up to 4c	-	-	-	-
5a to 6a+	18	4	1	-
6b to 7a	8	9	6	2
7a+ and up	-	2	5	-

Sirhowy is one of the best chunks of quarried sandstone in the area, made even better by its tranquil setting with little in the way of road traffic noise or onlookers. It also has its own picnic area complete with bench and tables! The best climbing is on The Rust Curtain with its brilliant line-up of fingery wall climbs, whilst the more recently developed Western Wall has plenty of excellent (slightly) easier climbing on some of the best rock around.

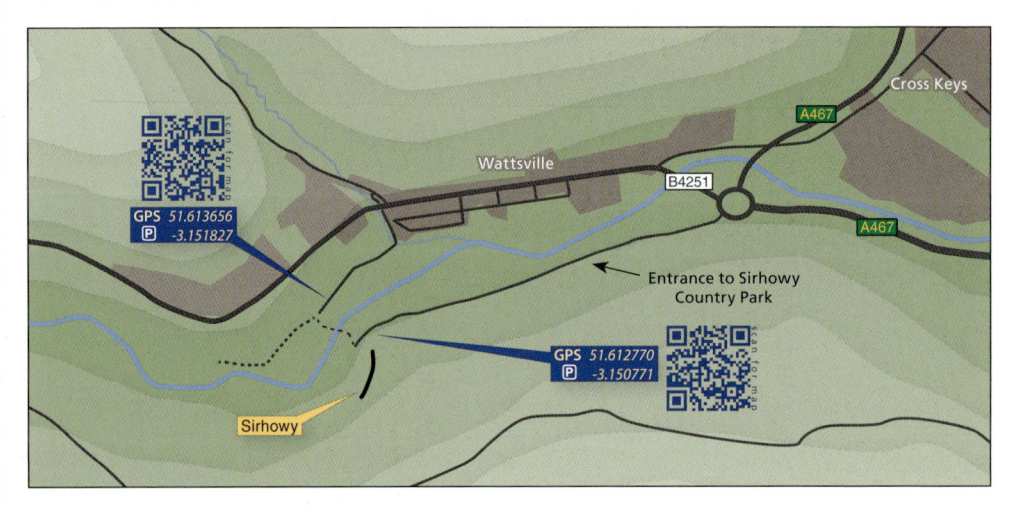

Approach   Also see map on page 254
From junction 28 on the M4, take the A467 dual carriageway north to the fourth roundabout. Take the first left at this roundabout, which leads directly into the Sirhowy Country Park. Park at the end (fee), next to the crag. The barriers to the park often close early, but the times for closure are posted on the notice board at the entrance.
Alternatively, in the middle of Wattsville, turn right off the main road onto Hafod Tudor Terrace. Go down it for 50m and turn sharp left under a tunnel then continue downhill and then turn right. In 200m a large parking area is reached on the left. Walk a short way further on the road and then go left over a bridge to arrive at the parking area in the Country Park - this way has no fee or problems with barrier closures.

Conditions
The crag faces west and receives afternoon and early evening sun although the tree canopy is dense in summer. It dries relatively quickly except in the winter months when seepage is present. Sirhowy can be a perfect venue in warm weather.

Access
There is no official right of access and the park does have a warden who is usually at the park entrance. Climbers are reminded that they climb at their own risk and should remember to park in the alternative spot across the river to avoid being trapped in the Country Park should the barrier be lowered when it closes. There are signs in place saying that climbing is not allowed - if asked to leave please do so courteously.

Sirhowy

Jen Stephens midway up the sustained thin cracks of *Strange Little Girl* (6c) - *page 360* - at The Rust Curtain section of Sirhowy. The Rust Curtain contains a great line-up of quality hard face routes. Photo: Tom Skelhon.

Sirhowy — The Rust Curtain

The Rust Curtain

One of the cleanest walls on the sandstone crags, offering some fierce and fingery face climbing with a very pleasant ambiance.

Approach - A simple stroll from the parking places.

Conditions - The wall takes relatively little seepage outside the winter months. The face picks up sun from mid afternoon and dries quickly.

Access - Climbing is not officially allowed. If asked to leave, please do so.

❶ The Waco Kid **6b**
The first bolt line on the far left of the wall.
FA. Alan Rosier 29.8.2016

❷ Gott in Himmel **7a**
A short fingery and desperate exercise.
FA. Roy Thomas, Simon Coles 9.5.1996

❸ Butcher Heinrich **7b**
Superb, technical face climbing on micro holds.
FA. Martin Crocker, Roy Thomas 1989

❹ Strange Little Boy **6c**
A tight filler-in line between two older routes.
FA. Alan Rosier 29.8.2016

❺ Strange Little Girl **6c**
A fine pitch up the crack-line. A good introduction to this section of the crag. *Photo on page 359.*
FA. Roy Thomas, Martin Crocker 1989

❻ 'King Ada **7b**
Quality wall climbing with a frustrating crux and perhaps the best move on the wall. Moving into *Strange Little Girl* at the break gives a decent **6c**.
FA. Gary Gibson, Roy Thomas 7.4.1996

❼ Skanderbeg **7b**
A good clean wall pitch with the difficulties lower down. There is a direct start at **7b+**.
FA. Martin Crocker, Roy Thomas 11.6.1989. FA. (Start) Oliver Burrows 9.16

❽ King Zog . . . . **7a+**
Excellent climbing. Start up a flake. Finish slightly left via a desperate move to pass the 'smooth band'.
FA. Martin Crocker, Roy Thomas 11.6.1989

❾ Face . . . . **7b+**
One of the best here with a reachy start, an overlap and a technical finale.
FA. Gary Gibson, Roy Thomas 6.4.1996

❿ Mawr, Mawr, Mawr **7a**
Tackle the intermittent crack-line direct. *Photo opposite.*
FA Gary Gibson, Roy Thomas 6.4.1996

The Rust Curtain **Sirhowy** 361

Tom Skelhon embarking on the wall and thin cracks of *Mawr, Mawr, Mawr* (7a) - *opposite* - on the Rust Curtain at Sirhowy. Photo: Jen Stephens

Sirhowy The Rust Curtain

11 The Crimson King .. 7a
Climb the wall finishing leftwards to the same lower-off as *Mawr, Mawr, Mawr*. Hardest at the start.
FA. Gary Gibson, Roy Thomas 6.4.1996

12 Sunstone 7a
The wall behind a tree stump has a fingery start and finale.
FA. Alan Rosier 2007

13 VIP Lunge.............. 6c+
The wall just right of the tree stump has a trying start.
FA. Roy Thomas, Gary Gibson 6.4.1996

14 Hostility Suite 6c
The wall just to the left of the prominent arete.
FA. Roy Thomas, Gary Gibson 6.4.1996

15 Aedan's Arete .... 6a+
The right-hand arete of the wall.
FA. Alan Rosier 2007

16 Brucifer .... 6a+
Climb through the left-hand side of the slim overlap.
FA. Alan Rosier 14.5.2005

17 Take Your Pants to Heaven 6c
Climb the crack up and over the roof.
FA. Alan Rosier 21.5.2005

18 Gouge the Unknown .... 6c+
The thin wall under the right-hand side of the roof.
FA. Roy Thomas 2007

The Dust Curtain Sirhowy 363

19 Knickerless in Hell.......... ⬜ 6b
A steep wall and groove to a large lower-off.
FA. Roy Thomas 2007

20 Holey Moses............. ⬜ 6a
Easier moves through the overlap's right-hand side.
FA. Pete Wardman 15.5.2005

21 Where the Arc is It?........ ⬜ 5c
Up a shield then left to the lower-off of *Holey Moses*.
FA. Pete Wardman 15.5.2005

22 Temples of Cwmaman....... ⬜ 5a
Climb the wall to a small roof.
FA. Alan Rosier 15.5.2005

23 Arch of the Last Craven Ant.... ⬜ 5c
Climb past a loose flake to a short arete.
FA. Roy Thomas 2007

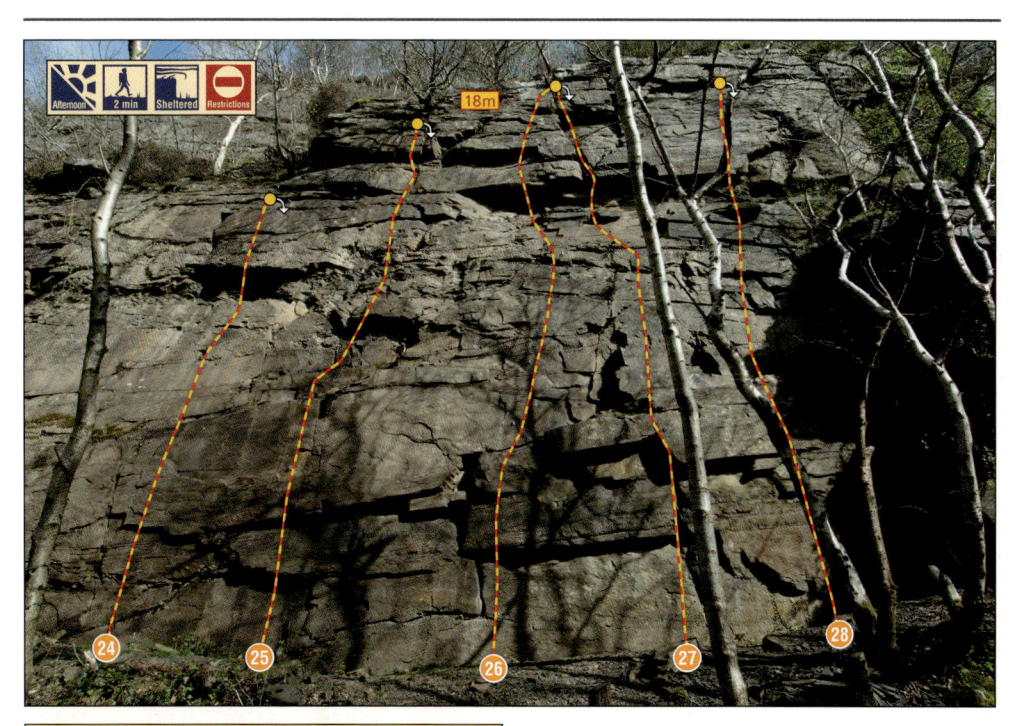

The Dust Curtain
A tall wall of variable rock quality.
Approach - Walk along the base of the crag a short way from The Rust Curtain.
Conditions - The wall takes relatively little seepage. The face picks up sun from mid-afternoon and dries quickly.
Access - Climbing is not officially allowed. If asked to leave, please do so.

24 OC/DC .... ⬜ 6a
Good pocket pulling through the overhang. The initial bolt hanger may be absent.
FA. Alan Rosier, Rob McAllister 17.6.2014

25 Shale I Compare Thee?.... ⬜ 5a
Positive holds and pockets lead up the fragile shale band to finish at a tree.
FA. Alan Rosier, Rob McAllister 5.9.2014

26 Play Dusty For Me........ ⬜ 5c
The line left of a loose looking block.
FA. Roy Thomas, Goi Ashmore 2013

27 Dustin Cough Man........ ⬜ 5c
The long crack-line starting just right of the loose looking block.
FA. Roy Thomas, Goi Ashmore 2013

28 Dustin Crime............ ⬜ 6a+
A bit of a mixed bag with good climbing high up but a poor lower wall and shale band.
FA. Roy Thomas 2014

Sirhowy — Western Wall

Western Wall

An excellent venue that has good rock and plenty of interesting routes which are generally easier than on The Rust Curtain. The base of the cliff is a pleasant spot to relax between climbs.

Approach - Walk a short distance along the base of the crag from the Rust/Dust Curtain walls.

Conditions - This wall needs time to dry out.

Access - Climbing is not officially allowed. If asked to leave, please do so.

1 Queen Bee 5c
The slightly fragile curving corner on the far left of the wall.
FA. Roy Thomas, Goi Ashmore 27.9.2013

2 A Poxy Queen 6b
A bouldery pitch. Make a long move to a reinforced protruding square-cut hold and then mantel onto the ledge above. Move right and finish up the interesting wall.
FA. Roy Thomas, Goi Ashmore 27.9.2013

3 Slip into the Queen . 6b+
A similar but slightly harder version of *A Poxy Queen* avoiding the glued-on rail. Finishes as for *A Poxy Queen*.
FA. Roy Thomas, Eugene Travers-Jones 29.9.2013

4 Little Queen 5c
A good pitch. Move left up ledges and then climb the steep crack using some off-balance moves. *Photo on page 367.*
FA. Alan Rosier, Rob McAllister 30.6.2013

5 Sheer Heart Attack .. 7a+
An intense bit of finger work up the steep wall above a ledge.
FA. Alan Rosier, Rob McAllister 10.7.2013

6 Deaf as a Post ..... 7a+
From the ramp, make a big move past an overlap to a crack. At its top, move left and up to good holds. Alternatively, follow the direct finish to the lower-off of *Killer Queen*.
FA. Martin Crocker, Roy Thomas 1989

7 Killer Queen 7a
Climb ledges and a crack to a tricky wall.
FA. Alan Rosier, Roy Thomas 2.7.2013

8 Queens of the Stone Age. 6b+
Teeter up the right-leading ramp and climb the sustained wall above it. Good moves from start to finish. *Photo opposite.*
FA. Alan Rosier, Rob McAllister 25.6.2013

9 Drag Queen .... 6a+
Start up the ramp of *Queens of the Stone Age* but continue up the groove at its end. Lots of interesting moves.
FA. Alan Rosier, Rob McAllister 30.6.2013

10 Raving Queen ...... 6b+
Nip up the thin crack and make a tricky sequence to get on the sloping ramp of *Drag Queen*. Finish up this.
FA. Alan Rosier, Rob McAllister 30.6.2013

11 The Queen is Dead .. 6b
Climb up past a shothole and continue up the smart wall above.
FA. Alan Rosier, Rob McAllister 30.6.2013

12 Drama Queen 5c
The unattractive corner on the right-hand side of the wall.
FA. Roy Thomas, Alan Rosier, Rob McAllister 10.7.2013

Western Wall **Sirhowy** 365

John Warner midway up the sustained and varied line of *Queens of the Stone Age* (6b+) - *opposite* - on the Western Walls at Sirhowy. Photo: Mark Glaister

Sirhowy — Upper Tier

Upper Tier
The most recently developed section of Sirhowy is a set of walls seamed with cracks.
Approach - Walk a little further on along the base of the cliff from the Western Walls and then head up the bank.
Conditions - Catches little sun.
Access - Climbing is not officially allowed. If asked to leave, please do so.

The first lines are just around the arete left of *Forgotten Ground* and not shown on the topo. There is a project up the narrow wall left of a corner.

1 Budda's Watching 5b
The sandwiched wall past ledges.
FA. Alan Rosier. R.Heirene 16.3.2016

2 Providence .... 6b+
The arete just right of *Budda's Watching*.
FA. Alan Rosier, Ollie Burrows, J.Williams 26.5.2016

3 Psilocybic 6c
The crack and face in the centre of the wall right of the corner.
FA. Alan Rosier, Ollie Burrows 10.9.2015

4 Zeitgeist E2 5c
The fine looking crack left of the arete takes plenty of gear.
FA. Alan Rosier, Rob McAllister 3.9.2015

5 Forgotten Ground 6a
Climb just to the right of the arete to a shared lower-off.
FA. Alan Rosier, Rob McAllister 9.7.2015

6 Approaching the Nadir 6a
The left-leaning crack joining *Forgotten Ground* at the top.
FA. Alan Rosier, Rob McAllister 25.6.2015

7 Hooker With a Penis .... 6a+
The finger-crack and face to a move left to a shared lower-off.
FA. Alan Rosier, Rob McAllister 25.6.2015

8 Lateralus 6b
Pass the tricky overlap and step right beneath the lower-off before a hard move gains the top of the wall.
FA. Alan Rosier, Rob McAllister 11.6.2015

9 Rosetta Stoned 6a
Skirt overlaps on their right to finish at a shared lower-off.
FA. Alan Rosier, Rob McAllister 17.6.2015

10 Stinkfist 6a
The corner-crack.
FA. Alan Rosier, Rob McAllister 30.6.2015

11 Intension .... 6b+
The narrow groove in the centre of the buttress.
FA. Alan Rosier, Rob McAllister 25.6.2015

12 Third Eye 6b
The arete of the buttress. Try not to bridge.
FA. Alan Rosier, Rob McAllister, Nick Goile 28.6.2015

13 The Grudge 6c
The left-hand crack in the buttress is a tricky number. Go right to a shared lower-off with *Jambi*.
FA. Alan Rosier 17.6.2015

14 Jambi 6c
The twisting right-hand crack of the buttress is hard low down.
FA. Alan Rosier, Rob McAllister 17.6.2015

15 Prison Sex 5c
The chimney to a shared lower-off with *Jambi*.
FA. Alan Rosier, Rob McAllister 30.6.2015

16 The Outsider 5b
The jamming crack in the tower. Shared lower-off with *Jambi*.
FA. Alan Rosier, Rob McAllister 30.6.2015

The brief but engaging *Little Queen* (5c) - *page 364* - at the Western Wall section of Sirhowy. Photo: Glaister collection

Tirpentwys

Tucked away at the end of a quiet valley is this pleasant quarried crag. The rock is generally solid and the climbing fairly sustained and pumpy with a good supply of crimps, jugs and cracks available. The base of the cliff is flat and grassy and, in good weather, this is a lovely place to relax between climbs.

	No star	★	★★	★★★
up to 4c	2	-	-	-
5a to 6a+	12	3	1	-
6b to 7a	3	5	2	1
7a+ and up	-	-	1	-

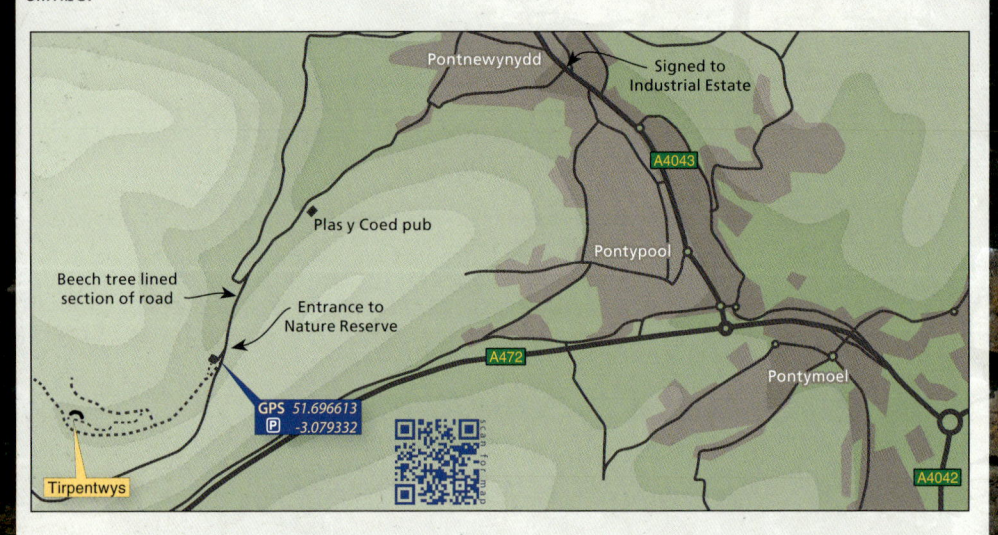

Approach   Also see map on page 254
From the A4043 Pontypool/Blaenavon road turn off into the Pontnewynydd Industrial Estate and drive straight through it to a T-junction. Turn left and continue to where the road becomes lined with ancient beech trees. A further 150m further on is the entrance to Tirpentwys Nature Reserve - park here. Just beyond the entrance to the Nature Reserve is another gated tarmac/gravel track - follow this for 650m until it bends to the right. Go straight on following another gravel track for 350m until the crag comes into view on the right. Cross a small drainage ditch and walk to a stile that allows easy access over a fence to the crag.

Conditions
The quarry faces southwest and gets sun for much of the day. It is very sheltered and dries quite quickly, making it a possible year-round venue. Seepage can become a problem after prolonged periods of rainfall.

Access
The cliff is on private land and a notice is posted stating that climbing is prohibited, though no reports of climbing being prevented have been reported. The issue is to do with civil liability - please leave if asked and report any information to the BMC and Rockfax. The inclusion of the quarry in this book implies no right of access to climb there.

Tirpentwys *369*

Jay Astbury moving up the final thin wall of *Hail Mary* (7a) - *page 372* - one of the many excellent well-equipped wall and crack climbs at Tirpentwys. Photo: Mark Glaister

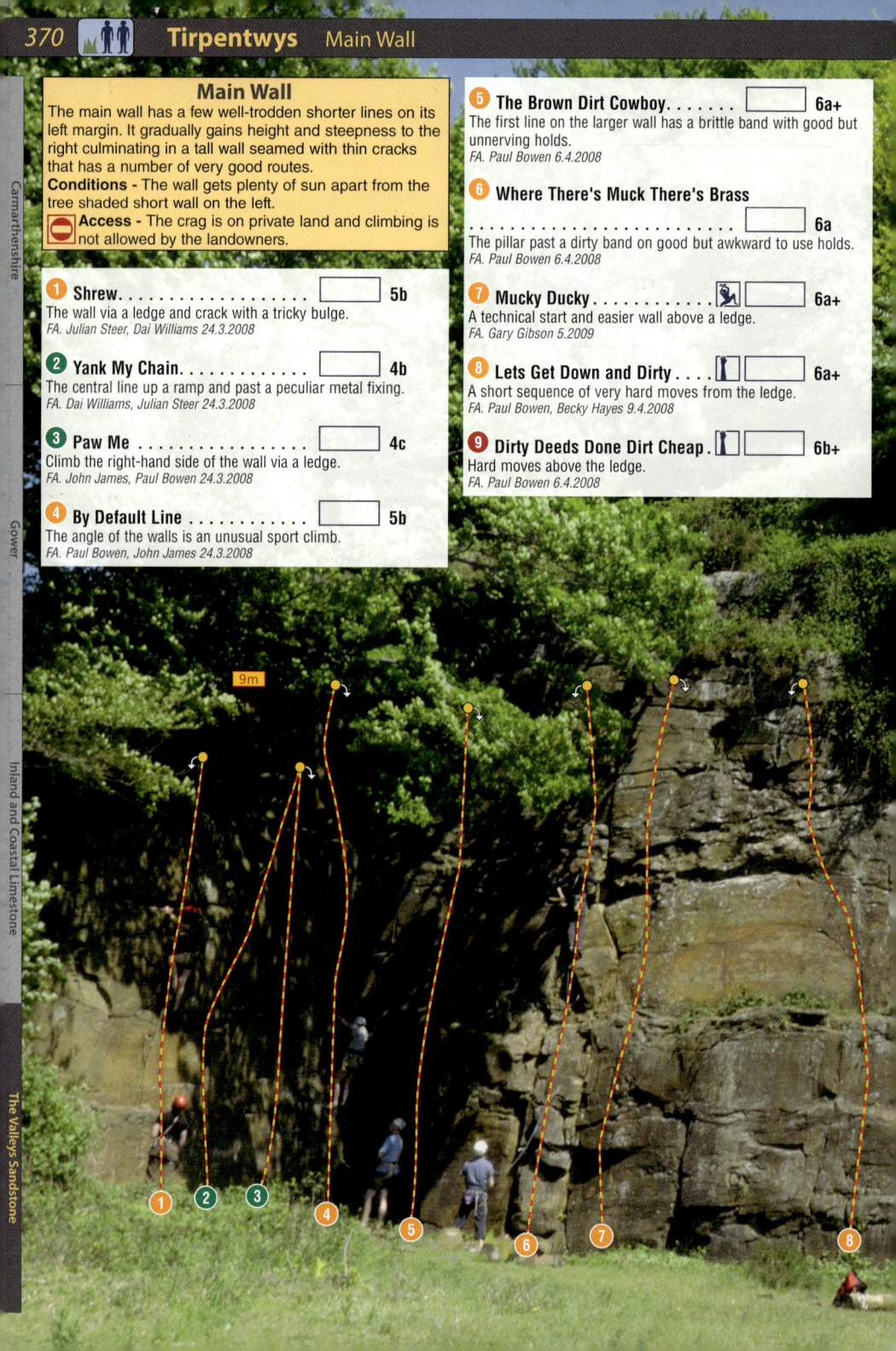

Tirpentwys — Main Wall

Main Wall

The main wall has a few well-trodden shorter lines on its left margin. It gradually gains height and steepness to the right culminating in a tall wall seamed with thin cracks that has a number of very good routes.

Conditions - The wall gets plenty of sun apart from the tree shaded short wall on the left.

⛔ **Access** - The crag is on private land and climbing is not allowed by the landowners.

1 Shrew 5b
The wall via a ledge and crack with a tricky bulge.
FA. Julian Steer, Dai Williams 24.3.2008

2 Yank My Chain 4b
The central line up a ramp and past a peculiar metal fixing.
FA. Dai Williams, Julian Steer 24.3.2008

3 Paw Me 4c
Climb the right-hand side of the wall via a ledge.
FA. John James, Paul Bowen 24.3.2008

4 By Default Line 5b
The angle of the walls is an unusual sport climb.
FA. Paul Bowen, John James 24.3.2008

5 The Brown Dirt Cowboy ...... 6a+
The first line on the larger wall has a brittle band with good but unnerving holds.
FA. Paul Bowen 6.4.2008

6 Where There's Muck There's Brass 6a
The pillar past a dirty band on good but awkward to use holds.
FA. Paul Bowen 6.4.2008

7 Mucky Ducky .... 6a+
A technical start and easier wall above a ledge.
FA. Gary Gibson 5.2009

8 Lets Get Down and Dirty .... 6a+
A short sequence of very hard moves from the ledge.
FA. Paul Bowen, Becky Hayes 9.4.2008

9 Dirty Deeds Done Dirt Cheap . 6b+
Hard moves above the ledge.
FA. Paul Bowen 6.4.2008

Main Wall **Tirpentwys** 371

10 Choosey Suzie.......... 6b+
The pillar has a technical section low down.
FA. Gary Gibson 5.2009

11 Lundy Boy............ 6b
Pumpy jug pulling marks out the quality of this line.
Photo on page 374.
FA. John James, Paul Bowen 5.4.2008

12 Supertramp.......... 7a
The leaning headwall is superb. Difficulties increase as height is gained, particularly after the large mid-height pocket.
FA. Laura Jones 6.4.2008

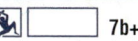

13 Strawberry Jam....... 7b+
The crack-line in the upper half of the face gives a stern test of ability from bottom to top.
FA. Bill Gregory 14.4.2008

14 The Cragmeister...... 6b
The central line of the face has a testing jamming crack after a steep, juggy start.
FA. Bill Gregory 24.3.2008

15 Rocky............... 6a
Tackle the sandy-coloured bulge with good blocky holds above.
FA. Becky Hayes, John James 4.4.2008

372 Tirpentwys Main Wall

16 The Tactless Teacher 6b
An easy start leads to a fingery finale.
FA. Laura Jones, Becky Hayes 5.4.2008

17 Hail Mary 7a
An easy start with crimpy face climbing above.
Photo on page 369.
FA. Bill Gregory 24.3.2008

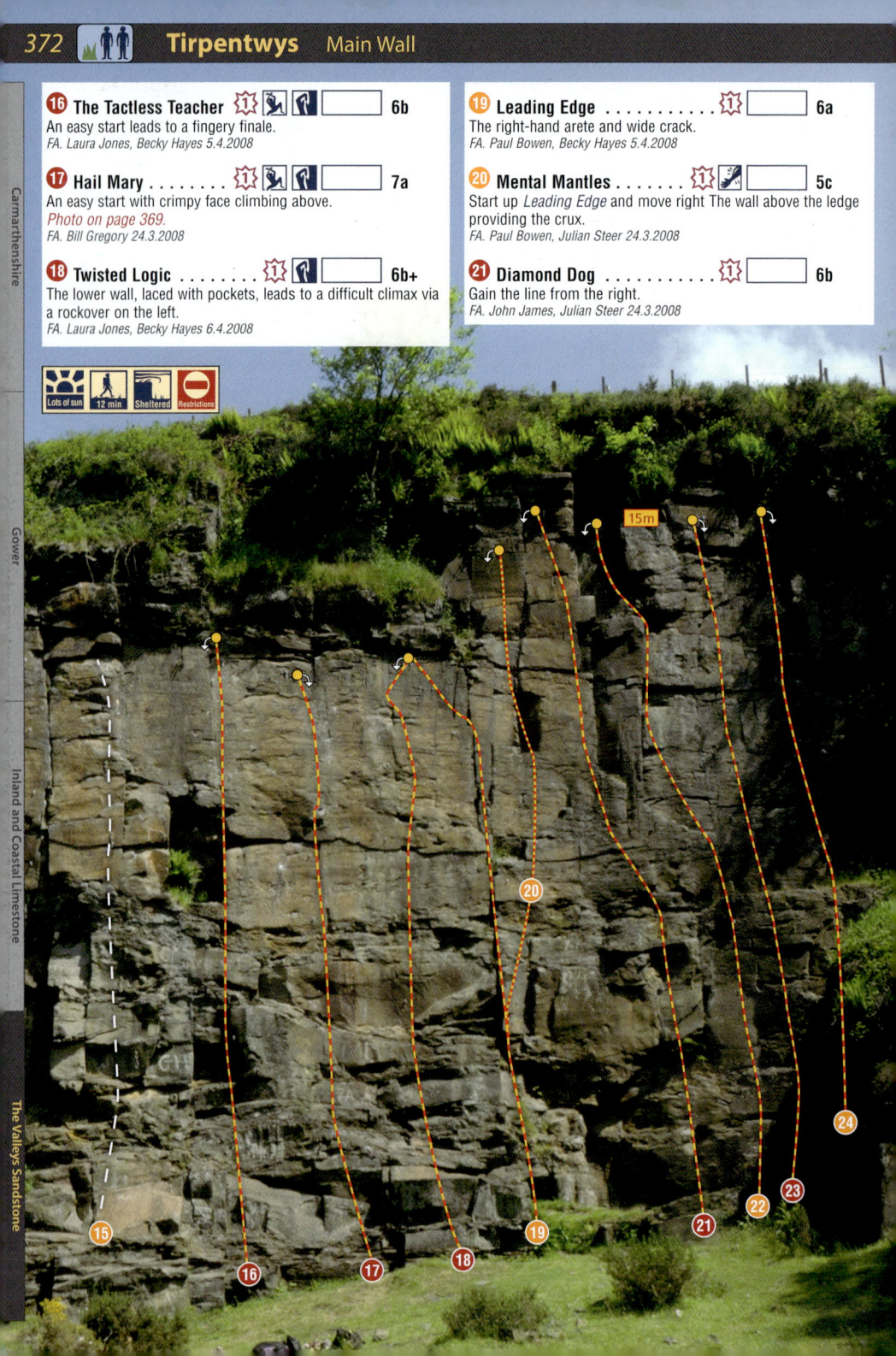

18 Twisted Logic .... 6b+
The lower wall, laced with pockets, leads to a difficult climax via a rockover on the left.
FA. Laura Jones, Becky Hayes 6.4.2008

19 Leading Edge 6a
The right-hand arete and wide crack.
FA. Paul Bowen, Becky Hayes 5.4.2008

20 Mental Mantles 5c
Start up *Leading Edge* and move right The wall above the ledge providing the crux.
FA. Paul Bowen, Julian Steer 24.3.2008

21 Diamond Dog 6b
Gain the line from the right.
FA. John James, Julian Steer 24.3.2008

Lots of sun · 12 min · Sheltered · Restrictions

Right Wall **Tirpentwys** *373*

Right Wall
The small buttress to the right also has a number of bolted pitches.

Access - The crag is on private land and climbing is not allowed by the landowners.

㉒ The Chimney Finish . . . . 6a+
An awkward and slightly bold start up the blank groove and pockets gains better holds above. Continue more steeply and step left to finish.
FA. Paul Bowen, Julian Steer 24.3.2008

㉓ Flakes and Chips . . . 6b+
Taking the wall direct past the bolts gives a fingery little number with three hard moves. It can be climbed on the left or right.
FA. Paul Bowen, John James 4.4.2008

㉔ Ledge and Braces 5a
The wall above the raised platform is slabby. Keep the bolt runners on your left.
FA. Paul Bowen, John James, Becky Hayes 4.4.2008

㉕ Fledgeling . . . . 6a+
The short hard wall.
FA. Roy Thomas, Gary Gibson 5.2010

㉖ The Yolk's on You 6a
The arete has a hard pull on small holds to get going.
FA. Roy Thomas, Gary Gibson 5.2010

㉗ You've Had Your Chicks 6b
An easy groove leads the way to a problematic pull.
FA. Gary Gibson, Roy Thomas 2.2010

㉘ Crumlin Towards England 5a
The juggy wall from the left side of the grassy ledge.
FA. Gary Gibson, Roy Thomas 5.2010

㉙ Crumlin at the Seams 6a
The thin crack above the grassy ledge.
FA. Gary Gibson, Roy Thomas 5.2010

㉚ Crumlin at the Edges 6a
The right arete above the grassy ledge.
FA. Gary Gibson, Roy Thomas 5.2010

Myles Jordan approaching the final moves of the pumpy *Lundy Boy* (6b) - *page 371* - at Tirpentwys. Photo: Mark Glaister

Tirpentwys

375

Route Index

Stars	Grade	Route	Photo	Page
	6c	30' is the new 20'		308
*	6b	300 Spartans		240
**	6a+	3D Dog		74
**	7b+	Abbatoir and Costello		348
	7a+	Abdominal Showman, The		318
*	5c	Abra-Ker-Fucking-Dabra		234
**	6c	Academy Awards		192
	6a+	Acatalepsia		346
	5c	Ace in the Hole		335
*	6b+	ACE Inhibitors		76
*	6b+	Achilles Hasn't a Foot		240
***	8b	Achilles' Wrath		89
	6b	Adam Hussein's Nan		211
***	E2	Adulteress, The		106
	6a+	Aedan's Arete		362
	6b	Affairs of Man		260
	5c	Affluenza		212
	E3	Ain't as Official		318
*	7a+	Air Display		170
***	8a+	Air Show		86
	4b	Al Perchino		98
	6a	Alchemy of Error		240
	6a	Alco-Troll		332
	5c	Alements		294
	4c	All Aboard My Dinghy		224
**	6a+	All For Nothing		64
	3a	All Hands on the Sea Cocks		96
*	6a	All of a Quiver		156
	6c+	All Sand Together		344
	6a+	All Talk		282
*	7b+	All that Glitters is not Gold		161
*	6b+	All the Pies Arete		216
	6b	All's Well		211
*	6b+	Alone and Blue		276
*	6a+	Alpha Blocker		76
	5b	Alys Rook		310
	6a+	Amber Leaf		353
	7a	Amnesia		346
*	6a	Amount of Fun to be had by a Bear with a Broken Baculum, The		76
*	6b	Anal Gesia		128
*	6c	Anal Retention		251
*	6b+	Anchors Away		230
	5b	Andre Marriner		94
	6a+	Andrew the Zebra		304
*	6c	Angel of Mons		202
*	5c	Angry Pirate		196
	6a	Anne's Stiff Entry		264
*	5c	Anniversary Walk		310
*	6b	Anoek Clear Missile		128
	6b	Anonymous Bosch		136
	6c	Anonymous Flare		128
	5b	Ant Frenzy		316
**	6c	Any Old Iron		212
**	7b	Anything You Can Do		324
	6a	Apples and Pairs		222
*	6a	Approaching the Nadir		366
*	6c	April Fool		276
**	7a	Aptitude Test		344
	E5	Arabesque		353
*	5c	Arch of the Last Craven Ant		362
*	6a+	Archimedes Screws		243
**	7a+	Arizona Stan		304
	6c+	Article 50		224
	5c	As it is		326
	VS	As it Was		322
**	7a	Ashes to Ashes		167
	6b+	Aspidistra		154
	6b+	Ass in the Hole		204
	6c	Asset Manager	30, 62	60
*	5a	Asteroids		220
*	5b	Atomic Wedgie		106
	6a	Atraumen		94
	6a+	Attrition (Cwm Capel)		38
*	E5	Attrition (Rhossili B)		86
	6b+	Attrocities		316
	7c+	Au		161
*	6a+	Aur of Glory		160
*	6a	Aur of Need		160
*	6c	Away With The Fairies		287
**	6b+	Away With The Mixer		287
*	E1	Axe, The		111
	6b	Babcock Test, The		280
*	6c+	Baby Bouncer		128
*	6b+	Baby Going Boing Boing		128
	5a	Back, Crack and Sack		225
*	6b	Bad Bad Boy		258
	7a+	Badger's Out!		72
	4a	Badness		351
*	5b	Baggle Brook Affair		260
*	6a+	Baldy Walks to Ponty		300
*	6b	Balthazaar's Ball Sac Bulges		338
	6c	Banal Pretention		251
*	6b	Banjo Versus The Pigeon		289
*	7a	Banog's Barmy Army		291
	6b	Barbara		260
	6a	Bargain Basement Bargoed		338
*	6b	Bargoed Blow Job		338
*	6b	Bargoed Bushwhacker		338
	6a	Bargoed Sideshow		338
	6a	Barnacle Bill		96
*	6b	Barnacle Bill, The		243
	6c	Barnacles at Dawn		52
*	6b+	Barry Freight		251
	E3	Bas Chevaliers		342
	4c	Basil Brush		142
**	7b+	Basildon Snapper, The		304
**	7b+	Basilica		184
*	6c	Battle of the Bulge		222
*	6b	Beat A Block, Ha!		76
*	6a+	Beautiful People, The		111
*	7a	Beauty School Drop-out		300
*	6a+	Beavers at Bargoed		338
	5c	Bedraggled Trousered Misogynist		234
	HVS	Beef Curry and Chips		300
**	7a+	Before Planck's Time		72
**	6c	Behind the Lines	293	294
***	7c+	Bellerophon	166	167
*	7b	Belly Up		355
	7a+	Berlin	1, 174	188
***	7b	Berlin Extension		188
*	6a	Besetting Fears		100
*	6b+	Between the Lines		344
*	6c+	Beware of Poachers		182
*	6b+	Beware the Burly Butcher of Bargoed		338
*	6c	Beyond All Resin		130
*	6b	Beyond the Fringe		149
	6b+	Biffa Bacon		268
	6b+	Big Ears Takes Flight		180
*	E6	Big Time, The		191
*	6b+	Big Tissue, The		355
	HVS	Billy the Fish		272
*	6c+	Birth Canal		353
	5b	Birthday Bulge		260
*	6b	Bit of Nokia on the Side, A		260
**	6b	Bitch		74
	7c	Bitchin'		130
*	E3	Bizarre Geetar		269
**	6c	Black Adder		84
*	6b+	Black Dog		338
*	7a	Black Friday		111
**	6b	Black Magic	3	331
*	6a	Black Night's Rein		216
***	8a	Black Pearl, The		188
	5a	Black Sea Shanty		96
	5b	Black Tide		222
**	7b+	Black Wall		106
	8a+	Black Wall Direct		106
	6c	Blackberry Crumble		353
	6c+	Blacker than Black		314
***	E4	Blackman's Pinch		106
	6c	Blagdon		291
	6c+	Blagdon Direct Finish		291
	6a	Bland Of Four		276
	4c	Blandess		351
	E3	Blank Abstract, A		331
*	6b	Blank Dark Thirty		69
**	6b+	Blinded by Love		344
*	5b	Blockbuster		111
***	6b	Blockiness		90
	6a+	Blood Spunker		74
*	6b	Blood Sweat and Beers		331
**	8a	Bloody Sport Climbers		188
*	5c	Blow Me, Another One	239	238
*	7a+	Blowing For Tugs		338
	VS	Blowing The Ram's Horn		243
*	6b	Bluster		322
*	6b	Bob's Birthday Party		180
*	7a	Bolder Boulder		116
*	6b+	Bolt Fund Blues, The		331
**	6b	Bolus Feed		64
*	7b	Bonacci's Sequence		64
*	6b	Bone Hard Start		264
	5b	Bonehead		180
*	6a	Boney King of Nowhere Direct		208
*	4b	Border Control		94
	3c	Bore Hole		356
	6c	Bored of Brackla Becomes Benefactor of Bargoed		338
	6a	Bored of Toad Hall		94
*	7b	Boston Strangler		342
*	6b	Bottom Drawers		92
	VS	Boulevard De Alfred Turner (1926)		304
*	6a	Bowen Arrow		156
**	6a	Bowen to the Inevitable	28	156
*	6a	Branch Line		251
	6c+	Branch Manager		314
**	6c+	Brazilian Blend		192
*	6c	Breakout		192
*	6b+	Breccial Motion	153	154
	6a	Brexit Legacy, The		224
	5b	Bring Back the Birch		316
	6a+	Bring out the Crimp		216
*	7a+	Bringeth yon Leach		348
*	6b	Bringing The Brane Theory To Bargoed		338
*	7a	Bristol Beat		209
*	6b	Brittania		338
*	4c	Brittle Biscuit		225
*	6b	Broken on the Rocks		230
	6a+	Brown Dirt Cowboy, The		371
**	6c	Brown Eyed Girl		353
	6a+	Brucifer		362
	7a	Brush Down, The		344
	7a	Brush Off, The		344
	6b	Bucket of KFC and Two One Armers		285
*	5b	Buckets of Bubbly		106
	5b	Budda's Watching		366
	4b	Buen Culo		356
*	6b	Buff the Happy Lamp		310
*	4b	Bulbus Tara		198
**	7b+	Bull Fighter		154
	6a	Bull Market		60
	6b	Burdock		344
*	6c+	Burn After Reading		60
	6b+	Burning Brush		272
**	6b	Burning Glass, The		243
	5b	Burton Line		251
	5c	Bush Trimmer's Corner		251
	5c	Buster Gonads		272
**	7b	Butcher Heinrich		360

Route Index 377

Stars	Grade	Route	Photo	Page
	5c	Butt Out		326
**	6c+	By Appointment Only		285
*	5b	By Default Line		371
	7a	By Proxy		183
*	6b+	Bye Bye Eddy		161
*	6b+	Bye Dad		98
**	7b+	Caerphilly Contract, The		346
	6c+	Caerphilly Cop Out, The		344
*	6b	California Freeming		251
*	6c	Call a Spade a Spade		186
	6a+	Campaign For See Through Bikinis	40	294
*	6c	Can the Can		208
*	5a	Can't Swallow That		111
	HVS	Canaan Grunts		243
*	6a+	Canine League		324
**	8a+	Cannonade		89
***	7b+	Capstan	303	304
**	8a	Captain Barbarossa		188
**	7b	Captain Hook		170
*	6b+	Captain Jacque Hoff		94
*	4c	Carpetbagger, The		246
*	5b	Cartesian Dualism		243
*	6c+	Cascade		346
**	5b	Cash in the Attic		98
*	6a+	Cast Adrift (Telpyn Point)		51
*	6c	Cast Adrift (Witches Point)		230
*	6c	Cast Me Away		92
*	4b	Catapult		94
*	6b	Catch The Pigeon		289
	6c+	Catching Fire		92
*	6b	Cauldron of Satyr		128
	4a	Ceasg		98
*	7b	Celestial Being		202
*	6b	Cenotaph Norm Carter		300
*	6b	Central Deviator		72
**	6b	Central Integrator		69
*	6b	Certain Peace, A	317	318
	6b	Chain Reaction		264
	6a	Chargeable Event		243
*	7a	Charlie Barking		116
*	6c	Charlie's Rusks		180
***	7a+	Chattery Teeth		335
	6b+	Cheapskate		216
*	5b	Checkpoint Checkout		94
	S	Cheeky Arete		355
	5c	Cheesy Flaps		173
**	6c	Cheesy Rider		178
	6c+	Chicken Licken		144
**	7b+	Chilean Flame Thrower		115
*	6a+	Chimney Finish, The		373
*	6c+	Chinese Whispers		208
**	7c	Chives of Freedom	36	191
**	6b	Chock a Block		120
	E2	Choice Cut		314
	6b+	Choosey Suzie		371
*	7a	Christendom		202
*	6a+	Christian Broke My Flake		222
	6b	Chubby Rambo		353
*	6b	Cigarillo		280
	6a	Cilly Arete		310
	6a	Cinders Catch		92
	6a	Circus Clowns		310
*	6b	CJD		200
	6a	Clair de Lune		209
*	6c	Clampetts, The		163
**	6b	Clapham Injunction		163
*	7b	Clart Mountain Project, The		353
**	6c+	Clear Conscience and a Blow Job		308
*	6c	Clear Head and a Blow Lamp	306	308
*	7a	Cleft Stick, A		355
	HVS	Climb a Sycamore Tree		243
*	6c	Clip Joint		138
*	4c	Clock Sucker		272
*	6b+	Closed Shop		264
*	6a+	Clot Thickens, The		92
	5c	CND		264
*	6b+	Cock and Ball Story		287
*	6c	Cocky Black Chauffage		89
*	6b	Cod Liver Oil		225
	7a	Coffee Shop		335
	6b+	Coggars Lane		314
	7a+	Cointreau	26	314
**	6b	Cold Inconvenience		120
*	6c+	Cold Rolled		264
	5c	Community Spirit		264
	6a	Concrete Cows		94
*	7a	Confidential, LA		198
*	7a	Conglomeration	159	163
*	7b	Connard Canard		142
	6a	Connect One		180
**	7a+	Conneticut Connection, The		198
	HVS	Consequentialist Perfectionism		243
*	6c+	Constant Gardener, The		170
	5c	Constantinople		316
	6a	Continued Nursing Care		69
***	7c	Contraband		342
**	6c	Controlled Emission		326
*	7a	Cool Crux Clan, The		170
	7a	Cop the Lot		344
	6a+	Coprophagic Canine		273
*	6c+	Cordoba Express		251
	HVS	Corner, The		289
***	E3	Crack Basher		264
*	6b+	Crack Liqour		251
	4a	Crack Me Up		224
	E2	Crackatoa		220
	6b+	Cracker Barrel		92
**	6a	Cradle Snatcher		128
**	6b	Cragmeister, The		371
	5b	Crash and Dash		60
*	6a	Crash Landing		332
	4a	Crass Word Pizzle		98
*	7a	Crawling Chaos, The		204
	7a+	Crawling King Snake		150
	6c	Creaming Dream, The		211
	6b+	Credit Squeeze	59	60
	6b+	Creme de Rockfall		178
*	6b+	Creme de Roquefort		178
	5c	Crescent Wanker		272
*	6c	Crest of a Wave		56
***	E5	Crime and Punishment		106
	6a	Crime of Omission		78
*	6c+	Crimes of Fashion		197
*	6b+	Crimp Paddle		98
*	7a	Crimson King, The		362
*	6c	Crock Block		167
*	6b+	Crock Licker		272
*	7c	Crock of Gold		191
*	6b+	Croeso I Gymru		230
*	6b+	Crooked Little Pinky		210
*	7a+	Cross Country Booty Call		74
*	6c	Cross Incontinents		89
	7b+	Cross the Rubicon		167
	6a	Crumlin at the Edges		373
	6a	Crumlin at the Seams		373
	5a	Crumlin Towards England		373
*	6c	Cujo		180
*	6b	Culture Vulture		285
*	5b	Cunning Ling		51
	5a	Cunning Little Fox		142
*	5c	Cure for Crabs		51
	5a	Cymru Euro		316
*	6a+	D'ya Hear Ma Dear		200
	HVS	Daft Nutter		64
**	6c	Daggers		200
**	7b	Dai Hard		297
	6b	Dai Horrea		326
**	7c	Dai Vinci Coed, The		229
	6a	Dai's Dalliance		276
*	5c	Dai's Route		120
	6a+	Damp Digits		260
*	6a	Dan Dix		289
**	6b	Dan'ds-Inferno		289
	6b	Dandelion		344
	7a	Dandelion Slab, The		184
	7a+	Danny La Rue		192
	4a	Dark Art of Banana Magic, The		204
	6a	Dark Force of Glamorgan, The		240
***	5a	Dawson's Corner		98
	5b	Dawsons Creek		98
	5b	Day The Drill Conked Out, The		272
*	6b+	Day the Sky Fell In, The		144
*	7a+	De-Regulators, The		182
*	7a	Dead Man's Shoes		56
*	6c	Deadly Nightshade		180
*	7a+	Deaf as a Post		364
*	E2	Death Wish		331
	6c	Debauching Deborah		118
	6a+	Debbie Likes It Wet		116
**	7a	Debbie Reynolds	21	116
	6c+	Deborah		118
**	6c	Decades Apart		167
**	6b	Decimus Maximus		202
*	6b	Deflated Dickhead, The		180
**	8a	Delta Dagger		89
*	7a	Demi Moore		300
	6a	Democratic Republic of Maesteg		180
	6a	Demolition Gang		260
	7b+	Department of Correction		116
**	7b+	Deputy Dawg		116
*	6c	Deri Made		335
*	5c	Descartes' Dithers	244	243
*	7a+	Desert Storm		343
	6a	Destination Brynmawr		222
**	6c	Deus Ex Machina	328	331
	6a+	Devil's Brew		128
	6c+	Diagnosis Made Easy		222
*	6b	Diamond Dog		372
*	5c	Dicky Dyson		287
*	6b	Didymo Clogs Yer Tackle		234
**	7c	Digitorum Brevis		210
*	6c	Digue, La		285
***	E9	Dina Crac		186
***	8a	Dinasty		188
*	6b	Direct Start (Black Night's Rein)		216
*	6b+	Dirt Box		128
*	6b+	Dirtbag Arete		287
*	6b	Dirty as a Dog		343
*	5c	Dirty Deeds		258
	6b+	Dirty Deeds Done Dirt Cheap		371
*	6b+	Dirty Drawers		92
	5c	Dirty Innuendo		92
**	6a+	Discount Included in the Price	299	300
	6c	Dish the Dirt		60
	5c	Dishonourable Discharge		74
*	6a+	Dismal Differentiator		69
*	7a	Disraeli's Curl		69
	7a	Disraeli's Curl Direct		69
	4a	Dissertation Distraction		204
*	6b	Diving for Pearls		52
*	7a+	Dixienormous		289
	5b	Dodecanese Dalliance		240
***	8a+	Dog Days are Over		116
	6a	Dog Leg		74
*	6b	Dog Wuff		74
	6a	Doggy Bag		74
**	6b	Doggy Style		74
*	6a+	Doggy Style Deviant		74
	6a	Dolphin Snoggin'		220
*	7a	Don't Bark Yet		324
*	6b	Don't Blame Me		322

Carmarthenshire · Gower · Inland and Coastal Limestone · The Valleys Sandstone

Route Index

Stars	Grade	Route	Photo	Page
***	6a+	Don't Jis on My Sofa		173
	6a+	Donkey Work		282
*	6b+	Double Bore		318
	6c	Double Dutch		173
	6a+	Double or Squits		343
*	6c	Doux Parfum de la Lingerie Utilisé, La		92
	5a	Down in One		111
	5b	Down the Drain		258
*	4c	Down Under		280
*	7a	Down Under Deborah		118
	7a+	Dr Van Steiner		191
*	6a+	Drag Queen		364
	5c	Drama Queen		364
*	6c	Dream Academy		192
**	7a	Dreaming in Colour		348
*	7a	Drilling Fields, The		136
	5c	Drinks at 'The Dog and Hammer'		272
*	6b	Dross of 86		238
	6a	Dry Blood Beast		92
**	7a+	Ducky Lucky		144
*	6b+	Dulce Et Decorum Est		243
	6b	Dumbfounded Dunderhead, The		180
*	7c	Durbin Two, Watson Nil		186
*	7a+	Dusk		314
	5a	Dust Devil		287
	5c	Dustin Cough Man		363
	5c	Dustin Crime		363
*	7b+	Dynamo Kiev		128
*	6b+	Each Way Nudger		186
*	6a+	Earl of Porth		300
**	7a+	Eastern Block Rock		332
*	6a	Ed's Folly		260
	5c	Ed's Triumph		260
***	7b+	Edge-Hog		230
	7c	Edge-More		230
**	7a	Ego Sanction, The		57
*	6c+	El Camino Del Roy		192
	4b	El Cino		94
*	E4	Elastic Retreat, The		331
	5c	Electra's Revenge		246
	HVS	Electrolux		287
	6a	Elephantacino		94
*	6c	Elf and Safety		300
*	6a	Empty Talk		282
	7b+	Encore Magnifique		324
*	5c	Enema Affair, The		115
*	6c+	Enema of the Affair		356
*	6b	Enigma		258
*	6c+	Enter the Darren		304
*	6a	Euclid's Theorem		240
*	7a	Eugene Genie		251
	7b+	Eugene's High Point		183
	8b	Euro Fighter		89
*	E2	Evening Light		332
	7a	Evil Eye, The		348
***	7a+	Evil K'nee Full		234
	6a	Evil Ways (Cwmaman)		310
**	7b	Evil Ways (Witches Point)		234
*	5a	Excavation		136
*	E3	Expansionist, The		346
*	E4	Exterminate All Bolt Thieves		273
***	7b+	Face		360
	6a+	Fach Roo		297
	6a+	Fach Roo Too		297
	6a+	Faecal Finger of Fate, The		273
*	6b+	Fair Cop		344
	4c	Fair Enough		287
**	6c+	Fairies Wear Boots	357	355
*	4c	Fairy Godmother		287
*	6c	Fairy Ring		287
*	4c	Fairy's Liquid		287
	7a+	Falling Freely		346
*	6b	Family Day		260
	6a+	Family Values		186
**	E4	Far Cry from Squashim, A		318
	5c	Faster! Pussycat		212
	5c	Fat Controller, The		251
	8b	Fata Morgana	91	89
	3c	Fatman and Nob In		234
*	6c+	Fats Waller		84
**	7a+	Fe 500		264
*	6a	Feeling Lucky		280
	7b	Feeling Sheep		332
*	6b	Fergie's Folly		216
	5b	Fermat's Last Theorem		246
*	7a	Ferndale Revisited		314
	6b	Feud For Thought		156
	4c	Fickle Finger of Fate		251
**	6b	Fiesta		115
	VS	Fiff and Faff		111
*	5c	Filial Duty		98
*	6b	Filthy Snatch		128
***	8a	Fin		167
	5c	Fin End of the Wedge, The		106
	6a+	Final Plot		318
*	5b	Final Relief of the Blue Ball Artist		276
	5c	Finger Flicking Good		251
	6a	Fingertip Mistress		251
**	7b+	Fings Ain't What They Used To Be		183
	7a+	Firepower		220
	6b	Firewater		291
	6a+	First Handout		90
	5a	First Step To Enlightenment, The		184
	5c	Fish Called Rhondda, A		272
	6b	Fisherman's Tackle, A		51
	6a+	Fishermen Pump Their Rods		234
	4c	Fistful of Tenners	102	98
**	6c+	Five O'Clock Shadow		229
**	6b+	Flakes and Chips		373
	6a+	Fledgeling		373
**	7b+	Float Like a Butterfly, Sting Like a Bee		72
*	6b	Flounder		100
**	6b	Flow Job		222
*	6a	Flue Liner		258
*	6a+	Fluster	323	322
*	6b	Fly		154
	VS	Fly Me to the Moon		331
	7a+	Foamin' at the Gusset		130
**	7a+	Food for Parasites		348
	6a+	Fools on Horses		280
**	6c+	Fools Rush In		238
	6a	Footsie		111
	4a	For Fonting Friends		204
*	E1	For King Trad Prawn		154
	HVS	For the Love of Ivy		182
*	6c	For Your Hands Only		291
	6a	Forgotten Ground		366
	5c	Forgotten Route, The		310
*	5c	Fought To The End	97	98
*	7b	Four Minute Tyle, The		355
**	7a	Fowl Play		144
*	7a	Foxy Lady		144
	4b	Frappacino		94
	6c	Free Lunch		280
**	6b	Freem of White Horses, A	248	251
	5b	Freem Team, The		251
	6a	Freeming at the Gusset		251
	HVS	Freeming of Jeannie		251
	5c	Freempie		251
*	7a	French Undressing		115
*	5c	Fromage Frais		178
	6b+	Fruitless Pair		222
*	7a+	Fuelled by Pies		225
	7b	Full Dog		335
	6a+	Full Metal Jacket		212
**	7a	Future Holds, The		316
**	7b	G.L.C SAF		211
**	5c	Galena Puts Lead In Your Pencil		251
	5c	Gallow's Step		273
*	6a+	Galvanised		280
*	6b+	Games of Ambivalence		204
*	6a+	Garden of Eden		220
*	6b	Gary's Talking Climbs		150
	6a+	Gathering Gloom		260
	5a	Gay Batman		234
**	6b+	Gaz 316		264
**	6c+	Geef onze fietsen terug		173
*	5c	Geez Louise		92
*	6b	Generation Bitch		324
*	5c	Generation Gap		324
	6c+	Genghis Khan	194	198
*	6a	Gentleman's Relish		156
*	6a	Gentleman's Retreat		156
*	6c+	Gentlemen Prefer Bolts		156
*	6c	Get Down on This		200
**	7a+	Get Flossed		324
	2c	Get Out Claws		64
	6c+	Get The Hence		200
	5c	Get Your Fist In		258
*	E6	Giant Killer		186
**	7a	Giant Sand		346
*	6b+	Gift of the Gods		240
	5c	Gift Wrapped at Bargoed		338
*	6a	Gilding the Lily		282
	5c	Giraffacino		94
	E4	Girdle Traverse		170
	7b	Give It Some Belly		211
	6c	Give It Some Wellie		211
	5b	Give the Dog a Bone		74
*	7a	Giving it all Up		348
	4c	Gladness		351
**	7b	Gladstone's Deficit	71	72
**	6c	Glucosamine and Chondroitin		225
*	7a	Glue Year		130
	6a+	Glug, Glug, Glug		52
*	6a	Go With The Flow		222
*	6b+	Goblin Girl		332
*	6a+	Godfather, The		327
	6a	Gods of Long Ashton		240
*	6c	Going Down On Deborah		118
	5c	Gold Block		331
**	5c	Gold Digger		161
*	7a	Gold Rush, The		160
**	6a+	Gold Teeth In Them Thar Hills		163
*	5c	Golden Boy		160
	5c	Golden Hour		160
*	5c	Golden String, The		64
*	6c	Golden Tower, The		218
**	7b	Golden Wonder		161
*	6b	Good Gear, Good Cheer		200
	5c	Good Ship Venus		94
	6b	Good Tradition		308
	6c+	Goose in Lucy	80	142
*	7a	Gorilliant		186
*	6c+	Gorki's Zygotic Mynci		300
*	7a	Gott in Himmel		128
	6c+	Gouge the Unknown		362
*	7a	Grab Some Tree and Follow Me		291
	6a+	Grated Expectations		128
	6a+	Grave Concern		318
*	6a	Grazed and Transfused		92
*	6b	Greased Balls		326
**	6c+	Great Expectations		331
**	6b	Great Expectorations		234
	HS	Green Arete		280
*	6b	Green Ginger Wine		353
	5a	Green Shoots of Recovery		60
***	7a+	Grit Box		346

Carmarthenshire / Gower / Inland and Coastal Limestone / The Valleys Sandstone

Route Index

Stars	Grade	Route	Photo	Page
**	E2	Groovy Tube Day		191
📷	6a	Groping For Jugs	337	338
*	6a	Grout Expectations		324
**	6c	Grout Of San Romano, The		327
*	7c	Grow-Up!		230
*	6c	Grudge, The		366
	6b+	Grunter Ass		273
	8a+	Gunshow		89
	6b	Guto Nythbran		300
	6b	Gutted		304
	6b+	Gwest y Gymru 7 Inch Mix		200
	6b+	Gypsy Eyes		144
**	8a	H1N1	185	188
*	7a	Hail Mary	369	372
*	6c+	Hair of the Dog		291
*	6b	Half Man, Half Machine		331
***	6c	Half Pipe Dream		218
*	6b	Hand in Pocket		220
	6a+	Hand Shandy/Make a Splash		90
	4c	Hands that Do Dishes		287
*	6a+	Hanger Them High	264	163
📷	6c	Hanging by a Thread		230
*	7a	Hant, The	105	106
	6c+	Hard Prawn		154
***	7b+	Harlem		191
	4b	Harris's List		251
	6b	Has the Fat Lady Sung?		326
*	6b+	Hatchet Man		111
*	7c	Hawaiian Chance		191
**	6a+	Hawk's Cheep		338
**	7c+	Hayabusa		188
*	5a	He Sawed		314
*	5c	Heading for a Sea of Tears		246
*	5c	Heading South		60
	E1	Heart Throb		332
*	7a	Heavenly		202
	5a	Helmet Man's Day Off		316
	E1	Help the Aged		276
**	7c	Help, Help Me Rhondda		229
📷	8b+	Helvetia		89
*	6a	Hey Mister		310
	6b	High Jinx		264
*	6b	High Moon		356
*	6a	Hirsuit Ulvula		198
	5c	Hoarse Breather		282
	4c	Hoarse Trader		280
	6b	Hoarse Whisperer		282
*	6b	Hogging the Mid Lane		243
**	5b	Holds May Spin	101	98
	5c	Hole in One		282
	6a	Holey Moses		362
*	6b	Hollow Feeling		343
	5c	Homebase		316
	5b	Honeybucket Supreme		212
**	6a+	Hook, Line and Stinker	50	51
**	6a+	Hooker With a Penis		366
**	7a	Hooker, The	146	144
	6a+	Horn of Plenty		342
*	5c	Horse Flavoured Shadows		100
	6b	Horses Bolted		280
*	6c	Host, The		348
**	6c	Hostility Suite		362
*	7b+	Hot Cross Guns		314
**	6b	Hot Flush		120
*	6a	Hot Fuss		297
*	7b	Hot Mill		264
*	7a	House of Cards		335
	6b	House Training Catwoman		338
*	6b	Howling Hadrons		209
*	6b	Hubble, Rubble		128
	6a	Hullabaloo		56
*	6b+	Hundred Years of Reflection		243
*	6a	Hung Like a Donkey		282
📷	6a+	Hung Over	122	120
	7a+	Hush Money		342
**	7c+	Hydraulic Lunch		118
*	6a+	Hypertension		76
*	7b+	Hypocritical Mass		170
	6b	I Am What I Am		344
	6c+	I Bolt, Therefore I Am		136
*	6a+	I Came		314
	6a+	I Conkered		314
	6b	I Wish My Wife Was This Dirty		353
	7a+	I.K.M.E.N.K.		173
***	7b+	I'm Spartacus		202
	6a	Ianto's Bargoed Bumblers Blind Spot		338
*	7a+	Ice Cream Sunday		211
*	6a+	Ice Station Gelli		282
	6b	Id-iot		200
	6b	Illegal Congress		186
*	7b	Imp, The		220
*	7a+	In Blood, of Life, of Sin?		348
*	7a+	In Search of Bedrock		229
	6c	In the Groove		216
	6a	In The Sidings		251
*	6b+	Inch Pinch		220
	6b+	Incidentally		344
*	7b+	Incidentally X		192
	E1	Industrial Relations		264
	5c	Industrial Salvage		212
*	7a+	Inflated Roundhead, The	179	180
	6a	Innocents Abroad		57
*	7b	Innuendo		308
*	6c+	Inscrutable Umberto Manteca		353
	6c	Insider Dealer		60
	6c	Insomnia		346
	7a	Inspector Glueseau		130
	5c	Instead of This		310
*	6b+	Intension		366
	6a	Internal Reflection		351
*	6c	Is it What You Are That Is?		344
**	7a+	It's a Black World		209
*	6a+	It's A Sine		327
	5c	It's all Greek to me		240
*	7a+	Its Tufa at the Bottom		230
***	7a	Jacky Fisher's Phobia		72
*	6b+	Jaded Locals	137	136
*	7a	Jalapeno Desperado		353
*	6c	Jambi		366
	6a+	Jap's Eye		173
*	6c	Jesus Wept		202
*	6c	Jet Lagged		318
	5a	Jetison Bilge		222
**	7a+	Jezebel		167
	6a	Jockey Club		280
	S	Joey's Full Pint		280
**	6b	John's Route		90
	6b	Johnny Fartpants		268
*	6a	Johnny Takes a Tumble		225
*	6c	Joker in the Pack		335
📷	7a	Joy de Viva	139	144
**	6b	Joys of a Tethered Goat		69
*	4b	Jug Fest		222
*	5c	Juice Runs Down My Leg		72
	4c	Jump on the Gravy Train		251
*	7a	Jump Over My Shadow		163
	7a+	Jump the Sun		149
*	7a	Jump to Conclusions	135	138
	4c	Jumping Jack Flash		356
	5c	Jurassic Shark		196
*	6b+	Just Another One Move Wonder		300
*	E1	Just Hanging Around		322
**	7c	Just In Time		188
*	7a+	Juvenile Justice		304
*	6a+	Kabuto Mushi		322
*	4c	Kant Hooks		246
	6b+	Keelhaul		56
	7b+	Kennelgarth		183
	VS	KES		280
***	7c+	Kestrel		150
	4a	Kestrel for a Knave		280
	5c	Keystone Kraps		276
	4b	Kickback Tar		96
**	7a	Kicking Ass and Taking Names		335
📷	6b+	Killer Arete	14	297
**	7a	Killer Queen		364
**	7b	'King Ada		360
**	7a+	King George verses the Suffragettes	39	89
**	7a	King Prawn		52
***	7a+	King Zog		360
*	6b	King's Shilling, The		94
*	7a+	Kings of New York		198
*	5c	Kiss the Gunner's Daughter		196
📷	6c	Kissin' the Pink	132	130
*	7a+	Kitchener's Nabla		69
*	6a+	Knackers Yard		212
	6a	Knee Jerk		64
*	6b	Knee Trembler		251
	6b	Knickerless in Hell		362
	4a	Knuckle Down		251
	7a	Kosovo		304
	6a+	Labrynthitis		69
	6a	Ladyboy's Cage	279	282
	4c	Lager Lout		294
**	E2	Lamb Leer Disease		269
*	6a	Lamisil		94
**	6b	Land of the Dinosaurs		324
	6a	Landfill Tax		212
	4a	Landlubber		98
	6a+	Lane Discipline		243
*	5a	Lara		98
	E3	Lasting Impressions		238
**	6b	Lateralus		366
	7b+	Laughing Boy		128
	6b+	Laughing Policeman, The		344
	6a	Leading Edge		372
	5a	Leaky Ball Cock		287
**	6c	Leave it to Me		324
*	7a	Leave it to me		258
**	7a+	Leave it to The Dogs		230
	5a	Ledge and Braces		373
*	6b	Ledger		120
	6b+	Left line		111
*	6b	Left Wing Rebolt		138
	5a	Leftover		331
	5a	Leger System		51
📷	6a	Lemon Soul	82	98
	6a+	Leonidas' Last Breakfast		240
	2a	Leopard Cannot Change His Spots, A		142
*	7a+	Less is More		60
**	E2	Let Me Play Among the Stars		331
	6a+	Lets Get Down and Dirty		371
*	6c	Letters of Life		348
*	7a	Liassic Lark		229
	HVS	Life and Soul		238
*	6b+	Life in the Slow Lane		243
	6b+	Life on Planet Earth		218
	6c	Life's Too Short		128
*	6a+	Light Cruiser		258
	3c	Lily of The Valleys		356
	6a	Lip Service		260
*	6a+	Lips Off My Shofarot	247	243
*	7a	Listing Badly		60
	E2	Little Big EGO		268
*	6b	Little Kurd		297
*	7a	Little Miss Lover		144
	5c	Little Polvier		318
*	5c	Little Queen	367	364
	6a	Little Runt		74

Carmarthenshire

Gower

Inland and Coastal Limestone

The Valleys Sandstone

Route Index

Stars	Grade	Route	Photo	Page
	6a+	Little Shrimp		51
**	6b	Little Something I Prepared Earlier, A		282
*	6a+	Little Taff		282
	6a+	Little Treasure		280
**	6c+	Little White Lies		346
	6a	Little Wrasse Cull		234
	6a+	Load of Bullocks		128
*	E2	Load of Rubbish, A		318
*	7b	Lobster Bisque		52
**	7b+	Loctite		324
*	7b+	Loneliness of the Long Distance Runner, The		170
	6c	Long Awaited		238
*	6b+	Long Forgotten		280
**	6c+	Look Over Yonder		200
*	5b	Looking for Leather		310
*	6c	Lucas Numbers		64
**	6b	Lundy Boy	374.	371
	7a	Luxury Gap, The		351
**	7a+	Lyddite		338
	E5	Lynch 'Em		273
*	5b	Ma Maid's Mermaid		94
	5c	Ma Moule Don't Like U Laffin		52
*	7a+	Ma's Strict		192
**	7c	Mad at the Sun		324
*	7a	Madame X		304
	6b	Madness		351
	6b+	Magellan's Straight		342
**	6b	Magic Carpet	219.	218
*	6b	Magic Circle		64
**	6b	Magic Touch	232.	229
	4c	Mal Culo		356
*	6c	Malice		353
*	6c+	Man Machine		74
	5a	Man on a Mission		78
*	7b	Man or Mollusc		52
*	7b	Man or Mouse		331
*	7b	March Of Progress		291
	5a	Mare Tranquilis		209
	4a	Marinated Goat Cheese		280
***	7a+	Marine Layer		86
	6a+	Marinieri		94
*	6a+	Marlin on the Wall		200
*	7a	Marmalade Skies	11.	142
	6b	Marooned		230
**	7a+	Mars Attacks		130
*	6b+	Mary Hinge's Close Shave		76
***	8a+	Masada		229
*	6c	Mastic Mick, The		327
*	6c	Matalanafesto		251
*	6a	Matt of the Iron Gland		238
	6c	Matt's Ice Bucket Challenge		200
	6b	Maud		154
	7a	Maurice Chevalier		342
	7a	Mawr, Mawr, Mawr	361.	360
*	6c	Maximus Extensicus		202
**	7b	Maybe Tommorow		308
*	6c+	McGoohan Loses Six		76
*	4b	Me Harty's		96
	6b	Meat Seeking Missile		338
	6a+	Medusa Spares No Head		240
*	6a	Meg (a) Skater Girl from Gelli		300
	6a	Mega Mix		200
*	6a	Megalodon		196
***	7a	Melting Man		198
*	7a	Melty Man Cometh, The		198
	6b	Memory Man		260
	E2	Men From Boys		57
*	7a+	Menage a Chien		335
*	5c	Mental Mantles		372
*	6b	Mental Message		57
*	6b	Mermaid's Footwork, A		100
**	5b	Mermaid's Tale, A		98
*	6c	Merthyr Infill, The		344
***	8a	Methuselah		229
*	6c	Michelle Pfeiffer		300
*	6c	Microwaves		216
**	6c+	Midas Touch, The		160
*	7c	Milkier Way, The		130
*	6b	Milkin' the Link		130
	6a	Milking the Snake		74
	6a	Milky White		260
*	7a	Millennium Thug, The		163
	E5	Million Destinies, A		210
	6c	Minchkins, The		150
	HVS	Mind like a Sewer		258
	6b+	Mine's a Pair		335
	5b	Mini Mission		78
	5a	Mini the Minx		92
***	7a+	Minnesota Nice		198
*	6c	Minsir		240
*	6a+	Mint Sauce Dressing		269
*	7a	Misadventure		318
**	7a	Mislivings		355
*	6b	Miss Alto		182
	4a	Miss Halfpenny		280
*	6c	Miss You		173
	7b	Missin' the Drink		130
	6b+	Missing Link		300
	6b+	Missing Quarter, The		344
**	7a+	Mistaking Cassini's Identity		64
	6a	Mister Faraday		324
*	7a	Mister Foothold		335
	6c+	Mister Polite Goad		173
*	6c	Molybdenum Man		314
**	7b+	Momentary Lapse of Reason, A		324
**	5c	Monica's Dress		111
*	7a	More More More		60
*	6b	More than a Feeling		316
*	7a	More than Enough		60
*	7a+	Moreland		60
	7a	Morfa, Morfa, Morfa		60
**	7b+	Morgue the Merrier, The		130
	8a	Mortal Kombat		186
	6a	Mortar Life		327
	7a	Morticia		182
*	6c	Moses Supposes His Toeses Were Roses		297
***	7a+	Mother of Pearl		308
*	6a	Moule Mariniere		52
*	6b+	Mountin' Ass Crack		318
*	E3	Mouse Trap		332
*	6c	Mouton Dagger		342
	S	Mr Farthing		280
*	6a+	Mr Potato Head		180
*	6a+	Mr Softy		216
	E3	Mr. Gorrilla's Got a Big Nose		338
**	8a+	Mr.T		229
**	7c	Muchas Maracas		191
	6a+	Mucky Ducky		371
	6a	Mud Lark Crack		264
*	7a+	Munsterosity		182
*	5c	Mussel Man		52
*	E4	Mutiny Crack		86
	6a+	My Blue Bell		344
*	6b	My Inheritance		128
*	5c	My Little Pony's on the Job		280
	6a+	My Little Routy Wooty		344
	6b+	My New House		304
*	6a	My Slice of Pie		64
*	7a	Nailbiter		269
	5b	Names from Roger's Profanisorous		98
*	6a	Napier's Bones		69
*	6b	Nappy Rush		343
*	E1	Narcissi		316
	4a	Naughty Corner, The		98
	6b	Naughty Step Direct Start, The		100
*	6a+	Naughty Step, The		100
**	7a+	Neil Kinnock's Last Stand		208
*	6b+	Nematode		120
*	7a	Nervous Nineties		297
	7b	Nether Edge		264
	5a	Never Out Fox the Fox		142
*	7a	New Day Today		202
	6a+	New Zawn		118
	5c	Newton's Apple		327
	5c	Nia Miss		138
	7a+	Niart Thgin		304
*	6a+	Nice Groove		128
**	6c	Nick to the Rescue		260
	6a	Nick's Dilemma		260
*	5c	Nietzche's Niche		243
	6a	Nifty Fingers		260
	7b+	Night Train		304
	6a	Night Watchman		353
*	6a+	Nil By Mouth		64
**	6c	Nine Green Bottles		285
	5b	No Barking up this Tree		316
*	6a+	No Beer, No Fear		200
**	7b	No Chips Round Here		316
*	6b+	No Epoxy Au Oxley		144
*	5c	No Father Day		98
*	7a	No Rest for the Wicked		138
*	5a	No Tar		96
	5b	Noah's Arse		64
	6b+	Nocturnal Emission		78
	6a	Norbert Colon Meets The Fat Slags		272
*	7a	Normal Norman		211
*	6b	Norman's Knob		268
*	6c+	Nose Job		222
	7a	Nosepicker	267.	269
***	7b	Nostradamus		170
*	6b	Not my Fault!		200
*	6b	Nothing in it		76
	4a	nside a Half-Cooked Chicken		204
*	7a	Numbers Game, The		308
	6a	OC/DC		363
	5c	Occam's Razor		276
	6a	Oceanus Aches		240
	6b	Ockers Delight		260
*	6a+	Off at a Tangent		64
***	6b+	Off the Peg		120
	4c	Off the Rails		251
	5b	Off to Oz		260
	E3	Ol' Blue Eyes		332
	6c	Old Firm, The		314
	7a+	Old Slapper		167
*	7a+	Olympic Doctor		335
*	5c	OMG She's a Squirter		272
**	E1	On Jupiter and Mars		332
	5a	On White Horses		224
*	6b	Once Bitten		343
*	6a	Once Upon a Time		208
*	6b+	One in Her Eye		282
	4c	One Less for the Spoiler		240
*	E3	One Small Step		170
	6b	One Step Beyond		216
	7b+	One Ton Depot		86
*	7a	One Track Mind		326
*	6b	Open Groove		200
*	6b+	Open Roads		182
	6a	Opening Batman		353
	5a	Operation Seaman		96
	4c	or the Prudes of Pontypridd		197
*	6a+	Orestes' Suffering		64
**	6c	Organised Chaos		198
**	7c	Original Start (Life on Planet Earth)		218
**	7b	Orion		157
	5b	Our Man From Hyder		258
*	6c+	Our Man In Bargoed		338
	7a+	Out Come The Freaks		183

Route Index 381

Stars	Grade	Route	Photo	Page
	4c	Out of the Pit		197
*	5b	Outsider, The		366
**	7a+	Outspan		314
***	7c+	Outta Time		191
*	6b	Oveleaf		348
*	E3	Over the Moon		332
*	7b+	Overlook, The		230
	7a	OW!		240
***	E2	Owl and the Antelope, The		332
*	6a+	Ox-Over Moon.		128
*	7a	Oyster Party		52
	5c	P.E.G Feed		69
	5c	Paddock Full of Ponies, A		224
**	8a	Palace of Swords Reversed	25, 33.	142
*	7a	Palm.		208
	E5	Palm Springs		210
*	6b	Pampered		343
*	6c	Par 3		90
*	6a+	Parabola.		318
*	7a	Paradise Row		355
*	7c	Parlour Français.		154
*	7b	Parlour Games		154
**	6a+	Parlour Vous le Sport		156
*	7a+	Party Animal.		210
*	7a+	Pastis on Ice		314
	4a	Pasty = Man Boobs		230
*	6b	Paternal Love		98
	4c	Paw Me		371
	6a	PCB		230
**	6b+	Peachy		355
	6b+	Pearlescence		216
***	7c	Pegasus		157
*	6a+	Pelagic Mush		229
*	6b	Pepperatzi		338
*	5b	Per Rectum		326
*	6b+	Perfect Prude		74
*	6c	Perfect Scoundrels		326
	HVS	Periscope		220
*	6b	Petering Out.		218
*	6c	Philandering Fillipino		163
*	6c	Phlegmatic Solution.		234
**	7b	Physical Presents		285
*	6b+	Piano Dentist		353
	6a+	Pick up the Pieces.		326
*	6c+	Pied Noir		111
*	6c+	Pig Iron		264
	4c	Pilgrim		200
*	6a+	Pillars of the Earth.		106
*	5c	Pinch a Minch		150
*	7a+	Pinch is On, The		60
	6c	Pinheads		180
*	6c+	Pink Lady, The.		355
	7b	Pioneers of the Hypnotic Groove	5, 140.	142
	6b	Pis En Lit		186
*	7b	Pissin' the Sink		130
	6a+	Plankwalk		56
*	6b+	Plaque Attack		344
	5c	Play Dusty For Me.		363
*	6b+	Play The Joker.		204
	7a+	Playing Away		206
**	7a+	Pleasant Valley Sunday	321.	324
*	5b	Plum Bob		251
*	5b	Plumb, The	217.	220
*	7a	Plumbing the Depths		287
*	7b	Plus ça Change		230
**	5c	Pocket Battleship		258
	6b	Poire, La.		222
	6a+	Poker in the Eye.		324
	5a	Polishing the Turd.		282
	7b	Popped In, Souled Out		115
*	5c	Poppin' in the Poop Deck		196
	5c	Porcellena.		222
	6b	Pork Sword		310

Stars	Grade	Route	Photo	Page
*	6b	Porno Text King	256.	258
	6c	Posh and Becs		222
*	6b	Post Expressionist		346
*	6b+	Pot Black		258
	5c	Pothead		180
**	7b+	Poultry in Motion		144
*	7b	Pour Marcel		192
*	3c	Power of the Leopard Skin Leg Warmers, The.		142
*	7b+	Power Struggle		144
*	7c	Powers That Be		188
*	6b	Poxy Queen, A.		364
*	7a	PR Job		264
	E3	Practice What You Preach		343
*	6a	Prawn Cock Tale.		154
*	6b+	Prawn Star		154
**	6b	Prawnsite		154
*	7a+	Pray for the Cray		52
	6b+	Pre Nups		289
*	6b	Predictive Text.		260
	5a	Premonition		78
	7a	Principles of Rock Mechanics		332
**	7b	Prison Bitch.		116
	5c	Prison Sex.		366
	3b	Probate Pending.		98
	6a	Probing Proctologist		246
	5c	Prometheus Bound		240
**	7a	Promises		197
	7a+	Propaganda		308
	6b+	Providence		366
*	6c	Psilocybic		366
*	7a	Psychotherapy		297
**	6b+	Pubic Enema		251
*	7a	Pugsley		182
*	7a+	Pump Action		138
	6a+	Pump and Dump		60
*	6a	Pump My Bilge		96
	6a	Pure Cino		94
*	4b	Puss Off.		186
*	7a	Pwll Du Crack	215.	222
	5a	Pysgodwibblywobbly		98
	5b	Quadcam of Solice		251
	6c	Quakering		216
**	7b+	Quantum of Lydon's Feelings		72
***	7b	Quantum of Lydon's Future		72
	7a	Quartz Bicycle, The		210
	5c	Queen Bee		364
*	6b	Queen is Dead, The		364
**	6b+	Queens of the Stone Age	365.	364
**	6b+	Quest for the Origins of Place Holder Notation, The		69
	6b+	Question of Rabbits, A		64
	5b	Quiet Flows The Jordan		243
*	7a+	Race You Up The Wallbars		285
*	7b	Rag and Bone		212
*	7b	Rage, La.		308
*	7b	Rain Dance		170
*	7a	Raindogs		210
*	7b	Rampage		170
*	6c+	Rancho La Cha, Cha, Cha		202
*	4c	Raspberry Ripple		287
***	7b	Rat on a Hot Tin Roof		184
*	6b	Rattle Those Tusks		324
	7a+	Raven, The	151.	150
*	6b+	Raving Queen		364
*	6b+	Reach for a Peach.		216
	6b+	Reaction Series		156
	5a	Recurring Nightmare		64
	6b+	Red 'erring		344
**	7b+	Red Letter Day		130
*	7b	Red River Rock		130
*	7b+	Red Snapper		130
*	6b+	Red Square		198
	7b	Red with Rage.	126.	130

Stars	Grade	Route	Photo	Page
*	7c	Regulators, The		182
*	7a	Reign of the Deer		163
**	6c	Relaxed Ladybird, The.		331
*	6c+	Renaissance.	168.	170
*	6a+	Repetitive Strain Inquiry.		258
	6a+	Requisition		78
**	7a+	Resin d'être		130
	7b+	Resisting Arrest		116
*	E3	Restricted Practices.		264
***	7b	Retrobution	cover.	106
*	6a+	Reverted Revisionist	237.	243
	6b	Rhod Above the Bridge		289
	6a	Rhondda Leader.		300
*	7a	Rhondda Ranger		285
*	7a	Rhubarb Lets Fly		300
	6b	Richter Scale, The		56
	5c	Ride on the Chocolate Unicorn, A		204
**	7a	Ride the Funky Wave, Babe		170
	6b	Right		111
	4c	Ring Finger		251
*	6b	Ring of Confidence		324
	3c	Ring, The		356
*	7b+	Ripe 'n Ready		314
*	3a	Ripple Slab		287
*	7b	Rise		304
	6a+	Rising Sap.		316
	HVS	Roaches Revisited.		300
*	5a	Road to Eldorado, The.		186
*	6b	Road To Nowhere, The	275.	276
*	7a	Road Whore.		289
*	6b+	Roaring Forties		344
*	7a	Rob Roy.		178
*	5a	Robin's Yoghurt Supper.		234
**	6b+	Rock Bottom		120
*	5c	Rockover Beethoven		331
*	6a	Rocky		371
	6a+	Root Canal		355
*	6c	Roraima		343
***	7b+	Rose-Line		184
*	6a	Rosetta Stoned		366
**	7b+	Rotbeest.		173
	5c	Rotters Club.		258
**	7a+	Round Are Way		304
	5b	Rounding the Mark		224
*	7b	Route with Two Pockets, The		84
*	5c	Rowan Jelly		269
	6b+	Royal Flush		204
	5b	Rubble Escalator		74
*	6a+	Rudaceous Ramble		154
	HS	Rude Buoys		246
*	6b+	Rum Thieves		84
*	6a	Rump and Scoop		355
*	7a?	Running Man, The.		182
**	7b+	Rush Hour.		154
	6c	Saboo.		344
	HVS	Sad Little Nutter.		64
	5a	Sadness.		351
	5c	Safe Connection.		57
	6a+	Saga Louts		300
	5c	Sailing to Freedom		224
**	7b+	Salem's Lot		191
**	7b+	Salisbury's Crowd.		72
*	5c	Sallies of Youth		156
*	7b	Salmon Running, Bear Cunning		324
*	5c	Salty Dog		74
	5c	Sam Sparrow		310
*	6b	Sand Man		90
***	7b+	Sangreal.		184
	7b+	Sangria Finish		184
	Mod	Sartre Flies		246
	VS	Sartre's Underlay		246
	6c+	Savant.		204
	E3	Save a Mouse Eat A Pussy		332
*	6c	Scandal (in the bin)		294

Carmarthenshire

Gower

Inland and Coastal Limestone

The Valleys Sandstone

Route Index

Stars	Grade	Route	Photo	Page
**	7a+	Scared Seal Banter		327
*	6b	Scarface		120
	5c	Scarfish		.98
*	4b	Schengen		.94
	6c+	Schmisse		264
**	7a+	Science Friction		308
	6a+	Scorpion		220
*	7a	Scram		202
	5c	Scrape the Bottom of the Barrel.		251
	6a+	Scraping the Barrel		178
*	7a+	Scream for Cream	206.	211
	6c+	Screaming Lampshades.		180
	6a	Scrotal Scratch Mix		268
*	6c	Scrotum Oil		326
*	5c	Scurvy Dog		.98
	4b	Scuttle		.98
*	6a+	Sea Fairer		.52
	4b	Sea Shanty Rib		.96
*	7b+	Seagull Stuka Strike		.72
	5b	Seaman in the Groove.		.96
	6a	Seaman Limbo		.96
	5a	Seaman's Sea Shanty		.96
	6b	Seamanship Mission		.78
	6a+	Seb Eats Sh**te.		273
	5b	Secret Drawers		.92
*	7b	Security Plus		211
***	6b+	Selling Short	62.	.60
	6a+	Send in the Specials.		282
	HVS	Sennapod Corner		318
***	7c+	Senser.		167
	5c	Serendipity		258
*	7b	Settin' Stone		130
***	7b	Seven Thirty at Arras		.72
*	6a+	Shackles of Love		324
*	7a	Shadow of the Sun		351
*	6c+	Shaken but not Stirred		304
	5a	Shale I Compare Thee?		363
*	4c	Sharktopus vs Megapotamus		196
	7b	Sharp Cereal Professor, The.	177.	191
*	7b+	Sharpy Unplugged		304
*	7a	She's Slipping Away.	46.	.60
	HVS	Sheepbone Wall		332
**	7a+	Sheer Heart Attack		364
*	7b	Shellin' Out		.52
*	7c	Shining Dawn		161
	6c	Short Sharp Manic Depressive		304
*	6b	Short Sharp Sock		.72
	5a	Shorter Life		327
	6b+	Should I Go		224
	6c	Should I Stay		224
	5b	Shrew		371
*	7b+	Siberian Husky		183
*	6b+	Sideburn		229
	6b+	Sidewinder		220
**	6b	Siege of Syracuse		243
	6a+	Sight for Saw Eyes, A		316
**	7a	Sign of the Times	263.	264
*	E1	Silent Echo		116
*	6a	Silent Mode		258
	HVS	Silent Movies		285
*	6c+	Silver Surfers Sermon.		.72
*	6c	Simple Addition		346
	E2	Simple Simon		163
*	6b	Simply Simian		338
**	7b	Sinister		348
*	7a+	Sink or Swim	213.	211
*	6a	Sister Mary's Blessed Finger	114.	115
	6b	Sixty Eight Plus One.		238
*	7a	Sixty Seconds Go See.		344
*	7b	Skanderbeg		360
	7a+	Skedaddle		167
**	7c	Skin Ed		180
	7c	Skull Attack		106
*	6b	Slab Happy		258
	6c+	Slap Happy		318
*	7a	Slap of Luxury, The		351
**	6b+	Sleeping Dogs Lie		324
	6a	Sliced Up at Thermopylae		240
***	7a+	Slip into Something Sexy	341.	351
*	6b+	Slip into the Queen		364
	6c+	Slipped		351
*	6b	Slippery Lip Trip, The		204
**	6b	Slipping into Luxury.		351
	5c	Slurp The Savoury Oyster.		229
	7a	Slytherin, The		216
	6c	Smack		304
*	6b+	Smack My Bitch Up		324
	6a	Small Fry		.51
	6a	Smart Keas		.64
***	7c	Smashed Rat		184
	5c	Smeaton's Stump		.94
*	4c	Smeghead.		180
**	6b	Smoke and Mirrors		234
*	6b	Snap Crackle 'n' Pop		225
*	6c	Snapper		348
	6c+	Snatch.		163
*	6b	Snatched from the Cradle		128
	E2	Sniffing Deborah's Pocket.		300
	E1	Snorting Horse		282
*	6b+	Snuffle Hound.		.74
*	6c	So Uncool		322
**	6b	Soapy Dahl	77.	.74
	5c	Socrates Sucks		246
	6a+	Soft Prawn		154
*	6a+	Soil and Shuvel		128
*	6b	Solihull Calling		276
	4a	Something That Came Up Much Later		282
*	6b+	Somewhere in her Smile She Knows		100
	6c	Sophie's Wit Tank.		.74
*	6a+	Sorcerer's Assistant.		234
	6c	Sore Wrasse.		234
***	6b	Sorry Lorry Morry.		304
*	6a+	Southeast Wall		115
	6b	Southwest Guru.		180
	6c+	Space Cowboys		202
	5c	Spades of Glory		106
***	E4	Spain		191
	5b	Spam Javelin		310
	6b	Spear the Bearded Clam.		229
*	6c+	Spectre of Love	54.	.56
	6c	Speechless		289
*	7a+	Sperm Wail		326
	6b	Sphagnum 45		346
	6a	Spic'n Span		111
*	6c	Spider		154
*	7a	Spirt of Ystrad.		276
**	6a	Spit it Out		111
**	6a	Spit'n Polish.		111
	6c	Spittle and Spume.		111
	6c+	Splashdown		346
*	6b+	Split the Equity		264
*	6a	Spoilt Bastard		268
*	7b+	Sport for All		318
**	8a	Sport Wars (Dinas Rock)		188
	6a	Sport Wars (Watch House)		136
	6b	Sporting Supplement		318
	5c	Sprats from the Captain's Table		.51
	6a	Spunk Welded.		.74
	6a	Squash Match.		331
*	6b+	Squash the Squaddie		182
	6c	Squeal Like a Hog.		163
	4c	Squeeze for Cream		211
	5c	Squeeze that Lemon.		.64
	5a	Squeezing the Curd		280
*	6c+	St. Vitus's Dance		136
*	6b	Stable Boy's Breakfast		280
*	5c	Stalag Luft.		204
*	6c	Standing on a Beach		355
	7b	Staple Diet.	13.	229
	6a+	Star Too Far, A.		353
**	6b	Starke Reminder, A		160
**	7c+	Starkly Nameless		130
**	7c	Starter for Ten		163
	7a+	Stay Hungry.		210
*	6b	Steel Yourself		130
	7b	Steely Dan.		289
*	6c+	Steroid John.		335
	4c	Sticky Fingers		251
	7a+	Sticky Tissue Issue		.92
	6a+	Sticky Wicket		353
***	7b+	Still Life		188
*	7a+	Still Nifty at Fifty.		154
*	6c	Stingray		.98
	6a	Stinkfist		366
*	6a+	Stinking of Fish		173
**	7a	Stoeipoesje		173
*	E5	Stone Wings.		229
*	6b+	Stonewall		120
	5c	Stool Sample		326
	6a+	Straight and Narrow		260
*	6b	Straight as a Dai.		.72
	7b	Strain Drain		138
**	7b	Straining at The Leash		230
*	7b	Straining Pitch		138
	6c	Strange Little Boy		360
	6c	Strange Little Girl	359.	360
**	7b+	Strawberry Jam		371
*	6c+	Stray Bullet		202
*	7a	Stray Cats		186
**	7b+	Streaming Neutrinos		209
	6c	Striking Twelve		304
	5a	String 'Em Up		273
*	6c	Stroke of Good Luck.		.74
	6a+	Stroking the Lizard		.74
	6b	Strongbow Flyer, The		.84
*	6c	Stuart's Line Left Finish		.86
	7a	Stubborn as a Mule		282
	6c+	Stuck On You		150
**	6c	Stuck Up Bitch		.76
	6a	Student Grant		268
*	6c+	Stump Stroker.		264
	4b	Sub Prime Market.		258
	7a	Sub-Contraction.		346
	E2	Submerged by Blubber		268
*	7b+	Subversive Body Pumping		188
	4a	Suction Power.		287
**	7b+	Sugar Bullets		202
	5c	Sultan's Spring		243
*	6b+	Sumo no Shiro		322
	E3	Sunday Sport		318
*	7a	Sunstone		362
**	7c+	Super Size Me.		229
*	6b+	Super Strung Direct		338
	6b	Super Strung Out at Bargoed		338
*	7a	Superposition		220
	6b	Superstition		.78
	6c	Supertramp		371
	6b	Supply on Demand		188
**	7b+	Support Your Local Sheriff		116
	4c	Suppose a Tree		356
*	6a	Suppose I Try		128
	6a+	Surly Temple		238
**	8b+	Surplomb de Ray		142
	7a	Sustainable Development		212
*	7a	Sverige		192
**	7a	Sweet Whistling Geronimo		289
**	7a	Swim With The Sharks		149
	5c	Ta-Ta Tata		264
	6a	Table Scraps.		.74
*	6b	Tactless Teacher, The		372

Carmarthenshire

Gower

Inland and Coastal Limestone

The Valleys Sandstone

Route Index 383

Stars	Grade	Route	Photo	Page
**	6c	Taffy Duck		211
*	5c	Take me up the Hindu Kush		225
	6c	Take Your Pants to Heaven		362
	7b+	Talk About False Gods		202
*	6b+	Talking Hands		220
	5c	Talking Hoarse		282
	6a	Talking Shop		282
*	6c+	Tall Dark and Handsome		294
*	6b+	Tallulah Dream		216
	5c	Tally Whore!		268
	6c	Tapping the Keg		178
**	6b+	Taurus Bulbous		198
*	7a	Taxi to the Ocean		.52
**	6b	Tea Leaves		222
	6c	Technitis		183
	S	Teen Prawn		154
*	6c+	Teenage Kicks		128
*	5b	Telefunken U47	172	173
	HVS	Telpyn Corner		.52
	5a	Temples of Cwmaman		362
	6b	Terry Forkwit	270	272
*	6a	Them's Be Barnacles, Them's Be		.96
*	6a+	Themis is Out of Order		240
*	6c+	Theory and Practice of Glue Sniffing, The		318
*	6b+	There's Life in the Old Dog Yet		230
	5c	There's No Business Like Flow Business		222
*	6a	Thieving Little Parasites		.84
	4c	Thin Drum, The		273
**	6c+	Thin Lizzy		234
*	7a	Thinner		182
*	6b	Third Eye		366
*	6c+	This ain't Pretty		.84
	7b+	This God is Mine	226	229
*	6b+	This Vicar's Tea Party		.98
	E2	Thorn in my Side		216
*	7b+	Thousand Bomber Raid		.72
*	6c+	Thousand Yard Stare		182
**	6b	Threadbare		120
*	6c	Three Men in a Goat		343
*	7a+	Three Minute Hero		118
*	6c	Thug Life		220
***	E5	Thumbsucker		269
*	5c	Tibial Plates Extension		276
*	5c	Tickety-Boo		136
**	6c+	Tidal Rush		.60
*	6c+	Tidy as Matt's Toolbox		200
	7c+	Tiger Cut		184
	6b+	Tikka-tikka Kiss-kiss		353
*	6a	Tinkers Dog		212
*	6c	Tip Ripper		240
	E1	Titanium Man		280
*	5c	To Dai or not to Dai		225
*	6c+	Tobacco King		280
	HVS	Toil		280
*	6b	Tom Tom Club		276
*	6c	Too Keynes by Half		346
	7a	Too Many Fingers		138
**	6b	Too Posh to Brush		276
*	5c	Top Drawer		.92
*	5c	Top Mouth Gudgeon		.51
	6b	Top Rail		251
*	7b+	Torch the Earth		343
*	7b	Tortilla Flats		192
*	6b+	Total Recoil		346
***	7c	Totally Clips		170
*	6c	Totally Radish	193	186
	6c	Totally Stumped		314
*	7a+	Touch and Go		138
	VS	Tough Carapace		.51
	4a	Toxic Assets		.60
	6c+	Toxicology		128
	6a+	Trad Man		136
*	E1	Tragedy		316
*	7a	Tragic Moustache		229
	7b	Trailblazer		211
	6b	Trainspotter, The		251
**	6b+	Tread Gently		136
	6c	Tremors		.56
*	4b	Trevena Fish Hotel, The		.98
*	7a	Tribulations		106
	7b+	Tricky Dickie Takes a Sickie		289
*	6b+	Triple Sigh		149
	5b	Triton Left		100
	5b	Triton Right		100
*	E2	Troilism Trouble		335
*	6b	Trolley Service Suspended		251
**	7a	Tufa at the Top		230
*	7a	Tufa Joy		230
*	6c	Tufa Tennis		230
	HS	Tumbledown		243
	6c	Turd Strangler		326
*	6c+	Turing's Sum		.69
*	7c	Turkey Lurking		144
	6a+	Turkey Twizzler		310
*	7a	Turn Off the Sun		297
	4a	Turtle Apocalypse		.98
*	7a	Twelve Inch Version!, The		200
*	6b+	Twenty One Ounces Of Blow		338
*	7a+	Twenty Second Chance		344
*	6a	Twice Shy		343
***	6c	Twilight World	119	115
*	6b+	Twisted Logic		372
	6c+	Two for Tuesday		308
	7a+	Two of a Kind		335
	7b+	Two of a Perfect Pair		130
**	7c	Ulrika Ka Ka Ka		200
	7c	Ultimatum		124
	6a+	Uncle Eddie Meets Modern Parents		268
*	5c	Under a Blood Red Sky		225
**	7c+	Under Arrest		116
	6b	Under the Axe		316
*	6a+	Under the Mattress		.98
**	8a	Underdog		116
	6b+	Underneath the Larches		128
	HS	Unearthed		282
	6a+	Unholy Alliance		142
	7b+	Uninvited Guest, The		229
**	6b	Uninvited Lines		294
**	7a	Uninvited, The		294
**	6b	Unleashed		.74
*	6b+	Up For Grabs		338
*	6a	Up Yours		327
*	7a	Urban Development		264
	4a	Ursula		.98
*	6c+	Valley Uprising		116
*	7a	Valleys Initiative		318
	8a	Vennerne	85	.86
*	7a+	Vera Figner's Lost List		.72
	4a	Vile Proposition		.78
	6c+	VIP Lunge		362
*	7a	Vitamin Z		192
	6c	Vladimir and the Pearl	49	.52
*	7a+	Voice From The Pulpit		150
	5b	Voyage of the Zawn Treader		118
	6c	Waco Kid, The		360
*	6b+	Wake, The		180
**	7a	Wandelende tak		173
	4a	Warmth of Man, The		204
***	7b	Watchmen, The		184
*	6b+	Waxing Lyrical		.76
*	7a	Wayne Fell in Do Do		222
	6c+	Weak Lemon Drink		251
*	5b	Wedge Dew Bin	108	106
	6a	Wedge-egade Master		106
*	5b	Wedgling		106
	5b	Weeping Stump	313	316
**	7a	Western Front Direct	252	332
**	7b+	Wet Afternoon		200
	E1	What No Metal		280
	6a	What's The Arc De Triomphe For Then?		314
	E2	What's the Craic		216
	6b+	Whatever Floats Your Boat		224
**	7a+	When I'm 64		154
*	7a+	When Push Comes To Shove		186
	7b	When Push Comes To Shove (Direct Finish)		186
	7a	Where Did You Get That Bolt		331
**	6c+	Where Has Stu Gone?		.86
	5c	Where the Arc is It?		362
**	7b+	Where the Fox That?		144
	6a	Where There's Muck There's Brass		371
*	4a	Whispering Whelks		.96
	7a+	Whistle Dixie		289
*	5a	White Noise		225
	E5	White Witch		234
*	7a+	Whiter than White Wall		318
	6a	Who Dunnit		258
*	6c	Why Did I Bother		260
***	7b	Wide Eyed and Legless	113	116
	6b+	Wij zitten nog in een sneeuwstorm		173
**	6c+	Willie The Pimp		234
*	5a	Wisdom of Age		156
*	4c	Wittle Thieving Lankers		.84
*	6c	Wonderful Land		111
	6b	Working on Commission		.78
	4c	Working to a Budget		282
**	7b+	World in Action		115
*	6c+	World is my Lobster, The		308
*	6b	World Without End		106
**	7a	World-v-Gibson, The		230
*	6b+	Worzel Budgie Spunker		282
*	6a+	Worzel Cloaca Sniffer		282
*	6b+	Wrasse		.51
	6b+	Wrasse Bandit		234
*	6c	Wrasse Wipe		234
	6c	Wrasseputin's Hypodermic Typewriter		234
	6b+	Wrassetafarian		234
*	7a+	Wreckage		.60
*	6a	Wreckers ball		212
*	6a+	Wreckers Bay		238
**	7b	Wrecking Ball		.86
*	6b	Wristlock		.76
*	6b+	Writings on the Wall		264
**	7b	Written in Red		130
*	7c	Y Caled Caled		355
*	6a+	Y'All Come Back Now		163
*	5c	Yak's Back		297
	4b	Yank My Chain		371
*	6a	Yank the Plank		310
	5a	Yar!		196
*	6b+	Yikes		322
*	6a	Yolks on You, The		373
**	6b+	You Are What You Is		344
*	6c+	You Change Me		343
*	7b	You Dunnit		258
*	7a	You Never Can Tell		210
*	6a	You Sane Bolter	66	.64
	6b	You've Had Your Chicks		373
**	7a	Young Free and Single		294
	4a	Young Gifted and Beige		230
*	7b+	Your Future, Our Clutter!		.72
*	6b+	Zacchaeus Repents		243
	E2	Zeitgeist		366
	6a+	Zero Inclination		.64
*	6b	Zeuwit		.94
*	5c	Zoo Time		310
	8a	Zulu Wall	125	124

Carmarthenshire · Gower · Inland and Coastal Limestone · The Valleys Sandstone

Crag and General Index

Gower **80**
Barland Quarry...... 172
Bosco's Gulch Area.. 158
Bowen's Parlour Area.. 152
Foxhole............. 140
Minchin Hole........ 148
Oxwich............. 126
Pwlldu Bay.......... 166
Rams Tor............ 168
Rhossili Beach........ 82
Third Sister to Zulu Zawn 112
Trial Wall Area........ 104
Watch House........ 134

Carmarthenshire...... **46**
Cwm Capel.......... 78
Morfa Bychan........ 58
Pendine............. 70
Telpyn Point......... 48

Limestone **174**
Dinas Rock.......... 176
Gilwern............. 214
Taff's Well........... 194
Taff's Well West...... 206
Temple Bay......... 236
Witches Point....... 226

The Valleys **252**
Abbey Buttress...... 262
Bargoed............ 336
Blaenllechau........ 286
Coed Ely........... 292
Crymlyn Quarry..... 352
Cwmaman.......... 306
Dan Dicks.......... 288
Deri................ 334
Dyffryn............. 256
Ferndale........... 284
Gelli............... 278
Glynfach........... 296
Llanbradach........ 340
Mountain Ash....... 312
Navigation Quarry.... 328
Sirhowy............ 358
The Darren......... 302
The Gap........... 320
Tirpentwys......... 368
Ton Pentre......... 274
Trebanog........... 290
Trehafod........... 298
Treherbert Quarry... 266
Tyle y Coch......... 354

Access................28
Accommodation.........20
Acknowledgments.......12
Advertiser Directory......12
App Version............8
BMC RAD.............28
Bolting...............30
Bouldering............35
British Trad Grade.......32
Bunkhouses...........20
Buses................19
Cafes................24
Camping.............20
Climbing Shops........24
Climbing Walls........24
Coastguard...........16
Contents..............3
Coverage..............6
Crag Index....... *This page*
Destination Planner.....42
Emergencies..........16
Gear.................30
Gear Shops...........24
Getting Around........18
GPS Locations........18
Grade Colour Codes....32
Grade Table...........32

Graded Lists..........36
Guidebooks...........10
Introduction............4
Limestone Graded List...36
Logistics..............14
Lower-offs............30
Map.................18
Map Key....... *Cover flap*, 9
Mobile Phones........16
Mountain Rescue......16
National Park Centres...16
Parking Spots.........18
Previous Guidebooks....10
Public Transport.......19
Pubs.................22
QR Codes............18
Rainfall..............16
Rescue..............16
Restrictions..........28
Rockfax App...........8
Rockfax Books... *Cover flap*
Ropes...............30
Route Index.........376
Sandstone Graded List...40
Satellite Navigation.....18
South Wales Bolt Fund...30
Sport Grade..........32

Symbols....... *Cover flap*, 9
Technical Grade........32
Temperature..........16
Topo Key...... *Cover flap*, 9
Tourist Information Offices.16
Trad Climbing.........34
Trad Grade...........32
Trains...............19
UKBoltFund.org.......30
UKClimbing Logbook....8
Weather.............16
Websites............10
When to Go..........16
Where to Stay........20